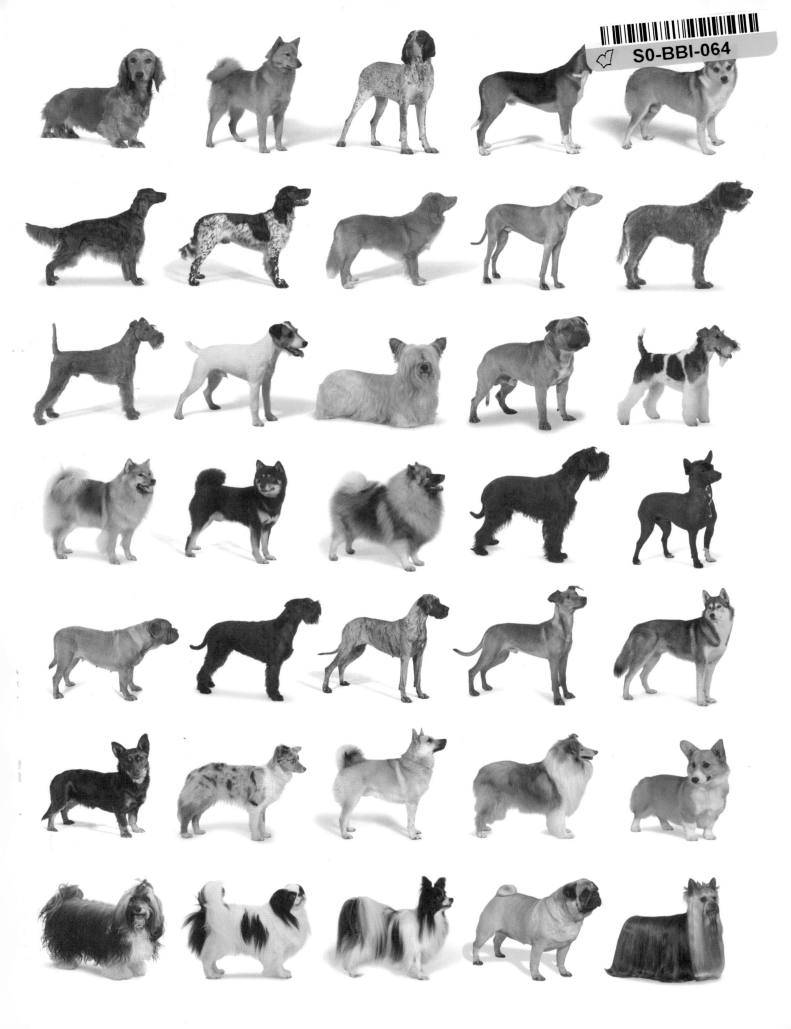

S0-BBI-064

THE COMPLETE BOOK OF
DOGS

THE COMPLETE BOOK OF
DOGS

BREEDS • TRAINING • HEALTH CARE

A comprehensive encyclopedia of dogs with a fully illustrated guide
to 230 breeds and over 1500 photographs

ROSIE PILBEAM

With Mike Stockman

Photography by Robert and Justine Pickett

LORENZ BOOKS

Contents

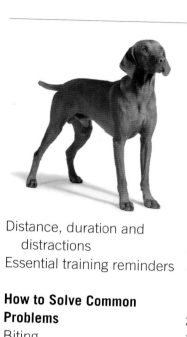

Introduction

The dog is our oldest companion. Humans and dogs came together thousands of years ago for mutual comfort, and slowly developed the interdependence seen today – caring for the dog in return for continuing companionship and a great variety of working functions.

The gradual recognition of the many different ways in which the dog could contribute to the association with mankind has led to the development of an enormous variety of dog types. All varieties of dog are members of a single species; it is the most varied of any species known, ranging from the tiny Chihuahua to the massive Irish Wolfhound.

So close has the association of dog and human become that there are now probably only two breeds of truly wild dogs left – the Cape Hunting Dog and the Australian Dingo. Many countries, of course, have roaming packs of wild dogs that lead an independent existence, but these are invariably domestic dogs that have 'gone wild' for one of any number of reasons.

To a remarkable extent, a dog of any breed can mate with another of any other breed and produce fertile offspring. This fact in itself has led to even more varieties developing over the centuries, as new functions and fashions were conceived. There are aound 100 known breeds in existence today. The precise figure is impossible to determine, because previously unrecognized breeds continue to emerge, and types of the same breed are recognized as distinct; or conversely, varieties previously considered as separate can become combined as one breed.

As part of this continuing evolutionary process, some breeds have also died out; several have disappeared even in the last 100 years, possibly due to reduced fertility or the

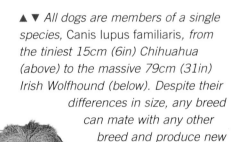

▲ ▼ *All dogs are members of a single species,* Canis lupus familiaris, *from the tiniest 15cm (6in) Chihuahua (above) to the massive 79cm (31in) Irish Wolfhound (below). Despite their differences in size, any breed can mate with any other breed and produce new varieties of dogs.*

▲ *The bond between dog and human can be very strong and rewarding.*

particular type ceasing to be fashionable. Loss of the traditional function of a breed may be another reason, but more often the breed has changed in conformation to such an extent as to be almost unrecognizable as the original breed. The war dogs of old, for instance, have developed into the civilized mastiff types.

Although every breed of dog, in the Western World at least, is expected to be domesticated, certain type characteristics tend to persist through many generations, and these are not just characteristics of conformation. Everyone realizes that if you buy a Great Dane puppy, for instance, small though it may be at eight weeks old, it will grow into a very large dog. If you buy a terrier of any breed, it will have terrier behaviour characteristics, inherited from its working ancestors.

If you have decided to buy a dog, look into all the breed characteristics, and consider them carefully before you decide which type of dog you want to live with. A dog may live for 10–20 years; it is yours to care for over a significant portion of your life.

IN THIS BOOK

This book is organized into four main sections. *Getting Started* gives advice how to choose the right dog for your lifestyle, with practical information about equipment, safety, nutrition, feeding, grooming, bathing, breeding, whelping and rearing puppies.

The Breeds is an illustrated directory of 230 of the main dog breeds of the world, including hounds, gundogs, terriers, utility, working and herding dogs and toy breeds, and also unrecognized breeds and hybrids. For every type of dog, a 'Breed box' panel summarizes the animal's size, grooming and feeding requirements, exercise needs and temperament.

Training Your Dog provides step-by-step instructions for how to turn a new puppy or untrained animal into a well-behaved member of the family. All the most important commands are included, including 'sit', 'down', 'leave it', 'stay', 'wait' and 'settle down', as well as walking nicely on a lead, coming back when called, and sitting quietly when visitors call. To keep your dog fit and happy, there is also a beautifully illustrated guide to the exciting sports and activities that are available, including breed shows, rally obedience, sheepdog trials, Schutzhund, flyball, canicross, gundog trials and dock jumping.

Finally, *Health Care* explains how to keep your pet in the best condition possible. There is veterinary advice on first aid, neutering, spaying and breeding, as well as holistic approaches such as massage, hydrotherapy and homeopathy.

▼ *With the right training and practice, your dog could become involved in fun sports and activities such as agility (left), heelwork to music (middle) and disc dog (below).*

GETTING STARTED

A great deal of thought and discussion should precede
your decision to get a puppy. It is important to choose
a breed that will fit in with your lifestyle; for example,
it would be foolhardy to acquire a dog that needs an
excessive amount of exercise if you lead a sedentary
lifestyle. You need to decide if you can put up with the
amount of hair some breeds shed; if not, you should look
for a non-moulting breed. Whittle down your long list to
a few select breeds, and try not to go for looks alone.
Ask around vet surgeries and other pet owners to find the
best breeder you can. It is also important to take into
consideration the costs of your puppy – not just the
purchase price, but the cost of vaccinations, health
checks, food and equipment. Good puppy classes are
an added expense. Owning a dog is not cheap, but
well worth the love and affection that you get in return.

◄ *Even the smallest of dogs will require a lifetime commitment from
its owner, who will be totally responsible for its wellbeing.*

Responsible dog ownership

Living with a dog is not just a privilege, but also a responsibility that should never be taken lightly. When you first decide to become a dog owner, there are many things to consider. Do you have the time for the dog? Will the breed match your particular lifestyle? Then you need to consider the costs, including training classes, vets' fees (including annual vaccinations), possibly groomers and a high-quality diet. Price is usually the best indicator of food quality; cheap food generally means poor-quality ingredients.

It is also your responsibility to make sure your puppy is good at socializing with other dogs and people, and that it gets regular, daily exercise – even when you don't feel like it because the weather is bad. It is important that your dog isn't a nuisance, either to other dogs or people in parks, or for people who live near you. Dogs that have to be left alone shouldn't be allowed to bark constantly and annoy the neighbours, and if they do, it's up to you to find a solution.

In short, make sure you can give your dog all the care and attention it needs. Owning a dog is a long-term financial and emotional commitment.

In many countries there is breed-specific legislation relating to the ownership of certain types of dog. Most European countries have lists of banned breeds (such as the Pit Bull, Japanese Tosa and Fila Brasileiro), and each state and county of the USA has its own laws. In general, an out-of-control dog is a liability and will be dealt with by law.

It is your responsibility to make sure that your dog is under control, which means training it on a daily basis

▲ Dogs should never be a nuisance to other dogs or people in the park.

so that it will come back when called, and won't launch itself at joggers, children and people in the park.

Vaccinations are a legal requirement in most countries, and there are particular laws applying to countries where rabies exists.

Next, you may be required to have your dog microchipped, or to wear a collar with an identity disc engraved

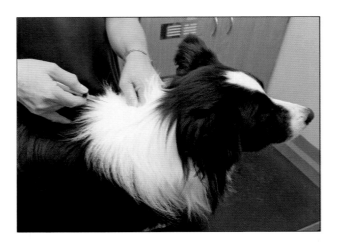

◄ Regular vaccinations are a must, to keep your dog healthy throughout its life.

► Your dog cannot speak for itself, so an identity disc is a necessity. It should be engraved with your name and address.

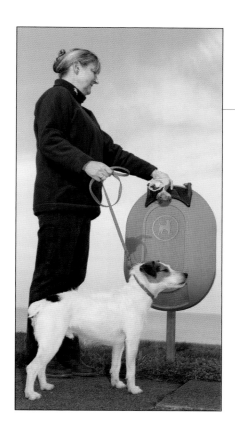

◄ *Always carry bags to clean up after your dog. Dispose of the used bags in appropriate bins for dog waste.*

Penalties vary from a fine to imprisonment, depending on the area fouled and the frequency of the offence. It is always the owner's responsibility to dispose of waste matter. It is not a legal obligation for authorities to provide appropriate bins, although most do. In the UK, councils can refuse to collect household rubbish if it includes dog faeces. Neighbours also have the right to complain to the local authorities if dog faeces in a nearby garden are causing a smell or health hazard. To deal with the problem, dog waste can be safely composted in the garden, or chemical 'toilets' can be purchased. These look like buckets that are partially buried in the garden, and they use chemicals to break down the solids that are placed in them.

Time requirements

If you are thinking about getting a dog, you should first look at your lifestyle. Consider whether you have the time needed, and whether you are prepared to give it, to ensure a happy human–dog partnership. Some dogs, such as the collie breeds, need a great deal of exercise; others, like some of the toy breeds, do not need so much. All require mental stimulation of some sort. This could take the form of a type of trained activity such as obedience or agility, or simpler games such as 'find your toy' in the home. Either way, this will take up part of your day, every day for the whole of your dog's life. Dogs also need company and must not just be banished to the garden; you should interact with them regularly. Their every need is your total responsibility. You cannot decide that you are too tired to bother; owning a dog is a lifelong commitment.

▼ *Regular, daily outdoor exercise makes for a happy dog.*

with the name of the owner and their contact details. Some countries require certain breeds to be muzzled in public places. It is the owner's responsibility to be aware of and conform to the regulations in force in the area in which they live.

You'll also need to pick up your dog's faeces when on a beach or in the street or park. You might not mind the mess, but other people will, especially those with children. Nothing gives dog owners a bad name quicker than dog faeces left all over the place, dirtying shoes and spreading disease – one very good reason why most beaches are now out of bounds to dog owners in summer.

Furthermore, in many countries – including most of Europe – it is a legal requirement to pick up and safely dispose of your dog's faeces. In some states of the USA, it is also an offence for a dog to urinate on or close to a public building. These regulations are enforced by dog wardens or officers employed by the county or state.

Benefits of dog ownership

There are many benefits of dog ownership for all types and ages of people. Owning a dog enforces a routine and a sense of responsibility that may be missing from a person's life. A dog provides companionship and unreserved affection, and many owners will say that their dog is good company. Our canine friends assist in fulfilling a basic human need of providing love and being loved in return.

Response to pets starts at a very early age, with young babies preferring something warm and cuddly to their own toys. In fact, many toddlers' first words are actually 'cat' or 'dog'. As the child grows, the dog becomes a friend and not just a pet. This friend never criticizes or chastises and always has

▼ *Most dogs are happy to join their owners in a 'keep fit' campaign. Having a reason to walk promotes fitness and also lowers stress levels.*

time for them. Owning a pet can help to teach a child about care and responsibility, and also how to communicate clearly. It is via their pets that many children learn about birth, life and death.

Dogs and children form a very strong

▲ *The family dog can become a playmate and a lifelong friend to adults and children alike.*

bond, but guidelines, for both dog and child, should always be taught and firmly enforced. A child should never be left unattended with a dog, even

▼ *Owning a dog provides companionship, mental and physical health benefits, a sense of responsibility and a social outlet.*

▶ Dog ownership can be a topic of discussion and an ice breaker when making new friends.

if it is only for a few minutes. Some dog training clubs run child handler classes, and this is an excellent way for the dog and child to learn together and to put in place the foundations of a lifelong partnership.

When older people retire or families reduce in size due to children leaving the home, the dog remains totally dependent on its master, and so encourages the owner to retain a feeling of self-worth. Studies show that dog owners who suffer from a stressful situation such a divorce, retirement or bereavement are better able to cope than those who do not own a pet. Simply walking a dog down the road to the local park opens opportunities to communicate with fellow dog owners and make new friends. The family dog, just like its ancestral wolf, also has an amazing ability to pick up on our moods, as it is very sensitive to atmosphere and emotion. If a human is sad or sick, their canine pet will seek them out and offer comfort by physical touch. In part, this explains the often-heard comment, "my dog understands me better than anyone else".

The health benefits of dog ownership are undisputed. Providing care for an animal gives a daily structure to life that can help to dispel feelings of loneliness, depression and isolation. Dependence on medication for depression and sedatives for sleep disorders is a lot lower among dog owners then those who do not own a pet. It is well documented that simply stroking a dog lowers blood pressure, slows the heart rate and reduces the risk of cardio-vascular diseases. Dogs also appear to diminish anxiety. Realization of the comfort and joy a dog can bring to those in hospitals

and nursing homes has led directly to the formation of 'Pets as Therapy' in the UK and Australia, and 'Therapy Pets' in America.

Most dog owners are fitter than non-dog owners because of daily exercise walking their pets. The dog also provides opportunities to interact socially with other people outside the home. This helps to reduce feelings of isolation. Ownership, care and the training of a dog encourages mental stimulation, and helps to keep a fit mind as well as a fit body.

A dog also promotes a feeling of security within the home. It does not matter if your pet is a tiny Chihuahua or a giant Mastiff, as the sound of barking will act as a deterrent to any would-be burglar. In some cases, dog ownership even reduces the premium payable for home contents insurance.

Some older members of the community feel that owning a dog gives them a reason to get up in the morning and become active. Dog training, and the friendship this activity provides, often starts as an interest in retirement and turns out to be an all-consuming hobby opening up a whole new and fulfilling world

after retirement. Older people worry about what will happen to their pet if they are rushed into hospital or the pet outlives them. It is important that this issue is addressed, both for the owner's peace of mind and for the welfare of the dog.

▼ A happy dog is a loving companion, and it will also give a valuable sense of purpose to the owner's life.

CHOOSING A SUITABLE DOG

Many households are just not suitable for a dog. If you work for long periods away from home and there is no one around while you are out, you need to consider very carefully whether the comforts of coming home to a dog are not outweighed by the lack of company that the dog will have to endure, with all the potential behavioural problems this may cause. Consider not just how the dog would fit into your own way of life, but how your lifestyle would affect the dog. Many aspects should be factored into your decision. Can you provide an appropriate, secure home for a dog for its lifetime? The size of your house and garden need to be considered. A large, high-energy dog is not best housed in a small apartment. Finally, check that everyone in the household wants a dog. If not, this may result in a dog unfairly having to be rehomed.

◄ *Before getting a dog, it is important to ensure that you can provide it with the environment it needs.*

What type of dog?

Dogs are companions. If you want one just as a guard, buy a burglar alarm. Dogs are usually effective burglar deterrents, whatever their breed, but their first function in a home must be as a friend – and there is no better friend. They don't criticize you (or not too unkindly), they don't sulk (or not for too long), and they are always there to comfort you and love you.

Choosing the right breed is an intensely personal matter, but there are broad guidelines.

The size of the fully grown dog is important, but perhaps not quite so critical as it may seem. Very large dogs need a lot of exercise, and once you have decided that there is room in your house for a large dog, exercise is the most important consideration. Most people, however, want a dog that fits reasonably into the home environment. A couple of Wolfhounds may be your ideal, but their bulk may make a small living space uninhabitable.

◄ Dogs enjoy the companionship of other dogs, with some surprising friendships emerging. Adult size is an important consideration when deciding which breed is right for you.

The Labrador Retriever, if not overweight, weighs about 30kg (66lb) when mature, and according to kennel club statistics it is the most popular dog in both the UK and the USA. Second in the USA is the German Shepherd, and third the Golden Retriever. In Britain the Cocker Spaniel is second, with the French Bulldog being the third most popular breed. These statistics can only be tracked by applications for kennel club registrations and take no account of the numbers of hybrids or unrecognized breeds, both of which have seen a dramatic increase in popularity in recent years.

▲ The Labrador Retriever belongs to the Gundog Group and loves long walks and splashing in water.

▲ Terriers come in a range of sizes, but most tend to be rather 'sharp' and are not afraid to give a warning nip.

▲ Many dogs in the Toy Group, such as this Cavalier King Charles Spaniel, are active and not just lap dogs.

◀ *Most dogs love chasing toys. This is helpful in exercising highly active breeds from the Working and Herding Groups.*

Looking at past statistics, there appears to be a gradual swing in the UK from owning large dogs to owning those of a smaller size. There is no clear reason for this, but it may be influenced by house size.

Breed or type behaviour is probably more important in choosing a dog than any other characteristic. It pays to ask not just dedicated owners, but also knowledgeable people outside the breed – your veterinary surgeon sees a wide variety of dogs every day.

Typically, the terrier types are lively, not easy to train, but very responsive dogs. If they are properly trained, they are good with children.

Toy dogs are usually better companions for owners who do not have young children. The dogs may be upset by what they perceive as large noisy humans rushing around. Their fear may make them snappy, with unhappy results. All toy dogs will enjoy as much exercise as you can give them, but they may be equally content with only a moderate amount.

Hounds need as much exercise as possible. If this condition is met, they make very good house dogs who love their comfort. Breeds in the other groups vary, but, in general, the working breeds are all better with an occupation that keeps them out of mischief.

The gundog (sporting) breeds are generally easy to train, and settle into the human environment without difficulty. They need exercise – and lack of exercise shows!

▼ *Some breeds, such as the Border Collie, spend hours looking for attention. Ignore them at your peril!*

Certain animals of the herding breeds, typified by the Border Collie, are, or should be regarded as, specialist working dogs. They demand more attention than other breeds if they are not to become neurotic pets. Outside their traditional working function, they have become the outstanding type in obedience work of all sorts. Provided you are able to give sufficient attention to them to keep their very active minds occupied, they are among the most rewarding of pets. But if you don't, they will find something to occupy themselves, and it will be trouble.

With so many breeds to choose from, as well as crossbreeds and mongrels, there really isn't a typical household pet these days.

▲ *The Otterhound will follow an interesting scent regardless of the owner's entreaties to come back.*

▶ *This charming Bernese puppy will make a beautiful house pet, but it will grow to 70cm (27½in) at the shoulder when fully mature.*

The cost of keeping a dog

Can you afford it? Buying a dog is just the start. Very few puppies can be acquired for nothing. Almost everyone will want to sell the litter they have reared, even if only to try to recoup the cost of feeding the puppies to weaning.

The cost of good pedigree puppies varies from country to country. In the United Kingdom, depending on breed, a puppy may cost from around £500, although probably the average cost of a well-bred puppy of most breeds is between £600 and £1,000. In the United States, asking prices are usually somewhat higher, from about $1,600 upwards. Australian prices are similar to those in the UK. Imported puppies in any country may cost a great deal more.

The initial examination by the veterinary surgeon, and the puppy's primary inoculations, will be around another £65, perhaps $95 in the USA, and you can spend as much as you wish on toys and other equipment.

A substantial part of the price of keeping a dog may be the cost of veterinary treatment. These days, veterinary surgeons are capable of sophisticated treatments of illness or injury, but they have no subsidy for the costs. If your dog ever needs complicated or prolonged veterinary treatment, the cost may be high.

There are many pet insurance companies catering for veterinary treatments; each has its own approach, and dog owners would be well advised to study what each company offers before deciding which policy to buy.

The premium-grade policies offer sums for the death of your dog, and for rewards to be offered if the dog is lost. They may include kennelling fees

▲ A fair return for the cost of keeping a dog may be the exercise it encourages its owner to take.

in case of your own illness, and even holiday cancellation costs. The level of veterinary fees covered is variable on most schemes, and it may be worth discussing this with your veterinary surgeon before you choose a policy. All additions cost money.

▼ Puppies need vaccinations and annual boosters, and this cost is not covered under any insurance scheme.

◄ When considering a puppy, the price of good training and socializing classes should be factored into the overall cost.

Some companies offer a basic veterinary fee insurance as an alternative to the premium schemes. It will be up to you to decide which of the various forms of insurance best fits your own needs.

Most insurers offer a puppy scheme, sometimes with an incentive to transfer to the adult scheme when it expires. Many breeders will offer puppy insurance to buyers, either as part of or as an extra cost to the purchase price of the puppy.

Feeding costs vary greatly. In theory, the smaller the dog, the less expensive to feed, but this is frequently offset by choosing more specialized, and therefore more expensive, foods for the very small pet. It is possible to feed a 14kg (31lb) dog very adequately for about £5.00 ($6.00) a week, provided that it is a healthy adult.

▼ A large dog such as this Great Dane will cost at least £1.50 ($1.80) per day to feed. As well as the cost of food, if you don't have a local safe place to exercise your dog, daily travel costs can also quickly mount up.

▼ Older dogs benefit from regular veterinary check-ups and may be prescribed ongoing medication.

▼ Buying budget food is not a saving if your dog won't eat it. Household scraps are not a healthy option.

▼ The superb grooming of this Maltese may be achieved by a professional at considerable cost.

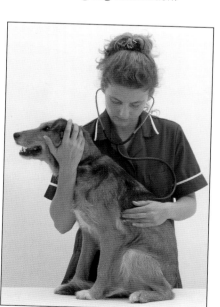

Pedigree or non-pedigree

Crossbred dogs, the most identifiable of which is the Lurcher, are usually not expensive to buy, which is an obvious advantage. They have their own 'mutt' charm, and their apparent type may be just what you are looking for. But remember that the tiny puppy may become an enormous adult. The best way to judge is to see both parents, but in the nature of things the father is likely to be 'away on business' when the puppies are ready to leave.

It is not necessarily true that crossbred dogs are healthier than purebreds, as many people believe. Every veterinary surgeon can tell you about crossbreds or mongrels suffering from recognizable, inherited diseases.

The advantage of choosing a purebred dog is that you know what you are getting. From a reputable

◄ If you choose a pedigree dog, you must still look for a strain in that breed that fits your lifestyle. Gundogs, such as this Irish Red and White Setter, can come from a 'working' or a 'show' strain.

breeder, a Cocker Spaniel puppy will grow up into a Cocker Spaniel dog, of a size and weight that is within the breed norm, and with potential behaviour characteristics typical of the breed. There is, or should be, advice

available to deal with whatever problems may arise as a particular feature of the breed.

There is no doubt that many breeds have inherited problems associated with that breed, although these have often been exaggerated in the press. It is up to the potential owner to enquire about these problems, and to take independent advice on their significance. It is worth bearing in mind that no species of animal, including human beings, is free from inheritable disease. Dogs may actually be less afflicted than most.

◄ A lovable mongrel. Did its owners know how it was going to turn out, and have they the time and inclination to give that coat the attention it demands?

► Crossbred dogs are often the basis for new working types. A cross between two recognized breeds is likely to have characteristics somewhere between the two.

Dog or bitch

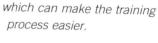

▼ Unless you are planning to breed a litter, it is wise to have a bitch spayed.

Choosing whether to have a male or female – a dog or a bitch – is one of the earliest decisions you will make.

Dogs tend to have a more 'macho' outlook on life than bitches, and if that attracts you, the male of the species will be your choice. Dogs are possibly more outgoing, certainly on average a little harder to train, but often more responsive once trained.

They do not, of course, come into season twice a year, with the attendant bother of oestrous discharges, and the attraction of all the dogs in the neighbourhood. But don't forget that it is the male dogs that are attracted, and if you have a male, it could be yours that has to be dragged home each night from his wanderings.

▼ In general, a male dog – such as this Airedale Terrier – is broader, heavier and more muscular, and therefore stronger, than a bitch.

On balance, if there is such a thing in this particular choice, the female is likely to make a better family pet. She is less likely to be aggressive, although dominance is as much a breed characteristic as it is related to the gender of the dog. Bitches are much less likely to try to wander for most of the year, and they are inclined to be more loving to their human family.

▼ Both dogs and bitches can be equally aggressive if not trained and socialized correctly. Bitches are more focused on their owners, which can make the training process easier.

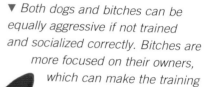

▼ Neutering a male dog is cheaper than spaying a bitch, because the former operation is less intrusive.

Buying a puppy

Let us assume that you know more or less the type of dog you feel you can best live with. Even though you may have no intention of ever showing your pet, dog shows are good places to visit while you are finally making up your mind. Talk to the people showing, and find out what their views are about their breed – you may find that many of the exhibitors are remarkably frank about the drawbacks as well as the virtues of their breed. In the long run, it pays them to be so.

The next step is to look for the right breeder – not necessarily the top one in the breed, who would, quite fairly, expect a premium price for puppies of show standard. Top breeders, however, will often be the most genuinely encouraging to the potential new owner.

Many dogs are still sold through so-called 'puppy farms' and pet shops. Neither is a suitable place to find a puppy. Young dogs cannot be treated as commodities to be traded at the convenience of their breeder, and serious health problems regularly arise from this form of mistreatment of young animals.

▲ *A 'pedigree puppy' should always come with a kennel club registration certificate, but this is not a guarantee to its health or temperament.*

Take your time, and be prepared to wait to get the dog you really want. Above all, visit the kennels and make sure you see the dam with the puppies in the litter (and other litters), and, if possible, the sire. Make your own mind up about the conditions in which the puppies have been reared.

There is some argument about the right age to buy a puppy, although the general consensus seems to be that about eight weeks is right. Much before that may be too early to remove the puppy from the nest, while leaving it later can give rise to socialization problems, with the time between six and eight weeks regarded by behaviourists as a critical period in the puppy's development. Certainly, if the puppy is much older than eight weeks, you need to be satisfied that it

◄ *This West Highland White Terrier puppy will not be ready to leave the breeder for its new home until it is at least eight weeks old. By this time it should be ready to meet and play with other dogs and people.*

◄ *Retrievers tend to have very large litters, often ten or more. Weaning can start as early as three weeks with suitable supplements. Pups should be plump and active with no sign of illness.*

has been exposed to a sensible social environment and not simply left in its rearing kennel to make its own way.

Be honest with the breeder. If you are looking for a dog that you may later want to show, don't pretend that you are only looking for a pet puppy, in the hope that the price might be lower. Explain truthfully and carefully the life that the puppy will lead, especially its home environment. At worst, the breeder will explain why your home may not be suitable for rearing a puppy; at best, you may get much good advice.

Never expect a guarantee that your puppy will be a show winner. Even though it comes from the very best show stock, with a pedigree as long as your arm, no one, including the most experienced breeders, can pick a 'cert' at eight weeks.

The breeder should provide you with the puppy's pedigree and a receipt for its purchase. If the breeder has already taken the puppies for their first inoculation, this may be included in the quoted price or regarded as an extra. You should ask.

You may be expected to sign a contract setting out the limitations of the breeder's liability in the event of the puppy later developing an inheritable condition. We live in a litigious society, and several court cases have made it plain that if a breeder fails to warn a purchaser of conditions that are recognized in the breed and the puppy later develops such a condition, the breeder may be held liable, even though they are unaware of the existence of the problem in that puppy, and have taken reasonable precautions to avoid the condition.

The contract you may be asked to sign must be reasonable, and it is likely to consist of a statement drawing your attention to the known inheritable diseases of the breed and an expectation that you will have discussed the significance of the condition with your veterinary surgeon. Your vet may be advised to make their comments in a written statement.

The breeder should always provide you with a feeding chart for the next stage of rearing your puppy. It is

▼ *The best way to decide on the suitability of a particular kennel is to see as many of their dogs as possible, both at home and at work, or in the show ring.*

▼ *Large breeds, such as these St Bernard puppies, generally have a shorter lifespan than their smaller counterparts.*

▼ *Ex-racing greyhounds make wonderful pets, but they occasionally have problems socializing after years of living in a racing kennel.*

worthwhile taking this to discuss with the veterinary surgeon when you take your puppy for its first visit. Many breeders give the new owner some sample feed to start the puppy off in its new home.

You should expect a healthy puppy, which has been wormed adequately, probably twice, and is free from skin parasites such as fleas or lice.

Pet insurance companies have short-term cover schemes, available to

breeders for issue to new owners. Ask the breeder if they have such cover. If not, arrange your own as soon as you have bought the puppy. Puppies are at their most vulnerable during the first few weeks in their new home.

◄ *The age to leave home is a compromise. A critical socializing time is about six weeks, when ideally the puppy should meet its new family, but other factors usually dictate that eight weeks is probably the best practical age at which to buy your puppy.*

Choosing a puppy

Never accept excuses about a puppy's condition or behaviour, and never buy a puppy because it's the last one left and you feel sorry for it.

It is often said that puppies choose their new owners rather than the other way around, and there is much truth to this claim. An overly shy puppy may have socialization problems later, and the puppy that comes forward from the nest, asking to be chosen, is probably the right one.

The puppy must be alert and have bright, clean eyes. Its nose must be clean (but forgive a little crust of food), its ears must be free of wax, and its coat must be clean and pleasant to handle and smell. There must be no sign of sores or grittiness on the skin and coat. Black 'coal dust' is usually flea dirt – fleas themselves are more difficult to spot. Examine all the puppies briefly to ensure that they have been well cared for.

▲ Make sure there is no discharge from the eyes. Forgive a scratch or two on the face – puppies in the nest don't always agree.

▲ The membranes of the nose must be clear and free of discharge. There must be no sign of a runny nose. Check the puppy is not coughing or wheezing.

▲ The inside of the ears must look pink and shiny, without inflammation or dark-coloured wax. The area should not look sore.

▲ Soreness or inflammation of the rims of the eyes, or eyes that are not completely clear, may be serious signs of present or potential disease.

▲ The puppy's coat and skin should feel loose and soft. The skin should be free of sores. There should be no baldness or patches of hair loss.

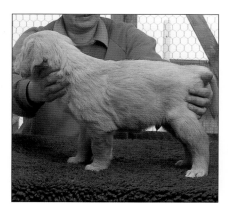

▲ Sturdy, strong limbs are a must for any breed, although if you fancy an Italian Greyhound, don't expect it to be this sturdy.

▲ Puppies should have a clean bottom. Signs of diarrhoea are obvious from a quick examination behind. The whole litter should be examined.

Children and dogs

Parents often boast that their children can do whatever they like to their dog, and that it is so good-natured it puts up with almost anything. What such parents often ignore is that this child–dog relationship must be fixed around certain rules.

BASIC GUIDELINES

A child must respect the dog's space and leave it alone when it is sleeping, not pick it up and carry it around like a teddy bear, and never hug it tightly around the neck or kiss it repeatedly, because the dog might respond with a bite to the child's face. In fact, constant cuddling and carrying can easily make your puppy grumpy and snappy, causing owners to think they have an aggressive dog, when really the child is to blame. Remember, not all dogs are keen on close contact. Nor should a puppy be

dressed up like a doll. If that's how a child wants to treat a puppy, then buy them a doll instead. Also make it clear that it is forbidden to pull a dog's ears, tail or nose, and that there's no prodding or poking, even if the dog is blocking the way.

Rewarding children when they are well-behaved with the dog, and vice-versa, will help create a good relationship. Even better, help children to develop a positive relationship with their dog by including them in the dog's training sessions. The dog will learn to take commands from and respect the child.

Young children also need to be taught how their natural exuberance can affect a puppy's behaviour. If a child becomes hyperactive – jumping up and down, shouting, yelling and waving their arms – their dog will also become overexcited, and suddenly

▲ *With supervision, children can take an active role in dog training.*

both are out of control. Worse, the child might hit the puppy when trying to control it. Neither is renowned for patience, especially when tired, so supervise any occasion when children and pets are together.

It goes without saying that a dog, no matter how much you think you can trust it, should never be left alone in a room with a young child. Accidents do happen. Be vigilant outdoors, too, and don't let a young child be responsible for a dog on a walk. Could the child really cope if another dog approached their dog aggressively, and be relied on to pick up the faeces and stop their dog from dashing out into the road? Finally, make sure your child never pats strange dogs. Always get permission from the owners first. Other people's dogs might not be as child-friendly as yours.

GET CHILDREN INVOLVED

Fortunately, it is easy to get children involved in all aspects of the day-to-day care of a dog and its training. Many dog-training classes encourage

▼ *Building a relationship is good for the dog's and children's well-being.*

▲ *If play becomes rough, it is best to move the dog away to a safe place.*

▲ *Teach children to give dogs space and peace when they are resting.*

▲ *If there is mutual respect, a good relationship can be built.*

children to attend with their parents, so they can learn how to handle the family dog effectively, and develop a relationship based on mutual respect and trust.

Safety

If you have crawling babies in the home, your dog's food bowl should be picked up as soon as the dog has eaten. Not only might a child try to eat the contents, but the dog may become protective over its food.

However sensible your child is, their friends may not have a good awareness of dogs. Watching both small children and a dog can be an impossible task. On these occasions, it is best to put the dog into another room or in a dog crate. This way, neither the child nor the dog will be at risk.

HEALTH ISSUES

A lot has been written about the health risks associated with children handling dogs, but these are actually slight and arguably outweighed by the benefits gained by both child and dog. The main risk is contact with and transmission of round-worm eggs that are passed in the dog's faeces. Worm eggs are tiny and can't be seen with the human eye. However, note that the risk of contamination is far greater when in contact with cats rather than dogs.

Dogs must be wormed regularly with a prescribed wormer, and your vet will advise on how often to do this. Children should be taught to keep their hands away from their faces and to wash their hands after handling their pet, applying the normal rules of commonsense and basic hygiene.

▼ *In time, your dog will learn to respond to what your child asks of it.*

Settling in

Bringing home a new puppy or even an older dog is an important family occasion. Everyone wants to touch, hold and stroke the new member of the family, especially the children. But you should take things slowly.

In the case of a puppy, this will be its first time away from the only environment it has ever known, and away from its mother and litter mates. The world is huge and frightening. For an older dog, there is still a lot of adjusting for it to do.

Bring it home when there are not too many people around, and introduce it to its new environment in as relaxed a manner as possible. Let it look and sniff around, offer it a little something to eat, which it probably won't accept, and allow it to have a run around the garden. Bring your family and friends to meet the dog one or two at a time, and give it time to make friends before introducing anyone else.

▶ *Puppies hate to be left alone until they are confident that you will quickly return.*

▶ *Puppies' curiosity about new toys helps to overcome their awe of strange surroundings.*

At some stage, you have to cause a little more trauma by taking the dog to the veterinary surgeon for a health check. If at all possible, take it to the vet on the way home from the breeder or kennels. If there should be a problem that necessitates returning the dog to the seller (fortunately, a very rare occurrence), it is going to be much easier if the family haven't met and already fallen in love with it.

Once the settling-in process has begun, interrupt the dog's established routine as little as possible. For a puppy, follow the breeder's feeding regime, giving the same number of feeds at the same time each day. To start with, give the food the dog is used to – the seller might have provided a 'starter pack' – even if you have decided eventually to use a different type of food. Make any dietary changes gradually.

Clean water should always be available; show the dog where it is. Make sure that not only is the water bowl always full, but that it is washed regularly – dogs are messy drinkers, and the bowl soon gets dirty. Most dogs, some breeds more than others, are also very splashy drinkers, spilling more water around the bowl than they

Safety guidelines on toys for dogs

The jaws and teeth of nearly all dogs are much stronger than you think, so toys should be very tough.

Fluffy dolls will be torn to pieces without fail, so if you must provide them, make sure that they do not have parts that can be detached and swallowed.

Balls are popular toys for dogs because the owners can throw them and join in the game. Fine, but make sure the ball is large enough not even to be half-swallowed by the dog. A dog being rushed to the veterinary surgeon choking on a tennis ball that is stuck in its throat is a common emergency.

The use of a bone as a toy is controversial. Most veterinary surgeons advise against it, unless the bone is so big that the dog cannot break pieces off and swallow them. There is no doubt that a good chew at a bone is a dog's delight.

▲ *Toys should be solid enough not to risk pieces being chewed off and swallowed.*

swallow. So it is important to choose the site for your water bowl carefully.

The ideal water bowl may be made of ceramic or non-rust metal, but it must be non-spill, and preferably too heavy for the dog to pick up and carry around. If you start with a heavy bowl, the puppy will soon get the idea that this is not a toy to be picked up and carted around, and it will look for something else to play with.

Feed bowls may be much the same as water bowls, with the same idea: the dog should not regard the bowl as a toy. Apart from anything else, if the bowl gets carried around, you can never find it when you want to feed the dog!

The new dog's bed is also very important – the bed is the dog's own special place. It is important to introduce the dog to its bed as soon as it arrives, and to insist that the bed is where it sleeps. This may be difficult, but if you give in and let it

◄ Hygiene is important for feed bowls. Never add another meal without first thoroughly cleaning the bowl.

▼ Rawhide chews are usually an excellent substitute for bones.

sleep on your bed "just until it settles in," you have lost the battle – and probably the war!

To make sure the dog uses its bed, the best way is to shut it into a 'bedroom' on the first night with nothing else to choose for a comfortable sleep but the bed. Make sure it is sited away from any draughts. Young puppies will miss their litter mates and perhaps their dam. A useful tip if the puppy doesn't settle – that is, if it is crying pitifully just as you are getting to sleep

– is to provide it with comforters. Traditionally, these are a hot-water bottle and a ticking clock, and like many traditions, they often work well.

Toys are important, whatever the age of the dog, but particularly for a young puppy. There is an enormous range on sale, from fluffy dolls that amuse the owner but soon become unrecognizable once the puppy has had a chance to tear them apart, to specifically designed training aids.

Some dogs are obsessive about a particular toy – this occurs more in the terrier breeds than in other types – but mostly dogs have a rather short attention span, dropping one object for another after a short spell of play. There is no certain winner. Each dog has a different fancy, but do provide choice for a puppy, bearing all safety guidelines in mind.

▼ Puppies take great comfort from a hot-water bottle, but beware leaks from chewing. A ticking clock seems to soothe them at night.

Beds and bedding

The dog must have a bed of its own. From the owner's point of view, washability is the priority. Plastic beds made for this purpose are not expensive and easily cleaned, but they must have soft bedding for comfort.

Providing a mobile cage as a bed and a private place for your puppy has several advantages, not least of which is that there is somewhere to put the puppy when non-doggy friends, who may not appreciate dog hairs all over their clothes, arrive.

Cages may be the completely collapsible type, useful for folding and taking with you when you are travelling with the dog, or, probably better in the long run, the 'sky kennel' type, which is fastened by nuts and bolts around the middle. This enables the cage to be divided in half for travelling, but provides a more permanent kennel for the dog to use at home.

There are plenty of choices of bedding. The most satisfactory from the hygiene point of view, as well as for comfort and warmth, is veterinary

◄ Flexible dog beds seem to pass the comfort test. They are usually insulated against cold floors and are easily cleaned. They may be destructible by determined dogs, and can be expensive.

bedding, sold under a number of brand names, made of synthetic fur backed by a strong woven base. These veterinary beds may be machine-washed, they stay dry as moisture goes straight through them, they are long-lasting, and they are

▼ Left to right: An old blanket is best in a bed rather than just on the floor; synthetic veterinary bedding is probably more hygienic than any other soft bedding; the bean bag is

resistant (but not if the dog is really determined!) to being chewed up. They can be bought or cut to any size, and using the principle of 'one on, one in the wash', you can easily keep the bed clean and free from doggy odours. Wash on a 30°C (85°F) cycle.

supremely comfortable and warmly insulating; a plastic basket is easily cleaned, but it does need a comfortable lining to be given the dog's personal accolade.

◄ Dogs all appreciate a warm covering to lie on, wherever they choose to sleep. Ideally this should be in a quiet spot away from traffic, but where the dog can still keep an eye on its family. Every dog needs a place to call its own.

Behaviour tip
Dogs will often accept your displeasure if it means you are paying attention to them rather than ignoring them. To ignore your dog is the most severe punishment you can inflict. So for peaceful nights for you and your dog, make it sleep elsewhere.

▼ *A dog's bed should be a place of safety and comfort, not somewhere to be sent to as a punishment.*

Cushions filled with a memory foam or orthopaedic pad are possibly the most comfortable beds. Those filled with polystyrene granules are popular but difficult to wash. Some dogs enjoy chewing their bed, and this results in a myriad little polystyrene balls rolling around the floor, which are almost impossible to sweep up.

Still probably more used than anything else is a square of old blanket or a blanket off-cut. There

▼ *An outside kennel must always be dry, warm and of an adequate size to ensure your dog's comfort.*

is nothing wrong with them, provided you have enough so that you can wash them regularly, bearing in mind that they leave a fluffy deposit which needs to be removed from the washing machine, and they take forever to dry.

WHERE TO SLEEP
The kitchen or a warm utility room are the best places for a dog to sleep. The kitchen floor often has non-absorbent flooring, useful for a puppy before it is able to avoid accidents. Once it has become accustomed to the kitchen, if it remains convenient to you, this is possibly the best place for the dog to stay. The kitchen tends to be one of the warm places in the house, and dogs like warmth.

Most dogs are not kennelled outdoors. There is no particular reason why they should not be, and if that is your intention, it must be instituted from the start. Use plenty of warm bedding and pay attention to

draughts and waterproofing. One problem with outside kennels is that it becomes too easy to ignore the dog. Few owners would indulge in the outright cruelty of neglecting to feed their dog, but if the weather doesn't look too good, plenty would put off the walk until another day. If a dog is to be confined in a kennel, you must ask yourself if you really want a dog. At worst, the kennel must provide an adequate exercise area, as well as the essentials mentioned here.

▼ *A basket containing a cushion and a washable fleece makes a comfortable and practical bed.*

Equipment

Pet shops and online sites sell a wide array of basic equipment, and it is essential that you have done your homework in advance, knowing the most suitable collars and the best types of lead to buy. Under UK law your dog will need to wear a flat collar with an identification disc containing your name and address, and without these details you could be fined £5,000. Even if your dog has been microchipped, it will still need a collar and disc. Microchipping of all dogs became compulsory in the UK in 2016. In many European countries, dogs need to be microchipped and/or tattooed An identification tag is required in the USA, while some states also require that your dog has a licence.

◄ *There is a vast array of basic control equipment on the market, such as flat collars, head collars and body harnesses.*

FLAT COLLARS

A flat collar with a buckle or clip fastening is by far the best piece of equipment for training your dog.

▼ *A flat collar with either a buckle or clip fastening is suitable for training.*

When your dog is fully grown, it is a good idea to buy the best you can afford. A leather collar is the most hard-wearing and is kind on your hands and the dog's neck. Puppies tend to grow quickly, so an ajustable collar for them is a wise buy.

If you buy a collar with a clip fastening, regularly check that it doesn't become loose and that you cannot pull it apart, because if your dog pulls away and the clip fastening comes undone, your dog could end up in the road, causing an accident.

HEAD COLLARS

These are devised to work in the same way as reins on many large animals such as horses, bulls and camels: they steer the animal from the head instead of the strongest part of the body – the neck and shoulders. There are varous types and designs of head collar available, and it is worth trying several to find the one that your dog feels most comfortable in.

▼ *A body harness has thick straps, but may encourage your dog to pull more.*

▼ Retractable leads are popular, but a leather lead is better for training.

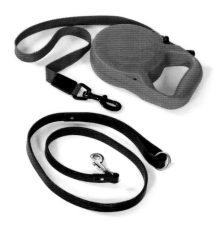

All head collars must be correctly fitted and be the right size for the dog.

There are positive and negative sides to head collars, and they can take some getting used to. It is worth putting one on your dog before giving it a treat, so that it associates it with pleasure, then take it off. Gradually let your dog get used to it. Some dogs scratch their faces along the floor, trying to get the head collar off, or rub themselves up and down your legs because they do not like the feel of it. The problem is it can be hard for the dog to concentrate on what you want it to do if it is uncomfortable wearing a head collar. If it keeps pulling on it while being trained, it could end up walking sideways, which can damage its neck.

Head collars are often mistaken for muzzles, and so other dog walkers may give you a wide berth when out walking. On the other hand, a head collar is useful for stopping an aggressive dog from staring at other dogs. A head collar should not be left on an unattended dog, as it might get caught up on something, causing the dog stress or injury. If your dog really does not like a head collar, then you could consider using a body harness instead.

BODY HARNESSES

There is a wide choice of body harnesses on the market, but choose wisely. The best kinds have a front and back or side attachment, and need a double-ended lead, which means that your dog cannot pull you from its strongest point – its shoulders. The weight is evenly distributed by the lead being attached to the front and side of the harness. The harness stays away from the dog's neck area and won't interfere with its natural body language when approaching another dog.

Avoid those with very thin harness straps, because they can chafe under the dog's legs and cause pain and discomfort. Look for a body harness with wide straps and padding.

Most basic harnesses are unsuitable for training your dog to stop pulling, and you only have to watch a team of huskies to understand how the harness lets them pull. A fixed harness without the use of a double-ended lead can only encourage your dog to pull, the lead being attached to the back and front of the harness in the middle of the chest. Specialist harnesses are available to help stop a dog pulling while on the lead, but these are not generally available in smaller pet shops.

LEADS

Always buy the best you can afford. Avoid chain leads, as these can hurt your hands. A range of materials is available, from leather through to braided fabric; they should be soft and pliable while still retaining strength. Always check that the clip that attaches to the collar is both strong and of good quality.

Retractable leads are very popular but are not suitable for training, because they can actually encourage dogs to pull, since they allow the animal to go to the end of the lead. In some situations they can be dangerous, with the lead getting tangled around your legs or another dog's feet, which could lead to a fight. Your dog could also run out into the road if you are not quick enough to put on the lock, and the lock mechanism could fail, resulting in a car accident.

Retractable leads are made in differing breaking strain, so check that the one you intend to use is suitable for the weight of your dog. A retractable lead should only be put on your dog when you have arrived at the location where it is going to be walked.

CRATES

A crate is absolutely essential for the puppy owner. It is an invaluable aid to house-training, because you can contain your puppy when you cannot watch it – puppies dislike messing the

▼ A crate is useful for house-training and for taking your dog in the car.

area that they sleep in, and so will cry to be let out to go to the toilet.

A crate also provides a safe place for times when you cannot supervise your dog. It makes a snug sleeping space and an area of safety in the car. However, never keep your dog locked up in a crate for hours, and don't use it as punishment. Get a crate that is large enough for when your dog becomes an adult, and in which it will be able to stand up and move around.

Light-weight fabric crates are ideal for travel but are not as easily cleaned as the folding metal type. They are not suitable for a dog that is not used to being crated, as they can turn over if the dog makes any energetic moves inside. They are also not the best option for puppies or for dogs that are likely to chew the fabric.

FOOD AND WATER BOWLS
There are many types of bowls on the market. The best are the stainless steel bowls that are hard-wearing and tough. Cheaper plastic bowls should

be avoided – they can be easily chewed, and splinters could cut your dog's mouth or be swallowed.

Some dogs benefit from specialist bowls. Spaniel bowls have a wide base, narrower top and sloping sides that cause their long ears to fall outside of the bowl and not get covered with the contents. Some food bowls have plastic ridges or knobbles at the bottom, which make it harder for a greedy dog to bolt its food. Stands are available to raise the bowl to a comfortable level. This is helpful for the veteran dog that may have back ache or a stiff neck. Many vets recommend the use of raised bowls for all dogs.

TREAT BAGS AND WASTE BAGS
Any small bag that can hang around your waist can be used to carry treats. Waste bags should also be carried at all times. Eco-friendly biodegradable waste bags are available at most pet shops. Nappy (diaper) bags are an economical alternative.

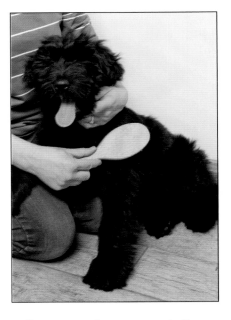

▲ *Groom your dog every week. Its coat will benefit, and it will enjoy the attention and get used to being held.*

BRUSHES AND COMBS
Even if you have a short-haired dog, it is a good idea to brush it once a week to keep its coat in good condition and to stimulate the skin and circulation.

▼ *Match the size of the food bowl you choose to the size of your dog.*

▼ *There are many types of food bowls, including stainless steel and ceramic. Both of these are strong, long-lasting and easy to keep clean.*

▼ *Single or double raised bowl stands are available in different heights and diameters to accommodate the particular needs of your dog.*

▼ *A huge range of toys and equipment are available that allow the owner and dog to interact together. These can be used as rewards when training.*

▼ *Some toys allow the dog to self-reward, by making a noise when they are played with. These are fun for the dog, but can become annoying for the owner.*

CLICKERS, WHISTLES AND TOYS

Useful training aids such as clickers and whistles are available from most pet shops, and there are more toys on the market for dogs now than there have ever been before. There are tug toys, interactive toys, educational toys, home-alone toys, teething toys, training toys and ball-on-a-rope toys. There are squeaky toys for terriers, fetch toys for retrievers, and balls for collies.

One of the best-selling dog toys is the Kong, an interactive stuffable toy that can keep any dog quiet for hours. Stuffing it with some of your dog's daily diet will teach it that it is rewarding to be left home alone. It can also be used to reward your dog for being calm when you have visitors, and will keep it busy if it has to be shut in its crate for any amount of time.

It is neither wise nor economical to buy cheap plastic toys, especially for puppies. Cheap toys are easily ripped apart by sharp teeth, and they are usually made of hard plastic that can lodge in the puppy's tummy and cause an expensive trip to the vet.

Do not throw sticks for dogs – these can puncture the skin, damage the mouth, and even prove to be fatal.

CLOTHING

From the bizarre to the practical, there is an almost unlimited choice of dog clothing. For dogs that live in centrally heated homes, protection against the cold and rain is an important issue. Duvet-style coats come in all shapes and sizes, and will keep your dog warm on even the coldest winter day. Older dogs and those with arthritis will benefit from the additional warmth. Heat-reflecting or cool coats stop your canine companion from over-heating on hot summer days.

Waterproof apparel serves two purposes: the dog is comfortable, and the home is not spoiled by wet mud. Water-resistant fleece jumpers are very popular and easy to clean after a county walk. Boots are available to prevent or to protect sore feet.

Designer products command high prices, but as long as the clothing is comfortable to wear, easy to clean and fit for purpose, your dog will not mind what name is on the label.

▼ *The range of dog clothing is enormous and includes everything from heat-reflective coats to faux fur jackets.*

Home, garden and car safety

Of immediate interest to most new dog owners is the need to make the home and garden dog-proof. This may prove to be a difficult and very expensive undertaking.

INSIDE THE HOME

Prior to bring a puppy or dog into your house, look around and try to eliminate some of the dangers. All electrical flexes should be tidied away or clipped neatly to the wall. Don't forget the phone cable too. Fitting safety covers to unused floor-level power sockets is a good idea.

Some houseplants are toxic to dogs including African violets, calla lilies, hyacinth bulbs, mother-in-law's tongue and poinsettia. The Internet is a useful source of information, and any suspect plants should be removed or placed out of reach.

Puppies are no respecters of your ornaments, and these also need to be placed out of reach. Not only can they get broken, but the resulting shards

▶ *Electric flexes and cables are dangerous if they are chewed.*

of china or glass can cause injury to you and your dog.

Cleaning solutions are poisonous to humans and animals alike. They are often stored in low-level cupboards that are not lockable, for example under the kitchen sink. It is possible to buy childproof catches for kitchen cupboards, and these work equally well for dogs too. If your dog manages to get hold of any of these items and pierces the container, there is a strong likelihood that they may have inhaled, swallowed or got splashed with corrosive chemicals. Prompt veterinary advice should be sought. Remember to take the container with you if you have to visit the vet, so that they know what they are dealing with.

Childproof locks should be used on the refrigerator or freezer if the door opens at or just above floor level. We store many foods that are potentially

lethal to dogs. Chocolate, blue cheese, grapes and any food containing raisins can, at best, cause sickness and diarrhoea, and at worst, death. Food waste needs to be stored safely. Dogs quickly learn how to operate a pedal or swing bin. Gorging on the contents may be fun at the time, but the resulting stomach problems from eating plastic, sharp bones and food that is well past its best are not so pleasant, and can be life-threatening.

Internal glass or patio doors are often not seen by an excited puppy, who may well run into them. Most doors of this type contain safety glass, but it is worth checking whether this has been installed. Dogs must be trained to be calm in the house and not to charge through doors in front of their owner.

Prescribed human medication is often left lying around. The top of a bedside cabinet is a common choice, but very execrable to an inquisitive dog. Place all medicines in a drawer or high cabinet. If you drop a tablet, look for it straight away – do not leave it for your dog to find.

◀ *An easily opened refrigerator is irresistible to dogs, but it may be a potential deathtrap.*

◄ *A childproof gate designed for children also works well for puppies.*

Small children have a habit of not putting their toys away. These brightly coloured objects are irresistible to child and dog alike, and are a choking hazard. Keep small toys in a safe place.

Keeping your home safe for your dog takes a little time, lots of common sense and some financial investment, but it will be a cheap price to pay for peace of mind.

FENCING

You have a responsibility in law to keep your dog under control. This means that your garden must be fenced in such a way as to prevent the dog escaping. As the puppies of almost any breed other than the very smallest grow, so does their ability to jump over fences. There can be no hard and fast rule for the height needed to prevent this; even within the same breed, one will be a jumper and another may never learn the skill. However, the minimum height for any dog-proof fence for anything but toy breeds will be 1m (3ft). Often, for dogs from the smaller terrier breeds, such as Jack Russells, and the more agile larger breeds, this will not be sufficient. Plenty of dogs can scale a 2m (6ft 6in) fence. A fence this high starts to make the garden look like Fort Knox, and the usual compromise is a fence of about 1.5m (5ft). If it is a wire fence,

▼ *The easiest way for a dog to get out of the garden is via the gate. The gate must be rigid and placed over a hard standing.*

Behaviour tip

Any response to unacceptable behaviour may be taken by the dog as encouragement. The sensible response is to ignore it, providing it is safe to do so.

▼ *Dogs may escape despite all precautions. Identity discs for collars should have a contact telephone number as well as your name and address.*

it must be tightly strung. Many gardens are close-fenced to this height, and close fencing has advantages as a dog fence. Being unable to see the world outside often removes the temptation to investigate it.

There are two ways through a fence, even if it is in good repair. One way is over the top, and the other is underneath. Dogs enjoy digging. You need to be sure that there is no way under. Wire fencing is particularly vulnerable to the tunnelling dog, unless it is firmly attached to some sort of hard, impenetrable base.

GARDEN SAFETY

Even if you feel that the garden is securely fenced, it still contains other dangers. Young puppies can drown in the shallowest of ponds, and so these should either be covered with a mesh frame or fenced off.

Garage and shed doors need to be kept shut, and items such as pesticides, antifreeze, fertilizers and herbicides stored on a high shelf. Make sure your dog can not access areas treated with weed killer.

There are many commonly grown plants that are poisonous to dogs. Even the best-trained dog may nibble at leaves and flowers, or dig up roots and bulbs. Websites, or your vet, will be able to give a comprehensive list of dangerous plants in your country. Daffodil flowers and bulbs, cyclamen, day lilies, foxgloves, delphiniums, azalea, amaryllis and asparagus fern are just a few examples of plants that are harmful to dogs, and should either be removed from the garden or carefully fenced off.

It is wise to shut your dog indoors when using electric or power tools in the garden. The electric flex of a lawnmower snaking across the grass may prove irresistible to the curious puppy or playful dog. Sadly, many

Plants that are toxic to dogs
- African violet
- Amaryllis
- Asparagus fern
- Azalea
- Calla lily
- Cyclamen
- Daffodil
- Day lily
- Delphinium
- Foxglove
- Hyacinth
- Mother-in-law's tongue
- Poinsettia

dogs are electrocuted each year by biting live power cables.

Preventing the dog from escaping from the house is usually a matter of care rather than built-in precautions. The 'perfectly trained' dog will not push past its owner when the front door is opened unless required to do so, but in real life plenty of dogs try to. The family has to learn to keep

▼ *The garden is full of interesting and potentially dangerous items for the curious puppy.*

the dog shut in the kitchen when anyone answers the door – one reason for not restraining the dog's barking when someone knocks at the front door; at least the dog is reminding you to shut it away. Downstairs windows, and occasionally upstairs windows, may attract the dog. It is a matter of vigilance unless you are prepared to barricade yourself in.

DOGS IN CARS

The idea of travelling with a dog in the car is very appealing, but in the event it sometimes becomes a nightmare. Part of the very earliest training for the puppy must be to learn to travel in a safe and socially acceptable way in the car. For the smaller breeds, a collapsible cage is ideal.

If your car is a hatchback, a dog guard is an obvious and sensible investment. It needs to be well fitting and strong enough to prevent a determined dog from climbing through it into the front of the car. There are dozens of dog guards designed specifically for each make and model of car. They are advertised in dog

magazines and are available from most of the larger dog shows.

Unrestrained dogs in cars cause accidents. If you are not able to use a dog guard or cage, the puppy must be taught to sit on the back seat and never to climb into the front. It will soon learn if you gently and patiently restrain it, and scold it firmly if it comes forward. This is one piece of training where the immediate 'no' can work, but not if you sometimes relent and let your pet sit on the front seat. Harnesses, designed to clip to the rear seat belt fastening, are another way to keep the dog on the back seat.

▲ *It is less distracting for the driver if dogs are safely contained in the rear of the vehicle.*

Some dogs become 'barkers' when in the car. This is dangerous and distracting, and steps to remedy it must be taken before the behaviour becomes totally engrained. Specialist advice may be necessary, but the first step is to restrain the dog with a short lead below the window level of the car. It's no good shouting at your dog to keep it quiet – the dog's response will be to redouble its efforts to be heard above its owner's voice.

◀ *The interior of a car with closed windows may easily reach 55°C (130°F) on a hot day. Install grills so that you can keep the windows open.*

▶ *In the event of an accident, an unrestrained dog could be thrown forwards through the windscreen.*

Consideration to others

When you are out and about with your dog, you should always be aware of other dog owners around you, and the effect your dog will have on them. Being a responsible dog owner means consideration to others at all times.

BE THOUGHTFUL

Learn to read the signs. If another dog is friendly and its owner is willing to let it play with your dog for a while, then everything is fine. But if they call their dog back and put it back on the lead, there is usually a good reason. Their dog may have a problem socializing with other dogs or people, and just because yours is friendly towards other dogs, that does not mean you should let it run over while you call out, "he just wants to play". Be thoughtful – put your dog back on the lead before asking if your dog can socialize.

If, however, your dog is the problem, then it is your responsibility to keep it under control at all times. If it is unsafe with people, make sure that it is muzzled, and never – even with a well-behaved dog –

▲ *Ask first before allowing your dog to socialize with other dogs in the park.*

let it loose in the countryside. This is for your dog's safety, the safety of livestock and wildlife, and even your own safety.

DOGS AND LIVESTOCK

The natural instinct of many dogs is to chase and attack sheep, and it pays to remember that sheep do not have to be caught by dogs to be killed. Sheep are 'flight animals', which means they run when they sense danger – possibly straight into a road

▼ *Keep your dog under control so that it is not a nuisance to other dogs.*

and an oncoming car or into barbed wire, where they may die slowly in great pain. They may even run into a stream and drown. Pregnant sheep can be so traumatized by an unfamiliar dog that they may miscarry, causing financial hardship to the farmer.

Many dogs are shot by farmers each year because they have been seen worrying or killing their animals. A farmer is well within their rights to shoot a dog that seems to be a threat, because it is an offence to let a dog disturb or scare sheep, cattle, wildlife or poultry while in the countryside. In the UK, a farmer is allowed by law to destroy any dog that poses a threat to livestock and wildlife. Most European countries also have laws against dogs that chase or kill livestock. In the USA, the livestock law allows farmers to kill dogs that worry livestock; farmers can also charge double the amount it would cost to replace their livestock.

▼ *Taking your dog out and about with you will improve its social skills.*

▲ *Well-socialized dogs will be able to play happily together off the lead.*

There have also been cases of dog walkers being killed, having been trampled by cattle protecting their calves from out-of-control, yapping, excited dogs. (If you are being chased by cattle, then escape immediately. Do not try to protect your dog; it will be able to escape much more quickly than you can.)

While on farmland, it's also your responsibility to make sure that your dog does not disturb the wildlife living in the hedgerows. In the UK, a dog must be kept on a lead while on common land and access land between 1st March and 31st July, and all year round on farmland. In the USA, many states require that dogs are kept on a lead at all times, except in designated dog parks.

Wherever you walk, always follow simple rules of courtesy. If you go through a gate, make sure you close it properly. Open gates mean that animals can get out and cause harm to themselves or others. Take your litter home with you. The dropped wrapper from your snack could kill if swallowed by an animal. Always keep to footpaths; don't wander through fields of crops. Not only will you damage the plants, but they may have

been sprayed with chemicals harmful to you or your dog. Pick up your dog's waste and take it with you until you can dispose of it correctly. Bags of dog faeces hanging on a hedge do not enhance the countryside. Enjoy your dog-walking, but remember that other people and animals have the right to enjoy the great outdoors too.

Respect farm animals

Farm livestock does not just include the commonly seen cattle, pigs and sheep. Deer and game birds are farmed commercially as well. They are naturally shy creatures, and you may not see or hear them. If you suspect they are in the area, walk quietly on the designated footpaths. Always keep your dog on a lead. Do not take any risks.

▶ *Prevent your dog from worrying horses by keeping it on a lead.*

▼ *Sheep are wary of predators, so keep your dog well away from them.*

Your dog and holidays

Dog owners who wish to have a holiday have three options: find alternative care for their dog; take the dog with them; or have a vacation at home. Each option takes some organization and should not be left to the last moment.

If you decide to put your dog into boarding kennels, careful research is required. Ask other dog owners for recommendations on kennels that they use. The best advertisement is word of mouth. When you have a short list, visit each kennel in turn. Look for good accommodation, cleanliness, happy dogs and friendly staff. Check on prices and find out if the cost is all-inclusive or if you have to pay for added extras such as on-lead walks and special diets.

▼ Most dogs will start to settle into boarding kennels when they can no longer see their owner.

▲ Canvas or fabric portable kennels are easy to transport and provide a safe haven for your dog on holiday.

Kennels will expect vaccinations to be up to date, and most insist that dogs are vaccinated against kennel cough. Ensure this is all in order several weeks before your holiday, especially as some dogs can feel under the weather, for a short period, after a vaccination. It is a good idea to book your dog into the chosen kennel for a day, a few weeks before your holiday, to see if it settles. This will give you peace of mind too.

Do not leave kennel bookings to the last moment, as the best kennels are booked months in advance. Ideally, arrangements for boarding should be made as soon as you have booked your trip.

Some owners prefer to organize dog care within their own home. This is often undertaken by family members or friends on a reciprocal basis. Those not lucky enough to have this option can investigate businesses that provide staff to move into the home and care for the house, plus all pets, and even the garden too. Again, word of mouth is the best recommendation.

▼ A pet 'sitter' will care for your dog as well as all the other animals in your household while you are away.

Ensure that the person moving in is insured, licensed by appropriate authorities, and has had a police check. Always ask for references, and follow these up.

If your dog is accompanying you on holiday, check that booked accommodation is dog-friendly. Lists of hotels and campsites that welcome dogs are available in specialist publications and on the Internet.

When planning the journey to your destination, factor in extra time to allow your dog a comfort stop and a chance to stretch its legs. Try to avoid travel during the hottest part of the day, and provide your dog with frequent opportunities to have a drink. Take familiar items with you, such as the dog's bed and toys, to ensure your pet's comfort and to help it settle into its new surroundings.

If you plan on going abroad with your dog, make sure that you are able to meet any entry requirements. Many countries insist on 'pet passports' and up-to-date rabies vaccinations. Your vet, local authorities, or the Internet will be able to give information on requirements relevant to the country you wish to travel to.

Some holiday periods, such as Christmas, might be taken at home, often in the company of friends and relatives. Many dogs enjoy the bustle and excitement of these events, but some do not. Provide your dog with a quiet place that it can retreat to if it wishes. Make sure guests understand that some food items, such as chocolate, Christmas cake and alcohol, are toxic to dogs and should be placed out of reach and not offered as treats. Ask everyone to tidy gift

packaging away and not to offer it to a dog as a toy. Insist that doors and gates are closed after use. Never leave visiting children and dogs alone together.

Some holidays involve noise. Fireworks are not only heard on Bonfire Night or Independence Day, but also as part of New Year celebrations. These, and Christmas crackers, can terrify noise-shy dogs. If you suspect that loud noises may be part of your holiday celebrations, shut your dog away somewhere safe and comfortable.

▲ *Never leave your dog alone in a room with a Christmas tree. The tree, lights, decorations and some presents could all prove fatal if chewed.*

Whichever choice you make for your holiday, check that your dog has the required identification on its collar and that microchip details are up to date. If you dog gets lost or is startled and runs off, these are essential elements to reunite owners with their dogs.

◄ *Specially designed dog playpens are easily assembled and provide a place of safety for a puppy.*

NUTRITION AND FEEDING

The diets of yesteryear, of home-mixed meat and biscuits, have long gone. Nowadays, professional nutritionists produce feeds of a variety and quality that should satisfy any dog, packaged in forms convenient enough to suit any owner. Nutrition is a complex subject, and there is a simple question: do you know more about the nutrition of the dog than the experts? Teams of nutritionists form part of a booming industry involving science, marketing and, most importantly, competition between feed companies. For modern dogs, palatability is considered to be of great importance, and the professional feed laboratories spend a great deal of time getting the flavour just right. Commercially produced food is carefully balanced to provide the correct level of components to aid and support the dog through the various stages of life. Breed-specific diets are also available, and even kibble size is variable to suit the needs of large or small dogs.

◄ *It is important to provide your dog with a nutritious diet that is appropriate for its age and activity level.*

Types of food

Dogs are carnivores. Their digestive system, from the mouth through their intestines, is designed to cope with a meat diet. The dog's teeth are adapted to tear food into swallowable-sized chunks rather than to grind the food, and their stomachs can digest food in this state.

Dogs have probably evolved from animals that lived on a diet of other animals. However, as with the fox in modern times, meat was not always available to them, and the dog is also able to digest and survive on a diet that is mostly vegetable; but a complete absence of meat is likely to lead to nutritional deficiencies.

Foods, whether for dogs or humans, have to supply energy, from which, as well as being the means of movement, the animal's body derives heat, materials for growth and repair, and substances that support these activities. For dogs, this involves a satisfactory mixture of the major nutrients – carbohydrates, fats and proteins – in proportions similar to those required for a healthy human diet. They must also have a sufficient intake of the minor nutrients – vitamins and minerals – in proportions that do differ significantly from the needs of humans.

Dog foods may be divided into several broad categories. For many years, the so-called 'moist' diets held the major part of the market. They are the tinned foods seen on every supermarket shelf.

Over the past few years, other types of food have infiltrated the market. Complete dry feeds are becoming increasingly popular. They need minimal preparation – if desired, they can simply be poured into a dog bowl and given to the dog. It is only very slightly more demanding to pour hot water on to moisten the feed.

Semi-moist diets are not intended to provide a balanced diet on their own. They hold a small but significant place in the market, largely, in all probability, because they involve some degree of preparation before feeding. It is still fairly minimal, involving the addition of carbohydrate supplements as a mixer, often some form of biscuit, to balance the nutritional quality of the food. This is a psychologically important exercise for the owner, who likes to think that they are doing something for the dog, as previous generations did when they mixed a bowl of table scraps with some meat and gravy. The one thing to remember is that too much mixing of modern foods can result in nutritional problems. What happens too often is that the concerned owner adds not just a carbohydrate mixer, but high-protein feed as well, resulting in a diet that is unbalanced, with too much

▶ *If a dog is hungry and healthy, it will eat. If it is healthy but won't eat, it isn't hungry, so take the food away and let it miss a meal.*

Nutrients

The major nutrients, required in substantial quantities by every animal, include the following.

- Carbohydrates, which provide the body with energy, and in surplus, will be converted into body fat.
- Fats, which are the most concentrated form of energy, producing more than twice as much energy, weight for weight, than carbohydrates, and which will also convert to body fats if supplied in excess.
- Proteins, which essentially provide the body-building elements in the diet.

The minor nutrients include the vitamins, minerals and trace elements, which, although critical to the animal's health, are required in comparatively small amounts. The vitamins are usually divided into two groups:

- Fat-soluble: vitamins A, D, E and K.
- Water-soluble: the B complex vitamins and vitamin C.

▼ *Puppies should be introduced to solid food from about three weeks. This food needs to be soaked and mushy.*

▼ *Each dog should have its own bowl, although the food is often more interesting on the other dog's plate.*

protein. There is usually no harm; animals, like humans, can deal with an astonishing variety of diet, but too high levels of protein can occasionally exacerbate an existing metabolic problem. There is an old adage, 'When all else fails, follow the instructions.' It is worth bearing this in mind when feeding your dog.

One feature of all modern compound dog foods is that they will contain adequate minor nutrients, which did not always happen in the meat and biscuit days. The outcome is that there is rarely any need for the proprietary feed supplements that are still widely advertised. Calcium, for instance, may have been lacking in some traditional diets, and a bonemeal supplement often used to be recommended. Today, such a supplement may do harm in certain circumstances, such as pregnancy in the bitch.

Special diets have been developed over the years. These are generally of two types: first, those that target healthy dogs with special requirements – puppies, for instance, with special growth needs, especially active dogs and older dogs; and second, those designed as supportive diets for various illnesses. There are kidney diets, for instance, which control the amount and type of protein the dog is given. These latter special diets are dispensed strictly under the control of a veterinary surgeon, many of whom are trained specifically in the use of such diets.

◄ *Canned food must be used within 24 hours of opening and kept refrigerated. Cover open cans with plastic lids, and reserve an opener and fork just for dog food.*

► *Dogs love bones, but vets don't because of the risks of bowel stoppages or choking. Very large bones minimize such risk. Never give a dog a chop or chicken bone.*

Food requirements

Dogs are adaptable creatures. They can, for instance, utilize protein foods for energy if their intake of carbohydrates is deficient. They must, however, be provided with a minimum level of each of around 30 nutrients, including the vitamins and minerals, if they are to stay healthy. All the modern prepared foods, and the great majority of home-mixed diets, will provide an adequate supply of essential nutrients.

Some animal protein is essential to maintain a dog's health. A vegetarian diet for dogs can be devised but requires skill, although there is no doubt that dogs do not need the level of animal protein in their diet that is commonly provided.

Some fats are also vital in the dog's diet, providing certain essential fatty acids, and acting as carriers for the fat-soluble vitamins.

Carbohydrates form the bulk of most diets, including normal dog foods, whether commercially compounded or home-mixed.

Provided your dog's diet has a reasonable balance of the major nutrients, and the foods are not themselves wildly out of the ordinary, the owner's concern need only be with the actual quantity given to the dog, and the total calorie provision.

▲ Butcher's scraps, canned or fresh, is not a complete feed.

▲ Canned chicken must be balanced with other foods.

▲ Cooked chicken is a cheap way of providing meat protein for small dogs.

▲ Commercial canned food may be a complete feed or mixed.

▲ Rice is a source of carbohydrates for home-mixing.

▲ Dry complete feeds have become very popular in recent years.

▲ Semi-moist feeds must be kept in sealed packets to keep them fresh.

▲ The traditional, old-fashioned dog feed of biscuits with gravy.

▲ Wholemeal biscuits are not adequate on their own as a dog's only food.

Average calorie requirements for 24 hours

Growing puppies	6 weeks	3 months	6 months
Terriers, mature weight 10kg (22lb)	330	530	700
German Shepherds, mature weight 30kg (66lb)	1,200	1,800	2,600
Giant breeds, mature weight 50kg (110lb)	1,950	2,500	4,000

Adult dogs	Maintenance
Terriers	400
German Shepherds	1,600
Giant breeds	2,400

The table gives average amounts and should be regarded as a guide only. Take account of whether the mature dog on this level of food intake is gaining or losing weight. Puppies should gain weight steadily, without becoming too fat.

At first sight, the figures in the table here suggest that the obvious and cheapest way to feed a dog is to give it biscuits alone. Dog biscuits offer the highest calorie content, weight for weight, of any food except pure fat, and they are cheaper to buy than canned foods. But this is misleading – a diet consisting solely of dog biscuits would be seriously deficient in protein, as well as fats, vitamins and minerals.

▲ Meaty treats make excellent rewards when training your dog.

▲ Most dogs enjoy bone-shaped biscuits, and hard-baked (safer) bones.

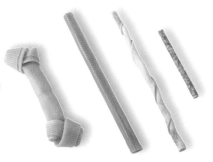

▲ Raw or processed hide chews are a safe substitute for bones.

▲ Give only special-formula dog drops (see panel for chocolate warnings).

▲ Some biscuits include a charcoal variety, to help digestive problems.

Chocolate and canines

Experts agree that certain chemicals in chocolate can be toxic to dogs, especially in large quantities. The chemical theobromine, found especially in dark (bittersweet) and baker's chocolate, can cause a toxic reaction, while caffeine may also lead to digestive problems.

Reactions will vary according to dog weight and sensitivity, and although most owners report few or no ill effects where only small amounts have been consumed, it is safest to avoid giving your dog any chocolate at all.

Calorie content of common food per 100g (3½oz)

- Dog biscuits used as mixer feeds — 300–360
- Fresh meat — 140
- Soft, moist, complete feeds — 320
- Dry complete feeds — 270

Manufacturer's declared calorie content per 100g (3½oz) in their canned foods (Hill's Science Diet)

- Canine Growth — 136
- Canine Maintenance — 126
- Canine Performance — 140
- Canine Maintenance Light — 87
- Canine Senior — 117

SPECIAL DIETS

Quality of feed is particularly important during puppyhood, to provide nutrients for the rapidly growing animal. Similarly, an in-whelp bitch needs high-quality food if she is to produce healthy puppies without putting undue strain on her own bodily resources. Pregnant animals will deplete their own tissues to provide sufficient nutrients for their puppies, both in the uterus and afterwards when they are suckling. A bitch with a litter of several puppies will almost inevitably lose some weight; her condition needs to be watched carefully. However, there is no point in over-feeding the bitch while she is pregnant.

◄ *Regular veterinary examination of older dogs will reveal the possible existence of nutritionally controllable diseases.*

► *If puppies share a bowl of food, it is difficult to be sure they both get a fair share.*

There may be specific demands for particularly active adult dogs, for the older dog, and for the overweight dog. Scientifically formulated diets are designed to provide for these various special requirements.

Several pet food manufacturers provide prescription diets that, used under veterinary supervision, aid in the management of a number of diseases. They are only obtainable through a veterinary surgeon.

The range is wide and includes products that may either contain greater proportions of certain nutrients than usual – one is a high-fibre diet, for instance, which may be of benefit in cases of diabetes, and in fibre-responsive intestinal problems – or smaller elements of the normal diet. Low-protein diets assist in the control of chronic kidney disease; low-sodium diets are used in the management of congestive heart failure.

OBESITY

One of the commonest afflictions in the dog is simple obesity. Owners will frequently not see it and, once acknowledged, it may still be extremely difficult for them to understand that reducing the dog's food intake is not cruel. The obesity diet has its part to play by enabling the owner to feed a low-calorie diet to the dog, which will satisfy the hunger pangs while reducing its intake of nutrients.

The table here indicates a suitable intake of calories for an overweight dog, with a target weight indicated in the first column. The diet needs to be balanced by sensible variations of other nutrients. Cooked green vegetables can be added to provide bulk to the ration.

Daily calorie requirement for the overweight dog

Target weight	Scale 1	Scale 2
2.5kg (5½lb)	120	90
5kg (11lb)	200	160
7kg (15½lb)	275	220
10kg (22lb)	350	270
12kg (26½lb)	400	320
15kg (33lb)	470	375
20kg (44lb)	600	470
25kg (55lb)	700	550
30kg (66lb)	800	650
40kg (88lb)	1,000	800

You can see from this just how few calories, and consequently how little food, a dog really needs if it is to lose weight at a satisfactory rate. Scale 1 will cause reduction in body weight at a fairly slow rate, and even with ordinary foodstuffs the dog should not be too drastically hungry. Scale 2 is necessary when a more rapid reduction in weight is called for. It is still not a drastic diet regime.

As an example, if you wished to reduce your dog's weight to 20kg (44lb), using the slower scale you would need to feed not more than 600 calories a day. Without resorting to a special diet, this could be achieved by a total daily feed of 115g (about 4oz) of meat and 130g (4½oz) of biscuit mixer. This is not a lot of food on a large dog's plate, and it explains why special reducing diets, which provide bulk to fill the dog's stomach, are popular.

▼ *Obesity is best controlled by careful attention to diet before the dog's weight gets out of hand.*

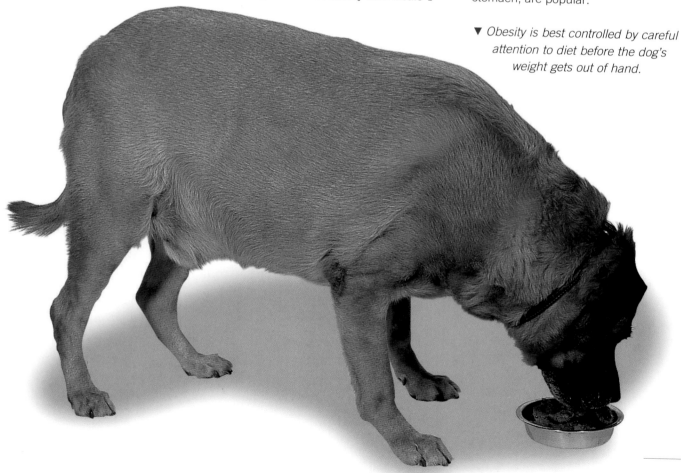

Recipes for dog treats

The advantage of making home-made treats is that you know exactly what is going into your dog. Shop-bought treats can be high in sugar, over-processed and full of artificial colours, chemicals and preservatives, causing your dog to put on weight, and too many sugars can be detrimental to behaviour. Home-made treats are a much healthier option, and they are usually a lot more enticing and exciting than anything you can buy from the shop.

Liver cake is an old favourite of many dog trainers, and is very easy to make. On the downside, it doesn't smell very nice and doesn't keep well, so when you make it, cut it into cubes immediately and freeze what you are not going to use.

LIVER CAKE
450g (1lb) liver
1 garlic clove
1 egg, beaten
225g (8oz) flour

Preheat the oven to 180°C (350°F). Line a baking tray with baking parchment or grease well. Liquidize the liver, garlic clove and egg. Pour into a bowl and add enough flour to make a scone-like consistency. Pour on to the tray and smooth out. Cook in the oven until you can insert a knife blade and pull it out cleanly. Leave to cool, cut into cubes and freeze whatever you do not use.

LIVER TREATS
450g (1lb) liver
1 garlic clove

Preheat the oven to 150°C (300°F). Bring the liver and garlic to the boil in a little water; simmer for 5 minutes until thoroughly cooked. Drain on kitchen paper and cut into small pieces. Spread on a baking sheet and bake in the oven for 30 minutes. Turn off the oven and leave until cold. Liver treats do not keep well, so freeze what you are not going to use immediately.

▼ *Some dogs have a big appetite. Regulate food intake to suit activity.*

HOME-MADE DOG BISCUITS
225g (8oz) sausage meat
225g (8oz) wholemeal (whole-wheat) flour
50–85ml (2–3fl oz) stock or water

Preheat the oven to 180°C (350°F). Mix the sausage meat and flour with the stock or water to form a scone-like dough. Roll the dough out to 1cm (½in) thickness, cut into squares and put on an ungreased baking tray. Bake in the oven for 30–50 minutes, depending on size.

TUNA BROWNIES

2 x 175g (6oz) cans tuna in water
2 eggs
1 garlic clove, crushed
115–175g (1–1½ cups) wholemeal
(whole-wheat) flour
Parmesan cheese

Preheat the oven to 180°C (350°F). Liquidize the tuna, eggs and garlic, pour into a bowl and add enough flour to make a scone-like consistency. Spread on to a greased baking tray, or one lined with greaseproof paper. Sprinkle with Parmesan cheese. Bake in the oven for 15 minutes. Cut into small squares. This recipe freezes well.

CHEESE AND GARLIC BITES

115g (1 cup) flour
115g (1 cup) grated cheese
15ml (1 tbsp) garlic powder
15ml (1 tbsp) margarine, softened
120ml (½ cup) milk

Preheat the oven to 180°C (350°F). Mix the flour and grated cheese, add the garlic powder and softened margarine, then slowly add the milk to form a stiff dough. Knead on a floured board and roll out to 1cm (½in) thickness. Cut into shapes and bake in the oven on an ungreased baking tray for 15 minutes. Keep in the refrigerator to maintain freshness.

TUNA TRAINING TREATS

2 x 175g (6oz) cans tuna in water,
undrained, or sausage meat
2 eggs
1 garlic clove, crushed
115–175g (1–1½ cups) wholemeal
(whole-wheat) flour

Preheat the oven to 250°C (480°F). Mix the tuna or sausage meat, eggs and crushed garlic together, adding the flour gradually until the mixture has the consistency of a ball of dough. Flatten the dough out to about 1cm (½in) thick on a baking sheet. Bake in the oven for 30 minutes. Cut into 1cm (½in) cubes.

Garlic

Many dogs are attracted to garlic – the bulb of a plant that is from the lily family – because of its strong taste and pungent smell. A few dogs intensely dislike it, however, and some people find the smell unpleasant as it can linger on the hands. If this is the case, it can be safely omitted from any of the treat recipes shown here without detracting from the finished result. Find out what your dog likes best.

▲ *Reward your dog with praise and a treat when it responds to your cue.*

▲ *Use extra-tasty rewards to keep your dog focused on its training.*

GROOMING

Grooming your dog performs two functions. The obvious one is to keep it looking, and smelling, acceptable to you and to other people. The second function is just as important: grooming between dogs establishes and maintains the relative status of each animal, so by daily grooming you are telling the dog, in the most gentle terms, that you are in charge. The whole ritual of insisting that your dog stands while you brush and comb it emphasizes that when push comes to shove, what you say goes. Regular grooming sessions also provide the opportunity to go over your dog's body thoroughly and check for any potential health problems. Sore or flaky patches of skin and the presence of parasites, such as fleas or ticks, are easily detected while brushing the coat. Regular inspection of the teeth, ears and eyes will reveal any abnormalities, and unusual lumps and bumps will be felt when handling the dog's body. All of these problems, if found at an early stage, can be treated straight away before they become too serious.

◄ *Grooming should be an enjoyable interaction between dog and owner. Get your dog used to having all parts of its body handled.*

Handling and grooming

From an owner's, a vet's and a groomer's point of view, being able to handle your pet is vital. It makes it easy for everyone to do their job, so that the dog doesn't have to be pinned down (which is alarming for both pet and owner), and ensures that the dog is relaxed. If your dog feels nervous and threatened, on the other hand, it might bite.

BENEFITS OF HANDLING AND GROOMING

About 20 per cent of dog bites are directed at the owner's hand when they are trying to grasp their dog's collar, while many children have their faces bitten when they try to give their dog a hug. Research has shown that dogs that have been handled by many different people when they are puppies become better socialized and are rarely aggressive with people or

▼ If your dog is used to being handled, vet visits will not be so traumatic.

other dogs. If you train your dog to tolerate being handled, the number of bites will be a lot lower.

Getting your dog used to being handled regularly also means you can feel if there are any lumps and bumps emerging, locating potential health problems at an early stage. For an illness to be diagnosed correctly, a dog needs to be happy with an invasive examination.

One advantage of checking your dog's teeth, for example, is that if it picks something up in its mouth that is dangerous, you'll be able to get it back without a fight. Sometimes twigs get trapped between the teeth, and you should be able to get these out without too much fuss. Likewise, if you need to give your dog medication or handle it when it's in pain, it shouldn't see that as a threat.

Similarly, getting your dog used to grooming means that you'll be able to wipe the mud from its feet and comb

▲ Grooming your dog several times a week gets it used to being handled.

out tangled knots without any fuss. It is equally as important to groom a short-haired dog as a long-haired one, to get rid of any dead hair.

Regular grooming will help eliminate fleas or ticks that might cause health problems, but this should not be limited to giving your dog a quick going-over with a brush. Get it accustomed to having its teeth, ears, eyes, paws and area under the tail examined, so that when it has to go to the vet to get its temperature taken, this will not be such a shock.

BE GENTLE

Not all dogs are instinctively happy at being examined closely. Some like having their ears and tummy stroked, but draw the line at having their feet or teeth examined. Don't make this a battle, forcing the dog's mouth open, because you'll alarm and possibly even hurt it. It also means that next

▲ *It is important to be able to regularly clip your dog's claws without stress.*

time you go near your dog, it will know what's coming and try to warn you off with a snarl and maybe even a bite. Be gentle, rewarding your dog at each stage. Let it realize that nothing awful is happening. Build up its confidence. It doesn't matter if it takes several sessions before it lets you check its teeth. There's no rush.

HOW TO BEGIN

The best way to get your dog used to being handled closely is to begin by stroking it gently, letting it get used to the feel of you. With a young puppy that tries to bite, wait until it is tired. While you are stroking it, play around with its ears and have a look inside them. Stroke it down the front legs and gently feel between its toes. If it pulls its foot away, it needs to be desensitized to your touch. If it doesn't

▶ *Build up your dog's confidence by praising it while gently handling its paws.*

like you looking at its teeth – and not many dogs do to begin with – again you need to desensitize it to your handling. Let it lick a piece of cheese held between your thumb and finger, and lift its lip up to look at its teeth while it is busy.

You could also try smearing some soft cheese on the refrigerator door or, if you have a tiled floor, squash some cheese on to the surface so that while your puppy is busy licking it off, you can examine it thoroughly, including its back, belly and under its tail. When it is happy to let you handle it, get your friends to give it a once-over. If you have children, you can supervise them, but make sure they are gentle. If your puppy complains or pulls away from any area being handled, reward it well when it lets you touch it there. Be especially gentle around its mouth while it is a puppy, because its gums may hurt when it is losing its puppy teeth and the adult teeth are coming through.

▲ *Get your dog used to handling its mouth, so you can look at its teeth.*

▲ *Reward your dog with a tasty treat when it lets you check it all over.*

▼ *Once your dog is used to being handled, it should enjoy being towel-dried after it gets muddy.*

Grooming for different coats

Short-coated dogs may need less attention than other types, and usually require no professional care at all. The downside to owning a short-coated dog, however, is that they moult all the time, sometimes more than long-coated dogs. Dedicated owners of the short-coated breeds, especially those with white coats like Bull Terriers, will tell you that there is no colour or type of clothing that you can wear that does not get covered in dog hairs.

Daily grooming helps. A brush with stiff but not harsh bristles is all that is required, and it takes about 10 minutes. Be careful to avoid the eyes, but otherwise brush the entire body.

Rough-coated dogs may need more attention. Some rough coats do not moult in the way that short coats do, but they 'cast', which is a more substantial moult, every 6 months or so. When they cast, hair is lost in mats, especially if the dog has not been regularly groomed throughout the rest of the year.

Regular, daily brushing and combing will prevent the coat from matting. Again, a stiff brush is the main piece of equipment, but a comb is also useful. It is essential to brush or comb right through the thickness of the coat. Just skimming over the top is of very little use.

Some rough-coated breeds need occasional attention from a professional groomer, particularly if you are intending to try your hand in the show-ring. All those artfully dishevelled creatures you see at major shows are the result of hours of attention by their dedicated owners.

The silky-coated breeds – such as Cocker Spaniels and Irish Setters – need exactly the same attention as

SHORT COAT

1 A short-bristled brush is being used to clean the coat of this Brittany.

2 A wire-bristled glove makes easy work for short-haired breeds that need minimal attention.

ROUGH COAT

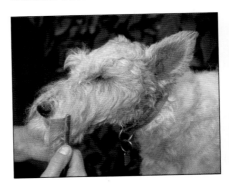

1 Rough-coated terriers need more attention to their coats than might sometimes be realized.

2 Regular, daily brushing out is essential. This dog looks about ready for a professional trim.

SILKY COAT

1 Dogs with long, silky coats demand much grooming. Their coat should never be clipped.

2 Careful grooming right through the coat with a not-too-stiff brush should be a daily task.

▶ *A Standard Poodle in perfect show trim, called the 'lion trim'.*

▼ *No breed is more difficult to keep in trim than the Old English Sheepdog.*

Trimming a Poodle

The Poodle is generally thought of as a trimmed dog, and the prospective owner usually realizes what is likely to be required. Daily attention is necessary, and a monthly visit to the dog parlour may become a welcome ritual.

The exaggerated trim, derived from a working cut of long ago (the Poodle was originally a gundog), is not essential to these breeds, and a version of the puppy trim can be carried on throughout the dog's life. This is simply a closer trim all over without the topiary of the show dog. Many owners feel it still keeps the essential nature of the breed. It takes less grooming than a show trim, but nevertheless needs daily attention. It also still needs regular attention from a professional to keep it in shape. The coats of ungroomed Poodles quickly get into an appalling state.

the skin to keep it socially acceptable. A beautifully groomed dog is seen on television advertisements and the family all cry, "That is the dog we want!" But none of them has the time or the inclination to spend a long time every day, brushing and combing and cleaning up their new dog; and still less after the novelty has worn off.

So if you must have a dog that needs a lot of daily work, be sure you are going to be happy to spend time on it. Before you make up your mind, go and see the breeder to find out exactly what is involved.

Expert owners and breeders will usually trim their own dogs, but if you are getting one of the trimmed breeds as a family pet, it is sensible to contact your local grooming parlour with your puppy as soon as it is allowed out. The groomer will give you advice on daily care of the puppy's coat, discuss with you when to start trimming, and suggest what you can best do to keep the dog's coat in good shape between professional visits.

◀ *The coat of the Afghan is long and very fine-textured. Gentle but thorough grooming is necessary to maintain this breed's condition.*

rough-coated dogs. Some tend to grow rather heavy coats and need to be trimmed regularly.

The breeds that demand really skilled attention are, of course, the long-coated ones – Poodles of all sizes, Old English Sheepdogs and the trimmed terriers.

Question one, therefore, is, "Do you want the expense and the trouble of professional grooming for your dog every four weeks?" This is the question that many prospective dog owners fail to ask themselves. Sadly, the typical result is the Old English Sheepdog that has its coat trimmed to

Bathing a dog

Dog owners in temperate climates are generally reluctant to bathe their dogs, remembering all sorts of old wives' tales regarding the adverse effects of doing so. These are probably the same arguments that people used in the Middle Ages about their own personal hygiene.

Some dogs may not need to be bathed, especially the short-coated breeds that tend to shrug off dirt; but the smell may remain.

There are, in fact, very few breeds of dog in which regular bathing causes any ill effects, although these are sometimes cited by breeders whose dogs' coats are less than ideal for the breed. "The new owner must have over-bathed or over-groomed the puppy" can be a convenient excuse. Some breeds should never, according

BATHING TIPS

1 Early training makes the task of bathing a dog easier, but few of them actually enjoy it. In time, the dog will learn to accept the procedure.

to the breeders, be bathed. These are the dogs that veterinary surgeons can smell through the door when the dog is brought to the surgery!

2 A double-drainer sink is suitable for small breeds, while the family bath can be pressed into service for larger dogs. A non-slip bath mat is helpful.

In many tropical or sub-tropical countries, dogs must be bathed weekly, without fail, if certain tick-borne diseases are to be avoided. There is no evidence of poor coats in show dogs in these countries.

There are three types of dog shampoo: cleansing or coat-enhancing shampoo; the anti-parasitic variety of shampoo; and specialized veterinary shampoos that may be prescribed for particular skin conditions. If a dog is prone to allergies, any of these may precipitate one, but rarely. In all cases, it is extremely important that any shampoo residue is carefully rinsed from the coat. Shampoos from a reputable source will minimize such problems. Information can be obtained from the Internet or other dog owners.

◀ *Nail-clipping is a regular necessity for many dogs. If you are not confident of your skill, ask a professional to do it – if you clip into the quick of the nail, you will never be able to persuade the dog to submit to the task again.*

3 A tiny dog may fit in a basin. Choose shampoo with care, and ensure all residue is rinsed out of the coat.

4 Rubbing the dog semi-dry will prevent some of the water splashing all around the room when the dog shakes itself.

5 A good shake should be followed by some vigorous exercise to complete the drying-out process.

6 Avoid getting water into the eyes during bathing, and wipe around them once the dog is out of the bath.

7 Grooming while the coat is still slightly damp, but not wet, will help make the job of removing tangles much easier.

8 (right) Clean and sweet-smelling, until some more horse manure is found!

Using dog clippers

If you decide to clip your dog yourself, you will need to buy clippers as well as the blades, snap-on combs, oil and blade cleaner. Patience and practice are required to achieve a smartly turned-out dog. Online tutorials are available for most breeds. These are a helpful aid to achieving the correct trim, and give the owner confidence prior to clipping.

There are two main types of clipper: fixed-blade and snap-on blade. The former is generally cheaper. These come with a set of blades that are screwed to the head, and a lever that lifts the height of the blades to change the length of retained coat. They are fairly restrictive in the choice of coat length, and for many breeds will leave the coat too short.

This is remedied by using snap-on combs which clip on to the underside of the clipper blade, lifting it up from the dog's body, thus giving a longer length of coat. It is difficult to use snap-on combs if the dog is not

▼ *Clippers come in all weights and sizes, but they should be comfortable to hold and not feel too heavy.*

CLIPPING WITH A FIXED BLADE

1 Place the dog on a stable surface at a comfortable work height, and secure it so that you are able to use both hands.

3 Clipper blades can become hot, so check them regularly, oil frequently, and clip the face when the blades are cold.

2 Hold the clipper so that it feels balanced. Lightly push the blade through the fur in the direction of coat growth.

4 After use, thoroughly clean the blades to remove hair, then lubricate with clipper oil to prevent rusting.

thoroughly groomed, as the comb will catch in any knots and pull off.

Clippers that use snap-on blades have different blades for each length of coat. These fit into the clipper head and are released by a button on the clipper. Snap-on combs can also be used with this type of clipper so that any length of coat can be achieved.

Prior to clipping, the dog should be well groomed to remove dead hair, knots, mats and dirt. It is easier to clip a dog if it is on a table and you do not have to bend over it. The clipper is

held like a pencil and should feel balanced in the hand. If a wrist strap is provided, use it, as dropping clippers will damage them.

Turn the machine on and gently but firmly place the clipper against the dog's body, letting the blades clip in the direction of coat growth. Do not force the blades through the fur, but apply gentle pressure following the line of the dog's body. Lubricate the blades regularly with a light oil to stop over-heating and to prolong the life of the blades. After use, clean and oil, and store the clippers in a dry place.

Getting the perfect finish

Using the correct brushes or combs for your dog will avoid damaging the hair, so that the coat will remain in good condition. Your breeder can advise you on which items to buy. Regular grooming helps stimulate hair condition and improves the look of your pet. The use of grooming sprays will help to freshen coats and reduce any coat damage.

Scissoring is the real skill of grooming, and when propererly done it can transform the look of your dog. It is possible to buy a range of scissor types, but a novice may be more comfortable buying those that have rounded tips so that they are less likely to stab the dog. Some breeds, such as the Cocker Spaniel, have furry feet that need regular trimming, and learning to do this can be very rewarding. Tails in the Retreiver breeds look nicer if the straggly hair is trimmed into a nice clean line. Other breeds require the hair around the eyes and mouth to be removed or styled.

Great care should be taken when working near the eyes of a dog, always ensuring you use blunt or rounded-tip scissors to avoid accidents. Mixed breeds benefit from a 'tidy-up' too.

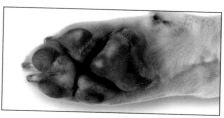

▲ Gently pull hair upwards and trim tufts from between the toes to prevent matts or balls of mud causing sores.

▲ Trimming hair between the pads gives the dog better grip and reduces the amount of dirt brought indoors.

There are many products on the market that can enhance the grooming experience. Shampoos are available for all coat colours and types. Using the correct one for your dog will always give a better finish. Carefully read directions before use. Some products need to be diluted with water before use, while others need to be left on the coat for a period of time. Dogs with long or silky coats benefit from the use of conditioners. These are available to use either after shampooing when the coat is damp, or in spray form to use on dry fur. Coat shine products can be purchased and worked through the coat using a soft brush. A high gloss can be obtained on smooth-coated dogs by 'polishing' them with a piece of velvet or soft pre-washed chamois leather. Dog deodorants or perfumed finishing sprays are fun, and help to remove doggy smells, leaving your pet smelling as if it has just returned from the groomer's shop.

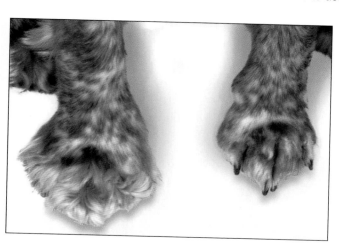

◄ There is a clear difference in the untrimmed and neatly trimmed feet of this spaniel.

▲ A selection of scissors comprising (left to right): blunt-ended scissors, thinning scissors, trimming scissors and long-bladed shears.

63

BREEDING

There are tens of thousands of four-legged reasons for not breeding from your pet. Dogs occupy hundreds of welfare and rescue kennels, so consider very carefully indeed whether you are at risk of adding to the large number of unwanted dogs. If you decide to go ahead, breeding is a most rewarding experience, however never decide to breed in the expectation that you will make money. This is almost certainly not true – the appetites of eight unsold 12-week-old puppies are devastating – and you would be breeding for all the wrong reasons. The cost of worming, vaccinations, health care and screening, registrations plus advertising must be factored into the overall cost. Introduction to noise and household activity is also an important and time-consuming activity that must not be neglected. Time also needs be given to interviewing potential purchasers to ensure they can offer the puppy a suitable home forever. All of that is before taking into account the hours wasted in waiting for people who make an appointment but never turn up.

◄ *Breeding from your dog can be very satisfying. However, it does entail a lot of hard work and should never be entered into lightly.*

To breed or not to breed

When considering whether to breed from your pet, the first thing to acknowledge is that you cannot expect a crossbred dog or bitch to produce puppies in his or her own image. If you own a crossbred, and your reason for breeding is that friends have said that they want one 'just like her', remember that the chances of a litter producing even one puppy that is just like its mother are small to very small.

Crossbred dogs, by reason of their own breeding, have a wider genetic pool than purebred animals. Any selection of the characteristics of either parent is a matter of chance, and the greater the variety of characteristics for nature to select from, the greater will be the differences between puppies in the litter, and the greater the difference between the puppies and their parents.

▶ *The Standard Schnauzer, the middle size of the Schnauzer breeds, is not very common in English-speaking countries, but is a delightful dog.*

▼ *Looking after a litter of puppies is very demanding work for bitch and owner alike. For both, it may easily involve many 24-hour days.*

If you breed from parents of mixed ancestry, you will produce puppies that may not even remotely resemble the dog or bitch that your friends were looking for. Potential buyers may well melt away.

But it is not only with crossbred dogs that the phenomenon of the melting buyer exists. Many litters of purebred dogs are bred on the apparent promise that several friends are anxious to have a puppy of that breed, just like yours. From the time of your bitch coming into season there will be about two weeks before she is mated, nine weeks before the litter arrives, and another eight weeks before the puppies are ready to go to their new homes. That's 19 weeks since the friends made their remarks – over four months for the enthusiasm to wane, for their circumstances to change, or for them to become really keen and buy a puppy from elsewhere. If you think this is a cynical attitude, try asking for a small deposit.

There are, however, good and sensible reasons for breeding. The dog or bitch should be purebred. One or other should either be of a good working strain – and have shown itself to be a good working dog in the field – or be a sufficiently good show dog for the breeder or an expert to recommend that you should breed

◀ *The Airedale Terrier is an old-fashioned breed. It is less spoiled than most, but has the terrier temperament.*

▼ *In every healthy litter the puppies are looking for mischief as soon as they are able to run around.*

from it. The most straightforward way to determine the animal's show quality is to exhibit at shows with success.

The reason for restricting breeding to these two groups of animals is that there is much less likelihood of your being left with puppies on your

hands, or worse, running the risk of sending them to unsuitable homes. No reputable breeder would ever do this. Remember that buyers of purebred puppies want the best, which means that both parents have shown their quality.

A litter of puppies is great fun. But after seven or eight weeks the fun may become an expensive and exhausting chore. Being left with six or more 14-week old crossbred puppies that are starting to reveal that they had Great Dane somewhere in their ancestry is not as amusing as it sounds.

The same applies whether you own the dog or bitch. There may not be the same imperatives if you own the dog and the bitch belongs to someone down the road, but you both have the same responsibility for the outcome.

There is no truth in the commonly held belief that siring a litter will settle a dog down. Neither is there any truth that a bitch needs to have a litter. There is no medical reason for either belief. The reverse may very well be true as far as the male is concerned.

▶ *The pregnant bitch needs special care and feeding, but should continue exercising regularly until the day she whelps.*

▼ *Cleanliness in the litter box is, as they say, 'next to dogliness'.*

Choosing mating partners

Stud dogs are always selected from the best. This may mean nothing more than being currently the most fashionable, but to be among the fashionable always means that the dog has sufficient merit, either as a working dog or as a show dog, to have attracted widespread attention.

It would be unusual for someone's pet dog to become a stud dog, but if a number of fellow enthusiasts ask if they can use your dog, take advice from someone you trust in the breed. Handling matings is a skilled job. If you want to learn, become an apprentice to an expert.

The better, or more fashionable, the stud dog, the higher will be the fee payable for its services. As a guide, the stud fee is likely to be somewhat lower than the price you might expect to get for a puppy. Special arrangements such as 'pick of litter'

are by no means uncommon. This means the stud dog owner has the right to pick whichever they regard as the best puppy from the litter, either in lieu of the fee, or as a consideration for a reduced fee.

However, it is not necessary or even desirable to go to the most fashionable stud dog for your bitch's mating. An experienced breeder will advise on which dog to choose, using the physical appearance and pedigree of your bitch and the available dogs as a guide. Some breeders take more notice of pedigree, others of conformation. Learn about the breed, and decide how close to your ideal each breeder's stock is.

PEDIGREES AND CHAMPIONS

In the UK, the Kennel Club (KC) has sole responsibility for registration of pedigree dogs. National clubs have

► *This outstanding Rough Collie may be the ideal stud dog.*

the same responsibility in their own countries throughout the world. The American Kennel Club, although not the only registration authority in the United States, reciprocates its registrations with the Kennel Club and the Federation Cynologique Internationale (FCI), to which the Australian Kennel Control is federated.

Most kennel clubs have reciprocal arrangements, and dogs registered in one country can be re-registered in another if the dog is imported. Official pedigrees are derived from the registration particulars of all purebred dogs that are themselves registered with the kennel club. Unless a dog is itself registered, its offspring cannot in turn be registered, except in certain special circumstances. Pedigree records are held for at least four generations, although some breeders will be able to show you much longer ones than that.

Different countries have different criteria for awarding the title of Champion. In the UK, the title is awarded to show dogs and working dogs. Some aspire to, and some achieve, both titles.

▼ *The Boxer is a very popular breed. There should be no difficulty in finding a dog to suit your bitch.*

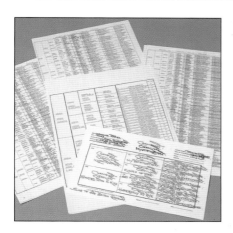

▲ *Careful noting of pedigree and breeding records is essential if you are serious about breeding.*

▶ *All breeding programmes start from small beginnings, but may end with a Champion like this Yorkshire Terrier.*

To become a Champion in the UK, a show dog must have been awarded three Challenge Certificates under different judges, with at least one of the certificates being awarded after the dog has reached the age of 12 months. Challenge Certificates are awarded to the best dog and bitch in each breed at specified Championship Shows. The term 'Challenge Certificate' derives from the fact that the judge may invite any or all unbeaten dogs from earlier classes to challenge the winner of the open class for the certificate.

The Australian system is identical to that of the UK, but in the United States, Championships are gained under a points system with points awarded in different fields: breed, obedience, field and herding.

The qualifications for Champions in working dogs take account of the dog's success in the working trials.

Finding homes for puppies

There is no point in breeding from a bitch unless you can expect to sell the puppies. Your best bet is to produce a litter that will be acceptable to enthusiasts, unless you have firm orders that ensure the sale of your puppies. The breeder of your bitch may be able to help.

▲ *At three weeks old, all puppies are delightful, but this pair is likely to get into mischief next week.*

▼ *A 'rough-and-tumble' is a vital part of puppies' learning process.*

In many breeds, good puppies are at a premium. Reputable breeders will be asked regularly when or where there is a litter due. Your bitch's breeder may be happy to pass on applicants to you, and to explain to them about the breeding of your bitch.

Mating, conception and pregnancy

Male dogs become sexually mature at about six months of age. From that time onwards, their sexual behaviour is not cyclical, and they are capable of mating at any time and almost any place!

The bitch usually comes into season for the first time when she is aged about nine months, and fairly regularly every six months thereafter. It is not unusual, nor is it in any way abnormal, for the first season to be earlier, even as young as six months, or for it to be postponed until the bitch is over a year old. Neither is it unusual

▼ Dogs will be interested in the bitch from day one of her season, but she will usually refuse to mate until she is in full oestrus.

or abnormal for the interval between seasons to be longer than six months. If the interval between one season and another is very much less than six months, and particularly if it has become irregular in this respect, there may be some abnormality, and advice should be sought from your veterinary surgeon.

A bitch's season lasts for about three weeks. She will show some swelling of her vulva shortly before presenting a blood-stained discharge. The discharge is usually very bloody at the start of her season, becoming paler after about ten days.

Although no risks should be taken from the first signs of season, the bitch will normally not accept a dog until about halfway through the

season, at which time she will become fertile (i.e. capable of conceiving). There is normally no odour detectable to a human from a bitch in season, but there is a very powerful one detectable by dogs a considerable distance away. Do not assume that because you live a long way from the nearest male dog, your bitch will not be mated.

Do not assume, either, that a dog that lives together with a bitch, even although they may be brother and sister, will not be interested.

True oestrus begins at about 12 days from the first signs of the bitch coming into season. From that time she will accept the male's attempts to mate her, and will be fertile for about five to seven days. Ovulation – the

▼ *Mating takes place when the bitch has ovulated. Ejaculation occurs quickly, and the tie is not necessary for conception. A mating without a tie is called a slip mating.*

▼ *Although not essential, the tie – when the male dog climbs off the female and faces the other way – has a physiological function in helping the sperm to move up the genital tract.*

release of eggs into the uterus – takes place during this period. The timing is variable, and the dog and bitch are the best practical arbiters of the bitch's fertile period, although laboratory tests are available to help timing if the bitch fails to conceive.

The mating act may be prolonged. Once the dog has ejaculated, the bitch continues to grip his penis in her vagina, by means of a ring muscle,

for up to about 20 minutes. The dog may climb off the bitch's back and turn to face the other way, but both stand 'tied'. The tie is not actually essential for a successful mating, although all breeders prefer to see it.

Pregnancy lasts for about 63 days from mating. The normal variation is about 60–67 days. Outside this range veterinary attention should be sought, although it does not necessarily indicate

a problem and may simply be an extension of normal variation. Bitches should not be bred from until they are physically mature. The ideal age for a first litter is about two years old.

▼ *The bitch should be introduced to her whelping box at least a week before whelping is due, in order to give her time to become comfortable with her surroundings.*

▲ *Bitches should continue with normal exercise throughout pregnancy, although they are likely to become increasingly placid for its duration.*

Whelping

Giving birth, known as 'whelping', is a natural event. Nine times out of ten there is no need for interference; in 99 cases out of 100, interference takes place before it is necessary.

Be prepared. Let your veterinary surgeon know well in advance. They may have confirmed that the bitch is in whelp, but ask the vet to note the expected date on the calendar.

Make sure that you have decided where the bitch is to whelp, and that she has agreed with you. If it is to be in a special place and in a special bed, introduce her to it a week or two in advance, and teach her that it is now her bed. The ideal place is a quiet corner without passing traffic, and away from where children might play. Bear in mind that you, or the vet, may have to attend to her at some stage. Under the stairs may not be a good idea, for this reason.

She should have a whelping box. It needs to be large enough to accommodate the bitch and a litter, which may number as many as 12 puppies. Most breeders will show you a suitable box with a rail around the edge to prevent the bitch from lying on her puppies and squashing them – some bitches are very clumsy.

Bedding for the box needs to be disposable – whelpings are accompanied by a great deal of mess. Almost universally, the basic bedding for a whelping box is newspaper in large quantities, so start saving these some weeks in advance. You can always do the crossword while you are waiting for the puppies to arrive!

Most bitches give warning of imminent whelping by going off their food. If you have a thermometer, you may use it at this stage. A dog's normal temperature is approximately 38.5°C (101.5°F). A drop in temperature of two or three degrees nearly always indicates that the bitch will start to whelp within 24 hours.

For several days before whelping, many bitches will start to make a nest somewhere, usually somewhere inappropriate. Most bitches become very restless a few hours before they start to whelp.

Right up to the point of producing her first puppy, a family pet that in the nature of things is used to human company will probably want the comfort of human attention, but once she starts to strain for the first puppy, the great majority of bitches will become uninterested in the people around them and just get on with the job of producing their litter.

It may take several hours from the time the bitch starts to strain until the first puppy is delivered. Provided she is continuing to strain, there is no panic. If, after serious effort for an hour or more, she stops trying, ask your veterinary surgeon for advice.

The first sign that a puppy is due is the appearance of the water bag. This is an apt description for the foetal membranes; they look just like a small bag of water, which appears through

GIVING BIRTH

1 Bitches do not normally need human assistance to produce their puppies, although whelping may be a prolonged business.

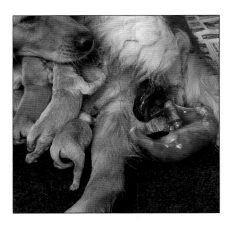

2 The bitch breaks the puppy out of the foetal membranes and often eats the membranes. It is not usually necessary to tie off the cord.

3 The puppy needs plenty of stimulation by licking from the bitch or, if necessary, by rubbing in a towel, to be sure that it is breathing satisfactorily.

▼ *New-born puppies spend virtually all their time drinking or sleeping. If the litter is restless, urgent attention should be sought. It is always better to be safe than sorry.*

the vagina. Do not attempt to remove it; it has the function of enlarging the birth canal to permit the following puppy to pass through.

The puppy may be born either head or tail first. Each is as common as the other, and the appearance of the tail first does not indicate a breach birth.

The first puppy may take some time to be born after you get first sight of it, and it may often seem to disappear back up the canal. The time for concern is when the puppy is obviously stuck fast with no movement up or down despite continued straining, or when the bitch appears to have given up straining and is lying exhausted. If this happens, veterinary attention is needed urgently.

CAESARIAN OPERATIONS

Veterinary assistance at a whelping is as likely to involve a caesarian operation as not. The bitch is too small to allow very much manipulation if she has problems producing her puppies. In earlier times, assisted whelping

involved the use of instruments inserted into her vagina, but this has largely been discontinued in favour of surgery. Caesarians are now more popular, partly for humane reasons, but mainly because of the existence of low-risk anaesthetics coupled with surgical techniques that have improved so much over the years that

a successful outcome of the operation can usually be anticipated.

To produce live puppies and a healthily recovering bitch, the operation must be carried out earlier rather than later. The subject should

▼ *With a large litter, you should make sure all the puppies get their share.*

▲ *Any puppies that do not get their share may be bottle-fed successfully with a suitable bitch-milk substitute.*

be discussed with the veterinary surgeon well before the whelping is due, so that both parties know the other's feeling about the operation. The vet must be called in before the bitch has become exhausted from straining unsuccessfully to produce her puppies.

Sadly, some breeds have such a poor reputation for natural whelping that caesarian operations are carried out routinely, without waiting for indications of failure by the bitch.

Breeders of these breeds must reconsider their whole outlook on dog breeding if their breeds are to continue to be popular.

Other than in these special circumstances, caesarian operations are usually carried out as a matter of emergency. Most veterinary surgeons will ask you to bring the bitch to the surgery if there are whelping difficulties, rather than visit the house, so that operating facilities are at hand.

The otherwise healthy bitch and her puppies will thrive best back in her home environment, and the veterinary surgeon will release them as soon as possible. Once home, the dam may need a little coaxing to accept and feed her puppies; as far as she is concerned, they just appeared while she was asleep. Careful introductions almost always work, but she may need some help initially to attach the puppies to the teats. Once they are sucking normally, the bitch will realize what she is supposed to do.

After the first day or two, a bitch who has had a caesarian may be treated the same as a bitch who has produced the puppies naturally.

AFTER WHELPING

The puppies must be cleaned behind every time they feed. This stimulates the passage of urine and faeces; without this stimulation they will not pass excreta, and may become fatally constipated. This is one of the bitch's jobs. If she has been under anaesthetic, she may not realize this. Holding the puppy tail first to her will quickly teach her the routine.

Normally, the bitch remains with her puppies constantly for at least the first couple of weeks. There may be difficulty in persuading her to leave them even for her own natural functions. If this is the case, don't worry. She will go eventually. Let her do it in her own time.

A healthy bitch with puppies quickly develops a large appetite. For the first few days it may be necessary to feed her in or very close to her bed, but you should make sure there is plenty of food available, and particularly plenty of fluids. She may prefer milk. Forget the usual once-a-day feeding routine; let her have food whenever she wants it. She has an enormous task.

▲ *A puppy that is not nesting with its littermates needs watching because it could be sick or too hot.*

▲ *The whelping box needs to be high enough to stop puppies escaping, but low enough for the dam to get out.*

▲ *Puppies' claws need trimming weekly to prevent them from making the bitch sore when they are feeding.*

Rearing puppies

The first two weeks are the easiest, when the puppies are relatively inert. They will wriggle around the bed a great deal but are incapable of recovering the nest if they accidentally fall out. Most whelping boxes have high fronts for this reason.

At this stage the puppies need no supplementary feeding, just their mother's milk, and should spend most of their time sleeping quietly. If they do not, seek help urgently.

Puppies open their eyes at about ten days old, though some breeds are notoriously lazy about this.

By about three weeks old, the puppies are moving around much more; they will mostly have fallen out

▲ At three days old, the puppy's eyes are still closed, and its only active movement is likely to be towards its dam for feeding.

▲ By three weeks old, the puppy will be trying to get out of the nest box.

► Five-week-old puppies are active and alert, and learning lessons about the world.

of the box several times, indicating that it is time to add another layer to the barrier at the front. It may also be time to start supplementing their diet. This is done by hand-feeding.

Although most people think of the puppies' first hand-feeding as an occasion for something delicate and perhaps milky, just try putting a little raw beef on your fingers. You will be lucky to have a finger left!

The main reason for starting to wean puppies at three weeks is to spare the bitch. With a large litter

► By eight weeks, it is time for the puppies to leave home, usually to the relief of their dam and often their owner as well.

there is a tremendous physical demand on her, and she will certainly lose a lot of weight during the course of rearing a litter. By starting to wean the puppies relatively early, she will be spared some of this load. Puppies do, in any case, start to look for more solid food at this age, if given the opportunity.

At three weeks of age, the litter must have its first worming dose. Take advice on this. Modern wormers cause no side effects.

From three weeks to about five weeks, a gradually increasing proportion of the puppies' diet should be supplied from sources other than their dam. By six weeks, they should be completely weaned, although the dam may take some convincing of this, and may keep trying to feed the pups. The action of sucking by the puppies prolongs the production of milk by the dam, and after six weeks this should be discouraged.

At six weeks, the puppies should be feeding on a puppy food of your choice. It is also time for a second worming dose to be given.

THE
BREEDS

For thousands of years, dogs have been selectively breed
to perform a function to assist mankind, and many can
trace their lineage over several generations. This section
looks at registered breeds – dogs with documentation
to certify that they are a certain 'breed'. Breeds are
generally grouped according to functional type, such as
herding dogs, hunting dogs or guard dogs. From country
to country there is great diversity within these groupings,
with dogs not necessarily being in the same groups. For
the purpose of this book, dogs have been placed in the
group that is, overall, the most consistent grouping for
that breed. These pages give a 'snapshot' of each breed,
and the breed boxes provide statistics for the average
dog. In some cases, there is a difference in size between
dog and bitch, and where this occurs it has been
indicated. It is strongly recommended that all potential
purchasers contact responsible breeders to gain
in-depth information prior to buying a dog.

◄ *Decades of careful selective breeding have gone into producing this
stunning sledge dog. Breeds that pull loads are in the Working Group.*

Dog breeds

The enormous number of breeds recognized today are derived from a creature that first associated with humans thousands of years ago. The precursor of the dog must have been keen to share the shelter, warmth from fires and left-over food that people provided. It was soon discovered that dogs could be put to good use as hunters, guards and companions. Humans realized that some dogs were better at one job than another, so they selected the best for each task and bred them together. This policy has been happening ever since.

Some breeds, such as the Ibizan Hound, are virtually unchanged from their predecessors thousands of years ago. Others breeds have developed very recently – the Eurasier has only been in existence since the 1960s.

A pedigree is the written record of a dog's genealogy for at least three generations. A purebred dog is a dog whose parents belonged to the same breed and who share unmixed descent since the recognition of the breed.

Dogs are divided into 'groups', and in some cases sub-groups, depending on type and the job they have been bred to do. There is a great variation within these groups worldwide. Some kennel clubs call the groups by different names, and dogs that are listed in one group may appear in a different group in another country.

For the purposes of this book, the dog breeds have been divided into seven broad categories: Hound; Gundog (Sporting); Terrier; Utility (Non-sporting); Working; Herding; and Toy. This is a generalization and should not be taken as a firm indication of the grouping of any particular breed. A final eighth category looks at unrecognized breeds and hybrids.

HOUND

Dogs in this group are hunters. Sighthounds such as the Greyhound see their prey and chase. Scent hounds such as the Beagle sniff out a trail left by their target and follow it. The Tree Walking Coonhound is among a number of breeds that find and indicate the presence their quarry by barking. Generally, hounds are not known for their obedience, and are more intent on hunting than listening to their owner. Some have very loud voices indeed.

GUNDOG (SPORTING)

These dogs work in a number of ways, and help the hunter by seeking, indicating, flushing or retrieving game, as well as acting as decoys. The group contains kind and gentle creatures that adapt well to the role of family companion. They are not all suited to town living rather than rural areas.

TERRIER

From the Latin *terra* meaning 'earth', terriers are the diggers of the dog world. They hunt anything that they consider fair game. If this means digging to get to their prey, so much the better. Feisty and trainable, they are sharp in character and appearance, if you have the patience.

▲ *Basenji – a sighthound.*

▲ *German Wirehaired Pointer – a gundog.*

▲ *Lakeland Terrier – a terrier.*

▲ *French Bulldog – a utility dog.*

▲ *Portuguese Water Dog – a working dog.*

UTILITY (NON-SPORTING)

This group is very varied among worldwide kennel clubs, and in some does not exist at all. It really is a grouping for breeds that do not fit comfortably in any other group. There is a great diversity of size, type and temperament among the utility breeds. Many of them are considered as companion dogs, and their suitability is discussed under the individual breeds.

WORKING

This is one of the biggest groups, and includes dogs that guard, pull loads, perform rescues from water, and even those such as the Portuguese Water Dog that assist fishermen. Sizes,

temperament and trainability vary enormously within the group, as do exercise requirements. Many make excellent household pets and excel at canine sports.

HERDING

All the breeds in this group assist humans to move livestock. This is done in a variety of ways. Nipping at heels, imitating predators and/or barking are a few of the methods that are often employed. These are mainly high-energy, intelligent dogs, some of which are capable of performing their job independently from their owners. Breeds should be researched carefully before considering one as a family companion.

TOY

All the breeds in this group are small. They are usually kept as companions, but some make excellent watch dogs too. Bright and trainable, they are happy in country retreats or town apartments. Activity levels differ, but even the least energetic will require daily walks and mental stimulation.

UNRECOGNIZED BREEDS AND HYBRIDS

This book includes some dogs that breed true to type but are not recognized by any, or the majority, of the kennel clubs. It also includes hybrids and so-called 'designer dogs'. Incorrectly referred to as breeds by some owners, these are in fact a first cross between two different breeds.

▲ *Border Collie – a herding dog.*

▲ *Belgian Griffon – a toy dog.*

▲ *Goldendoodle – a hybrid.*

Breed societies and kennel clubs

Breed societies and clubs differ from kennel clubs in the fact that they focus on one breed only. The breed they represent normally forms part of the name of the society or club. Formed to promote and preserve the breed that they are concerned with, they become the guardians of that breed. They are responsible for producing the 'breed standard', which is a document that defines the breed and acts as a template for breeders and judges. Breed standards are continuously reviewed to ensure their defining characteristics are desirable features in the breed.

BREED SOCIETIES

The first dog breed club was formed in Victorian England in 1864. Interested parties got together and wrote a standard for the Bulldog to prevent 'undesirable changes to the breed'. Although this club was only in existence for three years, it was the forerunner of all the societies today.

Most societies or clubs have a code of ethics to which members must conform. This covers sportsmanship, the welfare of dogs, and also breeding practices. Unfortunately, they have no control over the breeders who own the breed that they are concerned with, but are not members.

Some societies that represent unrecognized breeds form their own registry, documenting breeding lines and issuing registrations. In these cases, the emphasis is often on working ability rather than conformation.

Clubs offer a broad range of services to members. Education is important, and covers aspects of the breed and breed-related activities.

Many raise funds for research in health or genetic matters affecting the breed. They hold lists of member's puppies for sale, and are able to give advice and support to potential purchasers. Some have social activities, and most hold competitive shows or trials. Additionally, they support their own breed rescue, and are ideally placed to access a dog's rehoming requirements.

Applicants for membership do not have to own to own a dog of that specific breed to join, but can just have a general interest. If you are considering buying a pedigree dog, this is a good way to get information on all aspects of the breed.

▼ *Breed societies have the welfare of a single breed at their heart, and many provide social activities.*

▲ *The rules and regulations for most canine sports are formulated and enforced by kennel clubs.*

KENNEL CLUBS

In contrast to breed societies/clubs, kennel clubs concern themselves with all the breeds that they recognize. In some countries, they are known as kennel councils or canine councils. Most countries have their own national kennel club which is often affiliated to those of other countries. The *Fédération Cynologique Internationale* (FCI), translated as 'World Canine Organization', represents over 80 countries.

The Kennel Club (KC) is the name given to official club of the United Kingdom. This is the oldest recognized kennel club in the world, and was founded in 1873.

The governing kennel club in each country is responsible for recording pedigrees and registering puppies born from purebred parents. In many cases this is reciprocal, so registrations with one kennel club will be accepted by another if a dog is imported. The clubs liaise with breed societies regarding breed standards, and list judges approved to judge each breed.

Many kennel clubs also issue registrations to non-pedigree working dogs on a working or active register so that awards can be recorded. A kennel club is the governing body for all canine activities. It will set the rules of all competitive events that take place under its guidance. These events include showing for confirmation (breed shows), obedience, agility, flyball and field or working trials.

Health and welfare issues concerning some pedigree dogs has placed some kennel clubs in a bad light, but over recent years work has been done to improve this. Close inbreeding is monitored and charities have been formed to investigate and

▶ *This Havanese is able to compete in a breed class because it is registered with the Kennel Club (KC) as a purebred dog.*

research diseases. Screening programmes for hereditary problems are encouraged and often recorded on registration certificates.

Education is, again, an important aspect, but has a broader remit. The aim is to offer advice to all members of the public and breed owners alike. Kennel clubs promote responsible dog ownership and support dog training such as Good Citizen programmes. Information is available on a wide range of topics, and seminars are often organized. A kennel club can supply lists of puppies for sale, locations of training clubs and contact details of breed-specific rescue organizations. Many publish dog-related books or magazines, and have libraries or art galleries that can be visited on application.

THE HOUND GROUP

The temperament of any breed should be as important to prospective owners as size or appearance, although it is one factor that cannot be exactly described or standardized. Official kennel club breed standards do contain clauses under the heading 'Temperament', but these describe the ideal. Included here are observed traits that may not always conform to the ideal. What is accepted by most dog-minded folk is that hounds are basically hunters that have been bred to work over all kinds of terrain searching out different quarries. To take on any hound as a companion or family animal and expect it not to behave as a hunter is misguided. Some hound breeds can more readily be taught new tricks than others, but it is never easy. Some breeds in the Hound Group, such as the Beagle and the Whippet, are extremely popular, while others are virtually unknown and unobtainable outside their country of origin.

◄ *The Greyhound is capable of travelling almost 20m (65ft) per second over short distances, making it one of the fastest dog breeds in the world.*

Afghan Hound

One of the most glamorous breeds, the Afghan has a superbly elegant, silky coat on an athletic frame, as befits a hunting creature originating in the mountains of Afghanistan.

Its expression is one of dignity and superiority, but it can have moments of hectic eccentricity, racing across gardens or fields. Not inclined to heed the wishes of an exasperated owner unless handled with firmness as it grows up, this is a dog that is not for the uncommitted. Treating one casually will not lead to a happy relationship in the household.

More than capable of acting as a watch dog, the Afghan may use its powerful teeth on intruders if its warnings are not heeded.

▲ *The Afghan is an ancient breed that was discovered by the Western world in the 19th century.*

In spite of standing over 70cm (27½in) at the withers, the Afghan is not a greedy feeder; in fact it may be a little finicky if allowed to have its own way. It is an athlete and needs a lot of exercise to cope with its restless energy.

The Afghan's silky coat will not look its best without constant care. It needs regular and thorough grooming, and

Breed box
Size: Male 70–74cm (27½–29in), 27kg (60lb); female 63–69cm (25–27in), 22.5kg (50lb)
Grooming: Frequent and thorough
Feeding: Medium
Exercise: Essential
Temperament: Wary of strangers

▲ *One of the truly glamorous expressions of dogdom, the Afghan's eyes look straight through you; they seem to defy you to resist them.*

any knots must be removed every day. The breeder from whom it is purchased will show the new owner how this is best done.

The Afghan is a dog for the true enthusiast who has the time and patience to get the best out of a canine glamour star.

◄ *A shining silhouette characterizes one of the most dignified of all the breeds.*

American English Coonhound

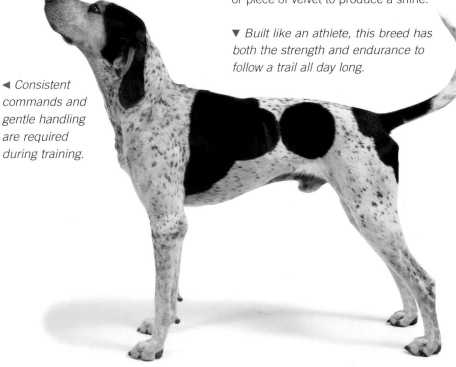

This breed was originally adapted from English Foxhound stock to produce a dog that would be able to work over rougher terrain. The American English Coonhound, also called the English or Red Ticked Coonhound, was bred in the southern states of America to hunt foxes and racoons by night. Nowadays it is also used to hunt larger prey, such as deer, cougars and bears.

This alert and confident breed has huge stamina and can work for hours at a time, covering the ground with a fast effortless trot. Possessing a very loud voice, it will 'bay' when hunting or if anyone comes to the door. This can cause issues if living in an urban area. The coat is short and can be red and white ticked, blue and white ticked, tricolour with ticking, red and white or white and black.

▲ *Although quiet in the home, the American English Coonhound needs to be exercised on lead, otherwise it will be off after a scent trail.*

The American English Coonhound is a very friendly breed, getting on well with other dogs and enjoying the company of both adults and children. It is very intelligent, but like all hounds, it lives to hunt. It is easy to train, but would prefer to explore and track than always come when called. This breed requires a securely fenced garden and is best kept on a lead when taken for walks. It makes an excellent jogging or biking companion that never seems to tire. The short coat needs little attention other than a weekly groom with a soft bristle brush and a rub over with a chamois leather or piece of velvet to produce a shine.

▼ *Built like an athlete, this breed has both the strength and endurance to follow a trail all day long.*

◄ *Consistent commands and gentle handling are required during training.*

Breed box

Size: Height 53–69cm (23–27in), weight in proportion to height
Grooming: Easy
Feeding: Moderate
Exercise: High
Temperament: Intelligent and sociable

American Foxhound

Bred from the Walker, Trigg and Goodman strains of Foxhound, this is one of the United States' rarest canine native breeds. George Washington was very fond of these dogs and ran a breeding programme to improve the stock. There are many references to these hounds in his journals. They were bred for four purposes: to hunt foxes; to work in a pack; as a trail or drag hound; and as a field trial dog. This resulted in some diversity.

Although similar to the Foxhound, this breed is taller, lighter and faster, and with a keener sense of smell. The smooth, hard coat can be any colour. With long, straight front legs, a slightly domed skull and an upward-curved tail, it is a very attractive dog. Said to have a very sweet expression, the brown or hazel eyes are large and wide-set. This breed will bay and bark.

It is gentle and loving in the home but extremely brave when hunting, making it an ideal sporting companion. It is excellent with other dogs and good with children, but should not be trusted with other pets or small animals because of the strong hunt instinct. This trait means that the owner must work hard to establish themselves as the pack leader. As this dog is very energetic and almost tireless, a commitment to giving it enough exercise is vital. It is best suited to a home with a very large, well-fenced garden and an active owner.

▼ When hunting, the musical barking and braying of the American Foxhound can be heard over great distances.

▲ The slightly domed skull is framed by large, long ears which help to sweep any scent towards the nose.

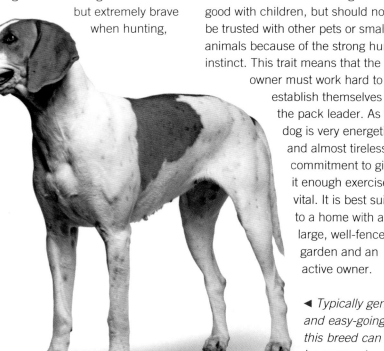

◄ Typically gentle and easy-going, this breed can be reserved around strangers.

Breed box
Size: 53–64cm (21–25in),
    29–34kg (65–75lb)
Grooming: Easy
Feeding: Moderate
Exercise: High
Temperament: Loving and energetic

Azawakh

▼ *The Azawakh moves with an effortless feline grace, and is capable of reaching speeds of up to 59km/h (37mph).*

This beautiful sighthound originates from the Sahel area of Africa. It is a desert dog that is used to hunt antelope, wild boar and hare. It is not suited to living outside in cold, damp countries. Unusually for a hound, this dog is also extremely protective and will form a strong bond with its family. This breed needs a home for life as it will have problems adjusting to a new owner.

The Azawakh is muscular with a thin skin that is stretched tightly over its frame. The coat is short and comes in a variety of colours, including shades of fawn, red, brindle, black, blue, grey and sand. Some dogs have black masks and may have white on the legs, chest and tail tip. Moving

▲ *This breed is also known as the Tuareg Sloughi, and similarities between the two breeds are easy to see.*

Breed box
Size: 61–74cm (24–29in),
    15–25kg (33–55lb)
Grooming: Easy
Feeding: Moderate
Exercise: Medium
Temperament: Loyal and protective

with a feline grace, this fast animal is an excellent coursing or racing hound. Because the muscles lie flat, the body looks thin and streamlined. The dog has a flat back and long legs, and the bone structure should show through the skin.

A very strong prey drive makes this dog unsuitable to live with cats, small dogs or other furry domestic pets. The Azawakh requires a well-fenced garden and should always be exercised on a lead. This protective dog will need lifelong socialization, as it is wary of strangers and unusual situations. As this dog does not carry any extra body fat, a well-padded sleeping area is needed to prevent pressure injuries. Loyal and intelligent, this dog makes an excellent companion for joggers and runners.

► *If an Azawakh senses danger, it will bark to warn other members of its pack, be they human or canine.*

Basenji

The Basenji may have originally come from the Middle East, but it is regarded as of Central African (Congo) derivation from some 300 years ago. Certainly that is the area from which the breed was exported in the mid-1930s.

A neat dog of sharp outlines with stiffly upright ears, it has a square frame standing around 43cm (17in) high, ending with a tightly curled tail. It attracts a small but enthusiastic following with its gentle, friendly attitude. It has a questioning look on its wedge-shaped face and a wrinkled brow; its curiosity is a real feature of

◄ With sharp outlines on a neat dog, the Basenji is renowned for its cleanliness and for being odour-free.

Breed box
Size: Male 43cm (17in), 1kg (24lb); female 40cm (16in), 9.5kg (21lb)
Grooming: Minimal
Feeding: Undemanding
Exercise: Reasonable
Temperament: Intelligent and affectionate

its temperament. It is known for the unusual fact that it does not give voice by way of a bark, but has a yodel-type cry.

The Basenji's short, close-fitting coat is sleek and very easy to groom; it comes in variations of black and white, and red and white, with an occasional tricolour, and it has a

tendency to carry out its own grooming in the manner of a cat. The Basenji's movement is clipped in style and suggests that it is quite tireless, although it does not require an excessive amount of exercise. It will not cost much to feed. All in all, it is a dog that will suit most households, because it is thoroughly companionable.

◄ Poised to spring even from a lying position, the Basenji gives the impression of constant restlessness. It will hunt any form of vermin.

▲ The Basenji is always alert, with a permanent frowning, quizzical expression on its face.

Basset Hound

The Basset Hound is the best known of the Basset Group, originating in France. Its normal prey is the hare, which it follows in a persistent, lumbering fashion. It can break into a run, but its natural pace is steady over long distances.

In spite of the fact that it stands about 38cm (15in) at the withers, it weighs around 32kg (70lb), which makes it a big dog on short legs. If it has to be lifted into the car or on to

◄ The Basset Hound is a cheerful character, even if its expression could be described as lugubrious.

At first sight, the Basset looks as if its skin was made for more dog than it contains, and there is a certain amount of wrinkles on its forehead. Its most exaggerated feature is the length of its ears; these have been allowed to increase to the extent that the dog can tread on its ears with ease. As a result, the flaps can be injured, and their weight can cause problems by interfering with the circulation of air into the ear canal. The droop of this breed's lower eyelids can also cause problems.

The Basset's forelegs tend to twist outwards below the wrist, and this may produce limb problems. Its short smooth coat is easy to keep clean and wholesome, even if it does enjoy rolling in various offensive-smelling farmyard and country substances.

The Basset is for the enthusiast who wants to take on a canine companion of great character as a member of the family.

Breed box

Size: Male 33–38cm (13–15in), 25–32kg (55–70lb); female 33cm (13in), 20–29kg (45–65lb)
Grooming: Relatively easy
Feeding: Has a hearty appetite
Exercise: Steady but necessary
Temperament: Placid but loud

the veterinary consulting room table, it may present a problem to the slightly built owner.

The Basset Hound has a reasonably hearty appetite, which may lead it to put on an inordinate amount of weight, especially as it can be idle, given the opportunity. As befits a hunting hound with a big chest, its voice is akin to the sound of a ship's foghorn. This can come as a distinct surprise to those in the immediate vicinity, but it should never give the impression that it is of an unfriendly disposition.

► The Basset Hound usually comes in black, white and tan, or in lemon and white. Its coat is easily kept clean and tidy.

Basset Bleu de Gascogne

One of the many French-bred hounds, as the name suggests, this dog originates from the Gascogne region. It is also called the Blue Gascony Basset. A coat of white ticked with black hair gives it a blue appearance. The word 'basset' means 'short-legged'. This dog is a slow but very enthusiastic hunter. Almost extinct in the 19th century, enthusiasts rescued the breed, but it is still considered rare. It has changed little from medieval times when it was used to hunt wolves and wild boar.

With a long back and short, strong legs, this is a tracking as opposed to a chasing hound. Solid patches of black are apparent on the short bluish coat, and the dog must have tan colouring on the ears and eyebrows. All face markings must be symmetrical. The low-set ears should be long enough to reach to the end of the muzzle. Eyes are dark brown in colour. The nails, pads and roof of the mouth are black.

Generally good with children and other dogs, this happy and affectionate dog makes an excellent family pet. Its deep voice also makes

▼ *The Bassett Bleu de Gascogne can be seen depicted in medieval French paintings and manuscripts.*

it a good watch dog in the home. Some breeders in France believe that this dog is susceptible to the life-threatening problem of gastric torsion, therefore it would be wise to feed it two smaller meals instead of just one, and to avoid exercise after feeding.

▼ *This dog is a real 'couch potato' in the home, but once it goes outside it may appear to go deaf and follow a scent for hours, regardless of its owner's instructions.*

▲ *The beautiful dark brown and expressive eyes of this dog have a melancholy and soulful look.*

Breed box
Size: 32–42cm (12–17in),
   16–18kg (35–40lb)
Grooming: Easy
Feeding: Moderate, but care
   needed
Exercise: Medium
Temperament: Good calm
   companion

Basset Fauve de Bretagne

This typical Basset-type breed, with its long back and short legs, comes from the Brittany area of France. The body shape makes it an ideal dog to flush game out from thick undergrowth and brambles. The Fauve de Bretagne is also known as the Tawny Brittany Basset. It is thought to have been derived from crossing large Brittany hounds with the short-legged hounds from the Vendee area. Early versions probably looked more like a terrier than the Basset-type dog of today.

Until fairly recently, this breed was relatively unknown outside France, but is now becoming popular in other countries, especially Great Britain.

The thick and harsh coat provides excellent protection against both weather and vegetation. The hair is varying shades of fawn, gold or red. With a wide chest and slightly barrelled ribs, the body gives the impression of great strength. The dog has a long muzzle with the ears

Breed box
Size: 32–38cm (13–15in),
    16–18kg (36–40lb)
Grooming: Medium to easy
Feeding: Moderate
Exercise: Medium
Temperament: Lively and
    affectionate

▼ A harsh, tight coat on the Fauve de Bretagne makes this breed easy to groom wherever it hunts. A quick brush-over is all that is needed.

▲ It is the ability to adopt such a relaxed pose while keeping the eyes 'on target' that makes all the Basset-type dogs look so loveable.

◄ The Basset Fauve de Bretagne is a very agile dog, capable of clearing quite large obstacles.

set below eye level. The tail is set high and is thick at the base, tapering to a point at the tip.

The Basset Fauve de Bretagne is a lively dog that can have its own agenda when it comes to obedience training. This dog enjoys physical activity but does not like being confined. It makes an excellent companion and would enjoy living with an active family. It is generally very affectionate, and its increased popularity is mainly due to the fact that it makes such a good companion dog as opposed to its use on the hunting field. This breed is suitable for a small house.

Bavarian Mountain Hound

Since the Middle Ages, dogs have been bred to follow the trail of wounded prey. Originating from the mountainous region of Germany, this hound was used to follow the smell of blood from larger animals, such as deer or wild boar. The Bavarian Mountain Hound is prized for its ability to track a cold scent over a great distance for long periods of time.

It is a balanced, lightly built dog that moves with an effortless springy gait. It is capable of covering rough

▶ The first Bavarian Mountain Hound Breed Club was founded in Munich in 1912.

▲ The head is broad with a domed skull, and it has high-set, heavy ears that are rounded at the tips.

ground with ease, and is a powerful hound that is fast, agile, persistent and very courageous. The red, fawn or brindle shiny coat is short and very dense, and lies flat to the body. Some dogs have a black mask. Eyes are dark, and the nose leather can be either black or dark red.

The Bavarian Mountain Hound remains one of the few hounds that is still kept predominately for working rather than being a companion animal. Although it will live happily with a family, it wil quickly become bored and destructive if it

does not have enough to do. This hound does not thrive in a kennel situation, as it is not happy away from its owner. Its strong prey drive means that it would chase cats and other small animals.

Although generally calm, confident and loyal, a natural stubborn streak can make this breed challenging to train. This is a dog for a dedicated and experienced owner who will be able to take it hunting on a regular basis. It would not suit an urban lifestyle or inactive owner.

▲ In its native Germany, this hunting dog is known as the Bayerische Gebirgsschweisshund.

Breed box
Size: Male 47–52cm (18½–20½in), 20–25kg (44–55lb); female 44–48cm (17–19in), 20–25kg (44–55lb)
Grooming: Easy
Feeding: Moderate
Exercise: Medium to high
Temperament: Confident, avid worker

Beagle

As a breed, the Beagles produce their puppies easily in reasonable numbers and seem to accept a life in kennels in philosophical fashion. As a result, they have been bred extensively for use in medical/veterinary research laboratories, making them victims of their own super-friendly temperaments.

From the point of view of life as a member of a human household, they are similarly accommodating. They enjoy being part of a gang in much the same way as they make good team members of a pack hunting hares. They are tidy creatures, although they are not always easy to house-train. Their short waterproof coat makes them drip-dry in the foulest of weathers. Even after a day running across clay, a quick sponge-down soon makes them acceptable visitors to the kitchen.

Breed box
Size: 33–41cm (13–16in);
  male 10–11kg (22–25lb);
  female 9–10kg (20–23lb)
Grooming: Easy
Feeding: Reasonable
Exercise: Considerable
Temperament: Genially stubborn

◄ *A natural hunter and explorer, the Beagle will need a well-fenced garden to keep it secure.*

The Beagle is not greedy, although life in hunt kennels tends to make it swallow its daily ration fast. It is not prone to veterinary problems, and lives to a reasonably ripe old age.

It is unusual to see a Beagle winning an obedience competition, as the breed has a tendency not to stay around for the recall once off the lead. This is a breed that pleases families who lead active lives.

▲ *Beagles are hunters with handsome muzzles designed to make a thorough job of sniffing out their quarry.*

► *Tough forelegs and tight feet make the Beagle able to last all day whatever the activity – in the field, the park or the garden – as long as there is human company around.*

Black and Tan Coonhound

This hound is one of the few all-American breeds and was bred to trail prey over any terrain. Coonhounds get their name from the fact that they are used to trail raccoons as well as larger animals. Hunting mainly at night, the raccoon is tracked until it goes into a tree. The dog will then stand guard and howl or bay to indicate to the owner the whereabouts of its quarry. This is called 'treeing'.

As the name suggests, these dogs are black and tan with markings similar to those of a Dobermann or Rottweiler. The tan marks above the eyes are sometimes referred to as 'pumpkin seeds'. The coat is smooth and glossy. Ears are set low and far back on the head and are extremely long, hanging well down the neck.

▼ *The Black and Tan Coonhound is a scent hound with coat markings that look very much like a Dobermann or Rottweiler.*

▼ *George Washington owned several Black and Tan Coonhounds, one of which was named 'Drunkard'.*

► *This very vocal dog has a lot of loose skin on the muzzle, which forms into heavy jowls.*

Although the tail is generally carried low, when excited it is lifted to form a right angle with the back. This hound moves with rhythmic strides and is happy to trail prey over great distances.

Tolerant with children, the Black and Tan Coonhound makes a good family pet. Its strong hunting instinct means that it will wander off, so a good fence and strong lead is required. This hound has a very loud voice and will bay or howl if bored. Although it is independent and at times stubborn, it does make an excellent companion. The coat only requires a weekly groom with a hound glove, but the ears need regular inspection and cleaning. This dog will drool, so the face needs frequent wiping, as will your furnishings.

Breed box
Size: 58–69cm (23–27in),
   29–34kg (65–75lb)
Grooming: Easy
Feeding: Medium
Exercise: High
Temperament: Calm and amiable

Bloodhound

▼ The Bloodhound's huge size requires solid bone. The 'Hound of the Baskervilles' of Sir Arthur Conan Doyle's book was based on this breed.

The Bloodhound is a big dog with a mind of its own. As it stands some 66cm (26in) at the withers and can weigh up to 55kg (121lb), it is heavy. It is also clumsy, with a tendency to pursue its path regardless of obstacles such as ditches, walls and fences. Once on collar and lead, it may choose to take its handler on without great regard to physical or vocal opposition.

Most people will be familiar with the breed's appearance: the Bloodhound has a super-abundant quantity of skin overhanging its eyes, and this is often accompanied by sagging lower eyelids. Its ears hang low on its skull in pendulous folds, and these are said to sweep scents from the ground into its large nostrils and over its highly efficient olfactory mechanism.

The large body is supported by enormous bones, but the Bloodhound has suffered over the generations from hip joints that cannot always take the strain of conveying it along, head down on the scent. Over the past few decades, much has been done by dedicated breeders to improve this.

▼ The deep chest gives this dog good lung capacity.

Bloodhounds eat massively and greedily. As with other breeds that have deep chests and wide bellies, the Bloodhound suffers from more than its fair share of a condition called 'bloat', in which the gases in the stomach tend to be produced in great quantities. For various anatomical reasons these cannot be belched in the normal fashion and may lead to torsion of the stomach, which is rapidly fatal unless veterinary intervention is prompt.

The general advice is to feed small quantities several times a day, and not to take a Bloodhound out for exercise on a full stomach. It is wise to ask a breeder offering puppies for sale about the incidence of bloat in the ancestry of sire and dam. Bloodhounds, like most giant breeds, tend not to live to a ripe old age.

Most Bloodhounds are dignified and affectionate, but this is not a breed with which to take liberties, as they can take exception to undue familiarity. Properly handled by those who are prepared to understand them, they are a fascinating breed to live with and a loyal, faithful companion.

▲ Also known as the St Hubert Hound, this tracker dog's long ears are said to sweep scent from the trail up into its large nostrils.

Breed box

Size: Male 63–69cm (25–27in), 41kg (90lb); female 58–63cm (23–25in), 36kg (79lb)

Grooming: Easy but extensive

Feeding: Demanding

Exercise: Ponderous but considerable

Temperament: Requires understanding

Bluetick Coonhound

This American hound originated in the state of Louisiana. Like all Coonhounds, it will track and 'tree' its prey. Originally thought of as just a colour variation of the English Coonhound, it is now recognized as a breed in its own right. A sub-group of the Bluetick is the Gascon Blue, which is larger and heavier but in other aspects the same.

▲ The Bluetick Coonhound is primarily used for hunting raccoon, but is now becoming popular as a companion dog.

Blueticks are prized for their ability to follow very intricate tracks, making them excellent hunters.

The breed name comes from the smooth black and blue mottled coat that looks as if it is navy blue. Solid patches of black hair are permissible, and this dog should have tan eyebrows and deep red on the cheeks. The feet are arched and cat-like. The paws are larger than those of most other dogs. The Bluetick is known for its very loud and relentless voice.

Thought to be easier to train than other Coonhounds, this dog needs to work. Although bred as a hunter, it is also successful in agility and obedience trials. It has excellent problem-solving abilities and is devoted to its owner. This breed

▲ This breed is intelligent, sensible, loyal and affectionate, but has a high exercise requirement.

makes a good companion, is very people-orientated and is generally calm around children. Enjoying canine company, it thrives best if there is another dog in the household. The strong hunting instinct means it is liable to chase cats and other small animals. Consideration should be given to neighbours, as these dogs are very vocal and will 'bawl' when greeting friends or sighting a stranger.

▲ When alert or on the move, the Bluetick carries its head proudly, with its tail high up in a 'half-moon' shape.

Breed box
Size: Male 53–69cm (21–27in), 20.5–36.5kg (45–80lb); female 51–63.5cm (20–25in), 20.5–29.5kg (45–65lb)
Grooming: Easy
Feeding: Moderate
Exercise: Medium to high
Temperament: Loyal and vocal

Borzoi

The Borzoi, as befits a hound from Russia that was dedicated to hunting wolves, is tall, aristocratic in bearing, and possesses a pair of impressive jaws. Its height at the withers is a minimum of 68cm (27in), which makes it tall by anyone's standards. Added to its height is a lean head, shaped to give an impression of

▼ Also known as Russian Wolfhounds, Borzois need their elegantly long and powerful jaws to snatch and hold wolves.

Breed box
Size: Male 75–85cm (30–33in),
    34–48kg (75–105lb);
    female 68–78cm (27–31in),
    25–41kg (55–90lb)
Grooming: Regular and thorough
Feeding: Not excessive
Exercise: Moderate
Temperament: Requires
    understanding

supercilious aristocracy, carried on an arched, longish neck that runs into well laid-back shoulders, all of which produces a superlative representative of the sighthound group.

The silky coat varies in length over different areas of the body; it requires enthusiastic handling from an owner willing to learn from an expert.

These dogs are capable of running at tremendous speed but do not demand great amounts of exercise. A Borzoi does not have a large appetite and is not particularly choosy.

▲ A gentle expression in the eyes belies the fact that the breed can have a slightly fierce temperament.

It is usually faithful to its owner and reasonably biddable.

The Borzoi gives the impression of being fond of people, but it is wise not to take liberties with such a creature; it is capable, on occasion, of becoming dangerous if it is annoyed. Such behaviour is rare, but there is some suspicion that certain strains inherit a less than perfect temperament. It would be as well to look into this further before deciding to take on a Borzoi.

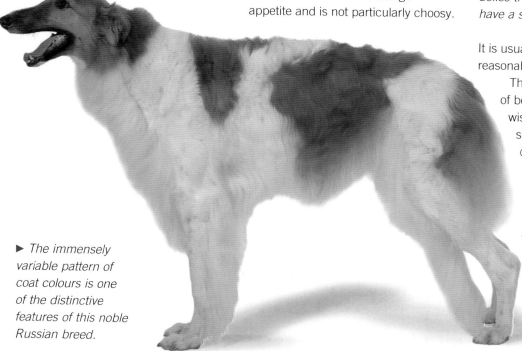

▶ The immensely variable pattern of coat colours is one of the distinctive features of this noble Russian breed.

Cirneco dell'Etna

The smallest of the Mediterranean hunting dogs, the Cirneco comes from the volcanic region of Mount Etna in Sicily. It is clear that this dog shares ancestry with both the Ibezan and Pharaoh Hound. Regarded as a primitive hunting breed, it has changed little over the past 2,500 years. Bas-reliefs from ancient Egypt show dogs with rigid erect ears and pointed muzzles that look exactly like the Cirneco today. This medium-sized dog was initially bred to hunt rabbits using sight, smell and hearing. It is also used as a lure racing hound in some countries. It is a real all-rounder and can be found equally at home in the show ring or competing at agility or obedience trials.

This dog has a square outline and a sculptured head, which gives an overall impression of elegance. It moves with a springy trot and has the ability to work for hours without food or water. The coat is smooth and either tan, chestnut or sand in colour.

◀ *The first Cirneco dell'Etna was imported into the UK in 2001. Since then, numbers have steadily increased, but this breed is still quite a rare sight in Great Britain.*

▶ *This is a friendly breed with an easily managed coat, but this dog does require a lot of exercise.*

The distinctive erect ears are set close together. Eyes are relatively small.

The qualities of high intelligence and a keenness to learn make this dog a good candidate for various canine activities and sports. It is friendly but can be rather mischievous. As with any hunting dog, the chase instinct is strong, but sensible training can temper this. The Cirneco loves all the comforts of home and makes an excellent companion. It appears to have no inherent health problems and is quite a hardy dog.

▼ *The word Cirneco is pronounced 'cheer-nay-co'.*

Breed box
Size: 43–51cm (17–20in), 10–12kg (22–26lb)
Grooming: Easy
Feeding: Moderate
Exercise: Medium
Temperament: Willing and attentive

Deerhound

The Deerhound, or Scottish Deerhound, is an ancient beed. It has a similar body type to a Greyhound, but is larger and heavier-boned. It is said that it has hunted deer for 1,000 years, and ancient depictions of it suggest that it has altered little over the centuries. It appears to capture the heart of all who fall under its spell, but in return it demands great loyalty.

It stands 76cm (30in) high and weighs around 45.5kg (100lb), so it is not a lightweight, but it has a surprising ability to curl up in a corner and not get in the way, even in a small house. It is not a big eater and gives the impression that ordinary oatmeal would be welcome, along with the venison.

Grooming should be regular, but this is not a chore as the harshness of the Deerhound's shaggy coat renders it relatively easy to keep tidy.

▲ *The Deerhound has been used to hunt red deer for 1,000 years.*

As far as its temperament is concerned, the Deerhound is a friendly, faithful creature with a dignified attitude to strangers. One of the most venerated among its current breeders travels with a team of Deerhounds from the outer regions of mid-west Scotland to shows all over Britain and does so by train, which must say something about the breed's charm and adaptability.

Breed box
Size: Male 76cm (30in), 45.5kg (100lb); female 71cm (28in), 36.5kg (80½lb)
Grooming: Moderate
Feeding: Medium
Exercise: Moderate
Temperament: Highly companionable

▲ *The shaggy coat comes in mainly pastel shades, from grey through brindle to fawn.*

▲ *The narrowish front of the Deerhound reveals the depth of chest that is displayed by all sighthounds.*

Dachshund

The Dachshund breed comes in six varieties, each named according to its size and coat type: Standard Smooth-haired, Standard Long-haired, Standard Wire-haired, Miniature Smooth-haired, Miniature Long-haired and Miniature Wire-haired. The dogs vary in weight from 9–12kg (20–26½lb) in the case of the Standards, down to 4.5kg (10lb) in the case of the Miniatures.

All six varieties are similar in body shape, being low to the ground in order to be able to go to ground after their prey, which is generally considered to be the badger (although

▲ *The Standard Smooth-haired – if any of the six varieties of Dachshund is to be considered the original, this is it. The body lines are neat and trim.*

they will do an equally good job if required to go after a fox).

In the past, all the varieties suffered from severe problems with their backs, basically because there was a tendency to breed for longer backs without due consideration being given to the musculature needed to cope with that structural build. Today there is a much better overall type, but it is wise to seek out breeders who can demonstrate a sound strain.

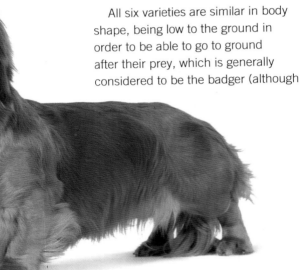

▲ *The Standard Long-haired is the glamour dog of the sextet – the same lines are masked by silky hair.*

Breed box
Size: Standard 20.3–22.8cm (8–9in), 9–12kg (20–26½lb); Miniature 12.7–15.3cm (5–6in), maximum 4.5kg (10lb)
Grooming: Varies with variety
Feeding: Undemanding
Exercise: Reasonable
Temperament: Independent

▼ *The Standard Wire-haired's coat was developed to protect these hunting dogs from thorn bushes and briar.*

▲ *The head of all six varieties tapers uniformly to the tip of the nose.*

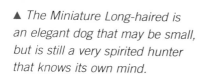

▲ *The Miniature Smooth-haired Dachshund may have been used to follow smaller animals to ground, such as rabbits, stoats and hares.*

Grooming of Smooth-haired and Wire-haired varieties is straightforward, but the Long-haired has a soft, straight coat that does need regular attention.

Exercise is accepted readily by all six varieties, but they are not over-demanding on the matter. From the feeding viewpoint, they are all also undemanding, good eaters.

▼ *The Miniature Wire-haired has a harsh coat and small moustache.*

Temperamentally they are sharp as far as acting as sentinels around the family premises and possessions is concerned, and they will not hesitate

to use their teeth if pushed. They are loud barkers, and the smaller sizes have a tendency to yap, but they stop once the intruder has been pointed out. They make excellent companion animals and deservedly attract a large following of devotees.

▲ *The Miniature Long-haired is an elegant dog that may be small, but is still a very spirited hunter that knows its own mind.*

▶ *All versions of the Dachshund should have a bold head carriage and an intelligent expression.*

Elkhound

The Elkhound (Norwegian Elkhound) hails from Norway, where it hunts elk, known as moose in the USA. The hound has to be solidly built to take on such a large form of quarry. The attitude of the Norwegians to this native breed is that it should be nimble, quick and courageous,

▶ *Elkhounds are solid, and their legs and feet must be powerful to carry them.*

Breed box
Size: Male 52cm (20½in), 23kg (50lb); female 49cm (19in), 20kg (44lb)
Grooming: Reasonably easy
Feeding: Has a reasonably hearty appetite
Exercise: Moderate
Temperament: Highly companionable

◀ ▼ *As well as being powerfully built to cope with hunting elk or moose, Elkhounds need intelligence too, as demonstrated by their bright, sensitive eyes and sharp ears.*

whether it is destined for the hunt or to become a household companion. It fulfils these dual expectations.

Within the group, the spitz types have prick ears and tails that curl up over their backs. The Elkhound is a true spitz; it has another characteristic of the type – a loud voice, which it enjoys using. It is essentially friendly, but intruders could be forgiven for doubting this.

The Elkhound's coat, which is predominantly grey, makes it weatherproof. It is a delight to clean by sponging off the worst mud, letting it dry and then brushing it vigorously.

It stands around 52cm (20½in) at the withers, and its body is solidly chunky at 23kg (50lb). To keep its powerful shape it eats well and may need careful rationing. Elkhounds tend to live to a ripe old age and are a good choice for the active family.

Finnish Spitz

The Finnish Spitz is the national dog of Finland, and the Finns are fussy about its appearance, which is very striking. It is reddish in colour, with shades varying from bright red to chestnut or honey. When it grows up, the dog has stiffly pricked ears and a tail that curls up over its back. Its coat is easy to clean off and brush up.

It grows to a maximum of 50cm (20in), but weighs at best a mere 16kg (35lb). It is a pocket-sized athlete, the nearest thing to perpetual motion, and it loves to be part of a

Breed box
Size: Male 43–50cm (17–20in);
 female 39–45cm (15–18in),
 14–16kg (31–35lb)
Grooming: Easy
Feeding: Undemanding
Exercise: Moderate
Temperament: Noisy and needs
 understanding

▲ The Finnish Spitz's outline is as sharp as its hearing.

pack. It is used in Finland to search out the whereabouts of birds, most particularly the capercaillie (a large grouse), and is the only member of the Hound Group whose objective is a bird. Its reaction to a successful hunt is to tell the world in a strident voice, which it also uses at home.

The Finnish Spitz is not greedy; it lives a reasonably long life, giving joy to its friends, and it expects to be

part of the household. In other words, it is a healthy extrovert and considers that those who own it should be similarly healthy and extrovert. Whether the neighbours would agree is a point to be considered.

▼ That appealing facial expression will change quickly if you relax.

◄ The breed has a loud voice which is used often. This picture shows a very characteristic pose.

Foxhound

The Foxhound (English Foxhound) is, as its name suggests, bred to hunt foxes. Hunters usually follow Foxhounds on horseback. These dogs are generally kept in packs in a kennel situation. These are strong and powerful hunters with the stamina to run for great distances. On sighting a fox, they bark and howl in a very musical manner. Rarely kept as companions in the UK, they are equally uncommon in USA.

The Foxhound has strong bones and a well-muscled body. The coat is short and white with irregular patches of black, lemon or tan that can be anywhere on the body. Over the years this dog has been selectively bred using only breeding stock with a strong prey instinct. It is seldom seen in the show ring or taking part in any canine sports other than hunting.

There is no reason why these dogs cannot be kept as companions. They

▲ *In some countries, this breed is known as the English Foxhound. It can be seen taking part in Foxhound Performance trials which grade its pack-hunting skills.*

Breed box
Size: 63–74cm (21–25in),
    29–34kg (65–75lb)
Grooming: Easy
Feeding: Demanding
Exercise: High requirement
Temperament: Tolerant and hentle

◄ *Foxhounds are much bigger in the flesh than when viewed in a traditional painted hunt scene. Hunting with dogs is now banned in the UK.*

▲ *The Foxhound generally works within a pack and uses scent to hunt its quarry over long distances.*

are friendly with both people and other dogs. Able to adapt to change well, they can be trained to become an amiable family member. The prey drive is high and owners would be advised to exercise them on lead and to keep them away from cats and other small furry pets. Foxhounds require at least two hours' exercise daily. They have huge appetites, and after eating from their bowl they will scavenge anything else they can find. It is considered that this striking and handsome dog may have a greater impact in the show ring in the future.

Grand Basset Griffon Vendéen

There is a full description encapsulated within this breed's name: 'Grand' indicates the size; 'Basset' means short-legged; 'Griffon' describes the rough coat; and 'Vendéen' reveals the area in France that it comes from. It is often referred to as a 'Grand', but despite the name it is really a medium-sized dog. There is also a 'Petite' or small, and 'Briquet' or medium-sized type of the hound. Used for hunting boars and deer, or to track hares and rabbit, this is a versatile hunter's dog.

With a sturdy body and short legs, this is a determined but athletic dog. Feet are large and well padded. The white coat is mixed with lemon, orange, tricolour or grizzle markings. A dense undercoat and wiry topcoat give it rather an untidy look, but this

provides protection against thorny vegetation. The face is well covered with hair, including a beard and moustache. Hairy eyebrows protect the eyes. Ears are long and should reach to the tip of the nose.

Increasingly popular, this boisterous and exuberant hound can make a good companion. Since Grands are pack animals, they do not like being left alone for too long. They enjoy having the company of another dog, or even a cat, in the home. This is an intelligent dog that can become

▲ The GBGV has a merry disposition and takes to any sort of canine activity with great enthusiasm.

destructive if bored. Renown for being a clever escapologist, a well-fenced garden is essential. Like all hounds, it will use its voice and easily become distracted by an interesting scent.

Breed box
Size: Maximum 45cm (18in), 18–20kg (39½–44lb)
Grooming: Relatively easy
Feeding: Undemanding
Exercise: Essential
Temperament: Friendly and humorous

▶ The coat should never be woolly or soft.

▲ The Grand is the largest of the Griffon Vendéen breeds. It is easier to keep the beard clean if it is regularly trimmed.

Grand Bleu de Gascogne

The Grand Bleu de Gascogne is an ancient French breed which is important in the ancestry of many other hounds. Traditionally, it was used to hunt wolves, but now it tracks hares in a very determined manner. Said to be one of the best hounds for following a cold scent, it works at a steady pace and seldom loses the trail.

This tall, long-headed dog has a sad, mournful expression. Long drop ears sweep the ground when the head is lowered, helping to push scent into

Breed box
Size: Maximum 70cm (27½in), 32–35kg (70½–77lb)
Grooming: Minimal
Feeding: Not excessive
Exercise: Necessary
Temperament: Gentle and acceptable

▶ The Grand Bleu de Gascogne is no stranger to breed show rings, and is recognized by many kennel clubs.

▼ In contrast with the traditional Foxhound, the Grand Bleu de Gascogne is much narrower in its head and body structure. It is a true aristocrat among hounds.

◀ This is one of the world's tallest scent-hound breeds.

the nostrils. Loose skin on the head forms one or two wrinkles on the cheeks. The white and black mottled coat appears to look blue, hence the name. Solid black patches of hair and tan eyebrows are part of the breed standard. A well-developed chest, long back and muscular body make this a powerful hunter. The loud baying voice is very powerful, and can be heard over long distances.

Preferring to be part of a pack and kennelled with its own run, this hound is now seen in the show, obedience and agility ring, as well as on the hunting field. Slow to mature, it can reach two years old before it achieves full maturity. Requiring at least two hours' daily exercise, this dog is ideal company for joggers. If living in the home, it will consider family members to be part of its pack. This dog does not like being left alone, and is happiest with canine company.

Greyhound

The Greyhound is, of course, the template for what are collectively known as the sighthounds. There is a physical difference between those Greyhounds that course hares and those that are seen in the show ring, but they all have the same instincts.

▶ The Greyhound is the fundamental sighthound – it is lithe, muscular, deep-chested and tight-footed.

◀ With its piercing searchlight eyes and an unwavering gaze, the Greyhound is also known as a 'gaze hound'.

Adult dogs that have been retired from chasing the electric hare make wonderful family pets, but they do retain their instinct to chase. This can mean that they may not be popular if let off the lead in public parks while surrounded by other dogs. Fortunately, however, they are easy to clean up after a long ramble down muddy lanes.

They stand as high as 76cm (30in), and can be surprisingly heavy for such a sleek dog. Their appetites are not excessive, but exercising them is fairly demanding if they have to be kept on a lead; owners need to be fit to walk fair distances each day.

A healthy Greyhound is beautifully proportioned and a fine sight, although as in all breeds of similar style, the pups go through a gawky, loose-limbed stage.

Breed box
Size: 71–76cm (28–30in), 36.5kg (80½lb)
Grooming: Minimal
Feeding: Medium
Exercise: Essential
Temperament: Affectionate and even-tempered

◀ The Greyhound is an ancient breed that may have originated in the Middle East.

▶ All colours – red, white and blue – are in favour. Anything goes, as long as it is fast.

Hamiltonstövare

The Hamiltonstövare is alternatively known as the Swedish Foxhound, and there is considerable similarity in type between this breed and the English Foxhound. In its native country, the Hamiltonstövare is a very popular hound indeed. It has a style of its own, with a mixture of black on its back and neck, and its mainly rich

▶ The Hamiltonstövare presents a wonderful contrast of colours in a classic pattern.

▲ A white blaze down the centre of the skull and around the muzzle is the typical head-marking.

Breed box
Size: Male 50–60cm
(19½–23½in); female 46–57cm
(18–22½in), 23–27kg (59½lb)
Grooming: Easy
Feeding: Medium
Exercise: Necessary
Temperament: Even-tempered

It has an appetite to go with its lifestyle, and it does not cause too much difficulty being cleaned up after a country ramble in mid-winter. This dog can be stubborn to train and requires patience and consistency, but it makes a thoroughly good canine companion for an energetic family.

brown head and legs. The white blaze on its head, down its neck, coupled with white paws and tail tip make it instantly recognizable.

It stands around 57cm (22½in) at the withers, but does not have quite as much body substance as the English version. It is a hunter with the same urgency in the chase as many other hounds. As such, it is truly a dog for the countryside, but it is very civilized if circumstances force it to become a temporary town-dweller.

◀ Although the Hamiltonstövare is just a touch lighter-framed than the English Foxhound, note the same classic white paws and tail tip.

Harrier

The Harrier is one of those breeds that has been written about for centuries. It is basically a hare-hunter, and enthusiasts speak about it as a specialist bred for the job. This hound is recognized by many kennel clubs worldwide, but not that of the UK. In fact, it is rarely seen in Great Britain, from where it originated. In the USA it is officially recognized, but it has no great show record.

Breed box
Size: 48–53cm (19–21in),
   22–27kg (48½–59½lb)
Grooming: Easy
Feeding: Medium
Exercise: Necessary
Temperament: Mild and kindly

▲ A good nose with well-opened nostrils is essential for this scent hound. Some Harriers will bray when hunting.

▼ This is a typical hound breed that has been specifically selected to chase the straight-running hare.

The Harrier stands in height between the Beagle and the Foxhound, and in general terms has some of the characteristics of both. Physically and mentally it leans more toward the Foxhound, as its whole inclination is to hunt and chase. It is a tolerant dog that is good with children, but is best placed with an owner who has some hound experience.

▲ The origins of the old Harrier breed are unknown, but today's dogs are thought to have been derived from the English Foxhound by selective breeding for a smaller dog.

Ibizan Hound

The Ibizan Hound is classified as a primitive type and has a very ancient lineage. The life-sized gold statue of Anubis found in the tomb of Tutankhamen is identical to the dog we see today. Hannibal took these hounds with him when he journeyed across the Alps. This very fast dog will hunt and kill rabbits to feed both its owner and itself. The female is considered a better hunter then the male. In the USA they compete at lure coursing and straight or oval racing.

The dog is elegant and exotic, with red and white, white and tan, or red or white colouring. There are three coat types: smooth, wire, and very rarely long-haired varieties. Amber eyes are

◀ The Ibizan Hound, with its characteristic prick ears, has a restless energy and can clear high fences from a standing start.

▲ ▼ This is a gentle dog that cannot cope with harsh commands. It is a breed that is generally tolerant of other dogs.

Breed box
Size: 56–74cm (22–29in),
　19–25kg (42–55lb)
Grooming: Easy
Feeding: Medium
Exercise: Essential
Temperament: Reserved and
　independent

set in long, lean heads topped with large, erect ears. The nose, eye rims, inside the ears and pads are tan in colour. Moving with a springy trot and able to clear 1.5m (5ft) from stationary, they need a well-fenced garden.

Unsuitable for outdoor living, this kind dog is good with children and makes an ideal home companion, but does have a high prey drive – it will chase rabbits, cats and rodents, and not return for hours. It is sensitive and responds to calm but firm (as opposed to harsh) commands.

Irish Wolfhound

The Irish Wolfhound is the largest breed of dog known, if not necessarily the heaviest. A magnificent creature, it is well proportioned even for a dog that may reach 86cm (34in) in height and weigh a minimum of 54.5kg (120lb). Its expression of quiet

◀ *This is the largest dog breed in the world, but it has no air of menace, even if those jaws are believed to have cleared Ireland of its wolf population.*

▲ ▶ *This massive creature illustrates the range of chest and body sizes seen among the sighthounds.*

the Wolfhound's youth. In adulthood, it will enjoy long rambles in the countryside, and it can achieve surprising speeds. The breed does not live to a ripe old age, but Irish Wolfhounds are such delightful dogs to live with that their devotees accept this with resignation.

Breed box
Size: Male minimum 79cm (31in), 54.5kg (120lb); female minimum 71cm (28in), 40.9kg (90lb)
Grooming: Regular
Feeding: Very considerable
Exercise: Regular
Temperament: Gently dignified

authority and its rough, harsh coat give it a look of invincibility, while its attitude towards people is kind.

It adapts to living under most circumstances, but those who own one must deal with the problems of transporting or lifting a dog of these dimensions, especially if it is immobilized by illness or injury. This breed is prone to suffer from bloat, and the feeding regime must be strictly observed to prevent it.

Rearing puppies of giant breeds is a skill in itself, and the advice of an intelligent, caring breeder should be followed closely. Growth is rapid, but over-feeding can cause as many problems as too low an intake, as can any tendency to over-exercise during

Norwegian Lundehund

Once a common sight in Norway, this little spitz dog was selectively bred over generations to hunt and retrieve puffins for its owner. The birds provided a source of meat and feathers for use as a fuel or warmth in the form of duvets. However, when puffins became a protected species in the early 1900s, Lundehund numbers declined dramatically. After World War II, five dogs were found on a Scandinavian island. These formed a breeding nucleus that saved this hound from total extinction, thus preserving a very unusual breed.

▼ *The Norwegian Lundehund's curious doubled dewclaw arrangement is particularly noticeable on the hind feet.*

Listed as one of Norway's national treasures, this dog is totally unique within the canine world. It has the ability to bend its neck backwards so that the top of the head touches the backbone. It can fold its erect ears closed, either forwards or backwards, at will. Each foot has at least six toes, and the front legs rotate slightly when moving. These characteristics are thought to be a process of adaptation that enables the dog to climb steep, rocky cliffs in pursuit of puffins.

Although recognized by many of the kennel clubs, the Lundehund is still quite a rare sight. They love the company of people and are good with children. This dog will alarm-bark and requires early socialization to ensure it does not bark at every new experience. It is very agile and needs at least one long walk every day. House-training can be a challenge. It does have a stubborn streak, so motivation and patience are needed.

▲ *This attractive, rare breed has a gentle expression, a very appealing head and a fun-loving personality.*

Breed box
Size: 31–39cm (12–15½in),
  6–9kg (13–20lb)
Grooming: Moderate
Feeding: Undemanding
Exercise: Medium to high
Temperament: Friendly and
  demanding

▲ *An excellent climber, this breed is starting to be seen in agility competitions in the USA.*

Otterhound

The Otterhound is a large dog with a rough, shaggy, oily coat. It is native to the UK and listed as a Vulnerable Native Breed by the KC. It is believed that there are less than 1,000 dogs in existence worldwide. The decline in numbers is largely due to the dramatic decline in otters, which are classified as a protected species within the UK, making the breed redundant.

Otterhounds seem to amble somewhat casually, and they give the impression of being extremely laid back in their behaviour. Owners should have a love of exercise and a relaxed view about dogs bringing twigs, mud and the like into the kitchen after a family outing.

The Otterhound is a typical pack hound in some ways, but unusual in being shaggy, massive and well attuned to the role of a house-dweller.

Breed box
Size: Male 67cm (27in), 40–52kg (88–115lb); female 60cm (24in), 45.5kg (100lb)
Grooming: Fairly demanding
Feeding: Considerable
Exercise: Essential
Temperament: Even-tempered

▲ *Otterhounds are able to track a scent in both mud and water, even when the odour is several days old.*

▶ *The Otterhound's imposing head has intelligent, gentle eyes, and its jaws are capable of a powerful grip on its prey. It loves water but tends to be a messy drinker, so it might not be ideal for the house-proud owner.*

▶ *Otterhounds have webbed feet. At their smartest, these dogs are still not stylish, but their genial character and adaptability make them a good choice for an energetic family with space to spare.*

Peruvian Inca Orchid

This dog has many different names, including Peruvian Hairless Dog, Moonflower, and Perro Sin Pelo del Peru. As an ancient breed unchanged for thousands of years, it has been given National Heritage Status in Peru. Ceramics decorated with or in the form of this dog have been dated back to AD300. Historical research shows that the Incas used it as a watch dog, foot-warmer and as a hunting sighthound. Rarely seen outside the Americas, visitors to Peru will have an opportunity to study it living in the grounds of most national museums.

Breed box
Size: 50–65cm (20–26in),
12–23kg (26–50lb)
Grooming: Medium, as skin
needs special care
Feeding: Moderate
Exercise: Medium
Temperament: Intelligent and calm

▶ *This breed comes in three sizes – small, medium and large – and, like the Chinese Crested, a coated variety is sometimes seen.*

This predominantly hairless dog may have small tufts of hair on the top of its head, tip of the tail and around the feet. Some litters produce coated puppies. Coat or skin can be any colour. To prevent the risk of sunburn, owners in Peru tend to shut their hounds indoors during the day and allow them to roam outside at night. The lack of hair increases the warmth

▼ *The Peruvian Inca Orchid is depicted on ancient Incan pottery, and on some items it is shown wearing a jumper.*

emanating from the body, thus controlling their temperature in hot weather. Dogs exposed to cold conditions need human intervention to prevent them from getting chilled. The Inca Orchid has the ability to lay its erect ears flat to the head.

In modern-day Peru, many believe that close physical contact with this hound will cure asthma, rheumatism and arthritis. Increasing in popularity in USA, the Peruvian Inca Orchid can be seen taking part in lure coursing, rally and agility. It is a fast and intelligent dog that can be wary of strangers. It is generally good with children and dogs, but does not like being left alone. As with all hounds, training is required if you wish to introduce it to other small, furry pets.

Petit Basset Griffon Vendéen

The Petit Basset Griffon Vendéen, or PBGV as it is known to its multitude of admirers, has rapidly increased in popularity since the 1970s, when it began to be exported from its native France. All French hounds are expected to be able to do their job, and this breed is no exception. It is a bustler of a dog, seemingly never able to sit still, so it is suitable for the active and tolerant owner only. Bred to hunt hares, this scent hound is easily distracted and won't always come when called.

▶ *Cheeky-faced PBGVs positively swarmed across the Channel between their native France and the UK in the mid-1970s, and it was not long before they migrated on to the United States.*

Breed box

Size: Male 34–38cm (13½–15in), 19kg (42lb); female 35.5cm (14in), 18kg (39½lb)
Grooming: Necessary
Feeding: Reasonable
Exercise: Essential
Temperament: Happy and extroverted

▲ *Fur on the face resembles a moustache and beard, and they usually have long eyelashes.*

The PBGV stands up to 38cm (15in) at the withers; its length is greater than its height, but not to an exaggerated degree – in other words, it does not suffer from problems with its intervertebral discs to any extent. On its sturdy, well-proportioned body it sports a rough, harsh topcoat with a thick undercoat, which together make it weatherproof. It is inclined to get muddy on its country rambles. It has lengthy eyebrows, so a curry comb is a good grooming tool. It needs good feeding to supply the energy that exudes from it at all times. The PBGV is not a dog for a town-dwelling family that never visits the countryside. It is a breed that will use its voice and will howl if it gets bored or is left home alone.

▶ *The Petit Basset Griffon Vendéen is a rough-and-ready breed, built to face all weather and ground conditions.*

Pharaoh Hound

◀ The general appearance of the Pharaoh Hound is one of power, grace and speed.

One of the oldest domesticated dog breeds, archaeological evidence suggests that this hound has lived alongside humans since 3000BC. Writings and artefacts show that dogs of striking similarity were kept by the Kings of Egypt. It is thought that the Phoenicians colonized the Isle of Malta around 1000BC, taking their hounds with them. The Pharaoh Hound is the national dog of Malta, where it is called Kelb Tal-Fenek, which translates as 'dog of the rabbit'. This breed is both a sight and scent hound.

With a clean outline and straight front legs, this tall elegant dog is a true athlete. The red or tan coat is smooth and glossy. White markings are permitted, and show judges prefer a white tip to the whip-like tail. The ears are erect and broad at the base, tapering up to a point. Both the Pharaoh and Ibizan Hound 'blush' when they are excited, with the skin on their nose and ears turning a glowing deep pink.

This dog is suited to indoor living, as it is liable to feel the cold outside. While some males can be dominant, it is generally good with other dogs. Liable to chase small animals, it should not be let off the lead unless in a safe, enclosed space. Willing to please, this is not only an excellent hunter but can also be seen in the competition obedience ring. Although hardy, the Pharaoh Hound can be sensitive to insecticides and some medication.

Breed box
Size: 20–25kg (44–55lb);
  male 56cm (22in);
  female 53cm (21in)
Grooming: Easy
Feeding: Reasonable
Exercise: Medium
Temperament: Alert and intelligent

▲ The Pharoah Hound has the characteristic prick ears and light body of a Mediterranean hound, but the penetrating eyes show why this breed is one of the sighthounds.

▶ This animal could have come from the frieze of a temple in the Nile valley, so little has this breed altered in thousands of years.

Plott

The only American breed that does not originate from English hound stock, the Plott is the National State Dog of North Carolina. It made its first appearance in the USA Westminster Show in 2008. This breed has a unique history, and is named after

▼ *This hound can be wary around strangers, but after sensible introduction it will make friends with other people.*

▲ *The Plott has a very loud and ringing voice which it uses when hunting and in moments of excitement or stress.*

▼ *This breed is loyal and eager to please, but can be aggressive with other dogs.*

the Plott brothers who brought the original ancestors from Germany to the United States in 1750. This fearless hound is capable of holding at bay – or 'treeing' – large game such as wild boar, mountain lion or bear. It is a courageous dog which will track a trail that may be up to three days old, over mountainous terrain and through water. This hound is not well known outside the American Smoky Mountain area.

With its wide chest and muscular body, this powerful and athletic dog is typical of the Coonhound sub-group. The coat is various shades of brindle or solid black in colour, and short, smooth and shiny. White markings are permissible on the chest and feet, but should not occur on other parts of the body. The voice is loud with a bugle-like musical sound.

Although bold and aggressive on the hunting field, the Plott is loving

and eager to please in the home. It is protective of its family and loyal to its owner. Intelligent and quick to learn, it can make a good companion. It requires regular daily long walks and obedience training. As with all trail dogs, exercise should either be in a safe, enclosed area or on the lead. Potential owners need to be aware that it is a large, powerful and sometimes noisy dog.

Breed box
Size: Male 55–71cm (20–25in), 23–27kg (50–60lb); female 53–63cm (20–23in), 18–25kg (40–55lb)
Grooming: Easy
Feeding: Moderate
Exercise: Medium to high
Temperament: Intelligent and fearless

Portuguese Podengo

This breed comes in three sizes: Peqeuno (small), Medio (medium), and Grande (large). The sizes are not interbred, but all originated from the Grande. The Grande looks similar to a Pharaoh Hound, and is very rare even in its home country of Portugal. The Medio is probably the fastest of the three sizes, and is popular with hunters as a sight and scent hound. As well as using traditional hunting methods, it likes to watch prey from above and then jump down on it in a cat-like manner. The smaller Peqeuno has rapidly become popular in the UK and the USA.

◀ *Podengo means 'rabbit dog', and the Peqeuno is thought to be the smallest hunting dog.*

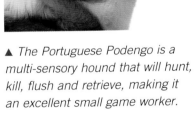

▲ *The Portuguese Podengo is a multi-sensory hound that will hunt, kill, flush and retrieve, making it an excellent small game worker.*

▶ *The three sizes of Podengo are not interbred, but each has its own breeding programme.*

All three sizes have two coat types: short and smooth, or longer and wiry. A wire coat tends to give the dog a more chunky appearance. Ears are erect and able to swivel forwards to catch sound. The chest is very muscular, and a prominent feature.

The tail is carried low but is lifted when the dog is excited.

The Peqeuno is a bright, lively little dog, and is seen in show, agility, flyball and rally competitions, as well as making an excellent companion. Due to its small size, it is suitable for urban living. The Medio also makes a good sport dog, but requires more exercise and would benefit from an owner with dog-training experience. All sizes are hardy, with the Peqeuno having a lifespan of 14–17 years.

Breed box
Size: Peqeuno 20–30cm (8–12in), 4–6kg (9–13lb); Medio 39–56cm (15–22in), 15–20kg (35–44lb); Grande 56–70cm (22–27in), 20–30kg (44–66lb)
Grooming: Easy
Feeding: Moderate
Exercise: Medium to high, dependent on size
Temperament: Loyal and fearless

Redbone Coonhound

This agile hound was bred to cold nose-trail raccoon, bear, bobcat and cougar over any terrain. The Redbone Coonhound is capable of working over mountainous regions or swampland. It is an excellent and fast swimmer, and can be used as a waterdog. Possessing a loud, deep voice it will bay when it has cornered or 'treed'

Breed box
Size: 20.5–31.75kg (45–70lb);
male 56–68.5cm (22–27in);
female 53–66cm (21–26in)
Grooming: Easy
Feeding: Moderate
Exercise: Medium to high
Temperament: Boisterous and even-tempered

▲ The glorious red coat is a feature of this breed. The ears of this dog should extend to the tip of the nose.

provide protection from undergrowth. Red-coated, this is is the only solid-coloured dog in the Coonhound group. Small amounts of white on the chest and feet are permitted. Some dogs have black on the face or muzzle, but this is not regarded as desirable.

Slow to mature, this handsome dog does not reach full maturity until it is two years old. It is quiet in the house and loves to be with its family.

These hounds are large and boisterous, and could knock over small children unless properly trained. Protective of their property, and with a very loud voice, they make good watch dogs. As with all hounds, exercise is best undertaken on the lead.

▲ The Redbone Coonhound has a pleading expression, black nose and dark brown or hazel eyes.

▶ Redbones are slow to mature, not gaining full maturity until they are at least two years old.

its prey. Favoured by hunters and companion owners in North America, it is virtually unknown in Europe and Australia. The name comes from one of the early breeders, Peter Redbone, not from its colour.

This dog is typical of the Coonhound sub-group, with long, straight legs and a wide barrel chest. The head and tail are held proudly high. Paws have thick pads, and the toes are webbed. The coat is short and smooth but coarse enough to

Rhodesian Ridgeback

The Rhodesian Ridgeback is a solidly built, upstanding dog of considerable presence. It is characterized by a dagger-shaped ridge of hair along its back from its withers to just above its tail root, which gives it its name.

In its native country, it is a guard dog, and its height – at close to 67cm (26in) – coupled with a very solid frame make it extremely powerful. Its quarry as a hound includes lions, and its dignified bearing suggests that it would not flinch from this task.

Without a difficult coat to keep clean, it will appeal to those who want an impressive canine member of the household. Nobody in their right mind would contemplate breaking into a house in the knowledge that there was a Rhodesian lurking within. This breed enjoys its exercise and its food; and it makes a handsome companion.

◄ *Rhodesian Ridgebacks are bold dogs that know no fear and have the physique to back up that attitude.*

▲ *The Rhodesian's expression sometimes gives the impression of being able to hypnotize.*

▼ *While these puppies are charming, they will grow into large, powerful dogs. With their ancestry as hunters and guards, it may not be wise to choose one as a first dog or as a companion for small children.*

Breed box
Size: Male 63–67cm (25–26 in), 36.5kg (80½lb); female 61–66cm (24–26in), 32kg (70½lb)
Grooming: Simple
Feeding: Fairly demanding
Exercise: Necessary
Temperament: Aloof and dignified

Saluki

The Saluki, or Gazelle Hound, is a dog of Middle Eastern origin. It is an elegant creature coming in a variety of colours, from white through cream and golden-red to black and tan and tricolour. It sports a smoothly silky coat that carries longer feathering on

◄ *The Saluki was much prized by the Arab sheikhs, who bred them as hunters to pursue wildlife over all manner of terrain.*

Breed box
Size: Male 58.4–71cm (23–28in), 24kg (53lb); female 57cm (22½in), 19.5kg (43lb)
Grooming: Essential
Feeding: Demanding
Exercise: Demanding
Temperament: Very sensitive

the backs of its legs and also from the upper half of its ears. It stands as tall as 71cm (28in) at its withers, but it is lightly built, carrying very little fat – the dividing line between accepted and under-nourished is sometimes hard to assess. In spite of this, it has great stamina in the chase.

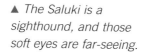

▲ *The Saluki is a sighthound, and those soft eyes are far-seeing.*

► *This is a lightly built breed in which speed is of the essence, hence those powerful thigh muscles. The feet are long, especially the middle toes, which makes the dog unusual.*

Its expression suggests that it is looking into the distance, and it certainly has a very acute sense of sight. It is not a dog for a rough-and-tumble family, as it is sensitive to loud voices and vigorous handling. It is admittedly highly strung, but its devotees rate it as extremely faithful to those whom it trusts.

Segugio Italiano

Once used to flush out boar, wild sheep and deer, the Segugio now mainly hunts rabbit or hare. It gets its name from the Italian word *seguire* meaning 'to follow', and works in a very distinctive manner by herding prey back to the hunter. This is the most popular hound in Italy for hunting, as it is versatile and capable of working all day.

There are two coat varieties: smooth or wiry. In Italy, the smooth-coated dog, the Sleuth, is classified as a separate breed, but the only difference between the two hounds is the coat type. Colours range from fawn and red to black and tan. White markings on

▲ *The length of ears is exaggerated with the same purpose as in the Bloodhound – to sweep scent up in front of the nostrils on the trail.*

the head, chest, feet and tail tip are permitted but not desirable. The head is narrow and elongated, with triangular ears that hang close to the cheek. This hound has a square outline and a muscular body. With a very fast galloping gait and a high-pitched musical bark, it is a very distinctive dog.

▲ *This dog is an ancient breed that is believed to be descended from Celtic and Phoenician hounds.*

Breed box
Size: 18–28kg (40–62lb);
   male 52–59cm (20½–23in);
   female 48–52cm (19–22in)
Grooming: Easy
Feeding: Moderate to demanding
Exercise: High
Temperament: Cautious and
   affectionate

► *The Segugio Italiano has a typically wiry body with its musculature providing stamina.*

Early socializing is required, as the Segugio is cautious in nature. It is a gentle and affectionate hound that is generally good with children and other dogs. Trainable but with a keen nose, this dog requires a lot of exercise. This is best under taken on the lead to avoid the dog following an interesting scent at high speed. The Segugio is an ideal jogging companion. It is an intelligent and active breed which will become destructive and bark if bored.

Sloughi

The Sloughi is an Arabian hound from the North African countries of Morocco, Tunisia, Libya and Algeria, and is also known as the Berber Greyhound. It is thought to have originally come from the Far East or Ethiopia, and travelled with early

▶ *The graceful Sloughi was once known as the Arabian Greyhound. Although similar in type, it is not related to the Saluki.*

▲ *The expression in the eyes warn that a period of formal introduction is considered to be* de rigueur.

traders. This sighthound is fast and sure-footed. It was originally bred to hunt jackal, gazelle, wild pig and hares in both the desert and mountainous regions. It is a popular breed in the European show ring and is seen in increasing numbers in the USA, but it is still relatively uncommon in the UK.

With its sad and melancholy expression, this tall hound is elegant yet robust. Body and legs should show

a defined bone structure. Muscles are long and flat, and not as rounded as seen in most other sighthounds. Feet are lean, with the middle two toes distinctly longer than the others. The shape of the foot is similar to that of a hare's. The coat is smooth, fine and tough. Permitted colours are sable, fawn, brindle, or black with tan points.

The Sloughi is a gentle dog that is quiet and calm in the house. Like all sighthounds, it will chase small furry animals and is best exercised on the lead. Responsive to training, it will make a good companion if treated kindly. This is a sensitive dog who needs praise as opposed to correction. In the USA, this breed can regularly be seen taking part in oval track and sprint racing, as well as lure coursing.

▶ *The Sloughi has something of the style of the thicker-coated Saluki, but it is even warier of humans.*

Breed box
Size: 12.5–13.5kg (27½–30lb);
   male 70cm (27½in);
   female 65cm (25½in)
Grooming: Easy
Feeding: Undemanding
Exercise: Necessary
Temperament: Indifferent
   to strangers

Treeing Walker Coonhound

The name of this breed comes from the fact that it is a 'treeing' dog – it will trail its quarry until the prey runs up a tree to escape pursuit. At this point, the hound will bark to alert the hunter to its position. 'Walker' refers to Thomas Walker, who imported English Foxhounds to America in 1742, and was pivotal in breeding this coonhound. Originally classified as an English Coonhound, some breeders

▲ *Bred to work and problem-solve, this dog can suffer from stress and behavioural issues if not given enough mental and physical exercise.*

▶ *The short coat makes grooming easy, but the ears need to be checked regularly for signs of infection.*

broke away to produce a hound with the qualities that they desired.

It is a striking dog that still retains some aspects of the English Foxhound. The short, dense coat is tricolour or bicolour, but the former is preferred by breeders. Predominant colours are white or black. Any tan colouring is never referred to as 'red', to distinguish it from the Redbone Coonhound. Large eyes have a soft, pleading expression. The upper lips hang well below the lower jaw. Oval or round-tipped ears hang gracefully towards the muzzle.

Often called 'the people's choice', this is an outstanding working hound that can be seen on the hunting field, tracking, assisting search and rescue teams, or as a companion. It is happy with children, other dogs and even, if properly introduced, the family cat. This dog is renowned for its problem-solving abilities. It enjoys learning and takes readily to consistent training. It requires a large amount of exercise and a well-fenced garden, and it will disappear after a scent if not on a lead. The Walker needs regular human contact and is devoted to its family.

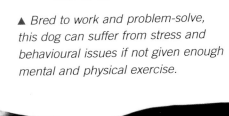

◀ *This is a fast and tireless breed that dominates at Coonhound field events. It has a loud voice that will carry for over 8km (5 miles).*

Breed box
Size: 51–69cm (20–27in), 23–32kg (50–70lb)
Grooming: Easy
Feeding: Moderate
Exercise: High
Temperament: Active and sociable

Whippet

▼ *This dog is a devoted, affectionate companion that is good with children.*

Affectionately referred to as the 'poor man's racehorse', the Whippet is the most popular of the sighthounds. This medium-sized dog is the fastest domestic dog of similar weight. It is capable of achieving speeds of up to 56km/h (35mph), with some animals able to run 180m (200yd) in 12 seconds. The breed is a mixture of Greyhound, terriers and the Italian Greyhound. It was popularized by English coal miners in the 19th century, who used them to race, kill vermin and catch rabbits. It is also known as the Snap Dog, because of its ability to 'snap up' rabbits.

This breed has long legs, a lean physique and powerful hind quarters, giving a balanced and graceful outline. A very deep chest provides plenty of heart room. The head is long and lean,

Breed box
Size: 12.5–13.5kg (27½–30lb);
  male 47–51cm (18½–20in);
  female 44–47cm (17–18½in)
Grooming: Easy
Feeding: Undemanding
Exercise: Average
Temperament: Gentle and affectionate

▼ *One of the most companionable of all the hounds, the Whippet comes in a great range of colours.*

▶ *The Whippet is the smallest of the true sighthounds, and is one of the fastest movers. Once considered a poacher's dog, the Whippet of today can be seen taking part in agility, flyball, rally and obedience, as well as gracing the show ring.*

and set on an arched neck. It has a short coat that is soft and silky, and can be solid-coloured, parti-coloured or brindle, in almost any shade or combination. This dog rarely barks.

Still used for hunting, coursing and racing, this breed is also a popular competitor in the show ring. As a companion, the Whippet is undemanding – provided it gets a good walk, it is happy to come home and sleep for hours. A warm and soft bed should be provided, otherwise it is liable to sleep on its owner. This dog is not suitable for outdoor living, as it feels the cold. It is an affectionate hound that is gentle with children and makes a devoted companion.

THE GUNDOG (SPORTING) GROUP

Dogs from this group are the most recognizable of all the breeds. The purpose of every breed in the group is to assist in hunting and retrieving game, be it furred or feathered. Common points include their very easy-going temperaments (although there are slight variations), and the fact that they do not make much noise. They range in size from the Irish Setter at 65cm (25½in) down to the Sussex Spaniel at 38cm (15in). One characteristic seen in several breeds is that the strains that are most successful in the shooting field are not necessarily similar to those that find favour in the show ring. It would be wise to ask the breeder about this if you are buying for a particular purpose. However, a high percentage of gundogs of every strain retain the intelligence and willingness to please for which they were originally selected.

◄ *The Golden Retriever is extremely popular worldwide, both as a working dog and a family pet. It is tolerant and intelligent, making it very responsive to training.*

American Cocker Spaniel

The American Cocker Spaniel is a derivation of the English Cocker Spaniel. In both countries, their own nationality is dropped in the official name of the breed.

The process of selection from the original stock has gone quite a long way. The American version has a very different head shape from the English – the muzzle is shorter and the skull is domed to the point of roundness, while the eyes are fuller and set to look straight ahead. The other huge difference is in the coat, which is exaggeratedly long and

Breed box
Size: 11–13kg (24–28½lb);
    male 36.5–39cm (14½–15½in);
    female 33.5–36.5cm (13–14½in)
Grooming: Extensive
Feeding: Small
Exercise: Medium
Temperament: Cheerful and
    intelligent

profuse on the legs and abdomen of the American Cocker Spaniel. If left untrimmed, this coat is impractical for the working dog. As a member of a household, its coat is likely to present a regular problem if it is not kept well groomed. Prospective purchasers must take this into account. The dog comes in a range of very handsome colours, including black, black and tan, buff, parti-colour and tricolour.

▲ Nobody could fail to remember a dog with a coat like this, but you should keep the grooming requirements in mind before succumbing to the enormous charm of those eyes.

► Note the characteristic peak to the hair over the eyebrows. This is one of the most popular breeds in the USA.

◄ These dogs were developed in the USA in the 19th century to flush out and retrieve quail and woodcock.

This breed is a thoroughly cheerful dog that does not eat ravenously. It enjoys its exercise, but is easily trained to behave in a suitable manner for suburbia. As it stands a mere 39cm (15½in) at its tallest, it does not need a mansion, but will be happy to live in one if given the opportunity.

American Water Spaniel

This Spaniel is one of the few breeds that originate from the USA. It was developed in the 19th century by crossing a variety of breeds, including both the English and Irish Water Spaniels, the Poodle and the Curly Coated Retriever. This dog is happy working on land and water, and is small enough to be transported in a rowing boat. It is capable of working as both a retrieving and flushing dog, and is used for duck, grouse, pheasant, quail and rabbit. It is the State Dog of Wisconsin, USA, but the breed is still relatively rare.

This medium-sized dog has a curly or wavy coat in various shades of brown, ranging from liver to chocolate. The outer layer is water-repellent and the inner acts as insulation to keep the dog warm. The coat is slightly oily and can have a 'doggy' smell. Eyes vary in colour, depending on the colour of the coat. Long ears hang close to the face and are covered in curls. The tail is well feathered, and is carried slightly above or below the back.

This breed makes a good family companion, and is willing but sensitive. It is a very active dog that needs plenty of mental and physical exercise. If bored, it may bark excessively and can become destructive. The American

▲ *Craving human companionship, this breed is best suited to a home where someone is around all day.*

▲ *The coat requires regular weekly grooming to keep it in good condition and free from knots.*

Water Spaniel requires a well-fenced yard or garden, as it will roam if given the chance. It is a friendly breed that is affectionate with family members,

although it can be aggressive towards strange dogs and will benefit from socialization and training.

▼ *The body of the American Water Spaniel is sturdy and its legs are well boned, but it is not so heavy that it is out of proportion.*

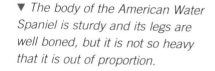

Breed box
Size: 38–46cm (15–18in),
    11–18kg (15–18in)
Grooming: Moderate
Feeding: Medium
Exercise: Medium to high
Temperament: Active and trainable

Boykin Spaniel

The Boykin Spaniel comes from the Wateree Swamp area of Southern Carolina in America. It was originally bred to hunt wild turkeys and ducks. It will also work as a flushing dog and is used to drive deer and to track wounded game. This dog loves water and will willingly swim to retrieve a fallen bird. There is much discussion about the origins of this gundog, but it is thought to have the American Water Spaniel, Springer Spaniel, Cocker Spaniel and the Chesapeake Bay Retriever among its ancestors. The breed was first recognized by the United Kennel Club in 1985.

Similar in size but much heavier than the Cocker Spaniel, the Boykin is a solid dog. The coat is liver or chocolate in colour. There is great diversity in coats, and any type is acceptable. Some are curly coated and others have straight fur, and a few Boykins are smooth-haired. A white patch on the chest is allowed, providing it does not cover more than 60 per cent of the chest area. The ears, chest, belly and legs are feathered, with the length depending on the coat type.

The Boykin is an easily trained, willing dog that makes an excellent family pet. Although very energetic, it will adapt to urban or apartment life providing it is given plenty of exercise. This friendly breed is good with children and other dogs. It has an even disposition, craves attention and is eager to please. The Boykin Spaniel can be trained to take part in a range of canine sports.

▲ *The web-toed Boykin Spaniel is larger than a Cocker Spaniel but more compact than a Springer Spaniel.*

Breed box
Size: Male 39–43cm (15½–17in), 13.6–18.2kg (30–40lb); female 35–42cm (14–16½in), 11.4–15.9kg (25–35lb)
Grooming: Medium
Feeding: Moderate
Exercise: High
Temperament: Energetic and willing

◄ *Since 1984, September 1 has been proclaimed as 'Boykin Spaniel Day' in the state of Southern Carolina.*

► *The high-set ears and distinctive amber-coloured eyes are characteristic features of this energetic gundog.*

Bracco Italiano

The breed has been in existence at least since medieval times, and there is some evidence that it may actually date back to the 5th century BC. Also known as the Italian Pointer, this is the gundog that looks most like a hound. In the Middle Ages, it was originally used to drive birds into nets. The Bracco is a very versatile worker that will hunt, point and retrieve.

It is a large, athletic dog that is almost square in shape. A drooping lower lip and long ears give the Bracco a very serious expression not unlike that of a Bloodhound. Coats are dense, short and glossy. White or white with orange, chestnut or amber markings are acceptable colours. Any black in the coat is considered a fault. Grooming is easy, as a weekly rub over with a hound glove is all that is required. Ears must be kept clean to reduce the risk of infection.

This dog loves the company of humans, especially children, and will form a very strong bond with its family, making it an ideal companion.

▼ This is a multi-purpose dog that will fetch and carry for as long as it is asked to do so, with evident enjoyment.

The Bracco needs to be trained with sensitivity and a positive incentive. It is willing to learn, but often thinks its own way is best. Like all dogs that were bred to work, it is happiest if it has a job to do. The breed is very active and requires both physical and mental stimulation. Exercise should be undertaken in a safe place as the dog is likely to disappear after a scent, given the chance.

▼ The eyes are large and oval with a soft expression, showing the even temperament of the Bracco.

Breed box
Size: 25–40kg (55–88lb);
    male 58–67cm (23–26in);
    female 55–62cm (22–24in)
Grooming: Easy
Feeding: Medium
Exercise: High
Temperament: Loving and active

▼ The Bracco Italiano is an excellent swimmer and is happy to retrieve from water. The head is held high to facilitate its ability to air-scent.

Brittany

The Brittany or Brittany Spaniel comes from north-west France, and has been used as a hunting dog since the 17th century. Paintings from this period often show the breed pointing partridges. As with many dog breeds, the Brittany suffered a serious decline during World War II. Numbers have greatly increased since then, as this is a very popular working gundog and competitor in most canine sports.

It is a medium-sized dog that moves with a fluid gait and has boundless energy. There are two types, although both are the same breed: the 'French Brittany' works close to the gun, while

Breed box
Size: 43–53cm (17–21in),
   14–18kg (30–40lb)
Grooming: Medium
Feeding: Moderate
Exercise: High
Temperament: Energetic and busy

▲ The Brittany comes in all sorts of colours and patterns. The American Kennel Club dropped the word 'Spaniel' from its name in 1982.

▶ The fine, dense and water-resistant coat should be flat or wavy, without excessive 'feathering'.

▼ The Brittany is a superb setting and flushing dog, as well as a retriever. It is a popular sporting breed in North America, and makes a good family pet.

the larger 'American Brittany' is faster. Coats are liver and white, black and white, orange and white, liver tricolour or black tricolour. The Canadian and USA Kennel Clubs do not recognize black colouring.

This is an extremely active breed, sometimes termed as hyperactive. If not given enough physical and mental exercise, it can become destructive and even neurotic. A rural home will suit this breed best, as it needs plenty of space for very long walks and free running. It excels at agility, flyball and hiking, and is affectionate and eager to please. It is not recommended for families with young children, however, as this dog's explosive energy could result in a child being knocked over or harmed. Potential owners should consider carefully if they have the time and commitment to give this dog the life that it requires.

Chesapeake Bay Retriever

The Chesapeake Bay Retriever is a strong, muscular dog. It stands up to 66cm (26in) high, which does not make it a giant among dogs by any means, but its purpose in life is retrieving ducks from its native Chesapeake Bay, which is usually cold. For this it needs much subcutaneous fat and a thick, oily-feeling coat, all of which add up to a look of substance.

It comes in a colour that is somewhat unromantically described as 'dead grass' (straw to bracken). It can also be red-gold or brown.

Its ability to work is prodigious. It loves people and is always ready to please, but it is not meant for the idle; rather it will suit a family that enjoys the countryside and does not mind having a fair amount of it brought into the

► *The Chessie is a burly dog that delights in leaping into water, whether asked to or not.*

house along with the dog. A very stiff brush and a chamois leather will repair the worst damage to its coat, but possibly not to the best carpet or the antique chairs!

► *The head shape is not very different from that of its Labrador cousin.*

► *There's no getting away from the fact that, of all the basic retrieving dogs, the Chesapeake Bay Retriever is the heavyweight. Its thick, oily coat protects it in the water and dries quickly, preventing it from getting a chill.*

Breed box
Size: Male 58–66cm (23–26 in), 31kg (68lb); female 53–61cm (21–24in), 28kg (62lb)
Grooming: Fairly demanding
Feeding: Considerable
Exercise: Demanding but simple
Temperament: Alert and cheerful

Clumber Spaniel

The Clumber Spaniel may only stand around 42cm (16½in), but it is a lot of dog. Admittedly, it was never expected to rush around the fields in the manner of the Cocker or the Springer, but it has increased in weight over the years up to 36kg (79½lb) or even more, and thus moves at a somewhat ponderous pace.

Its temperament is kindly even if a trifle aloof at times; it can be an attractive member of the household, but it should live in the country. Its mainly white coat, with some lemon or orange marking, is close and silky in texture, but abundant in quantity. This breed is not difficult to groom. Despite its size, it is not a particularly greedy dog, but it does need exercise.

▲ *These dogs will trundle through a day's shooting at a steady pace and never lose their cool.*

◄ *This breed has loose skin on its forehead, and it suffers from drooping lower eyelids. Both of these traits can cause veterinary problems.*

Breed box
Size: 42–45.4cm (16½–18in);
    male 36kg (79½lb);
    female 29.5kg (65lb)
Grooming: Reasonable
Feeding: Medium
Exercise: Medium
Temperament: Kind and reliable

► *The Clumber was bred at Clumber Park, Nottinghamshire, England, in the 19th century. It is thought to have originated in France, and includes the Basset Hound in its ancestry, hence its long back.*

Curly Coated Retriever

The Curly Coated Retriever is very obviously unusual in style, as its body is covered with tight, crisp curls, even down the length of its tail. The only part of the dog with smooth hair is its face and muzzle. It is most often seen in black, but liver is not uncommon either.

Its height is up to 69cm (27in), and it is well proportioned, so its powerful shoulders and loins do not make it appear clumsy or coarse. Those who employ it as a worker swear by its intelligence and ability in water, nosing out shot birds and bringing them to hand rapidly; it is noted for its prodigious shake.

It is energetic but not a greedy feeder. It makes a good guard for a retriever, it is not hard to control, and makes a good family dog.

Breed box
Size: 34kg (75lb); male 69cm (27in); female 63.5cm (25in)
Grooming: Fairly demanding
Feeding: Reasonable
Exercise: Demanding but simple
Temperament: Friendly and confident

▲ The coat is the mark of this calm, powerful water dog, with a mass of curls that lie tight to the skin.

▲ The aristocratically chiselled muzzle is smooth-haired. The head is wedge-shaped with ears set below eye level.

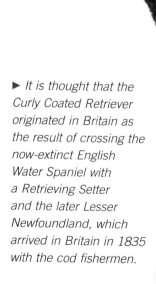

▶ It is thought that the Curly Coated Retriever originated in Britain as the result of crossing the now-extinct English Water Spaniel with a Retrieving Setter and the later Lesser Newfoundland, which arrived in Britain in 1835 with the cod fishermen.

English Cocker Spaniel

The English Cocker Spaniel is the original of the American breed. It stands around the same height as the American Cocker Spaniel at 41cm (16in), but its coat is shorter and therefore nowhere near such hard work to keep well groomed, provided adequate attention is paid to its fairly hairy feet and its longish ears. It can be found in whole colours such as red (gold) and black, and also in black and white, and in multi-colours.

A thoroughly busy dog, it is always searching and bustling around in the grass and bushes. Its name comes

◄ *The orange-roan colour is one of a huge range that this neat dog comes in. The breed is the basis of several of the land spaniels.*

from its ability to flush out game, particularly the woodcock. It also delights in carrying objects about, whether on command or purely voluntarily. It is often portrayed as the original slipper-fetching dog sitting by its owner's fireside, its tail wagging furiously. There is a clear difference between the heavier show English Cocker and the leggier working type.

▼ *Low-slung ears with long hair make regular grooming a must for this dog.*

Breed box
Size: 12.5–14.5kg (27½–32lb);
    male 39–41cm (15–16in);
    female 38–39cm (15–15½in)
Grooming: Regular
Feeding: Small
Exercise: Medium
Temperament: Merry and exuberant

▼ *The Cocker's job is to flush ground game for its handler. The tight body is essential for its bustling way of moving.*

▲ *This example shows a differently shaped eye, but still the gentle, relaxed expression.*

English Setter

The English Setter is a tall, handsome creature of comparatively slight build. It gives the impression that it knows it is attractive and intends to be noticed by all and sundry. As it stands 68cm (27in) tall, it is easily seen; it has a gloriously long, silky coat that can be a mixture of black, orange, lemon or liver with white. Like all such coats, it requires dedication to keep it clean after a day's work. The breed has a long, lean aristocratic head set on a long, muscular neck.

The English Setter can be trained to work in the field with speed and intensity, quartering large tracts in search of pheasant, partridge or grouse; once its relatively long nose recognizes an exciting scent, the dog comes to a rapid stop and sets on to the object.

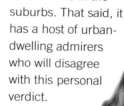

The sight of well-trained setters at full gallop suddenly screeching to a halt is, to say the least, memorable. There is no huge difference in shape and style between the show and working strains, but hunters have selected more for brains than beauty.

As a family dog, the English Setter is a natural because of its friendly nature, however it has a wildish streak in its make-up, even if it is not as

▼ *The flecked colours in the coat are referred to as 'belton', so you may have a lemon belton or an orange belton dog.*

▲ *Over the years, the English Setter has been bred in large numbers by top breeders, who have produced their own very characteristic styles, but the soft eyes are obvious in all strains.*

marked as in its Irish counterpart. It needs a firm, calm hand to turn it into a house dog, and it is not ideally suited to life in the suburbs. That said, it has a host of urban-dwelling admirers who will disagree with this personal verdict.

Breed box

Size: Male 65–68cm (25½–27in), 28.5kg (63lb); female 61–65cm (24–25½in), 27kg (59½lb)
Grooming: Demanding
Feeding: Reasonable
Exercise: Demanding
Temperament: A friendly enthusiast

▲ *This familiar pose is adopted by many dogs that are waiting for their owner to suggest a bit of action.*

English Springer Spaniel

The English Springer Spaniel was bred to flush or 'spring' game, hence their name. Flushing dogs, similar in looks to today's Springer, were in existence many years before the gun was invented. They would 'spring' on small game or birds to flush them out of cover so that they could be caught by hawks, hounds or in nets. Nowadays, there is a clear difference in both appearance and working ability between English Springers bred for the field and those produced for the show ring. Potential owners should satisfy themselves that they are buying from the correct bloodlines for the type they require.

▶ *Do not be deceived – this is a high-energy dog and requires long walks.*

This is a compact, medium-sized dog that has a very gentle expression and is well proportioned and balanced. Show-bred dogs are heavier and have longer coats and ears than the field-bred type. Working types maybe smaller and lighter than the guides given in the 'Breed box' on this page. In both types the coat is black and white, liver and white or tricolour. The white may be flecked or ticked. There is feathering on the ears, chest, belly, legs and tail.

This is an extremely popular breed worldwide. Affectionate and friendly, this dog makes a good companion in both the home and hunting field. It has great stamina and needs a lot of

▲ *The Springer has a charm that it is quite capable of using to its own ends. The coat requires daily grooming.*

exercise. It is generally tolerant with children, other dogs and small pets. Eager to learn, the breed excels in obedience, flyball and agility. The English Springer loves to work, and is used for drug and bomb detection, and also search and rescue.

▶ *The breed name 'Cocker' comes from this dog's use as a hunter of woodcock in England.*

Breed box
Size: Male 46–51cm (18–20in),
23–25kg (50–55lb);
female 43–48cm (17–19in),
16–20kg (35–45lb)
Grooming: Moderate
Feeding: Medium
Exercise: High
Temperament: Affectionate
and tolerant

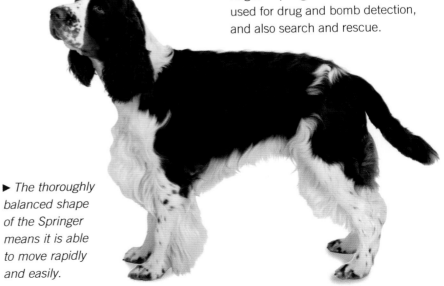

▶ *The thoroughly balanced shape of the Springer means it is able to move rapidly and easily.*

Field Spaniel

▼ The Field Spaniel is a dog for the country-dwelling family. It is steady and trainable.

This dog was once considered to be the same breed as the English Cocker Spaniel. It is said by some that due to the considerable diversity in size of the Cocker, it was decided in the early 20th century to split the breed. Dogs weighing above 11kg (25lb) were considered as Field Spaniels, while

▲ Several breeds of dog are liver coloured – this one shows that gleaming colour at its best.

those weighing less remained as Cocker Spaniels. Although the breed has changed since then, there are still some similarities to the working-type Cocker. This dog will retrieve from land or water, flush, hunt and track, as well as being a good watch dog. It is quite rare and is listed by the KC as a Vulnerable Native Breed.

The coat is silky and is coloured roan, solid black or solid liver. White markings are permitted on the throat and chest. Some dogs have tan points. The coat is darker with less white than other spaniels. The ears, chest, belly and the back of the legs are feathered. In size, this breed is between that of an English Cocker Spaniel and an English Springer Spaniel.

It is capable of being a good family dog, providing it has a job to do plus

Breed box
Size: 43–46cm (16–18in),
    18–25kg (40–55lb)
Grooming: Moderate
Feeding: Medium
Exercise: High
Temperament: Docile and
    intelligent

daily mental and physical exercise. The Field is not as excitable as some of the other spaniel breeds, but if bored it can become destructive.

▲ ▼ This breed is an ideal choice for an active family, jogger or agility enthusiast. Although friendly, it will bark to warn of an approaching strangers, and will benefit from puppy socialization.

Flat-coated Retriever

The Flat-coated Retriever is one of the lightest built of all the retriever family, and is a very agile dog. It is sociable and good-humoured, and always eager to please. The breed is most commonly black, but there are also a fair number of liver-coloured dogs. The odd yellow-coloured variation is frowned on by enthusiasts.

Breed box
Size: Male 58–61cm (23–24in),
    25–35kg (55–77lb);
    female 56–59cm (22–23in),
    25–34kg (55–75lb)
Grooming: Medium
Exercise: Medium
Feeding: Medium
Temperament: Kindly

▶ *The Flat-coated Retriever has a lighter body than other retriever breeds. It is a dog for the country rather than the town.*

Standing at most 61cm (24in) at the withers, it is not heavily built in the loins and hindquarters, hence its lighter appearance. Its coat is dense and flat, and positively shines with health after a good grooming. It is not a demanding dog to feed.

The Flat-coated Retriever is an excellent household dog who loves human company; its tail wags incessantly, and its intelligence is plain to see whether it is asked to work in the shooting field or play in the park.

▲ *This type of retriever has a less square foreface than other retrievers. Its deep bark gives a good warning of visitors or strangers.*

▶ *Flat-coats originated in Britain as the result of crossing several other breeds, including the Lesser Newfoundland. They originally had wavy coats.*

German Shorthaired Pointer

Of the three German pointers, the Shorthaired Pointer (GSP) is the best known. The mix of dogs that produced this breed is unknown, but is thought to include the English Pointer, Foxhound, Bloodhound and the German Bird Dog. The result is a superb all-round sporting dog that can retrieve, point and track. The GSP will retrieve from thick cover, open ground or water. Although predominantly a bird dog, it will hunt rabbits and racoons as well as trail deer.

Elegant and slightly streamlined, the GSP is a very striking dog. The short coat is solid liver, solid black, liver and white, or black and white. The American Kennel Club does not recognize any black colouring, and

▲ *The German Shorthaired Pointer is a superb worker of great intelligence.*

▶ *These dogs are strong swimmers. They have webbed feet, and delight in retrieving objects from water.*

would consider this a cause for disqualification. The hair lies close to the skin and forms a water-resistant layer. This enables the dog to stay warm when working in water or cold weather. The GSP has a broad muzzle, so it is able to retrieve large game.

This is a very energetic breed that requires vigorous exercise. It is best suited to active owners who have the time and stamina to take it for long, daily walks. It is a boisterous dog that that is generally good with children, but may not be the best choice for a young family. Care should be taken when introducing it to cats or other pets, as it has a strong hunting instinct. If bored or does not have enough exercise, it can be destructive or become an escapologist. A well-fenced garden or yard is essential.

▲ ▶ *This is a true sporting dog, full of athleticism – it has smooth lines, tight muscles and an all-seeing expression.*

Breed box

Size: Male 59–64cm (23–25in), 25–32kg (55–70lb); female 53–58cm (21–23in), 20–27kg (45–60lb)
Grooming: Easy
Feeding: Moderate to high
Exercise: High
Temperament: Boisterous and trainable

German Wirehaired Pointer

The breed was developed in the early part of the 1900s by crossing the German Shorthaired Pointer with a number of other breeds, including the Griffon. The aim was to produce a dog that was a robust and versatile hunter that could work in any terrain. Like all German Pointers, this dog has webbed feet. The coat is an important factor in the breed. It is made up of two layers – the outer is weather-resistant, and the undercoat is dense in the winter to provide insulation. This almost disappears in the warmer months. Dead hair needs to be removed to keep it looking tidy.

◄ *Although recognized as a breed in Germany in 1870, this dog is still relatively uncommon today.*

Breed box
Size: 27–32kg (60–70lb); male 60–67cm (24–26in); female 56–62cm (22–24in)
Grooming: Easy
Feeding: Medium to high
Exercise: High
Temperament: Playful and energetic

This is an affectionate and energetic dog that is loyal to its owner. It loves human companionship and, if properly trained, is tolerant towards children. It is prone to roaming and can become difficult to manage if not given enough exercise.

German Longhaired Pointer

This breed is rare and seldom seen in many parts of the world. It was devised in the 19th century by crossing German Shorthaired Pointers with English Pointers and Setters to produce a dog that could indicate by pointing the presence of flying prey.

It is closer to a setter then a GSP in appearance, with a medium-length, shiny coat. The fur can be solid liver or any combination of liver and white. It is an athletic dog that moves with a graceful gait. It is a very trainable and extremely affectionate dog that is prone to separation anxiety. Providing it is not left alone for long periods and has long daily walks, the GLP make a good family companion. This is a playful breed that gets on well with children.

◄ *The hair on the ears, tail, belly, chest and backs of the legs is longer than that on the body.*

▲ *Clean ears regularly to prevent a build-up of dirt and wax.*

Breed box
Size: 30kg (66lb); male 60–70cm (24–28in); female 58–66cm (23–26in)
Grooming: Moderate
Feeding: Medium to high
Exercise: High
Temperament: Athletic and friendly

Golden Retriever

The Golden Retriever is a canine all-rounder. It can turn its talents to anything, from its natural retrieving to acting as a guide dog for the blind, a detector of drugs or explosives, a reasonably laid-back obedience worker, or just being a most attractive member of a household.

Breed box
Size: 29.5kg (65lb); male 56–61cm (22–24in), 34kg (75lb); female 51–56cm (20–22in)
Grooming: Fairly demanding
Feeding: Demanding
Exercise: Demanding
Temperament: Intelligent and biddable

It stands 61cm (24in) at its tallest, but gives the impression of being a solid, comfortable dog. It is inclined to get its snout into the trough as often as possible, and owners need to watch its waistline. There is often quite a difference in appearance between those retrievers used in the shooting field and the type that are bred for showing and the home.

The Golden Retriever has a dense undercoat with a flat, wavy topcoat; the colour varies from cream to a rich golden, which is sometimes very deep.

It is easy to train, but needs to be kept interested because it is easily bored. Its ability as a guide dog for the blind demonstrates its temperament, as the work involves a great deal of steady, thoughtful walking.

It is one of the most popular household dogs because of its generous, loving nature. Such popularity is often a curse,

▲ *The Golden Retriever, one of the most popular of all dogs in the world, is a wonderful all-purpose breed, although guarding is not its forte.*

however, because dogs are bred by people who are not always conscientious in their dedication to producing truly healthy stock. As is true of any breed of pedigree dog, the best source of supply is direct from a reputable breeder who has the welfare of the dogs they produce at heart.

► *This breed was developed in Britain in the late 19th century. Becoming popular rapidly, it was imported to the USA, Canada, South America, Kenya, India and parts of Europe by the 1930s.*

▲ *These dogs have generous, soft muzzles that are able to carry shot birds, hares or even the newspaper without leaving a mark.*

Gordon Setter

Originating in Scotland, the Gordon Setter is the heavyweight of the setter section. It stands 66cm (26in) tall, but it is more solidly built than any of the others. As a result, it tends to move more steadily but still with considerable drive. It is a tireless worker that likes and needs its exercise; it does enjoy its food and can be heavy when fully grown.

It has a long, silky-textured coat of shining black with a pattern of chestnut-red tan on its muzzle and limbs. It grows slowly, as do all the setters, through a leggy, gawky stage, during which it can be the despair of its owner, but eventually it matures into a sound, dignified dog.

▶ *Setters vary in style, but nobody can fail to recognize the Gordon's solid build.*

Grooming has to be thorough, but is not over-demanding. This dog can make a good-natured companion as well as a reliable worker both in the field and on the moors.

Breed box
Size: Male 66cm (26in), 29.5kg (65lb); female 63cm (25in), 25.5kg (56lb)
Grooming: Reasonable
Feeding: Fairly demanding
Exercise: Reasonable
Temperament: Dignified and bold

◀ *This breed has a particularly powerful head and neck. The ears are heavily coated and hang down flat against the face.*

▶ *The Gordon may not have the glamour of its English and Irish cousins, but it is a trustworthy, steady working dog, and will last all day in the field.*

THE GUNDOG (SPORTING) GROUP

Hungarian Vizsla

The Hungarian Vizsla (often just called Vizsla) is a spectacularly coloured hunting, pointing and retrieving (HPR) breed from Central Europe. The short, dense coat of rich red russet only needs polishing with a cloth to keep it at its glorious best.

The breed stands up to 64cm (25in) at the withers, weighs some 28kg (62lb), and is strongly built with

Breed box
Size: 20–30kg (44–66lb);
male 57–64cm (22½–25in);
female 53–60cm (21–23½in)
Grooming: Easy
Feeding: Medium
Exercise: Medium
Temperament: Lively and fearless

▲ *The sight of a Vizsla in bright sunshine is a flash of the richest red.*

► *With one of the handsomest heads, the Vizsla is keen-eyed and has an intelligent expression.*

well-muscled limbs and a noble head that is not over-fleshed. The Vizsla is a worker with a great reputation in its native Hungary as both a pointer of game and a reliable retriever; it takes special delight in going into water in its quest for a shot bird. As a companion, it is a good, affectionate member of

the household, but it can be fairly protective so it needs a firm hand. Easily trained by those who set their mind to it, it is a truly all-purpose dog.

Hungarian Wire-haired Vizsla

The Hungarian Wire-haired Vizsla is another HPR breed, very much like the Hungarian Vizsla, with the exception that the coat is harsh. It sports definite eyebrows, which give it a sterner expression. Its height is the same as the Vizsla's, as is its

weight, and it demonstrates much the same characteristics of temperament. The coat on its legs is short and harsh, and possibly makes its limbs appear larger.

▼ *The harsh coat is the same russet red as the Hungarian Vizsla.*

◄ *Developed in the 1930s, the Wire-haired Vizsla is a popular gundog in Canada.*

Breed box
Size: 20–30kg (44–66lb);
male 57–64cm (22½–25in);
female 53–60cm (21–23½in)
Grooming: Relatively easy
Feeding: Medium
Exercise: Medium
Temperament: Lively and fearless

Irish Setter

The Irish Setter is known to its friends as the Mad Irishman, with a devil-may-care way about it. It is certainly beautiful, but to keep that long, silky coat of deep chestnut gleaming requires thorough and regular grooming, and the occasional bath.

▶ *The Irish Setter first appeared in recognizable form in the early 18th century.*

Breed box
Size: Male 65cm (25½in), 30.5kg (67lb); female 26kg (57½lb)
Grooming: Demanding
Feeding: Reasonable
Exercise: Demanding
Temperament: Affectionate and racy

▲ *Almond-shaped eyes with a kindly expression characterize this breed, which is also used as a therapy dog.*

It stands around 65cm (25½in), but the official breed standard does not contain a height clause because, according to those who have bred it all their lives, a good Irish Setter can never be a bad height. It is actually allowed to have a small amount of white on the front of its brisket, but nowhere else.

The Irish Setter does not carry a great deal of flesh, but its musculature has to be powerful because it is expected to work at top speed in the shooting field. It is not expensive to feed, although it can burn up a lot of calories, and it expects to be well exercised. It can be trained to curb its wildness by those who set out to be firm, and its attitude to one and all is of sheer friendship and *joie de vivre*. The recall exercise is not easily mastered by this dog.

The bitches of the breed tend to have very big litters of up to 16 puppies at a time.

▶ *The sheen on the deep chestnut coat is the reason why this dog is among the best-known and most popular breeds in the world.*

Irish Red and White Setter

The Irish Red and White Setter comes as a surprise to those who have always recognized the traditional Irish Setter, often incorrectly called the Red Setter. In fact, the Red and White is reputed by the Irish to have been the original version, but it became practically unknown outside its native Ireland for almost all of the early part of the 20th century.

Its success since the start of the 1980s has been gradual as breeders have become more selective and people have begun to notice this handsome, large red and white dog. It is similar in general appearance to the Irish Setter but has a slightly broader head and is more heavily built. It stands up to 65cm (25½in) at the withers and has a base colour of white with solid red patches on the head and body, and mottling on its limbs.

This breed does not eat greedily, and it enjoys human company. It makes a friendly family dog but, like a number of breeds with finely textured, longish coats, needs careful attention to keep it clean and wholesome after a run in the country. It is not temperamentally as racy as the Irish Setter, but it can still be quite a handful to control, and its training requires firmness and application on the part of its owners.

▶ The Irish Red and White Setter is a strong, athletic dog. It is good-natured and affectionate and is deservedly growing in popularity, but this breed requires patience to train it.

▼ Irish Setters are just red to most of us, but the original was probably this dog, often with more white than red.

▼ These dogs have a characteristic brilliant white blaze down the top of the muzzle, which adds to their appeal.

Breed box
Size: Male 65cm (25½in), 29.5kg (65lb); female 61cm (24in), 25kg (55lb)
Grooming: Demanding
Feeding: Reasonable
Exercise: Demanding
Temperament: Cheerful and biddable

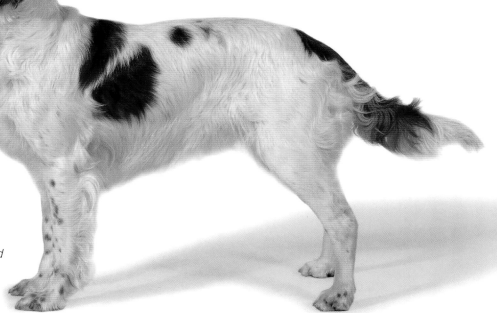

Irish Water Spaniel

The Irish Water Spaniel is one for the connoisseur. It is tall by spaniel standards, as it reaches 58cm (23in). The fact is that it is much more of a retriever than a spaniel. It is covered with tight liver-coloured ringlets, except for its muzzle, the front of its

▼ *This is a breed of great antiquity. A clear type emerged in the 19th century, from which today's dogs derive.*

◄ *The Irish Water Spaniel has a characteristic curly top-knot of hair just above the eyes.*

Breed box
Size: Male 53–58cm (21–23in), 27kg (60lb); female 51–56cm (20–22in), 24kg (53lb)
Grooming: Medium
Feeding: Medium
Exercise: Medium
Temperament: Affectionate if aloof

neck and the last two-thirds of its tail, which thus looks a bit like a whip. When it gets wet, its shake is a spectacular sight.

Aficionados regard it with great affection and enthusiasm, and consider that it has a good sense of humour. It is certainly energetic and revels in any amount of exercise, whether it is asked to be a household companion or fulfil its traditional role.

Grooming this spaniel requires skill and knowledge of the correct technique, as well as determination. Feeding is not a problem, as this dog is not greedy. It is a breed that could achieve greater acclaim.

▼ *Grooming is no easy task, and the art must be acquired from the start.*

◄ *Another water retriever, the Standard Poodle, has played a significant part in the Irish Water Spaniel's ancestry.*

Italian Spinone

The Spinone is an ancient breed from the Piedmont region of Italy. It is a versatile dog that can trace its heritage back to around 500BC. This hunter is capable of working on almost any terrain, and will point and retrieve. The breed name may have come from the word 'spino' which is a type of thorn bush that coarse-coated hunting dogs could push through without harm. The Spinone is often confused with the German Wirehaired Pointer, but it is very different in working style and character.

With a solid, well-muscled body and strong bone, it is easy to see how this dog can work in challenging

▶ *The Italian Spinone has recently arrived in North America, where the breed already has its devotees.*

▲ *This breed is a friendly, relaxed dog that is loyal to its owner, but it has a tendency to slobber.*

undergrowth. The coarse white, orange and white, brown and white, orange roan or brown roan coat protects the skin from brambles and thorns. The Spinone has pronounced eyebrows, and the hair on its muzzle forms a beard that provides additional protection to the face. Paws are large with webbed toes.

Not as fast or as energetic as many of the gundog breeds, the Spinone is well suited to life as a family dog.

◀ *A rough, tough all-purpose dog, the Italian Spinone's large hairy feet facilitate work in marshy terrain.*

Breed box
Size: 55–71cm (22–28in),
27–38.5kg (61–85lb)
Grooming: Easy
Feeding: Demanding
Exercise: Medium
Temperament: Loyal and placid

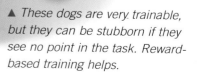

▲ *These dogs are very trainable, but they can be stubborn if they see no point in the task. Reward-based training helps.*

Kooikerhondje

This dog has many different names, including Small Dutch Waterfowl Dog, Kooiker Hound, Kooiker Dog and the Dutch Decoy Dog. Popular in the 17th and 18th centuries, it is featured in paintings by Rembrandt and Jan

◀ *The head should be in proportion to the body, and feature a well-defined stop.*

Steen. It was used to lure ducks into traps, by dancing around and waving its tail in front of them. Fascinated, the ducks would follow the dog and once in the trap could be caught by the hunters. This method of hunting is not employed nowadays, but the

Kooikerhondje is still used for luring ducks into traps for conservation and environmental purposes.

This beautiful medium-sized dog is red-orange and white in colour, with a well-plumed white tail. Some have a black ring encircling the tail where the red-orange meets the white. The ears should have long black hair at the tips, which are called 'earrings'. Other

▲ *The spectacular coloration and bushy tail helped the Kooikerhondje in its traditional role of luring ducks into netting traps.*

black markings are not permitted, but puppies are often born with some black hairs on their bodies that fall out as the puppy coat is shed. The unique adult coat can take up to two years to develop fully.

This dog is active outdoors but settled within the home. It is affectionate and naturally curious, investigating every new object that it finds. It is wary of strangers and will need socialization to overcome this trait. This is a cautious breed that does not like excessive handling, but with sympathetic training it will make a loving and loyal companion. Due to its sensitive nature, it is not recommended with small or noisy children. With correct training, it excels at activities such as dance and tracking.

◀ *Small and also supple, the Kooikerhondje's active frame makes it a good candidate for agility training.*

Breed box
Size: 36–41cm (14–16in),
   9–18kg (20–40lb)
Grooming: Moderate
Feeding: Medium
Exercise: Medium
Temperament: Sensitive and
   affectionate

Labrador Retriever

The Labrador Retriever is instantly recognizable. Thought to have originated in Greenland, it is a stockily built dog; its coat is short and hard to the touch, and it is entirely weather-proof and drip-dry. At one time the black coat was the best known, but yellow (not golden) became more widely seen from the 1940s onwards. Today there is quite a trend for chocolate, which is also called 'liver'.

▶ *Labradors were brought into the UK in the 19th century by the Earl of Malmesbury, to work the water meadows of his estate.*

Breed box
Size: Male 56–57cm (22–22½in), 30.5kg (67lb); female 54–56cm (21–22in), 28.5kg (63lb)
Grooming: Easy
Feeding: Reasonable
Exercise: Demanding
Temperament: Friendly and intelligent

▲ *Wisdom in a canine expression is difficult to define, but the true Labrador seems to get as near as any.*

The Labrador stands as high as 57cm (22½in), which is not very tall, but its body is extremely solid. Another characteristic is its relatively short, thick-coated tail, which is known as an 'otter' tail. Like the Golden Retriever, it is a multi-talented dog, being much favoured as a guide dog for the blind. (In fact these two breeds are regularly crossbred to utilize their combined skills.) It is also useful in drug-searching, and has been used by the army as a canine mine-detector. Undoubtedly its greatest skill is as a retriever from water.

The Labrador Retriever seems capable of taking all the knocks of a rough-and-tumble family, which is why it rates so highly as a household member. Its temperament is such that it does not seem to take offence at any insult.

It can consume any quantity of food, so needs rationing if it is not to put on too much weight. It must have exercise and, although it can live in town surroundings, it should not be deprived of regular, long walks. Without these it can rapidly become an obese couch potato, with all the health implications this implies.

▶ *With a frame like this, it is easy to see why the breed is famous for its stamina.*

Lagotto Romagnolo

The name of this dog is very descriptive: *lagotto* is the Venetian for 'duck dog', and Romagna is a region in Italy that the breed comes from. The breed type has been in existence in Italy since the 7th century BC. As marshlands were drained, the need for duck-hunting dogs diminished. But the Lagotto, with its exceptional scenting ability, was found to be able to 'sniff out' truffles. It is now the only breed of dog in the world that is recognized as truffle hunter.

It is an avid swimmer that has webbed toes and thick hair on the underside of the ear to prevent water from entering the inner ear. Eyes are large and round, and vary in colour

◀ *This breed has been employed for centuries in Europe and Scandinavian counties to hunt for truffles.*

◀ *Bright and happy, this dog responds well to training for a variety of activities.*

from dark brown to dark yellow. The Lagotto has a curly, non-shedding, waterproof coat that provides protection against thorns. This will require clipping several times a year. Left untrimmed, the hair on the head will grow across the eyes. Coat colours range from solid white, brown or rust to white with rust or brown patches.

Providing it is given sufficient exercise, this dog is an affectionate and loyal family companion. It is an intelligent breed that enjoys taking part in canine sports such as agility and flyball. It gets on well with other dogs and is tolerant towards children. It is a great digger, and will dig up the lawn in a matter of minutes given the chance. The territorial Lagotto will bark to sound an alarm, making it an excellent watch dog. Puppy socialization and training classes are recommended.

Breed box
Size: Male 43–49cm (17–19in), 13–16kg (28–35lb); female 36–41cm (16–18in), 11–14kg (24–31lb)
Grooming: Extensive
Feeding: Medium
Exercise: Medium
Temperament: Robust and intelligent

▲ *The Lagotto Romagnolo is often misidentified as a Poodle because of its similar coat.*

Large Munsterlander

The Large Munsterlander is a hunting, pointing and retrieving (HPR) dog that comes from the Munster region of Germany. It is a fearless hunter that has a total disregard of even the worst of weather conditions. Its boundless stamina and energy means that it is happy to work all day on the hunting field. Predominantly a bird dog, it will also hunt rabbits, hares and deer.

This breed has black head and white body that is flecked, ticked or patched with black. A solid black coat is considered a fault. Ears, tail and legs are feathered. There is a clear difference between males and

▶ *Excelling at obedience competitions, this breed is also used successfully as a therapy dog.*

females – the former are larger, with bigger heads, more feathering on the legs and longer hair on the chest. The Large Musterlander has a noble expression and moves in a fluid and effortless manner.

It is a very active breed that has a high exercise requirement. It is not suitable for an inactive owner, but ideal for someone who likes to spend a lot of time outdoors. A bored or under-exercised Musterlander can become destructive and may bark

when left alone in the home. This dog is very active both inside and outdoors. It is good with children, but unless properly trained to be calm in their presence, it may knock toddlers over. It is a keen hunting dog that must be taught not to chase livestock and other domestic pets. The breed is highly trainable, providing the owner is consistent, and responds well to reward-based training.

▼ *The Large Munsterlander is a keen, all-purpose gundog with a good nose and excellent stamina. Brown and white coats occur, but are uncommon.*

Breed box
Size: 58–65cm (23–25½in),
  23–32kg (50–70lb)
Grooming: Medium
Feeding: Moderate to high
Exercise: High
Temperament: Active and trainable

▲ *This breed always has a black head, but the expression is alleviated by the gleam in those golden-brown eyes.*

Nova Scotia Duck Tolling Retriever

The word 'toll' means 'to lure', and that is actually what the Nova Scotia Duck Tolling Retriever does. It rushes about in a playful manner at the water's edge while a hunter waits in a hide. Ducks are attracted to the spectacle, and swim towards the shore to take a closer look. When in range, the hunter stands up, causing the birds to take flight, and then shoots the ducks. The Toller retrieves the fallen birds from the water.

Breed box
Size: 43–55cm (17–21½in), 17–23kg (37½–50½lb)
Grooming: Medium
Feeding: Medium
Exercise: Medium to high
Temperament: Jaunty and trainable

◄ *The main purpose of this spritely breed is to tempt waterfowl to within range of a hunter.*

▲ *The Nova Scotia Duck Toller is devoted and loyal to its family.*

It is a medium-sized breed with a fox-like head. The coat is double, soft and water-repellent, and comes in rich shades of red. White markings are permissible on the feet, chest, tail tip and as a blaze on the head. The tail is well plumed and held high when active. The dog should be well muscled with medium to heavy bone. Tollers make a distinctive noise when excited; it is a cross between a bark and a howl, and is called the 'Toller Scream'. The breed is often mistaken for a small Golden Retriever.

The Toller is well suited as a family companion. It is a breed that enjoys the company of children, especially if they throw things for the animal to retrieve – this dog will retrieve for hours. It is a hardworking, intelligent and trainable dog that is devoted to its family. Excelling in canine sports, it can be seen enjoying obedience, dock diving and agility.

▼ *This type of dog is used with great success as a search and rescue animal.*

Pointer

The Pointer is an instantly recognizable breed. The clean-cut lines of its lean frame covered by a short, shining coat make a beautiful silhouette on grouse moor and in city parks alike, although its whole purpose in life makes it better suited for the countryside.

Breed box
Size: Male 63–69cm (25–27in), 29.5kg (65lb); female 61–66cm (24–26in), 26kg (57½lb)
Grooming: Minimal
Feeding: Demanding
Exercise: Medium
Temperament: Kind and reasonably biddable

▲ ▶ *The Pointer is built for speed and endurance. It uses its aristocratic nose to cover a great deal of moor or pasture remarkably rapidly.*

At 69cm (27in) in height, the Pointer is quite a tall dog. It does not carry much surplus flesh, so gives the impression of being bony. Its movements are fluent and athletic. This breed is not a big eater, it is a very easy dog to clean after a day's work, and it is relatively easy to teach it reasonable manners, though it is unlikely to win a top-standard obedience competition.

While most paintings depict the Pointer as white with a number of liver or black patches, it also comes in lemon and orange patterns. A kindly, gentle dog, it should appeal to the active owner.

◀ *The Pointer was developed in the UK in the 17th century to find and point hares for Greyhounds to chase. Dogs of a similar type are thought to have been bred in Spain at around the same time.*

Slovakian Rough Haired Pointer

The Slovakian Rough Haired Pointer, also known as Slovensky Hrubosrsty Stavac, is a relatively new breed that dates from the late 1950s and came from the former Czechoslovakia. It was created using the Weimaraner, German Wirehaired Pointer and the Cesky Fousek. The Weimaraner heritage can be seen clearly in the coat colouring. In its country of origin, this dog cannot be used for breeding

▶ This deep-chested dog should be well muscled and capable of great endurance.

unless it can prove its working ability by passing various hunting tests. It has the ability to hunt, point and retrieve, making it a good all-rounder.

It is a sturdy dog with a harsh, wiry, rough coat, and can work all day. White hair is permitted on the chest and feet, with the rest of the coat being any shade of grey or silver.

◀ The Slovakian Rough Haired Pointer is alert and has very expressive eyes.

The Slovakian has facial furnishings in the form of whiskers and a moustache. Nose leather, eye rims and pads must be dark. The breed is economical in movement and tirelessly covers the ground.

As with most sporting breeds, this dog needs a lot of exercise and is best suited to an active owner. Potential owners need to ensure they have enough time to give this breed the vigorous exercise that it will require. It makes an excellent canicross candidate or jogging companion. It is an affectionate dog that likes to please its owner and is tolerant with children. Many love water and would enjoy dock diving. This is an air-scenting dog that can be distracted by an interesting smell and take off to investigate. It is more suitable for rural living, but can adapt to town life if well exercised.

◀ In common with many breeds from the Slovakian region, numbers were much depleted between the two World Wars.

Breed box
Size: 57–68cm (22½–27in), 25–35kg (55–77lb)
Grooming: Moderate
Feeding: Medium to high
Exercise: High
Temperament: Active and affectionate

Spanish Water Dog

The Spanish Water Dog is a primitive breed whose origins are unclear. This animal has had a variety of jobs through the ages. In 18th-century Spain it was widely used as a herding dog, driving flocks of sheep and goats long distances in search of grazing pasture. The breed is still used today by farmers in the mountainous Andalucía region. In southern Spain it was used to tow boats to the shoreline, while in northern Spain it assisted the fishing communities by pulling nets. The Spanish Water Dog is also used for hunting, and is a good flushing dog capable of working on land or in water.

The coat of the Spanish Water Dog is non-shedding and termed as 'rustic'. This means that it should not be brushed or combed, but the hair allowed to grow into cords. If the cords mat, they can be pulled apart gently with the fingers. This may not be practical for working or pet dogs that would benefit from being clipped. Puppies are born with curly hair, and the adult coat is curly and woolly.

This breed can become protective, territorial and reserved with strangers,

▶ *This active breed is a willing worker and can be trained to undertake a variety of tasks.*

so early socialization and training is essential. It is very intelligent and learns quickly. Athletic, fast and very agile, this is a dog that needs to be doing a job. It excels on the hunting field, at agility, in the show ring, herding, therapy work, search and rescue, and at bomb or drug detection work, making it a true all-rounder.

Breed box
Size: Male 44–50cm (17–20in),
  18–22kg (40–49lb);
  female 40–46cm (16–18in),
  14–18kg (30–40lb)
Grooming: Medium to extensive,
  dependent on coat length
Feeding: Medium
Exercise: Medium to high
Temperament: Athletic and agile

▼ *Loving water, this dog is a strong swimmer; it has webbed feet.*

▲ *The face is well covered with hair, and the ears lie flat to the head.*

Sussex Spaniel

This dog is designated as a Vulnerable British Breed by the KC. After World War II there were thought to be only about seven Sussex Spaniels remaining. Numbers increased when breeding programmes were put in place, but this is still a fairly rare dog. It is a steady and careful hunter that is mainly used for flushing and retrieving upland game, and is a good watch and tracking dog. Unusually, this breed is the only gundog that bays when hunting.

It is a powerful, low and compact dog with a long body similar to that of the Clumber Spaniel. While being

▶ *The Sussex Spaniel has a heavier build and shorter legs than most other spaniels.*

Breed box
Size: 38–40cm (15–16in),
    18–20kg (40–44lb)
Grooming: Moderate
Feeding: Medium
Exercise: Medium
Temperament: Calm and steady

generally slow-paced, it can have bursts of extreme activity. Its rich red-gold coat is double, with a silky top layer and a dense water-resistant undercoat. The neck, chest, belly, legs and tail are feathered. Ears hang down, and are covered with silky hair.

This breed can be noisy, especially when bored or short of exercise. Training will teach the dog when this is appropriate and when it is not. It is generally accepting of children, other dogs and cats, and is calm in the home – not as active as other spaniels.

It is a good companion breed, but can be stubborn to train if not properly socialized. The breed is not recommended for an inexperience owner with small children, as this dog needs a person who is strong-minded with plenty of time to spare. The Sussex is prone to gaining weight if not getting sufficient exercise, so food rations need to be carefully monitored.

▼ *The head is broad with a wide muzzle. The ears are well furnished with protective hair.*

▼ *This ancient breed of slow-working spaniel survived by the judicious use of other spaniel blood in breeding programmes in the 20th century.*

Weimaraner

The Weimaraner is an outstanding dog. It stands tall in the Gundog Group at 69cm (27in). A highly unusual colour, the Weimaraner is nicknamed the 'Grey Ghost', although the grey can be slightly mousy rather than the silver-grey that experts crave. Possibly its most outstanding feature are its eyes, which can be either amber or blue in colour.

This is a hunting, pointing and retrieving (HPR) breed that originated on the European mainland. Its coat is short, smooth and sleek, although there is a rare version which sports a longer coat. In the more unusual coat it is no problem to groom – it is more a matter of polishing! Even when a Weimaraner spends a long day in the shooting field or on a country stroll through winter mud, it does not bring the outside world into its home.

This dog is not a big feeder, although it appreciates and needs a generously filled bowl on a cold winter's day. It does need exercise, because it has a temperament that requires plenty to occupy its very active mind. It can be trained fairly easily, but does not suffer fools gladly. It has a friendly attitude towards people but will act as an

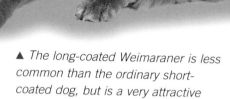

▲ The long-coated Weimaraner is less common than the ordinary short-coated dog, but is a very attractive variant of this breed.

impressive guard if its home or family are threatened. It is not a fawning, easy-going type of dog, even if it comes from a group that appears generally placid.

▲ This dog's piercing eyes are a distinctive feature. Normally shades of amber or blue-grey, they may appear black when dilated with excitement.

► The truly stylish Grey Ghost is built on racy lines, but with a stamina and turn of speed that emulate the thoroughbred stayer of the horse world.

Breed box
Size: Male 61–69cm (24–27in), 27kg (59½lb); female 56–64cm (22–25in), 22.5kg (49½lb)
Grooming: Easy
Feeding: Medium
Exercise: Demanding
Temperament: Fearless and friendly

Welsh Springer Spaniel

This breed is similar to the English Springer Spaniel, but is smaller and has a finer head. The 'Welshie' is used to find and 'spring' or startle game to take flight. Initially, the fleeing game would be caught by falcons or nets. With the development of guns, game is sprung to fly over the heads of hunters so that they can get a clear shot. Fallen game is then retrieved by the dogs who must not damage the bodies with their teeth. The Welsh Springer has great stamina and can undertake this job all day long.

With its red and white coat and fringed ears, the Welshie is a very striking dog. The coat is soft and lies flat to the body. Legs, chest, belly and tail are feathered. Eyes are almond-shaped and brown. The nose leather should be black or brown. A pink nose is considered to be a fault.

Friendly and loving towards family members, the Welshie can be wary of strangers. It is a fine companion, providing owners are active and prepared to give this dog long daily walks. It is a playful breed that is good with children, other dogs and pets. It does not like being left alone for too long and can exhibit signs of separation anxiety. It can be distracted when out and needs early training to ensure it comes when called. As well as being an excellent hunting dog, the Welsh Springer Spaniel does well in the show and obedience ring, agility, flyball and tracking, and as a therapy dog.

▲ *This is a gentle and sensitive breed that is widely used for therapy work.*

▶ *For sheer beauty, the sheen on the warm red of the Welsh Springer Spaniel's coat in the summer sunshine takes a lot of beating. The kindly expression is a mark of the breed.*

▲ *The Welsh Springer Spaniel is a much-loved breed in India, Australia and the USA, as well as the UK. It is a very popular all-rounder.*

Breed box
Size: 16–20kg (35–45lb);
male 46–48cm (18–19in);
female 43–46cm (17–18in)
Grooming: Moderate
Feeding: Medium
Exercise: Medium to high
Temperament: Loyal and willing

Wirehaired Pointing Griffon

There is some dispute as to whether the Wirehaired Pointing Griffon is a Dutch or German breed. The founder of the breed, Eduard Karel Korthals, was Dutch by nationality but was living in Germany at the time. He started his breeding programme in 1874, with the first animal entered in the American Kennel Club's stud book in 1887, just 13 years later. There is no certainty as to which breeds were used to devolve this dog, which is also known as Korthals Griffin. The 'Griff' is a pointer, flusher and water retriever.

It is a medium-sized, rough-coated dog that can exhibit a variety of colour combinations. Potential owners who wish to show this breed should consult the breed standard in their own country, as there is a variation in permitted colours among different kennel clubs. The dog's coat provides

▼ Referred to by some as the 'four-wheel-drive hunting dog', this breed is equally happy working on land or in water.

▼ This breed thrives on human company and prefers to live in a house where it can keep an eye everyone.

protection against dense or thorny undergrowth which, unlike some other gundogs, the Griff is quite happy to push through.

As the Griff is less excitable off the hunting field than some other sporting breeds, it is calmer, but still active, in the home. This is a people-loving breed that makes a good companion as well as a hunting dog. It is gentle with children and generally gets on well with other dogs. It tends to retain its puppy playfulness long into adulthood, and is a high-energy dog that requires plenty of exercise. It loves water and is a good swimmer. It is a breed that is loyal and trainable, and makes an excellent watch dog.

◄ The Griff is a highly intelligent breed that is quick-minded and good at working things out for itself.

Breed box
Size: 50–60cm (20–24in),
   23–27kg (50–60lb)
Grooming: Easy to moderate
Feeding: Medium
Exercise: High
Temperament: Loyal and energetic

THE TERRIER GROUP

The breeds that comprise this group are the pest-controllers of the canine world, having originally been used to find and kill rodents of all shapes and sizes. They possess fairly similar temperaments – they have to be tenacious as well as sharp in movement and reaction. They are inclined to act first and think afterwards, they tend to argue with the dog next-door, and they are not often the delivery man's best friend. But a terrier that is properly introduced is a delight as far as humans are concerned. A family who is seeking an alert, playful and affectionate friend will be well satisfied with a member of this group. The Terrier Group may be thought to include one of the most popular of all dogs, the Jack Russell Terrier, although this is, in fact, a cross-breed and therefore not registered by either the British or American Kennel Clubs. (In this book, it is featured in the chapter on Unrecognized breeds and hybrids.)

◄ *Although the Terrier Group is very diverse in type, size and weight, all have quick reactions and often act before they think. These are American Staffordshire Terriers.*

Airedale Terrier

Originating from northern England, the Airedale is the largest of the terriers, by some degree. It is a splendid animal with a genuine style about it that entitles it to its nickname, 'King of the Terriers'. It stands as tall as 61cm (24in) and has a head with an expression suggesting total command of any situation.

◄ These three youngsters will eventually grow into king-sized Airedale Terriers. They will reach maturity at about two years old.

its to look after. It has a loud voice that can be very convincing to any intruder. It is not a greedy feeder, but at the same time it is a well-built dog and naturally needs an adequate supply of nutrition.

◄ The Airedale greets friends with a laughing expression on an impressively bearded face.

Breed box
Size: 21.5kg (47½lb);
  male 58–61cm (23–24in);
  female 56–59cm (22–23in)
Grooming: Medium
Feeding: Medium
Exercise: Reasonable
Temperament: Friendly and courageous

The Airedale is somewhat less aggressive towards other dogs than some breeds in the group, but it will not back down if challenged. Few would dare to challenge it! It is reputed to be intelligent, but can be stubborn unless handled in a firm manner.

It has a black saddle, and the rest of it is mostly tan; the tan can be a gloriously rich colour. Its coat is harsh and dense and grows impressively, but can be kept tidy with regular brushing. It sheds its coat twice a year, and at such times it is good for it to be trimmed or stripped by a professional. The experts will frown on the use of clippers, but these can be an alternative if the dog is destined to be a household companion, not a show dog.

It makes a very good guard dog as it considers that its owner's property is

◄ This splendidly elegant, mature dog is ready to stand up to monster rat or human intruder alike. Although unable to go to ground, the Airedale displays all other terrier characteristics in abundance.

American Rat Terrier

The American Rat Terrier is believed to have originated initially from a cross between the Smooth Fox Terrier and the Manchester Terrier, and was a popular with American settlers coming from the UK during the 1820s. Other terrier breeds were then introduced. In the first quarter of the 20th century, an explosion in the population of jack

▶ *They may look cute, but these terriers are great escape artists.*

▲ *The American Rat Terrier is an intelligent dog that is a born worker, and can become destructive if bored.*

rabbits caused extensive crop loss and damage, so farmers crossed this feisty terrier with Whippets to increase their speed, and Beagles for a greater prey instinct and 'nose'. The result is a dog that can hunt both above and below ground, and also course.

The Rat Terrier comes in two sizes: miniature (25–32cm/10–13in) and standard (32–46cm/13–18in). These sturdy, compact dogs are smooth-coated and predominately white with coloured patches. The patches or 'pied markings' are acceptable in a variety of colours. The dogs can also have tan points. Ears may be either erect or tipped, as long as they are both even. Some dogs are born with bob tails, while others have long tails.

This long-lived, intelligent dog is happy living in a small home, as long as it gets plenty of exercise. Generally good with children, it makes an excellent family pet. Although it will shed its coats seasonally, a weekly groom with a soft brush is all that is normally required. As with all dogs, it requires training and socializing. The American Rat Terrier is highly trainable and excels in both agility and obedience competitions.

Breed box
Size: 25–46cm (10–18in),
  4.5–11kg (10–25lb)
Grooming: Easy
Feeding: Undemanding
Exercise: Medium
Temperament: Intelligent and loyal

◀ *This Rat Terrier is an import to the UK and has a docked tail. Docking is an illegal procedure in most countries around the world.*

American Staffordshire Terrier

The American Staffordshire Terrier, or Amstaff, gained recognition with the American Kennel Club in 1936. The breed originated from the Staffordshire Bull Terrier that had been brought to the USA by immigrants from the UK. The main visible difference between the two breeds is the size and weight. It is from this breed that the American Pit Bull Terrier evolved. In the United States this is now classified as a separate breed, but in many countries Pit Bulls are classified as one type. All Pit Bulls or Pit Bull types are subject to legislation and restriction, and potential owners should make themselves aware of rulings regarding these dogs within their own country.

American Staffordshire Terriers give the impression of great strength for their size. They are compact, well-muscled dogs with a broad, powerful head. The jaw is very strong. Ears are set high on the head and, in some countries, may be cropped. The short coat is made of thick, stiff and glossy hair. All colours are permissible, and can be solid, parti or patched. AKC regulations state that the coat should not be more than 80 per cent white.

This is a loyal and friendly breed that is often naturally obedient provided it has a firm, consistent and confident owner who understands the importance of becoming the pack leader. The dog is a courageous and persistent fighter who will fight to the death. A high degree of socialization is needed when the dog is young, to curb any aggressive tendencies. This is not a breed recommended for any but the most experienced dog owner.

▲ *If you are considering acquiring this breed, ensure that you are aware of the legal liabilities of its ownership.*

▼ *In most areas, laws makes it an offence for this dog to be let off the lead outside its own garden.*

◄ *Well toned, muscled and agile, this American Staffordshire Terrier portrays an impressive and confident presence.*

Breed box
Size: 20–30kg (57–67lb);
    male 43–48cm (17–19in);
    female 41–46cm (16–18in)
Grooming: Easy
Feeding: Moderate
Exercise: Medium to high
Temperament: Dominant and loyal

Australian Terrier

Initially called The Rough Haired Terrier, the Australian Terrier is thought to have originated from a cross of British northern terriers that travelled to Australia with the early settlers. This dog was bred to hunt and kill mice and rats. The breed is now recognized by the kennel clubs of all English-speaking countries. It rates highly in its native land, but has not yet achieved quite the same degree of popularity elsewhere.

The Australian Terrier is an alert, small dog of great character. It stands a mere 25cm (10in) high to the shoulder. The body shape is round rather than deep, with plenty of space for good lungs, which it needs in order

▲ In Australia, these feisty little terriers are prized for their ability to kill snakes.

to be as active as it always seems to be. The coat is relatively short and is harsh in texture, making it easy to groom. The dog has an intelligent expression and carries its ears pricked. The coat can have either steel blue on its saddle with tan on the rest of it, or an all-over red. The blue

and tan-coated dogs are often born with a blue-black coat that changes colour at around nine months of age.

Either way, the Australian Terrier is a smart little dog that is surprisingly tractable and anxious to please, although it can be rather bossy. It can be very useful as a watch dog and is able to use its vocal chords effectively in the home. Like all terriers, the male dogs can be aggressive in the absence of early socialization and training.

Breed box
Size: 25cm (10in), 6.5kg (14lb)
Grooming: Reasonable
Feeding: Small
Exercise: Undemanding
Temperament: Extroverted and friendly

◀ The Australian Terrier delights in using its sharp bark to warn its owner of a visitor's arrival. This breed is not often found in a relaxed mood.

▲ The 'Aussie' was recognized by the British Kennel Club in 1933. It has a black nose with an inverted 'V' above.

Bedlington Terrier

This dog comes from the northern counties of the UK, possibly Northumberland, and was bred to chase and catch rabbits and other small rodents. Often owned by poachers, it has also been known as the 'Gypsy Dog'. In the 19th century, this fast breed was used by factory workers to race, sometimes even against Whippets. Nowadays it is seen mainly as a family pet.

The Bedlington Terrier is a very distinctive dog with a somewhat tucked-up loin and an unusual non-shedding coat. The fur, sometimes described as 'linty', stands away from the dog's body and has a tendency to twist. Because this dog does not moult in the normal manner, it is considered less likely to cause allergic symptoms in susceptible people. The coat requires regular grooming and clipping, and when properly presented, this terrier looks like a shorn lamb. All Bedlingtons are dark in colour when born but lighten as they grow, and they become very pale shades of blue or sand that may appear white.

As this dog has a very strong prey instinct and is liable to chase other small furry animals, including cats, it requires a well-fenced garden. It needs moderate exercise and will

▲ Correctly presented, the Bedlington Terrier has a very distinctive trim.

happily join in with most family activities. The Bedlington is a quiet dog within the home provided it gets sufficient exercise, making it suitable for smaller dwellings or apartments. The breed is moderately popular in the UK and USA.

▲ The head is long and narrow, with low-set ears hanging close to the cheek.

▶ A terrier in lamb's clothing, the Bedlington is full of courage in the house or as a rabbit catcher.

Breed box
Size: 41cm (16in), 8–10.5kg (18–23lb)
Grooming: Reasonably undemanding
Feeding: Small
Exercise: Undemanding
Temperament: Mild

Border Terrier

The Border Terrier is originally from the borders of England and Scotland, and is popular as both a worker and a family dog. The fact that many veterinary surgeons choose to own this breed speaks volumes about the temperament and lack of hereditary health problems found in the Border Terrier. It is a friendly breed that appeals to many different people.

The maximum weight is just over 7kg (15½lb). This is a dog who is expected to work, however much it is adapted to living as a family companion. It fits that bill excellently. It has a cheeky otter-like head, a sound body clothed in a harsh, dense

▶ The Border Terrier is described as 'racy', which means it gives the impression of speed but without loss of substance.

coat, and its legs will carry it across country or urban park for as long as its owner requires. The official standard states that the dog should be capable of following a horse, hence its sufficient length of leg. It is not quarrelsome, but it is game for anything. It likes being with people.

The Border Terrier comes in a variety of colours, including red, wheaten, grizzle and tan or blue and tan. It is light enough to be picked up easily, and it does not require a great deal of food. It has a lot going for it.

◀ One of the most cheerful and companionable of all dog breeds, the Border Terrier makes an excellent family dog.

Breed box
Size: Male 30.5cm (12in), 6–7kg (13–15½lb); female 28cm (11in), 5–6.5kg (11–14lb)
Grooming: Undemanding
Feeding: Small
Exercise: Medium
Temperament: Game and friendly

▶ This breed has changed little since it first appeared in the late 18th century. It has found much favour in the show ring, but has still remained true to type. The breed standard describes it as having a head like an otter.

Bull Terrier

The Bull Terrier is an odd one out in the Terrier Group. It is not a pure terrier, even though its name is a combination of 'bull' and 'terrier'. In fact, it was originally more of a dog fighter than a small pest-controller.

The breed's shape contrasts with other terriers. The Bull Terrier is much more burly, and it has an egg-shaped

▲ The egg-shaped head of the modern Bull Terrier is hard as a bullet if the dog runs into you at speed.

head and a Roman nose. It gives the impression of being ready for anything and is nicknamed the 'Gladiator of the Terriers', a description that fits it perfectly.

Bull Terriers are the only dogs to have triangular eyes, which are dark in colour and deep-set. Ears are erect and set to the side of the skull. The tail should be horizontal when on the move, but carried lower when at rest.

The Bull Terrier is usually thought of as white, but even the white ones often have patches of red, black or brindle on the head. The dog can also appear as black, red, fawn or brindle,

▲ White is the most common colour for the Bull Terrier, often with coloured markings on the head.

▼ There is no wasted space on this attractive, power-packed bitch – just solid quality in the flesh.

Breed box
Size: 45cm (18in), 33kg (72lb)
Grooming: Easy
Feeding: Medium
Exercise: Medium
Temperament: Even but obstinate

with a certain amount of white mainly on its head, neck or limbs.

Its coat is short and flat, with a feel of harshness about it. It is simple to groom, by sponging the dirt off and then rubbing it down with a cloth.

The Bull Terrier is a very active dog. It likes its exercise and food, and is a grand dog to have about the home because it loves people – but woe betide any burglar!

The Pit Bull Terrier, originating in the United States, was also bred for fighting. As the result of deliberate training for illegal dog fighting, this breed has been deemed dangerous and has been banned in many countries throughout the world.

Bull Terrier – Miniature

Miniature Bull Terriers have been known since the early 19th century. In fact, most pictures of Bull Terriers painted around that time show the smaller variety. By World War I they had fallen from favour, and they were removed from the Kennel Club Register in 1918. This was because the reduced size resulted in dogs that did not look like Bull Terriers, but more like Chihuahuas with a tiny head and protruding eyes. Breeders worked hard to re-establish the breed type, and the Miniature Bull Terrier was reinstated in 1938; it is now classified as a British Vulnerable Native Breed. The breed was given full status by the American Kennel Club in 1991.

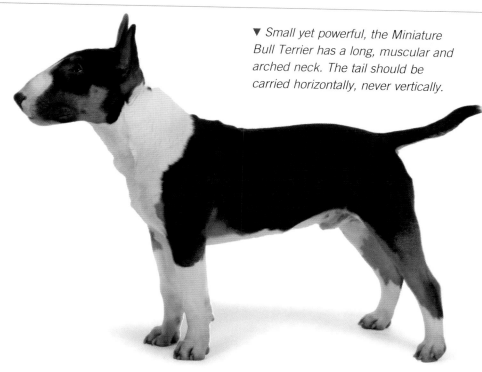

▼ *Small yet powerful, the Miniature Bull Terrier has a long, muscular and arched neck. The tail should be carried horizontally, never vertically.*

▲ *This photograph clearly shows the egg-shaped head and triangular eyes that are so typical of the breed.*

Breed box
Size: Height should not exceed 35.5cm (14in); weight in proportion to height
Grooming: Easy
Feeding: Undemanding
Exercise: Moderate
Temperament: Loving but stubborn

This strong and muscular dog should have a weight in proportion to its size, and must be carefully dieted to avoid obesity. All sizes of Bull Terriers have a very distinctive egg-shaped head. This dog moves in a free and easy manner with a characteristic jaunty gait. The coat is smooth and lies flat against the body, causing the fur to gleam. Grooming is easy, simply requiring a soft brush to remove any dirt and a polish with a cloth to make the coat shine.

► *Eyes should be dark. Blue eyes are a fault in either size of the Bull Terrier breeds.*

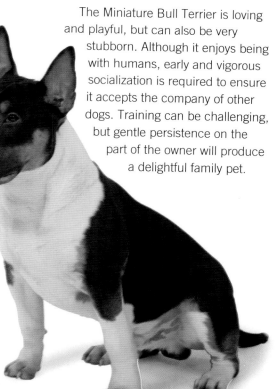

The Miniature Bull Terrier is loving and playful, but can also be very stubborn. Although it enjoys being with humans, early and vigorous socialization is required to ensure it accepts the company of other dogs. Training can be challenging, but gentle persistence on the part of the owner will produce a delightful family pet.

Cairn Terrier

The Cairn Terrier is an engaging creature, usually blessed with a fascinating character. Coming from the Highlands of Scotland, it is one of a group of breeds that is small in stature but large in heart. It stands a mere 31cm (12½in). Its coat, which is harsh and weatherproof, can be anything from cream through red or grey to almost black. The essential

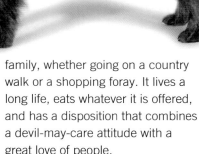

▶ *Most Cairns carry more coat; this example is in between coats, but shows the neatness of line and the reasonable length of leg.*

feature is that the dog should end up looking shaggy even after it has been groomed.

Its prick ears on top of a small, sharp-featured head give it a look of alert gameness, which is absolutely justified. It bustles everywhere at great pace, tending to catch unawares any small rodents that it chases. It is a tireless animal with an impressively sharp voice, and delights in accompanying its human

family, whether going on a country walk or a shopping foray. It lives a long life, eats whatever it is offered, and has a disposition that combines a devil-may-care attitude with a great love of people.

Breed box
Size: 28–31cm (11–12½in),
    6–7.5kg (13–16lb)
Grooming: Medium
Feeding: Small
Exercise: Reasonable
Temperament: Fearless

Czesky Terrier

The Czesky (pronounced "cheski") originated in the Czech Republic. It is a kind dog with a coat colour varying from black through dark grey to a silvery look. Sociable and relatively obedient, it tends to be less aggressive than many of the other terrier breeds.

It stands up to 35cm (14in) high and is slightly longer in the back than it is tall. Its coat is not shed and needs trimming regularly with attention from brush and comb. It is not greedy, but eats well. It enjoys exercise as a family companion.

▲ *The Czeskys were bred for underground burrowing work.*

◀ *The Czesky Terrier's traditional clip leaves a prominent beard and eyebrows, as well as long hair on the legs and underbelly.*

Breed box
Size: 35cm (14in), 5.5–8kg
    (12–18lb)
Grooming: Medium
Feeding: Small to medium
Exercise: Reasonable
Temperament: Cheerful but
    reserved

Dandie Dinmont

The Dandie Dinmont is a terrier whose appearance comes as something of a surprise. It has an expression that can only be described as soulful, with large, round eyes peering out of an equally large head that is covered with what seems to be a huge soft cap or top-knot of hair. The breed comes in two distinct colours: a reddish

▶ *The Dandie Dinmont is more docile than other terriers, but has a surprisingly deep and loud bark.*

▲ *This breed was named after one of Sir Walter Scott's characters in his novel 'Guy Mannering', written in 1814 – Dandie Dinmont was a farmer who kept these dogs.*

Breed box
Size: Male 28cm (11in), 10kg (22lb); female 20.5cm (8in), 8kg (18lb)
Grooming: Medium
Feeding: Small
Exercise: Reasonable
Temperament: Independent and affectionate

brown through to fawn, which is dubbed mustard; and a bluish-grey, which is known as pepper.

The dog is longer in its body than it is high at the withers. It may weigh up to 10kg (22lb), so is not a heavy dog. It is also not a big eater. It thrives on human companionship and certainly makes an attractive household member. It never looks as if it would do anything in a hurry, but it can be roused to action by the sight of any rat or squirrel unwise enough to invade its territory.

▶ *A faithful houshold member, the Dandie Dinmont has gentle eyes, a soulful expression and is good with children and a watchful guard dog.*

Glen of Imaal Terrier

The Glen of Imaal Terrier is the shortest and rarest of the Irish terrier breeds, and comes from County Wicklow. Used to control vermin, including foxes and badgers, this terrier is brave and fearless. Although still found working on Irish farms and small holdings, it is little known outside its country of origin. Numbers remain low, but there has been a small increase in recent years. This dog is recognized by the KC and AKC and a few other kennel clubs around the world.

Standing roughly 36cm (14in) at the withers, its back is long in proportion to its height. Small ears hang naturally on a powerful head that has a pronounced stop and tapered

▼ *This is the only Irish breed of terrier that stands low to ground.*

muzzle. Feet are slightly turned out with black nails, and the front legs should be slightly bowed to assist the dog while digging. The coat is wiry and not over-long, with a soft undercoat. It comes in shades of blue, brindle or wheaten. This sturdy dog has a 'shaggy dog' appearance that requires little grooming other than a daily brushing.

The Glen of Imaal Terrier is not a striking dog, but it has a happy and charming personality that makes it an attractive family pet. An affectionate and playful nature also makes this dog an ideal companion, but like most terriers the Glen will not back down in a fight. At home, this calm dog is very loyal and loving towards its owner, and is not as yappy as other small terriers.

▲ *It is suggested that this breed was the original 'turnspit dog' used to rotate meat over cooking fires.*

▼ *The Glen of Imaal has a surprisingly laid-back expression for a terrier.*

Breed box
Size: 35–36cm (14in), 16kg (35lb)
Grooming: Medium
Feeding: Medium
Exercise: Medium
Temperament: Game but docile

◄ *Short legs enable this fearless dog to pursue its quarry underground.*

Irish Terrier

The Irish Terrier is a handsome dog, standing up to 48cm (19in) at the withers. It sports a harsh and wiry coat of a sandy red colour, which may on occasion tend to be a paler wheaten tone. It gives the impression of being long in the leg, and it certainly is not burly in its body shape.

As a result of not being thick-set, it does not need a lot of food to sustain its frame. It enjoys exercise, but this should be under strict control if there are likely to be other dogs about. It is a first-class dog for people of all ages, and makes a fine house pet.

Its coat grows in a less bushy fashion than the Airedale's, and it is not hard to keep it looking neat,

▼ *This dog bristles through and through with a love of action. It is still used as a working terrier in Ireland, and is popular for field trials and lure coursing in the USA.*

Breed box
Size: Male 48cm (19in), 12kg (26½lb); female 46cm (18in), 11.5kg (25lb)
Grooming: Medium
Feeding: Medium
Exercise: Medium
Temperament: Good with people, but fiery with dogs

although it needs an occasional smartening trim by a professional groomer – unless its owner decides to take a course in the art.

▼ *The handsome and magnificent jaws of this breed contain one of the finest sets of teeth found in any dog.*

◄ *The Irish Terrier, from southern Ireland, is one of the oldest of the terrier breeds. In the 1880s it was the fourth most popular breed in England. The Irish Terrier Club of America was founded in 1896.*

Kerry Blue Terrier

This blue-coloured Irish terrier originated from County Kerry, hence its name. It was once considered to be a mascot for the Irish patriots, and is now the national dog of Ireland. Initially bred to hunt badgers, foxes and otters, it is thought to have bloodlines back to Irish, Bedlington and Bull Terriers. This dog is an excellent all-rounder capable of guarding, hunting, retrieving and herding, as well as being a good swimmer.

Breed box
Size: Male 46–48cm (18–19in),
  15–17kg (33–37½lb);
  female 46cm (18in), 16kg (35lb)
Grooming: Medium
Feeding: Medium
Exercise: Medium
Temperament: Game

All puppies are born black and should change to a shade of blue within the first 18 months of their life. A small patch of white on the chest is allowed. The profuse, fast-growing coat is soft and silky with no undercoat, and does not shed. This dog has a strong neck, lean head and powerful jaws, and the overall body is square in shape.

This dog requires extensive grooming and regular clipping or trimming. The beard will need constant attention to keep it neat and clean. The expense of trips to the groomer or the purchase of grooming equipment should be factored in when considering this breed.

The Kerry Blue is generally good with children and is very playful, but retains strong guarding qualities.

◀ *The Kerry Blue was first introduced to the breed ring in the USA in the early 1920s.*

It can display aggressive tendencies towards other dogs, and will need training and socializing to turn it into a suitable household pet. A confident owner who is prepared to continue obedience training is needed to temper this boisterous, headstrong and sometimes rowdy dog.

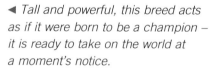

◀ *Tall and powerful, this breed acts as if it were born to be a champion – it is ready to take on the world at a moment's notice.*

▼ *This terrier is capable of catching and killing an otter in deep water.*

Lakeland Terrier

The Lakeland Terrier, from the Lake District of north-west England, is one of the group of square-built terriers. Standing 37cm (14½in) at the withers, it has a dense, harsh coat that can be all kinds of colours, from red through wheaten to liver, blue or black, with black and tan and blue and tan as alternatives.

Grooming it is not a huge task, but as the dog's coat grows relatively thick, it would be wise to have it professionally trimmed every now and then, or possibly learn to do the job yourself. In between, the use of an ordinary brush and comb will suffice.

This is an agile dog that loves freedom and exercise. A tireless working terrier, it delights in joining a family and taking part in any activity that is going on, and it is not over-noisy.

The Lakeland, like many terriers, is a great digger, as well as agile, so garden fences

need to be sound, higher than you might expect, and sunk into the ground to prevent under-digging. It makes an excellent alarm dog, quick to bark at the approach of a stranger.

▲ This is a good working terrier who nevertheless makes a good family pet. It can be dominating given the chance.

▲ Lakeland Terriers were originally bred in England to kill foxes that preyed on sheep and their lambs.

▶ The Lakeland Terrier has sufficient length of leg to cover rough terrain.

Breed box
Size: 37cm (14½in); male 7.5kg (16½lb); female 7kg (15½lb)
Grooming: Medium
Feeding: Medium
Exercise: Medium
Temperament: Friendly and self-confident

Manchester Terrier

The Manchester Terrier is a fair height, 41cm (16in), and looks as if it has a bit of Whippet in its make-up. It is jet black and tan in colour, and its coat is smooth, shining glossily after a good, hard polish with a cloth.

This dog does not eat a great deal, and might give the uninitiated the impression that it is a dilettante in its approach to life, but it was bred as

▲ *In Victorian England this dog was called the 'Gentleman's Terrier', as it was more well-mannered than most of the other terrier breeds.*

a ratter and, given the chance in modern society, will prove it still retains its old skills.

It is a sporting sort that delights in family activities, whether in town or the country. It is not aggressive either to human or dog, and it makes a good companion for anyone who likes a dog to be a bit out of the ordinary.

▼ *Being good with children and responding well to training make this breed an ideal choice for a novice dog owner.*

◄ *This breed is well loved by many devotees. With its Whippet connection, it is an unusual type for a terrier.*

Breed box
Size: Male 41cm (16in), 8kg (18lb); female 38cm (15in), 7.5kg (16½lb)
Grooming: Easy
Feeding: Undemanding
Exercise: Reasonably undemanding
Temperament: Companionable and relatively quiet

► *There is an obvious likeness in this stylish pair of Manchester Terriers.*

Norfolk and Norwich Terriers

The Norfolk Terrier and its older cousin, the Norwich Terrier, each bear the name of their place of origin in England. They are breeds of extremely similar type and style. They are eager, bustling, little dogs, low to the ground and thick-set in body. The essential difference is that the Norfolk Terrier's ears drop forward at the tip, whereas the Norwich Terrier's ears are pricked.

Their aim in life is to hustle foxes, badgers, rats and anything that moves in the countryside, except farm animals and people. In fact, they are both capable of keeping their family companions on the move, but from in front rather than behind.

They stand a mere 25cm (10in) at the withers, with hard, wiry coats that tend to be rougher around the neck and shoulders. The coat is red, wheaten, black and tan or grizzle, and it gives the impression that it is warm and thorn-proof. It does not present much of a problem when it comes to grooming, and after a country walk or a busy session down a handy hole, the coat is returned to its rough neatness very simply.

The two breeds are exhibited at shows separately in spite of the fact that there is little or no difference between them, except the ear carriage. In either guise, aficionados have adopted the attitude that docking of the tail is optional, and more and more are being seen with this appendage left as nature decreed it. Both terriers are good rough-and-tumble dogs with kindly personalities, and they will not go around looking for a fight.

▼ Both Norfolk (here) and Norwich are small, solid terriers and great diggers.

▲ There's a gleam in this Norfolk's eyes that speaks of fun and frolic.

Breed box
Size: 25cm (10in), 6.5kg (14lb)
Grooming: Simple
Feeding: Undemanding
Exercise: Medium
Temperament: Alert, friendly and fearless

▼ Wearing the look of a fun-loving breed, this is the Norwich Terrier looking its sharpest.

▲ An alert expression with prick ears is the hallmark of the Norwich.

Parson Russell Terrier

The Parson Russell Terrier is descended from the type of Fox Terrier favoured by a famous sporting parson from the West Country of England in the second half of the 19th century. Parson Jack developed what he considered to be the ideal hunt terrier, one that stood about 36cm (14in) high and weighed in the region of 6.5kg (14lb), easy enough to carry on his saddle and capable of going to earth to bolt a hunted fox.

First given breed status in 1990, this dog has rapidly gained in popularity. It is now recognized by most kennel clubs worldwide.

It has longer legs and is squarer in shape than the Jack Russell Terrier. Ears are V-shaped and drop down, with the tips pointing towards the eyes. Nose leather should be black in colour. The coat is either smooth or broken (i.e. smooth with some longer hair on the face, legs or body). Curly or rough coats are incorrect, according to the breed standards.

This is a feisty breed that requires both physical and mental exercise to prevent it from becoming bored and

▼ *The Parson combines dedication as a worker with a playful nature. It makes a good house dog, but requires plenty of exercise.*

destructive. It is very energetic and excels in most canine sports, especially agility and flyball. Provided it is well trained and socialized, the Parson Russell can make a good family pet, but it should not be trusted with small pets such as rabbits or hamsters.

▼ *This is a balanced terrier, and the rough-coated type has remained very much the same as it was when the famous sporting parson first bred it.*

Breed box
Size: 28–38cm (11–15in),
 5–8kg (11–18lb)
Grooming: Undemanding
Feeding: Medium
Exercise: Medium
Temperament: Cheerful and bold

▲ *This breed has sparkling eyes and an intelligent-looking head.*

Scottish Terrier

The Scottish Terrier has been popular for many years, but is not seen quite as frequently as it used to be. It stands some 28cm (11in) at the withers and gives the impression of being a neat, powerful dog for its size. It has a harsh, wiry and weatherproof coat that benefits from being kept tidy, whether professionally or otherwise.

The 'Scottie' has fairly large prick ears and carries a good deal of coat on its longish muzzle in the form of a beard. Most people would know it as black or very dark brindle, but on occasion it does come in wheaten

◄ Tall, erect ears of a neatly sculptured head are the essence of the Scottie, once known as the Aberdeen Terrier. This breed is popular in North America.

◄ The wealth of beard is one of the factors that sets this breed apart from the Cairn and West Highland White Terriers. Eyebrows are kept long.

▼ Solid and thick-set, the Scottie is surprisingly agile and active for such a short-legged dog. It is a proud dog that is very dignified in nature.

as well. Its well-boned legs look almost thick-set, and its deep frame makes it appear to be close to the ground. The Scottie moves with a smooth, level gait as if it is very important and, although normally gentle, this is not a dog with which to pick a fight.

Breed box
Size: 8.5–10.5kg (19–23lb);
   male 28cm (11in);
   female 25.5cm (10in)
Grooming: Medium
Feeding: Reasonable
Exercise: Undemanding
Temperament: Bold and friendly

Sealyham Terrier

The Sealyham Terrier is a small, sturdy terrier from rural Wales. It should not grow taller than 31cm (12in) at the withers, and the length of its body should be slightly greater.

It has a longer coat than some terriers, but it is also wiry. Since it is basically white with small patches of lemon or badger usually on its head and ears, it is not simple to keep clean in the breed's natural country home, especially if the weather is wet. For this reason, it does benefit from occasional professional attention.

The Sealyham can be a trifle cautious with strangers, but it is a superb companion or house dog and a very effective alarm-raiser. It is known as a self-sufficient dog that makes its own entertainment.

▶ The Sealyham is named after the Welsh village from which it originated. It has a marked independence of nature.

◀ The curtain of hair on this breed's face conceals a pair of very bright eyes that will not miss anything.

Breed box
Size: 31cm (12in); male 9kg (20lb); female 8kg (18lb)
Grooming: Medium
Feeding: Reasonable
Exercise: Undemanding
Temperament: Alert and fearless

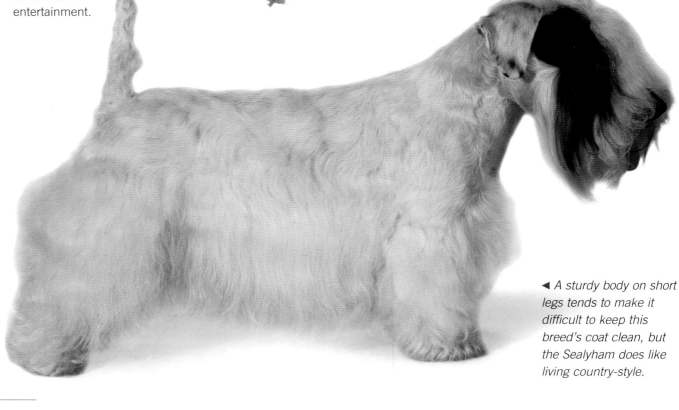

◀ A sturdy body on short legs tends to make it difficult to keep this breed's coat clean, but the Sealyham does like living country-style.

Skye Terrier

The Skye Terrier was developed from the same root-stock as the Scottish Terrier. It is a very long dog, being only 26cm (10in) at the withers but twice that from stem to stern.

The coat is hard and straight as well as long, and covers its eyes. It needs constant attention, which can be demanding, so it is something of a specialist's dog. The Skye Terrier is

Breed box
Size: Male 25–26cm (10in),
  11.5kg (25lb); female 25cm
  (10in), 11kg (24lb)
Grooming: Demanding
Feeding: Medium
Exercise: Medium
Temperament: Distrustful of
  strangers

▼ *Most Skye Terriers have prick ears that are gracefully fringed with hair.*

cautious of people it does not know, while being very loyal to its own family. It is very striking to look at and is certainly a good watch dog. It is designated by the KC as being a Vulnerable Native Breed.

▼ *From contemporary records it seems that this long-haired dog, with its beautiful flowing coat, is much the same as it was nearly four centuries ago.*

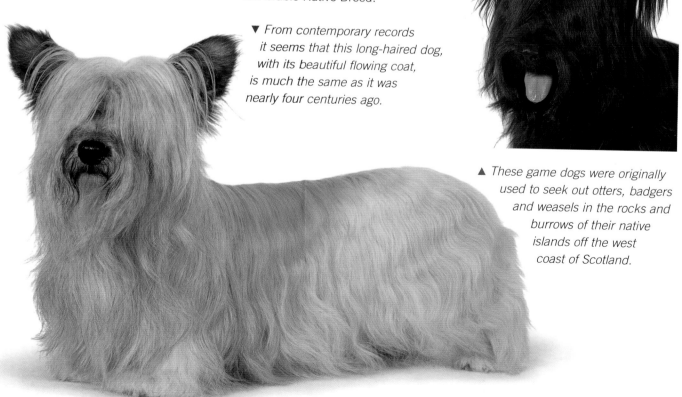

▲ *These game dogs were originally used to seek out otters, badgers and weasels in the rocks and burrows of their native islands off the west coast of Scotland.*

Smooth Fox Terrier

The Smooth Fox Terrier is a smart, alert dog. It stands about 39.5cm (15½in) at the withers and always gives the impression of being right up on the tips of its toes. A lethargic dog of this breed would be most unusual. It is typical of all the square-built terriers, ready to stand its ground

Breed box
Size: 39.5cm (15½in);
male 7.5–8kg (16½–17½lb);
female 6.5–7.5kg (14–16½lb)
Grooming: Undemanding
Feeding: Medium
Exercise: Medium
Temperament: Friendly and fearless

▶ *Most breeds of terrier came from somewhere in the British Isles; this one is the original hunt terrier used alongside packs of Foxhounds.*

and argue with any dog who may challenge it, but not the one to start proceedings. Its small to medium size and sharp warning bark makes it excellent as a house dog.

The Smooth Fox Terrier will take all the exercise offered, but will not spend any time nagging its owner to fetch its lead. It carries enough flesh to have a well-covered frame, but does not run to fat unless over-fed and under-exercised. It is not a dog to leave loose near livestock unless it has been very well schooled. It is easy to maintain in an urban area, and will keep the rodent population down.

Grooming its basically white coat, with tan or black markings, is simple – use a stiff brush followed by a comb and finish off with a cloth. This regular routine will keep the dog looking very trim throughout its long life.

▼ *The sharp outline and the way in which colour appears in distinct patches on an otherwise all-white dog is typical of this breed. This is a tough, no-nonsense dog.*

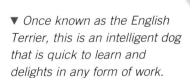

▼ *Once known as the English Terrier, this is an intelligent dog that is quick to learn and delights in any form of work.*

Soft-coated Wheaten Terrier

The Soft-coated Wheaten Terrier, as its name implies, sports a soft and silky coat that is always wheaten in colour. It stands up to 49cm (19in) at the withers. It originally came from Ireland where it was a hunter, guard dog, herder and a companion to farmers. In 1943 it was registered with the Kennel Club in Great Britain, and in 1973 with the American Kennel Club. Today it is recognized as an attractive pure-bred dog.

This breed has a good-natured temperament: it loves people and seems to get on well with other dogs too. It enjoys plenty of exercise – the rougher the better. In spite of the length of its coat, it is not hard to keep in order. It needs as little trimming as possible, and it only eats enough to keep its prodigious energy levels up to par. This is an easy-going breed, but due to its mud-trapping coat, it is possibly not one for the house-proud.

Breed box
Size: Male 46–49cm (18–19in), 16–20.5kg (35–45lb); female 45.5cm (18in), 16kg (35lb)
Grooming: Medium
Feeding: Medium
Exercise: Medium
Temperament: Good-natured and spirited

▲ The breed retains its happy-go-lucky charm, even in full show trim.

▲ It is hardly surprising that the Soft-coated Wheaten Terrier is sometimes referred to affectionately as a 'mop-head'.

▶ This square-built power-pack of a dog is full of confidence and humour. It makes a delightful companion.

Staffordshire Bull Terrier

The Staffordshire Bull Terrier is not just a breed; it is a cult. The devotees of this smooth, shiny-coated dog from central England often appear to be blind to the existence of any other sort. The breed is renowned for its courage, and certainly if any dog would be willing to defend owner and house to the death, this is the one. All it asks in return is adequate rations and a lot of love.

Officially, the 'Staffie' measures up to 41cm (16in) tall, but many bigger dogs are seen. Its head is fairly big,

▶ This solid-boned and well-muscled dog was originally bred for fighting and ratting.

▲ The power of the Staffie should never be underestimated. In the company of other dogs or animals, the Staffordshire Bull Terrier may need to be carefully controlled.

without being exaggerated. It views life as if everything is entirely for its own benefit. Its body is built on the lines of a muscled midget, and it walks with a swagger – for prodigious distances if invited. It can be groomed in a minute because it is short-coated, and it is brimming with vitality into the bargain.

It comes in red, fawn, black or brindle, with varying amounts of white. The colours can be predominantly in patches, sometimes over the eyes.

▼ The Staffie needs early socialization. A lack of training accounts for the high numbers seen in rescue centres.

Breed box
Size: Male 35.5–41cm (14–16in),
   12.5–17kg (27½–37½lb);
   female 35.5cm (14in),
   11–15.5kg (24–34lb)
Grooming: Easy
Feeding: Medium
Exercise: Medium
Temperament: Fearless and
   dependable

Welsh Terrier

The Welsh Terrier is a square-built breed from Wales, referred to by diehards as being built like a miniature Airedale, standing up to 39cm (15½in) tall. It has a coat of the same abundantly wiry type, and it requires the same professional care. It also comes with a similar black saddle and tan head and legs.

Perhaps slightly thicker-set than the Lakeland Terrier, it has that breed's style of standing right up on its toes. It enjoys exercise; it delights in its family and all their occupations, including any form of game. Above all, it is as biddable as any in the Terrier Group, and it is not fussy over food.

◄ *This is an old breed that was originally known as the Old English Wire-haired Black and Tan Terrier. It is possible that the Welsh and the Lakeland Terriers have common ancestry from pre-Roman Britain.*

Breed box
Size: 39cm (15½in), 9–9.5kg (20–21lb)
Grooming: Medium
Feeding: Easy
Exercise: Medium
Temperament: Happy and fearless

▲ *The set of the ears betokens intelligence and alertness. The hair around the muzzle is trimmed to form a beard.*

◄ *Standing four-square on tight paws, this is a neat, cheerful, workman-like dog, and also a good rat-catcher.*

West Highland White Terrier

The West Highland White Terrier, or 'Westie', has pushed its way steadily up the popularity charts, and this is no wonder – it is a handy size to pick up and carry when necessity requires, it has an outgoing manner, it loves people, and, although it will not buckle under when challenged, it does not go out of its way to pick a quarrel with other dogs.

It stands a mere 28cm (11in) at the withers, but packs a great deal of spirit into its small frame. It is not as stocky as the Scottish Terrier. As the name implies, the Westie's coat is white and can get dirty very easily, so this breed needs regular bathing. It is also prone

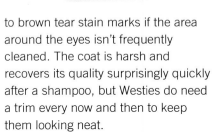

Breed box
Size: 28cm (11in); male 8.5kg
   (19lb); female 7.5kg (16½lb)
Grooming: Medium
Feeding: Easy
Exercise: Undemanding
Temperament: Active and friendly

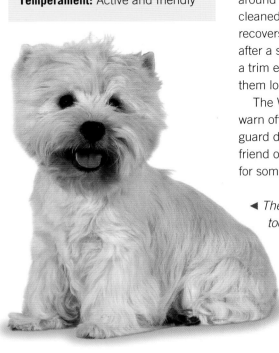

to brown tear stain marks if the area around the eyes isn't frequently cleaned. The coat is harsh and recovers its quality surprisingly quickly after a shampoo, but Westies do need a trim every now and then to keep them looking neat.

The Westie uses its sharp voice to warn off strangers, so it makes a good guard dog. It also makes a great family friend or a companion *par excellence* for someone living on their own.

◄ *The various predecessors of today's Westies were known as Poltalloch, Roseneath, White Scottish and Little Skye. These variations were all merged under one name, the West Highland White Terrier, in 1904.*

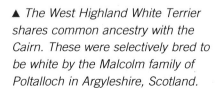

▲ *The West Highland White Terrier shares common ancestry with the Cairn. These were selectively bred to be white by the Malcolm family of Poltalloch in Argyleshire, Scotland.*

▼ *The Westie has a merry expression and loves company and attention. A devoted family member, its small size will not prevent it from fiercely protecting its hearth and home.*

Wire Fox Terrier

The Wire Fox Terrier is the rough-haired version of the Smooth Fox Terrier, with the same aptitude for rat-catching. It measures up to 39cm (15½in) and is square-built. Its harsh, wiry coat is white, usually with a black saddle and black or tan markings, or a combination of the two. The coat grows thick and it should be trimmed fairly regularly. This is probably best done by a professional, but it is perfectly possible for an owner to learn the art, given a good teacher. Well trimmed, this is a very smart dog indeed.

The Wire Fox Terrier is not a greedy dog and does not run to fat unless it is given insufficient exercise. A very good house dog, it will guard its domain noisily. It imagines that its family is there purely to provide it with company and fun, irrespective of whether it lives in the town or the country.

▶ *The Wire Fox Terrier is the wire-haired version of the Smooth Fox Terrier, with the same balanced body, short back and sharp features.*

▼ *The breed may be derived from the old Black and Tan Rough-haired Terrier of Wales and northern England, or some people consider it to have Foxhound and Beagle in the mix. It is one of the oldest terrier-type breeds.*

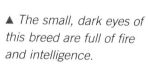

▲ *The small, dark eyes of this breed are full of fire and intelligence.*

Breed box
Size: 39cm (15½in), 8kg (17½lb)
Grooming: Medium
Feeding: Medium
Exercise: Medium
Temperament: Friendly and fearless

▶ *This is a bold breed that can be noisy and wilful, and it also loves digging. Affectionate and loyal to its owner, it is a quick and intelligent, and it enjoys learning tricks, as well as taking part in a range of dog sports. It can become destructive if bored or stressed.*

THE UTILITY (NON-SPORTING) GROUP

This group includes dogs of all shapes, sizes and functions, from the Dalmatian at the large end of the scale to the Lhasa Apso at the small. There are two common explanations for the composition of the group. The first is that the breeds cannot be fitted into any of the other five groups, which is quite an unflattering explanation. The second is that they are all companion dogs, which may sound politer but also suggests that the members of the other groups are not companions. To complicate matters, not all countries include the same breeds in this group. For example, the Japanese Akita Inu is classed as a utility breed in the UK but a working breed in the USA. Looking through this section will undoubtedly give you some sympathy for those who had to solve the problem of how to classify such a varied assortment.

◄ In the past, the Chow Chow been used as a hunter, guard dog and as a food source, but now is firmly a member of the Utility Group.

Akita

The Akita, or American Akita, is subject to debate. The American and Canadian Kennel Clubs consider the Akita and Japanese Akita to be two varieties of the same breed, but all the other clubs, including the Japanese Kennel Club, state that they are two separate breeds. The Akita is a large, strong dog that is capable of hunting and holding an Asian black bear at bay. This brave hunter was also bred as a fighting dog. The Akita found favour with US servicemen stationed in Japan during the World War II, many of whom brought dogs home with them.

This powerful dog is solidly built with a heavy bone structure. The head is large and bear-like, and set on a thick, muscular neck. Ears are upright and hooded. The coat comes in two types: standard or long. Long coats are considered a fault and not

Breed box
Size: Male 66–71cm (26–28in),
  45–59kg (100–130lb);
  female 61–66cm (24–26in),
  35–45kg (70–100lb)
Grooming: Medium
Feeding: Demanding
Exercise: High
Temperament: Dominant and
  fearless

accepted in the breed show ring. Both coats are very dense and can be any colour, including pinto. Some dogs have black masks.

Classified in some countries as a 'dangerous dog', this breed needs an experienced owner who will become the pack leader. The Akita is territorial

▲ *The name 'Akita' comes from the northern mountainous Japanese province where these dogs originated.*

and reserved with strangers. It is very dominant and can show aggression to other dogs, especially those of the same sex. A clean and fastidious breed, it can make a good companion with the right owner. As with all dogs, the Akita should be closely supervised around children and other animals.

▼ *The head of this dog is massive, but it must be in proportion to the body.*

◄ *The Akita became very rare during the 1930s, and the breed nearly died out.*

American Eskimo Dog

Despite its name, this dog has nothing to do with Eskimos. Its ancestors were brought to the United States with early German immigrants. It is thought to have originated from European spitz breeds, including the German Spitz, white Keeshond, Pomeranian and Italian Spitz. Originally called the German Spitz, the name was changed during World War I; 'American Eskimo' is believed to have come from the kennel name of one of the breeders. This dog is not a sled dog, but was bred purely as a companion. It became very popular in the 1900s due to its use as a circus dog.

The 'Eskie' is a white Nordic-type dog with a double coat consisting of a dense, soft undercoat covered with long guard hairs. Biscuit markings sometimes occur. The coat is thicker on the chest and neck, forming a mane. With dark, oval eyes and black nose, lips and eye rims, this is a very attractive dog. Ears are erect and triangular, and the plumed tail is carried over the back. There are three

▲ Once called a 'Deutsch Spitz', the Eskie was initially bred as an all-purpose farm dog.

◄ This dog is an eager-to-please and loving companion animal that really enjoys playing with toys.

▼ The Eskie is a highly vocal dog that will bark excitedly to warn its owner of an approaching stranger.

sizes of American Eskimo Dog: Toy, Miniature and Standard.

This breed is a loyal and alert companion that is also an excellent watch dog. It is a very trainable dog that enjoys learning tricks and excels in the show, obedience and agility ring. With training and socialization, it makes a wonderful family dog. It requires extensive, regular grooming and daily exercise. It is a dog that is slow to mature, and will not reach full adult maturity until it is two years old.

Breed box
Size: Toy 23–30cm (9–12in), 2.75–4.5kg (6–10lb); Miniature 30–38cm (12–15in), 4.5–7.75kg (10–17lb); Standard 38–51cm (15–20in), 7.75–11.5kg (18–25lb)
Grooming: Extensive
Feeding: Undemanding
Exercise: Moderate
Temperament: Intelligent and friendly

Boston Terrier

The Boston Terrier is a strikingly handsome dog. It is often described as the national dog of America, although its short muzzle confirms that it has Bulldog in its ancestry.

It stands around 38cm (15in) tall; it can vary considerably in weight – around the 9kg (20lb) mark – but it is easily handled and picked up. Its coat is short and shiny, and can be kept that way with the minimum of fuss. As its colour scheme requires brindle or black with white markings, it is instantly recognizable.

The Boston Terrier is compactly built with a square-shaped head, wide-set, intelligent eyes and prick ears. It is both dapper and boisterous, without being too short-bodied; it is strong-willed but nevertheless a thoroughly good-natured house pet.

▶ *Today's Boston Terriers are the result of a cross between the Bulldog and the English White Terrier (now extinct).*

▼ *Intelligence and watchfulness are the Boston's hallmarks.*

Breed box

Size: 23–38cm (9–12in); lightweight under 6.8kg (15lb); middleweight 6.8–9kg (15–20lb); heavyweight 9–11.3kg (20–25lb)
Grooming: Simple
Feeding: Undemanding
Exercise: Undemanding
Temperament: Determined

▶ *Boston Terriers were originally bigger and heavier, but careful selective breeding has produced the clean-cut dog of today.*

▲ *The Boston Terrier has a characteristically short muzzle and a square head.*

Bulldog

The Bulldog, often referred to as the British Bulldog to distinguish it from any other, is instantly recognized by eveyone who sees it.

It has a friendly if stubborn nature. Its devotees will not hear a word against it, but those who fancy taking one on must understand its special needs. Its physical characteristics, for example, mean that a walk should not be conducted at a great pace, especially in the heat of the day. The shape of its head and its breathing apparatus mean that it can easily become short of breath; it can, on occasion, put in a surprising burst of

speed, but over-exertion on a hot day can, and does, have serious side effects. In addition, it tends to breathe quite noisily.

The Bulldog was bred to get to grips with bulls by grabbing their noses using their front teeth. The design of the jaw for which it was bred, in the days when bull-baiting was legal, has been considerably exaggerated in recent times, even though it is no longer necessary to fulfil that role.

◀ *Affectionately nicknamed 'Old Sourmug', the Bulldog's face is definitely its fortune because of its uncompromisingly upturned chin. It has an undershot bite.*

Its coat is short and easily kept clean; it can be all manner of colours, from red through fawn to white or pied. It is a massively built dog, giving the impression that its muscles have been built up like those of a human weight-lifter. It weighs 25kg (55lb), sometimes more, and eats as befits its size. It is a superb guard dog and it adores children. It is reasonably good with other dogs as it simply appears to ignore them, but it can give a show of aggression towards strangers, human or canine, if provoked.

▲ ▶ *The Bulldog today is radically different from the bull-fighting dog of the past. The ferocity and viciousness of the breed have been bred out.*

Breed box
Size: Male 55–70cm (22–28in), 25kg (55lb); female 52–65cm (20–26in), 22.5kg (50lb)
Grooming: Simple
Feeding: Medium
Exercise: Undemanding
Temperament: Affectionate and determined

Canaan Dog

Considered one of the oldest dog breeds in the world, Canaans were used by Israelites to guard and herd livestock in biblical times. Originating from the feral pariah dog found in the Middle East, this breed may also share ancestry with the Indian Wolf. Caanan Dogs still exist in limited numbers in the wild. In the 1930s Dr Rudulphina Menzel captured some of these wild dogs and started working with them, initially to protect isolated settlements. They proved to be very responsive to training. During World War II, this was one of the first breeds that was used successfully to detect land mines.

With its square shape and brisk trot, this is a dog that looks balanced. The head is wedge-shaped with erect ears. The coat is short to medium in length, and the undercoat is profuse and covered with a harsh and dense outer layer of hair. Colours include black

▼ *These two alert Canaan Dog puppies belong to a breed that is relatively new to Western civilization, and will become watchful adults.*

▲ *The Canaan is believed to have changed very little since biblical times.*

▲ *Same-sex aggression can be a problem with this breed which, without proper training, may try to dominate its owner.*

correct training and socialization, it makes a loyal companion and can be seen competing at agility, flyball, obedience, herding, tracking and in the show ring. It is now firmly established in UK, USA and Western Europe, along with its home country of Israel, where it is the national dog.

through to cream, shades of red, and brown and white with coloured patches. The tail is curled over the back.

Early socialization from puppyhood is needed, as this is a reactive dog and can be wary of strangers. It makes a good watch dog. The Caanan is intelligent and quick to learn, but will get bored with repetitive exercises. With

Breed box
Size: 18–25kg (40–55lb), depending on height; male 50–60cm (19½–24in); female 45–50cm (18–19½in)
Grooming: Medium
Feeding: Moderate
Exercise: Medium to high
Temperament: Responsive and independent

Chow Chow

One of the first primitive dog breeds to have descended from the wolf, the Chow Chow is believed to have come from Mongolia or northern China. In China it is called 'Songshi Quan', which translates as 'puffy lion dog'. It has been used for hunting, pulling sleds, as a war dog, temple guard and as a source of food. In more recent times, it is primarily a companion dog.

▲ *The Chow Chow, Shar Pei and polar bears all have black tongues. Puppies are born with pink tongues.*

Legend has it that the first teddy bear was modelled on a Chow Chow puppy belonging to Queen Victoria.

It is a sturdy, square dog with a broad skull and small, triangular pricked ears that are rounded at the tip. It is the only breed of dog to have a blue-black tongue, lips and oral cavity. The Chow has very straight hind legs that give it a stilted action. The profuse coat comes in two types: rough and smooth. Both types are very dense and stand away from the body. Thick fur around the neck forms into a ruff or mane.

▲ *This breed was first exhibited in England in 1870. Early reports show that a Chow, listed as a 'wild dog of China', was housed in the London Zoological Gardens as an attraction.*

This a dominant breed that needs early and continual socialization and training. Ground rules must be clear and adhered to. Although not overly active, the dog will require a daily walk. This breed can be stubborn, and this trait appears to increase with age. It is very protective and may be hesitant with strangers. The hunting instinct is still strong, so exercise on the lead is recommended. Some Chow Chows may show aggression towards other dogs.

◄ *The Chow Chow is a distinctive Chinese breed with a scowling expression and upright gait.*

Breed box
Size: 43–51cm (17–20in);
    male 25–32kg (55–70lb);
    female 20–27kg (20–27lb)
Grooming: Intensive
Feeding: Moderate
Exercise: Low to medium
Temperament: Protective and quiet

Dalmatian

The Dalmatian is as distinctive a breed as any. With its white base colour and plethora of black or liver spots all over its head, body and limbs, it is the original 'spotted dog'. It has been known in the UK for well over a century, and was originally used as a carriage dog; it has a penchant for running between the wheels of a horse's carriage quite undaunted by the close proximity of the flashing hooves. In the USA it was used to control the horses that pulled fire appliances, and it is still a well-known firehouse mascot.

◄ The essence of the Dalmatian is that no part of the dog is ever still, especially its long and tapering tail.

◄ The Dalmatian is always ready for its next walk.

The Dalmatian is a handsome dog that is up to 61cm (24in) in the UK, or 58.5cm (23in) in the USA. It could not be more friendly to people. It lives to a ripe old age and never seems to slow down. It loves running and needs plenty of exercise, so owners need to be fit. Its coat, being short, is no problem to groom, and in spite of its size, it does not over-eat.

▼ This bitch is a youngster; a full-grown dog can be a handful to control.

▲ This is a dog of ancient ancestry and uncertain origins. The first undisputed record of it is in Dalmatia on the Adriatic coast, hence its name.

Breed box
Size: Male 58.5–61cm (23–24in), 27kg (60lb); female 56–58.5cm (22–23in), 25kg (55lb)
Grooming: Easy
Feeding: Medium
Exercise: Demanding
Temperament: Outgoing and friendly

Eurasier

A relatively new breed, the Eurasier was developed in Germany in the 1960s by Julius Wipfel. He wanted a dog that would be an ideal companion. He crossed Chow Chow with Keeshond (a Wolfspitz type), and later added Samoyed, to produce a spitz type of dog. The Eurasier, also called Eurasian, was recognized as a breed in its own right by the FCI in 1973. Since then the breed has found popularity in many countries, not only as a wonderful companion, but also in the obedience and agility ring.

▶ *Considerable work is required to keep this stunning coat in tip-top condition.*

▲ *The Eurasier is a very affectionate and people-orientated dog.*

This is a medium-sized dog. Spitz-type in looks, the Eurasier may have a blue-black or spotted tongue, which is a legacy from the Chow. It is double-coated with a dense and thick undercoat with longer guard hairs lying loosely over the top. All colours are permitted, with the exception of liver and pure white. It should not have any white markings or patches. This breed requires regular grooming.

◀ *This friendly dog breed is rapidly gaining recognition all around the world.*

Breed box
Size: Male 52–60cm (20–24in), 23–32kg (51–71lb); female 48–56cm (19–22in), 18–26kg (40–57lb)
Grooming: Extensive
Feeding: Moderate
Exercise: Medium
Temperament: Calm and devoted

The Eurasier has a calm and even temperament, but remains watchful and alert. It seldom barks, but when it does, this is for good reason, making it an excellent watch dog. Reserved but dignified with strangers, it is devoted to its family, and it bonds with the whole family rather than just one person. Quick to learn and keen to please, it is very trainable but does get bored with repetitive exercises. This dog is not happy in a kennel situation and needs to be considered as a valued family member. The Eurasier can be a picky eater.

French Bulldog

The French Bulldog is the French version of the British Bulldog. It has a similar square face, but without the exaggeration of the shortened muzzle. It carries its large ears erect, well up on its skull. Its dark eyes are full of expression – usually kindly, but capable of a glint that suggests it does not suffer fools gladly.

It can weigh up to 12.5kg (27½lb) and enjoys its food, so its diet must be controlled. It comes in dark brindle,

◄ *French Bulldogs can move very much faster than their solid frame might suggest.*

fawn or pied, and its coat is short, close and shiny, and is therefore easily groomed. It is compactly built with a slight concave curve over its loins and, like its British cousin, it has a short tail which can be corkscrew-shaped.

It rushes about when taking exercise, but finds hot days hard

going, tending to breathe noisily when under severe stress. It makes a charming house pet and gives the impression that it would guard hearth and home with its life. This breed has become increasingly popular recently.

▲ *The large, upright ears tend to swivel to pick up every sound.*

► *These dogs both have pied coloration; the most desired pattern comes with a neat central band down the forehead.*

◄ *French Bulldogs are one of the few breeds that have their loins higher than their withers; this helps them to launch themselves vertically, as if on springs.*

Breed box
Size: 30.5–31.5cm (12–12½in);
  male 12.5kg (27½lb);
  female 11kg (24lb)
Grooming: Easy
Feeding: Undemanding
Exercise: Undemanding
Temperament: Cheerful and
  intelligent

German Spitz

The term 'German Spitz' refers to both a type of dog and a breed of dog. The German Spitz type includes a number of breeds as diverse as the Wolfspitz and the Pomeranian. All have similarities in body shape and coat.

The registered breed now termed 'German Spitz' is subdivided into two sizes, the Mittel and the Klein. In conformation there is no difference between these, other than body weight and height, with the Mittel being the larger of the two. Both are alert, curious dogs that have a long lifespan and are game for anything.

▲ A pair of perky Kleins with intelligent eyes and good bone structure.

▶ This is a typical German Spitz head, which is fox-like in appearance.

▼ A coat like this Klein's will cope with the bitterest of winter weather.

German Spitzes are prick-eared, sharp-featured dogs with compact bodies and tightly curled tails. They have thick, harsh-textured coats that keep them warm in the coldest of winters. They come in many colours, from chocolate to white, as well as in all sorts of combinations. Their coats look marvellous after grooming, but they are not for the lazy owner. These sturdy, cheerful dogs are friendly but will alarm-bark at strangers. They make good companions for all ages.

▲ No matter which size you have, a German Spitz carries a great deal of coat which needs a lot of grooming. This example is a Mittel.

Breed box
Size: Mittel 30–38cm (12–15in), 10.5–11.5kg (23–25lb); Klein 23–29cm (9–11½in), 8–10kg (17½–22lb)
Grooming: Demanding
Feeding: Undemanding
Exercise: Medium
Temperament: Happy and lively

Japanese Akita Inu

The Japanese Akita Inu, or Akita Inu, differs from the Akita or American Akita in two main respects: size and coat colour. The Akita Inu is smaller, lighter and has a more fox-like face. The Japanese Akita Inu is at least 10kg (22lb) lighter and not as heavy-boned as the Akita.

The coat is very thick, and comes in red, fawn, sesame or brindle. All colours have 'urajio' markings, a whitish colouring on cheeks, muzzle, jaw, neck, chest, body, tail and inside of legs. Black masks are not permissible.

Very dominant and challenging, this dog is not suitable for a first-time owner. The Japanese Akita Inu rarely exhibits body language, so it can be difficult to predict. Some are food protective and aggressive towards other dogs. This dog is classified as a 'dangerous dog' in some countries.

Breed box
Size: Male 64–70cm (25–27in), 32–39kg (70–85lb); female 58–64cm (22–25in), 23–29kg (50–65lb)
Grooming: Medium
Feeding: Moderate
Exercise: High
Temperament: Protective and dominant

▲ The Japanese Akita Inu comes in a series of striking colours and patterns. White on the body is undesirable.

Japanese Shiba Inu

The Japanese Shiba Inu, or Shiba Inu, stands up to 39.5cm (15½in) tall. It is much the same shape as the Akita, including the hooded ears that tip sightly forward, continuing the topline of its neck. It has the same plush feel to the coat, but comes in less striking colours, including red, black, black and tan, and brindle, which do not have quite the same brilliance.

Its temperament is not as dominating, although its intelligence is just as obvious; a Shiba will think its way through to getting what it wants. It is not noisy but will spot the invader of its owner's property without making a scene about it.

It loves its family and joining in all activities, but this breed is not a restlessly demanding dog. It is trainable and enjoys learning.

▲ This is the smallest of the Japanese dog breeds, and is of ancient origin.

Breed box
Size: 8–10kg (18–22lb); male 39.5cm (15½in); female 36.5cm (14in)
Grooming: Reasonable
Feeding: Reasonable
Exercise: Reasonable
Temperament: Bright and intelligent

◄ The Shiba Inu's plush coat comes in a variety of colours. Note the hooded ears.

Japanese Spitz

The Japanese Spitz breed was developed as a companion in the 1920s, and is now well established. Standing about 36cm (14in) tall, it is a neat, sharply outlined dog with a stand-off coat that is never anything but brilliant white. Considering the thickness of its coat, it is not too difficult to groom or even to keep clean, although it will obviously need regular attention.

It is not overly noisy indoors or outside, but makes a good sentry. It is capable of being an extremely

▶ *This breed is recognized by major kennel clubs, with the exception of the American Kennel Club who consider it too similar to the white Pomeranian, American Eskimo Dog and the Samoyed.*

Breed box
Size: 30–36cm (12–14in),
   5–6kg (11–13lb)
Grooming: Medium
Feeding: Undemanding
Exercise: Medium
Temperament: Affectionate
   and alert

companionable and nimble character, whether it lives with a large family or a single householder. It is not greedy, and is not a picky feeder for what, at first sight, looks like a dainty dog.

The Japanese Spitz is a very proud, noble character who takes readily to training for a variety of canine sports. The breed standard regarding height varies from county to country, but it is always classified as taller than its close relation the Pomeranian. This energetic dog is good with children and other dogs. It would suit an active family, being happy to join in with all games and activities.

▲ *The pointed muzzle should be neither too thick nor too long.*

◀ *Three delightful Japanese Spitzes, with their coats gleaming like freshly fallen snow. It is possible that these small, nimble dogs have the same ancestry as the Samoyeds.*

Keeshond

The Keeshond is a spitz-type dog that comes from Holland, where it guards farms and barges, and is also known as the Dutch Barge Dog. It has smallish prick ears, a compact body and the most tightly curled tail of all the spitzes. It stands around 46cm (18in) and is solidly built; it can be a greedy feeder and needs rationing if it is not to put on excess weight.

Its harsh coat is thick, and it comes in what is officially called silver-grey – but in fact it sports long guard hairs that have black tips. It withstands freezing temperatures and snow, regarding them with contempt, and considers central heating in its owner's house to be a sign of weakness! Grooming it is hard work, but it has the sort of coat that rewards those who are conscientious and dedicated.

It loves human company and the exercise that goes with a busy family, but it is not demanding. It has sharp hearing and responds noisily to the arrival of visitors or the intrusion of strangers. Socialization is required.

◄ The Keeshond is a very solidly built, hardy dog that can live happily in the toughest of weather conditions. It was used as a guard dog and vermin catcher in its native Holland.

▼ Thoroughly trusting and cheerful, the Keeshond loves being with people.

◄ The coat does not look as good as this one unless someone has made a great deal of effort at grooming it.

Breed box
Size: Male 44–48cm (17–19in), 19.5kg (43lb); female 40–46cm (16–18in), 18kg (39½lb)
Grooming: Demanding
Feeding: Medium
Exercise: Medium
Temperament: Friendly and vociferous

Korean Jindo

▼ *Similar in type to the Japanese Akita Inu and Shiba Inu, the Jindo was originally used to hunt a variety of game.*

The Korean Jindo is native to the South Korean island of Jindo, where it lived feral for hundreds of years. Because the island was separated from the mainland by water, the breed has remained pure. Unique in the world of dogs, all Jindos are cared for, funded and technically owned by the South Korean government, who have listed this dog as a national treasure. These animals are avid hunters, working either in a pack or alone. Many have an aversion to running water and will avoid getting wet.

The Jindo breed is divided into two types: the Tonggol or Gyupgae is stocky and muscular, while the Hudu

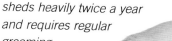

▲ *This is a fastidious breed that sheds heavily twice a year and requires regular grooming.*

► *The Jindo is courageous and highly intelligent. It is the most popular dog breed in Korea.*

or Heutgae is slender with less depth of chest and a longer loin. They move on fast, cat-like feet with an elastic trot. Speeds of up to 56km/h (35mph) having been recorded. Ears are triangular and pricked, although on puppies they remain down and flat until they reach the age of 5–6 months. The tail is curled or hangs loosely in a sickle shape over the back. The

thick, smooth coat can be red, white, fawn, grey, black and tan or brindle.

This is a dominant dog with a high prey drive and requires an experienced owner. It will chase and kill smaller animals and often shows aggression towards other dogs, so exercise should always be on the lead. Home fencing must be sound and high, as this dog excels at escaping. Extremely loyal to its owner, the Jindo is a one-person dog. It will seldom accept food from a stranger.

Breed box
Size: Male 52–60cm (20–24in),
  23–32kg (51–71lb);
  female 48–56cm (19–22in),
  18–26kg (40–57lb)
Grooming: Medium
Feeding: Moderate
Exercise: Medium to high
Temperament: Loyal and brave

Lhasa Apso

The Lhasa Apso is a native of Tibet, where these dogs were originally kept as indoor guards. With their intelligence and sharp hearing, they were ideally suited to the task. Their long, hard coats protected them from the severities of the climate. Nowadays, a Lhasa Apso can be glamour personified, the colour of the coat ranging from gold to grey, but that show-ring gleam is not

▼ The long hair falling over the Lhasa Apso's eyes protected them from the wind and glare in their native Tibet.

achieved without regular shampoos and lots of hard work.

The Lhasa Apso stands around the 25cm (10in) mark at its withers, but it sports a back that is a little bit longer than its height, although not as exaggeratedly as to make it prone to a weakened spine. Its appetite is appropriate to its small size. Its head, under all the hair that often covers its

▲ With the hair swept back from the eyes, the Lhasa Apso has a soulful expression and dark brown eyes.

Breed box
Size: 25–28cm (10–11in),
 6–7kg (13–15½lb)
Grooming: Demanding
Feeding: Undemanding
Exercise: Undemanding
Temperament: Companionable
 but haughty

face, is much more like that of one of the smaller terriers than one would expect. It is tough in cold weather, and it will cheerfully walk for long distances. It has an independent nature and is wary of strangers, although very affectionate with its owners. It makes a delightful family companion.

◀ The Lhasa Apso must be seen on the move to realize just how active the dog under that mass of coat really is. The long, dense, straight coat should never be woolly or silky, but fairly harsh to the touch. The tail is carried over the back.

Poodle – Standard

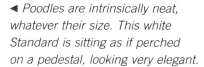

Although the Poodle is the national dog of France, it actually originated in Germany. It was first known as a Pudelhund, which roughly translates as 'splash-about dog'. It was bred as a water dog to retrieve game from lakes and rivers. Documentary evidence proves the existence of this breed as far back as the 15th century, and its use as a water dog declined through the ages until it was just thought of as a companion.

The Poodle comes in several sizes, with the Standard being the largest. This size is now making a comeback as a water dog in Northern America, where it can be seen on the hunting field and taking part in hunting tests.

All sizes of Poodle have the same body shape and conformation. They are very elegant dogs with a square-shaped outline. The Standard is 38cm (15in) or more in height (except under FCI rules where the minimum height is 45cm/18 in), but in reality it is usually considerably taller. The Poodle is clever, and is regarded as second only to the Border Collie in intelligence and aptitude. The Standard is considered to be a better family dog

◄ Poodles are intrinsically neat, whatever their size. This white Standard is sitting as if perched on a pedestal, looking very elegant.

than the smaller sizes because it is thought to be more tolerant. It is good with children and loves playing games, and this breed does not like to be left alone. The Standard Poodle is an active companion that is happy to take part in various canine sports, including agility, flyball, dock jumping, tracking and even Schutzhund, as well as competing in the breed show ring.

▲ An old breed from Germany, the Standard Poodle was originally a water-retrieving dog.

▼ This is the best-known show cut, and is meant to protect the dog's chest, kidney and leg joints.

Breed box
Size: 38cm (15in) or over; (FCI 45cm/18in and over); weight dependent on height
Grooming: Intense
Feeding: Moderate
Exercise: Medium to high
Temperament: Intelligent and quick-witted

Poodle – Miniature and Toy

Most kennel clubs classify Poodles in three sizes, Standard, Miniature and Toy, with Standard being the largest and Toy the smallest. The FCI is the exception, including a medium-size that is halfway between Standard and Miniature. It is thought that the original Poodle was a large dog and the smaller sizes were bred down, but this is disputed by some parties. The Miniature was widely used for scenting out and digging truffles, an edible fungus, in the 1700 and 1800s. Both the smaller sizes were favoured by upper-class Georgian and Victorian

Breed box
Size: Miniature 28–38cm
  (11–15in); Toy under 28cm
  (11in); these heights given as
  guidelines only as they vary
  within different kennel clubs;
  weight dependent on height
Grooming: Extensive
Feeding: Undemanding
Exercise: Medium
Temperament: Alert and active

▼ *Underneath the huge coat of this Miniature Poodle is a dog that measures less than 38cm (15in) high.*

ladies as a lap dog. These dogs had their fur dyed and sculptured into unusual shapes to match their clothing, and as a fashion statement.

The Poodle is often described as a non-shedding breed, but this is untrue. It does shed its coat, but at a slower rate than many other breeds. Because the coat is curly, dead hair and dander does not fall away, but is matted into the living hair. For this reason, the Poodle is less likely to cause allergies then most other breeds. The coat is solid-coloured or parti-coloured and comes in a wide variety of colours. Some colours or combinations are not accepted in the breed show ring.

Both the Miniature and Toy tend to live longer than the Standard. Bright and active, they are highly trainable and make lovable companions. The smaller sizes are less tolerant than the Standard, and may sometimes snap when afraid.

◄ *All Poodles dislike being left alone, and can become anxious if not properly socialized. Toys have the same herding, guarding and water-retrieving background as Standards.*

Schipperke

There is much discussion as to the original use of the Schipperke. Some believe that this breed is a small shepherd, while others think that it was bred as a barge dog. It does make an excellent boat dog, but will also guard and protect its family. It was used by the Belgium Resistance during World War II to carry messages from one group to another without detection by the Nazis.

This small fox-like dog has a double coat with a distinctive ruff of longer hair around the neck. This makes it look heavier at the front. The longer hair on the hind legs is referred to as 'culottes'. The coat can be black,

▶ Sometimes known as the Belgian Barge Dog, the Schipperke is both neat and sharp.

cream or gold solid in colour. The ears are pricked and carried high on the head. Some Schipperkes are born without a tail, while those born with one carry it loosely curled over the back. Sometimes the tail is docked, but this is now illegal in many countries.

Alert and active, this dog can be mischievous and stubborn. It is a naturally curious breed, and early socialization and training are essential.

It is loyal to its owner and generally good with children, with whom it forms a strong bond. It can be overly protective of places and property. Schipperkes are fast and will chase small animals, so they require a well-fenced garden. If bored or allowed to dominate, they can become demanding barkers. They are better suited to an owner with some experience.

▼ If asked to be on guard, this breed can stand like a sentry. They will bark to warn of an approaching stranger.

▲ This breed is sometimes referred to as the 'Little Skipper'.

Breed box
Size: 21–33cm (10–13in),
5.5–8kg (12–18lb)
Grooming: Medium
Feeding: Undemanding
Exercise: Moderate
Temperament: Active and mischievous

Schnauzer – Standard

The Standard is the middle size of three Schnauzers (Giant, Standard and Miniature). This German breed has been known since the 15th century, and the name comes from the German word for 'snout', referring to the beard on the muzzle. It was initially used as a farm dog for driving livestock, guarding, catching rats and pulling carts. All three Schnauzers are interesting in the fact that they are not all in the same Kennel Club group, and the grouping varies greatly from country to country. (In this book, the Giant Schnauzer is included in the

Breed box
Size: Male 48.5cm (19in), 18kg (39½lb); female 45.5cm (18in), 16kg (35lb)
Grooming: Straightforward
Feeding: Medium
Exercise: Medium
Temperament: Alert and reliable

▶ *All three sizes of the Schnauzer are very popular in the breed show ring. This is a Standard.*

chapter on the Working Group.)

Salt and pepper or black in colour, the coat is double with a soft undercoat and a wiry topcoat. White markings are not permitted. The Schnauzer has a stubby moustache and whiskers on the chin which form the beard. Long hair over the eyes gives the impression of fringed eyebrows. Neat and triangular ears drop forward towards the muzzle. The chest is broad and deep.

This terrier-type dog does not have a terrier temperament. Energetic, friendly and loving, it makes a good family companion.

Most enjoy the company of children and are gentle and patient. They will alert owners of potential danger, making them excellent watch dogs or guard dogs. This can lead to persistent barking if they have had inadequate training or socialization. The Schnauzer is an intelligent breed that needs daily exercise but is happy to join in with games and learn tricks. Primarily a companion, it excels at agility and tracking, and is used as a search and rescue dog.

▲ *Prominent eyebrows and whiskers are the hallmarks of the Schnauzer breeds. The eyes are dark in colour.*

◀ *The Standard Schnauzer is deservedly increasing in popularity. A lively and trustworthy companion, it makes a good house dog.*

Schnauzer – Miniature

The Miniature Schnauzer, one of the three Schnauzer breeds, gives the impression that it should be grouped together with the square-built members of the Terrier Group, which indeed it is in the USA. Standing around 36cm (14in) in a coat that is harsh and wiry, it must have one of the most stylish outlines of any dog.

To achieve the look that you see in the show ring takes a professional touch; for the companion at home, all that is required is a good instructor and a wire glove. The breed comes in black, black and silver or, most commonly, what is officially termed 'pepper and salt', but to most people this is actually a dark grey.

◄ Black is an officially recognized colour for the Miniature Schnauzer, although there are not many of them. This breed is reliable, robust and agile, and, above all, adaptable.

◄ Combing the whiskers and leg hair daily will keep the dog looking neat.

What makes the Schnauzer family so distinctive is their ears, which are set up high on the head and tip forward towards the temple; in addition, they tend to grow luxurious eyebrows and beards.

The Miniature Schnauzer gives the impression of doing everything on the double; it enjoys exercise but does not grumble if it is not out and about all the time. It is not noisy. It makes a handy-sized companion for people of all ages, from the busy family to the senior citizen who needs a friend. From the companion point of view, it is possibly the best dog in the Utility Group. It is follows you everywhere, even when you don't want it to.

Breed box
Size: Male 36cm (14in), 9kg (20lb); female 33cm (13in), 7.5kg (16½lb)
Grooming: Straightforward
Feeding: Undemanding
Exercise: Medium
Temperament: Alert and intelligent

► The likeness to a terrier is obvious. The Standard Schnauzer, Affenpinscher and Miniature Pinscher each played a part in the development of the Miniature Schnauzer.

Shar Pei

The Shar Pei, also known as the Chinese Shar-Pei, is a breed of great distinction. It has become well known because of its unusual appearance, with its characteristically wrinkly skin and frowning expression.

Its head shape is rectangular, with little taper from the back of the head to the nostrils, and its lips and muzzle are well padded. It has inherited a tendency to be born with in-rolling eyelids (entropion), and this can cause problems. It is also born with very wrinkled skin, and unfortunately these remain into its adult life; skin problems can occur as a result. The earliest exports were not blessed with the most perfect of temperaments.

Those people who like the breed obviously appreciate the Shar Pei's unusual appearance, while those who find it ugly will steer clear. The dog stands up to 51cm (20in) tall and is powerfully built, mounted on reasonably firm legs.

In any country where there is a very small pool of breeding stock, faults will multiply. Although the breed has improved in recent decades, it is wise to decide on this dog only after careful consideration and research. It is

▲ *The loose skin and wrinkles are abundant in Shar Pei puppies, but may be limited to the head, neck and withers of an older dog.*

essential that the Shar Pei is given early socialization and training if it is to be a family pet. Loving and loyal towards its owner, this breed is wary and very suspicious of strangers and unusual situations.

▲ *This breed has a large head and a well-padded muzzle.*

Breed box
Size: 46–51cm (18½–20in),
   16–20kg (35–44lb)
Grooming: Medium
Feeding: Medium
Exercise: Medium
Temperament: Independent
   but friendly

◄ *The Shar Pei almost became extinct in its native China following the prohibition of dogs. Breeders in Hong Kong kept the line going.*

Shih Tzu

The Shih Tzu is thought to have originated in Tibet and then been developed in China. It has a host of admirers who greatly appreciate its wide-eyed expression and distinctly cavalier attitude. It views the world from a fairly small frame which is only some 26.5cm (10½in) high, but it gives the impression of mental superiority in no uncertain terms.

▶ *Shih Tzus are sturdy, bouncy extroverts that make delightful family companions.*

▲ *The golden head typifies a breed that is convinced of its own distinction.*

The breed has a long, dense coat, which rewards hard work and gets distinctly ragged if neglected. It comes in a glorious variety of colours, often with a white blaze to its forehead, and it carries its high-set tail like a banner over its back. It definitely enjoys being part of the family, but this does not necessarily mean it is keen to partake in long, muddy tramps across the fields. It takes a fair deal of cleaning up if it does feel an urge towards outdoor forays in the middle of winter.

▼ *This beautiful coat gives a good idea of the work involved in grooming a Shih Tzu to show standard.*

Breed box
Size: 4.5–7.5kg (10–16½lb);
male 26.5cm (10½in);
female 23cm (9in)
Grooming: Demanding
Feeding: Reasonable
Exercise: Reasonable
Temperament: Friendly and independent

▲ *The hair grows upwards on the bridge of the nose, giving this breed its characteristic 'chrysanthemum' look.*

Tibetan Spaniel

The Tibetan Spaniel is a neat, tidy dog standing only 25.5cm (10in) high. Its coat is longish and silky, but does not take as much grooming to keep it looking good as you might expect.

This breed turns up in all sorts of colours, but a golden-red is the most common. It also comes in a mixture of fawn and white. It has slightly bowed front legs, but this should not be an excuse for it to be unsound.

It is accommodating in the household, being happy-go-lucky. It takes naturally to climbing over garden rockeries with abandon, or rushing around the garden with its family. It does not spend its time looking for food, and makes a delightful household companion.

◀ This is an unfussy breed that does not demand endless grooming. A brush-through is all that is required.

▼ This dog's original purpose was to act as a companion and watch dog in the monasteries of Tibet.

Breed box
Size: 25.5cm (10in), 4–7kg
(9–15½lb)
Grooming: Medium
Feeding: Reasonable
Exercise: Undemanding
Temperament: Loyal and
independent

Tibetan Terrier

The Tibetan Terrier is a profusely coated, square-built dog, standing as high as 40cm (16in). Its coat is fine, although with hard brushing it can be made to gleam like silk. It comes in a range of colours, from white to black, including golden. It loves people, enjoys plenty of exercise and is extremely nimble and energetic. It eats well, but not greedily. It will act as quite an impressive guard to house and family.

▶ A terrier does not usually have such a shiny coat as this, but the Tibetan Terrier is, in fact, more of a guard dog. It will bark as a warning.

◀ The coat needs regular grooming, which, together with its boundless energy and enthusiasm, means that this good-natured dog may be rather overwhelming for some.

Breed box
Size: 35.5–40cm (14–16in),
8–14kg (18–31lb)
Grooming: Fairly demanding
Feeding: Medium
Exercise: Demanding
Temperament: Outgoing and
intelligent

Xoloitzcuintle

The Xoloitzcuintle is also known as the 'Xolo' or Mexican Hairless Dog. Although it comes from Mexico, not all of these dogs are hairless, with roughly one puppy out of five born with a coat. Archaeological evidence shows that these animals were living in Mexico 3,000 years ago. Not genetically linked to the hairless Chinese Crested, it appears to be a

▶ *The Xolo is a playful and energetic breed with an inquisitive nature.*

▼ *In ancient times, the Xoloitzcuintle was believed to be able to communicate with the gods.*

mixture of Old World breeds. Sacred to the Aztecs, these dogs were first bought to Europe by Christopher Columbus, but their popularity dwindled. By the 1960s they were thought to be extinct, but a few were found in Mexico and a breeding programme was instigated.

The Xoloitzcuintle comes in three sizes, Toy, Miniature and Standard, although in Mexico the sizes are classified as Miniature, Intermediate and Standard. Similar in shape to a Pharaoh Hound, they are elegant and agile, and give the impression of strength. Hairless dogs may have some short hair on their head, feet and tail tip. Those born covered in hair have a short, sleek coat. All colours and markings are acceptable.

The hairless Xolo requires bathing and lotion to keep its skin clean and supple. It also needs suntan cream to prevent sunburn. As they come from hot climates, they require a warm indoor home. A hunter at heart, this dog must have a

well-fenced garden to prevent it escaping and chasing smaller animals. Puppies are energetic and very noisy. Slow to mature mentally, they do not settle down until two years old. This breed is affectionate but sensitive, and is best suited to owners with previous experience of dogs.

◀ *This striking breed does not have premolars, and the canine teeth grow into 'tusks'.*

Breed box

Size: 4–20kg (10–50lb),
  in proportion to height;
  Toy 23–36cm (9–14in);
  Miniature 37–51cm (15–20in);
  Standard 52–76cm (21–30in)
Grooming: Moderate
Feeding: Variable according to size
Exercise: Medium to high
Temperament: Sensitive and
  energetic

215

THE WORKING GROUP

This group of dogs was selectively bred to undertake a job of work to assist their owners. There is a great diversity in the activities that these breeds are capable of doing. Some, such as the Alaskan Malamute and Bernese Mountain Dog, haul loads over difficult terrain. The Dobermann and Rottweiler will protect their family and property, while the Portuguese Water Dog helps fishermen with their nets. Generally quick to learn, they make dependable companions. Most dogs in this group are large, and so may not be suitable for all homes. Many are protective, strong and very intelligent. Without correct training and early socialization, some can become difficult and even dangerous. The majority are highly or moderately active, requiring safe places to run. Service and security dogs generally come from this group.

◀ *The Working Group contains many giant breeds such as the St Bernard, which was originally developed to guard the grounds of the Swiss hospice St Bernard.*

Akbash

This Turkish breed is commonly mistaken as a herding dog, but is actually a working dog. It was bred to live with flocks of sheep, goats or other livestock, and to protect them from predators. Large but mainly non-aggressive, it will warn of danger by barking or growling, and will only chase or attack predators if really necessary. Gentle with its charges, it is not unknown for this breed to lick clean new-born lambs. This dog has been bred to think for itself and to assess situations without human intervention.

The Akbash has a strong body and long legs. A feathered tail curls over the back. The white coat is double

▲ *This breed's almond-shaped eyes vary widely in colour, from light golden brown to very dark brown.*

and can be short or medium in length. The skin under the coat is pink, blotched with black or blackish brown. V-shaped ears lie flat to the skull. Lips, nose and eye rims should be black. This dog has loose skin around its neck, which acts as protection against serious injury if attacked. Some dogs may have double rear dewclaws.

▼ *Due to its size, the Akbash is not recommended for potential owners with children under eight years of age.*

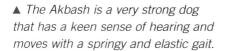

▲ *The Akbash is a very strong dog that has a keen sense of hearing and moves with a springy and elastic gait.*

This breed is a very independent worker and not normally kept as a companion. If socialized as a puppy, it will get on well with other dogs. The Akbash requires mental stimulation but does not take readily to obedience training. It is also reluctant to play with a ball or other toys. It is not suitable for urban living as it requires a large, well-fenced area to patrol. It is not recommended for a first-time owner; it is better suited to a working life.

Breed box
Size: 69–86cm (27–34in), 34–64kg (70–140lb)
Grooming: Moderate
Feeding: Demanding
Exercise: High
Temperament: Intelligent and loyal

Alaskan Malamute

The Alaskan Malamute is a big dog. At 71cm (28in), it does not stand as tall as some other giant breeds, but it is massively built as befits a dog that is designed to pull heavy weights over snow-covered terrain for vast distances in sub-zero temperatures. It can weigh in excess of 56kg (123½lb). Temperamentally it is normally friendly to people, but it can take umbrage with other dogs. A Malamute in full cry after a canine foe is an awesome sight, and requires strength and experience in those who have to apply the brakes.

This is a superbly built, handsome breed. Its relatively short, harsh, dense coat can be any shade of grey through to black, or from gold through red to liver, with areas of white on its underbelly, mask, legs and feet.

The breed was developed over many generations in Alaska and the Arctic fringes of Canada as a

◄ The heaviest of the sled dogs, the Alaskan Malamute has a distinctly watchful air.

'workhorse', and it uses its ability to pull to great effect when it is on the end of a lead. It needs training from early puppyhood to be controllable in a household situation, so training classes are essential.

This dog enjoys its food and needs a great deal of exercise from those owners capable of handling such a giant; it is a delightful dog for anyone who is ready for a challenge.

Breed box
Size: 38–56kg (84–123½lb);
    male 64–71cm (25–28in);
    female 58–66cm (23–26in)
Grooming: Medium
Feeding: Demanding
Exercise: Demanding
Temperament: Reasonably
    amenable

► The Alaskan Malamute is a powerful, dignified dog. Named after an Inuit tribe called the Mahlemuts, it was used as a draught animal long before Alaska became an American state.

▲ This dog displays a thoroughly handsome and trusting expression, but it is not an animal to be treated in a casual fashion.

Beauceron

The Beauceron, also known as the Berger de Beauce or Bas Rouge ('red stockings'), is a French shepherd dog. It is thought to originate from the plain region of 'La Beauce' near Paris. Dating back to the 1500s, it was primarily used as a livestock guardian and herding dog. Its willingness to

◄ *The Beauceron does not reach maturity until its third year, and should not be over-exercised as a puppy.*

▲ *This breed has featured in many films, including the James Bond movie 'Moonraker'.*

follow commands without hesitation is a great asset. In modern times, the breed is regularly used by the military and police, where it undertakes tasks such as mine and narcotics detection, search and rescue, protection and crowd control.

It is a large, athletic dog with a hard outer coat and a thick, woolly undercoat. The coat is black and tan

or merle (harlequin) in colour. Eyes are dark and slightly oval. Ears can be either half-pricked or dropped. The Beauceron has double dewclaws on the rear legs. These may be removed for working purposes, but any dogs without them will be disqualified from the show ring.

The Beauceron is a brave, protective and intelligent working dog, and is happiest in a home where it has a job of work to do. Due to its large size and need for extensive exercise, it is not suitable for apartment or urban living. It is essential that this dog is well socialized during its first year and that its owner is the pack leader. It excels in obedience, tracking, agility and protection tasks, but is not recommended for a first-time dog owner or anyone who does not have the time and energy to commit to train it. A large garden is required too.

◄ *The shiny coat is weatherproof and protects against both the cold and wet.*

Breed box
Size: 61–70cm (24–27½in),
   30–45kg (66–100lb)
Grooming: Moderate
Feeding: Demanding
Exercise: High
Temperament: Highly intelligent
   and brave

Bernese Mountain Dog

The Bernese Mountain Dog is a handsome, affable animal. At its tallest, it reaches a height of 70cm (27½in) and it is built on sturdy lines. Its laid-back temperament allied to a great love of its food means that it tends to be overweight.

Its coat is soft and wavy, and responds to vigorous brushing by producing a real sheen. The colour is mainly black with patches of reddish brown, with a striking white blaze on the head and a white cross on the chest.

▶ *The massiveness of the leg bones and the power of the shoulders show why the Bernese is a favourite choice for pulling dog-carts.*

▶ *The white blaze and cross on the head and chest are characteristic of this handsome Swiss dog.*

The Bernese Mountain Dog is an intelligent and trainable dog, full of *bonhomie* and courtesy, making it a very suitable member of a country household. This is not a dog for the town dweller, however. It was originally a draught dog, and will pull a light cart with evident enjoyment.

◀ *The cheerful nature of this ancient breed comes over clearly as this dog gazes attentively upwards at its owner.*

Breed box
Size: 40–44kg (88–97lb); male 64–70cm (25–27½in); female 58–66cm (23–26in)
Grooming: Medium
Feeding: Medium to large
Exercise: Medium
Temperament: Good-natured

Boerboel

The mastiff-like Boerboel is a South African dog that was bred to protect homesteads and as a hunter and holding dog. Stories abound of its courage in defending livestock and property from human or animal predators. This is truly a courageous dog that can instinctively detect an owner's unease. It is believed to have originated from the inter-breeding of native African breeds with mastiffs and bulldog breeds that were brought by early settlers. The Boerboel is banned in Denmark, where it is considered a fighting dog.

It is an impressive breed that is well muscled and imposing. The head is short, broad and square, with a fleshy upper lip covering the lower lip. The skin is loose, forming wrinkles on the forehead when the dog is alert. Ears are V-shaped and in proportion to the head. Dogs may have a black mask. The cream-white, tawny, red, brown

▶ *Not suitable as a first dog, this breed needs an owner who is experienced in dog training and behaviour.*

or brindle coat is smooth and sleek. Paws are well padded, with the hind feet being smaller than the front ones.

Although intelligent and obedient, the Boerboel has a strong protect and guard instinct. Loyal and loving towards its owner, it can be unwelcoming to strangers. If time is taken to introduce it correctly, this breed will live with other dogs, cats

▲ *These fearless dogs are capable of holding their own against lions.*

and domestic pets. Exercise and long walks are important to prevent boredom and destructive behaviour. Many breeders recommend that this dog is exercised on lead when off its own property. It is not a suitable breed for a first-time dog owner.

◀ *The Boerboel needs to be seen in real life to visualize the size and strength of this breed.*

Breed box
Size: 59–70cm (23–28in),
 70–90kg (154–200lb)
Grooming: Easy
Feeding: Demanding
Exercise: High
Temperament: Protective and calm

Bouvier des Flandres

The Bouvier des Flandres is a powerful and rugged-looking dog. Its basic role in life is herding both cattle and sheep, but over the years it has adapted to town life to a surprising degree. It has found favour with police forces not only in its native Belgium, but also in the UK and several other countries around the world.

It stands up to 68cm (27½in) and weighs solidly to match. It sports a coat that is coarse both to touch and to view. It also carries a beard and moustache, which add to its fairly fearsome appearance. Coupled with a colour that ranges from fawn through brindle to black, the Bouvier des Flandres might be thought forbidding, but, in fact, it is a trustworthy character and fully deserves its increasing popularity as a house companion for those who enjoy a strong dog.

Breed box
Size: Male 62–68cm (24½–27½in),
    35–40kg (77–88lb);
    female 59–65cm (23½–25½in),
    27–35kg (60–77lb)
Grooming: Fairly demanding
Feeding: Medium
Exercise: Medium
Temperament: Calm and sensible

▲ The Bouvier des Flandres is a solid and stable dog. That, combined with its size and forbidding expression, has encouraged several police forces to train it for service.

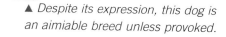

▲ Despite its expression, this dog is an aimiable breed unless provoked.

▲ Ears are small and high-set. Show dogs are trimmed every 3–5 weeks.

◄ The Bouvier was once a cattle dog in its native Belgium, and was also used to pull carts. It is balanced in body and limb – a true power-pack.

223

Boxer

The Boxer is one of the canine world's most popular characters. It is rightly recognized by its vast army of devotees as an extrovert. It is intelligent, but still needs to be convinced that its owner knows best – any other relationship is liable to be a disaster.

It stands up to 63cm (25in) high, and its supple limbs and body are well covered with muscle. It is full of stamina and considers its purpose in life be to guard its family household – and woe betide anyone who does not recognize this fact.

▲ *Nothing gets past those flashing eyes. The Boxer is one of the best of all the guarding breeds.*

◀ *Originating in Germany, the Boxer's ancestors were used for hunting wild boar and deer. Today, it has one of the most distinctive shapes of all dog breeds.*

Its coat is simple to keep clean and neat; its colour ranges from red-fawn through various shades of brindle, with degrees of white. Some Boxers are born entirely white; a percentage of these are deaf from birth, and as a result many breeders put them down.

The Boxer is not a particularly greedy dog, but its appetite needs control if it is not to become overweight. Its concept of exercise is that life is to be lived at speed. It can be trained to be obedient, but anyone who sets out to harness this canine power-pack needs to realize what they are facing.

Its pugnacious, upturned chin gives it the appearance of a pugilist; it does not start fights frequently, but it will never back down if challenged.

◀ *A relaxed Boxer is a rare sight, but this breed will still react in a flash if it needs to.*

Breed box
Size: Male 57–63cm (22½–25in), 30–32kg (66–70½lb); female 57–59cm (21–23½in), 25–27kg (55–59½lb)
Grooming: Easy
Feeding: Medium
Exercise: Demanding
Temperament: Biddable and fearless

Bullmastiff

The Bullmastiff evolved from crossing the Old English Mastiff with the Bulldog, to produce a very effective guard dog. In an age in which several large guarding breeds have been imported into the UK from mainland Europe, the original role of the Bullmastiff as a gamekeeper's assistant has tended to be forgotten.

This dog stands as much as 69cm (27in) high and weighs up to 59kg (130lb), which means it is both big and powerful. It is not to be trifled with and it does not suffer fools gladly, so it merits ownership by those who

▶ *This original gamekeeper's dog can achieve a truly awesome turn of speed, in spite of its size.*

▲ *The power of the Boxer's jaws is obvious. Note the short muzzle.*

◀ *As befits a reliable guard dog, the Bullmastiff is noted for its alertness.*

appreciate its cardinal virtue and utter faithfulness, and can handle a dog of independent nature.

It has a close-fitting, hard coat that can be brindle, fawn or red. It does not take a great deal of effort to keep

clean and neat. It is muscular all over, and its head is reminiscent of the old-fashioned Bulldog of the 19th century, which had a longer nose than the Bulldog of modern times. It does not therefore suffer the breathing problems that beset some brachycephalic breeds, and it enjoys exercise without being over-demanding. The Bullmastiff enjoys obedience, tracking and carting.

Breed box
Size: Male 63.5–69cm (25–27in),
  50–59kg (110–130lb);
  female 61–66cm (24–26in),
  41–50kg (90–110lb)
Grooming: Easy
Feeding: Demanding
Exercise: Medium
Temperament: Reserved and faithful

▶ *This is an extremely strong dog that may be stubborn and over-protective; it is not one for the novice owner.*

Canadian Eskimo Dog

The Canadian Eskimo Dog, also called Canadian Husky, is one of a group of husky types. It is smaller than the Alaskan Malamute, but thicker-set than the Siberian Husky. It was bred to haul fairly weighty sleighs over snow for the Inuit people; its temperament was not important, and it had to fight for its very existence. It is the classic dog portrayed in books about polar exploration.

This dog stands 68cm (27in) high and weighs up to 47kg (104lb), and when it decides to pull on lead or harness it does just that – it pulls. It has a thick double coat of any known dog colour, and grooming it is hard work. It eats well and voraciously, and training it takes time and patience. It requires a lot of exercise, so think carefully before choosing this breed.

▲ *The Canadian Eskimo Dog follows very much in the tradition of the polar-exploration dogs; it is willing to lie for hours waiting for the next task.*

▲ *This breed displays a watchful eye and has a somewhat reserved attitude towards people.*

◄ *The coat protects against the rawest of cold weather, but this means the dog is prone to heatstroke in summer.*

Breed box
Size: Male 58–68cm (23–27in),
34–47kg (75–104lb);
female 51–61cm (20–24in),
27–41kg (59½–90½lb)
Grooming: Demanding
Feeding: Demanding
Exercise: Demanding
Temperament: Wary and alert

Cane Corso

The name of this dog is derived from the Latin *cohors*, meaning protector or guardian. Originating from Italy, this ancient breed will protect people and property, as well as livestock. It is also a very capable hunter of large prey, including wild boar. The breed was used as a war dog in Roman times, and then later as a drover's dog. The multi-purpose Cane Corso went on to become a popular farm or yard dog in rural Southern Italy. It is closely related to the Neapolitan Mastiff, which it pre-dates.

Less bulky than most mastiff breeds, the Cane Corso is a powerful and athletic dog. The large head is striking, with a flat forehead and broad muzzle. Eyes are dark and almond-shaped. The body is strong, muscular and balanced. The long tail is carried

▼ Despite its size and thick-set body, this is a deceptively athletic dog.

erect, but should not curl over the back. Coats are smooth and come in shades of black, blue or fawn, including brindle. White markings on the toes, chest, bridge of the nose and

chin are acceptable. Eye rims, lips, nose, pads and nails should be dark.

Very loyal and willing to please, the Cane Corso is intelligent and trainable. It requires an owner who is highly experienced and able to commit to the ongoing training that this breed requires. Although not a fighting dog, the Cane Corso can be aggressive with other dogs if not socialized, and it will not back down if another dog tries to dominate it. Affectionate and gentle towards its owner, it is naturally suspicious of strangers and very protective of its family.

▲ In some countries, this breed is known as the Sicilian Branchiero.

◀ The Corso is an excellent cattle drover, and nips the animals' noses to turn them in the right direction.

Breed box
Size: Male 64–68cm (24–27in),
45–50kg (99–110lb);
female 60–64cm (23–25in),
40–45kg (88–99lb)
Grooming: Easy
Feeding: Demanding
Exercise: Medium to high
Temperament: Loyal and protective

Chinook

The name of this dog is derived from the Inuit word meaning 'warm winter winds'. This US breed is New Hampshire's state dog, and originates from that region. The Polar explorer Arthur Treadwell Walden wanted a dog that had the strength of heavier sled dogs but also speed and trainability. This was achieved by crossing German and Belgian Shepherds with Greenland Dogs and mastiff types. Recorded as the rarest dog in the world in 1965, numbers have steadily increased, with hundreds now registered in kennel clubs across the world, with a loyal core of devotees.

◄ *This breed's front feet turn slightly outwards, and its toes are webbed with thick hair growing between the pads.*

▲ *The Chinook is slow to mature and will act like a large puppy for a number of years.*

The Chinook ranges in colour from a pale fawn to red-gold. The medium-length coat is thick, double and lies flat to the body. Almond-shaped eyes are dark or amber-coloured. The nose, eye rims, lips and paws are dark-pigmented. This compact dog is muscular and has a deep chest. The oval feet are well furred with hair between the webbed toes. When stationary the Chinook carries its tail in a downwards position, but when the dog is moving the tail is lifted.

Bred as a sled dog, this agile dog also excels at flyball, agility, carting, obedience and search and rescue. Its non-aggressive nature makes it an ideal companion. It is tolerant of children and, if bought up with them, makes an excellent child's pet. This dog needs to be considered as part of the family and is not happy in a kennel situation. Provided the dog has a daily walk, it is suitable for urban living. A Chinook rarely barks, so it should not be used as a guard or watch dog. Nevertheless, it is quite talkative and communicates with a series of whines and 'woo-woo' sounds. This breed is rarely seen outside the USA.

◄ *Gentle and dependable, this dog equally enjoys exercise and curling up on the sofa.*

Breed box
Size: Male 58–69cm (23–27in), 32kg (70lb); female 53–64cm (21–25in), 25kg (55lb)
Grooming: Moderate
Feeding: Medium
Exercise: Medium
Temperament: Calm and tolerant

Dobermann

The Dobermann, still known as the Doberman Pinscher in the United States, originates from Germany and is a tough, fast-moving guard dog. It was bred selectively by Herr Louis Dobermann as an all-purpose tracking/police dog. It is built on clean, powerful lines and ideally reaches 69cm (27in) at the withers.

Its short, close-lying coat responds well to polishing, giving a true gleam. It is most commonly seen as black, with tan colouring on the muzzle, forechest, legs and feet, but the black can be replaced by red or blue, or, more rarely, with fawn. The tail is raised when moving or standing.

◄ *When well controlled, the Dobermann is as good a guard dog as any.*

This breed is energy personified, and at one time it had a reputation for being bad-tempered. Careful, sensible selection and training has altered this to a very large extent, but the Dobermann is still a dog that needs to know who is going to be the boss in any family or work place. As a house dog, it ranks with any breed for faithful performance. It demands exercise as a right, and needs to be provided with a sizeable amount of food as a result.

▲ *The Dobermann's soft expression is the result of leaving the ears uncropped, which is done in the UK.*

◄ *This elegant and powerful breed has an enormous following throughout the world, but frightens some people.*

Breed box
Size: Male 69cm (27½in), 37.5kg (83lb); female 65cm (25½in), 33kg (73lb)
Grooming: Simple
Feeding: Medium to demanding
Exercise: Demanding
Temperament: Alert and biddable

Dogue de Bordeaux

▼ *This breed was a common sight in Medieval France, with most large estates owning at least one.*

Also known as a French Mastiff, Bordeauxdog and Bordeaux Bulldog, this breed is thought to have descended from the Tibetan Mastiff or the Roman Molossoids. The breed has been in existence since the 14th century, and originated from the Bordeaux region of southern France. Through the ages, this dog has been used as a war dog, cattle driver, hunter, watch dog and guard dog, as well as, sadly, being trained for baiting bears, bulls and big cats.

This stocky mastiff has a massive head with a fairly short muzzle. The skin is loose, forming wrinkles on the head and a dewlap on the neck. Eyes are dark and set wide apart. The soft, short coat can be various solid shades of fawn to mahogany, with a dark red or black mask. White is permitted on the chest and toes. The ears are small and hang downwards, and are slightly

◀ *A Dogue de Bordeaux starred alongside Tom Hanks in the movie 'Turner and Hooch'.*

darker in colour than he body. The tail is thick at the base, tapering to a point.

The Dogue de Bordeaux is devoted to its family and generally good with children. It is fearless and very loyal to its owner, but early socialization is required to prevent aggression towards strangers and other dogs. Training can be a challenge, as this dog has its own agenda. A potential owner must consider carefully if they have the experience, room and physical strength to offer this large, strong dog the training and environment that it requires. Long daily walks and mental stimulation are needed to prevent behavioural issues. This dog tends to be inactive within the home, but it will snore and drool.

▲ *At one time there were two sizes of Bordeaux dog, but the smaller Doguin no longer exists.*

Breed box
Size: Male 60–69cm (23½–27in), 68kg+ (150lb+); female 58–66cm (23–26in), 57kg+ (125lb+)
Grooming: Easy
Feeding: Demanding
Exercise: High
Temperament: Loyal and calm

230

Dogo Argentino

Bred as a big game hunter by the doctor and surgeon Antonio Nores Martinez, the Dogo Argentino was based on the now-extinct Cordoba Fighting Dog. Crosses with Boxers, Spanish Mastiff, Irish Wolfhound, Great Dane, Old English Bulldog, Pointer, Bull Terrier, Great Pyrenees and possibly Dogue de Bordeaux were introduced to produce a fearless dog with great stamina.

The breed is banned in Ukraine, Australia, Singapore and Iceland, and cannot be kept in the UK without lawful authority. This dog is also known as the Argentinian Mastiff.

▶ *The Dogo is often trained for military and police service work, as well as for search and rescue in the country of its origin.*

▼ *The broad head of the Dogo Argentino is slightly domed, with the muzzle a little higher at the nose than the stop.*

▶ *This is a headstrong breed that requires training and sociliazing throughout its life.*

The Dogo Argentino is a strong, powerful and well-muscled dog. The body is compact and has a deep chest. The head is large, with very strong jaws. Eyes are brown or hazel, and the nose is black. It has a short, white glossy coat that requires little attention. Preference is given to pure white dogs. A dark patch on the head, near the eye, is permitted by some kennel clubs, as long as it does not cover more than 10 per cent of the head. On the move, this is a true athlete with powerful hind quarters propelling the dog forward at a gallop.

This is a highly intelligent and very powerful dog. Loyal and affectionate, it can become dominant if it does not have an owner who is experienced in pack leadership. Early

and ongoing consistent obedience training and socialization are required to establish clear guidelines and to prevent aggression with other dogs. This breed is not suitable for any but the most experienced dog owner.

▼ *In common with the Dalmatian, white Boxers and Bull Terriers, the Dogo may suffer from pigment-related deafness.*

Breed box
Size: 40–45kg (88–99lb);
   male 60–68cm (24–27in);
   female 60–65cm (24–26in)
Grooming: Easy
Feeding: Moderate to demanding
Exercise: High
Temperament: Dominant and
   intelligent

Entlebucher Mountain Dog

The smallest of the four Swiss Mountain Dogs (the others being Appenzeller, Bernese and Greater Swiss), this breed is also known as the Entlebucher Sennenhund or Entlebucher Cattle Dog. It was bred as a farm dog to guard, herd cattle and pull carts over mountainous terrain. The breed was under serious threat in the early 1900s due to repeated crossings with German Shepherds. Professor Albert Heim, a Swiss Mountain Dog enthusiast, found a small nucleus of purebred dogs, and the breed was saved from probable extinction.

It is a medium-sized, smooth-coated, tricolour dog. The body is mainly black, with symmetrical tan and white markings on the face, chest and legs. The tan is always between the black

◄ *With its robust and compact build, the Entlebucher is happy to work all day long.*

► *This dog is much respected as a fine herding dog by shepherds in the Lucerne area of Switzerland.*

and the white. There should be a white tip to the tail. Some dogs are naturally born with a 'bobtail'. The Entlebucher and Appenzeller are very similar in type, differing only in their size and weight, the latter being larger and heavier. Both are muscular, deep-chested and have broad hips. Although very striking, this dog is often mistaken as a cross-breed.

This dog needs plenty of exercise and a job to do. It takes readily to agility, flyball and disc dog, it likes to be with people, and it will bond well with the family group. It can be territorial, and therefore requires early socialization with strangers and other dogs. It is a very trainable dog that enjoys learning tricks and undertaking tasks. Due to its boisterous nature, it needs to learn to be calm around children and elderly people. It requires an active owner who is happy to walk it for at least an hour every day.

Breed box
Size: 48–50cm (19–20in),
  20–30kg (45–65lb)
Grooming: Easy
Feeding: Moderate to demanding
Exercise: High
Temperament: Active and alert

▼ *Although relatively uncommon outside its country of origin, this breed is starting to gain a devoted following worldwide.*

Giant Schnauzer

The Giant Schnauzer is the largest of the three Schnauzer varieties (the other two being the Standard and Miniature, covered in the Utility Group chapter in this book). This big dog is very similar in shape to its smaller cousins, being a clean-cut, square-built dog that can stand as high as 70cm (27½in) at its withers. It is found in the same colours – black or pepper and salt – as the smaller ones, but naturally it is a more imposing looking animal.

▲ *This dog has a distinctively moulded head and huge eyebrows.*

▼ *The Giant Schnauzer will defend its territory very keenly. It is not a breed to be treated casually.*

At one time employed as a cattle-droving dog, it has become popular as a household guard dog in Germany and the UK. It also has a role as a police dog in Europe, because it is highly trainable and loyal.

This breed needs regular trimming, it enjoys family life, it does not eat a vast amount considering its size, and its beard and moustache give it the sort of expression that will impress those with felonious intent.

▲ *This is a no-nonsense breed that is used in Europe for police work. It is not aggressive unless provoked.*

▼ *In some countries, the Giant Schnauzer's ears are cropped.*

Breed box
Size: Male 65–70cm (25½–27½in), 45.5kg (100lb); female 60–65cm (23½–25½in), 41kg (90lb)
Grooming: Medium
Feeding: Medium
Exercise: Medium
Temperament: Bold and good-natured

Great Dane

The Great Dane is a true giant among dogs; it stands an absolute minimum of 76cm (30in), but the adult male should be considerably taller. Its coat is short and dense, and therefore relatively easy to keep neat and sleek.

It has five official colours which are jealously guarded by the breed enthusiasts: brindle, fawn, blue, black and harlequin, this last one being a basic white with all-black or all-blue patches that give the appearance of being torn at the edges. Any other colour is incorrect, and it is unwise to pay extra money on the suggestion that "this unusual colour is very rare and therefore more valuable".

◀ The Great Dane is remarkably gentle for such a huge creature.

Breed box
Size: Male minimum 76cm (30in), 54kg (119lb); female minimum 71cm (28in), 46kg (101½lb)
Grooming: Simple
Feeding: Demanding
Exercise: Medium
Temperament: Kindly but dignified

This breed is a strong, deep-chested dog. It is used for chasing wild boar in its native country of Germany (not Denmark, despite its name). As it is intelligent, it can be trained to be reasonably obedient. It likes both exercise and creature comforts, recognizing the pleasure of occupying the major part of the hearth in front of a roaring fire. For those who see it as the dog of all dogs and can afford its large appetite, it is a must. However, like all giant dogs, it has a regrettable tendency to have a shortish life span.

▲ This breed's large head is carried high, giving the impression of great strength.

◀ This brindle bitch takes up a lot of space – she won't curl up easily in a small house.

Greater Swiss Mountain Dog

The Greater Swiss Mountain Dog, or 'Swissy', is the largest and oldest of the four Sennenhund breeds developed in rural Switzerland (the other three being Appenzeller, Bernese and Entlebucher). It is used as guardian, drover of livestock and carting dog. Until recently, this breed was virtually unknown outside its country of origin. It is believed that the Greater Swiss was used in the development of both the Rottweiler and St Bernard.

It is a large but agile dog that possesses both strength and balance. Bred to work on rough mountainous terrain, it moves with an efficient and powerful gait. It is generally tricoloured with a black body, white

▼ *It is thought that all four of the Sennenhund breeds can trace their ancestry back to the Alpine Mastiff. They have existed for hundreds of years.*

◄ *Although the Swissy is popular in the USA, it is less well known in the UK.*

symmetrical markings on the face, chest and feet, and tan between the black and white and above the eyes. This is the desired colouring for the breed standard, but blue tricolour or rust bicolour puppies are sometimes produced. The coat is short with a dense undercoat, and the tail is long with a white tip.

Craving attention, the Swissy loves people and is gentle with children. It is confident, observant and accepting of other dogs. The breed is slow to mature both mentally and physically, and can be difficult

◄ *The shiny coat is weather-resistant, providing the animal with protection from wet and cold.*

to house-train. With a deep bark, it makes an excellent watch dog. As with all working dogs, it is happiest when it has a job to do. Early socializing and obedience training is needed, as the breed is very boisterous. The Swissy needs regular long walks and a large garden. It enjoys taking part in many canine sports, including hiking, carting, obedience trials, agility and search and rescue.

Breed box
Size: Male 65–72cm (25½–28½in), 54–70kg (120–155lb); female 60–69cm (23½–27in), 45–52kg (100–115lb)
Grooming: Easy
Feeding: Very demanding
Exercise: Moderate
Temperament: Faithful and sociable

Greenland Dog

The Greenland Dog is a spitz-type dog that can trace its ancestry back over 12,000 years. Originating from the Arctic regions of Greenland, Canada and Northern Siberia, it is one of the oldest breeds in the world. Its behaviour is closer to that of a wild dog than any other breed within the spitz family. It is a hunter and

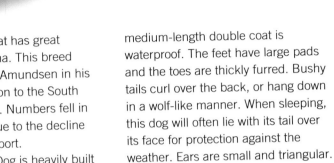

▼ *This is a relatively rare breed, with few litters born. It is gaining popularity in Norway and Sweden.*

sled or pack dog that has great strength and stamina. This breed was used by Roald Amundsen in his successful expedition to the South Pole in 1910–1912. Numbers fell in the 20th century due to the decline in dog-drawn transport.

The Greenland Dog is heavily built and covered with thick fur to prevent frostbite. The outer layer of the

◄ *The Greenland Dog is also known as the Greenland Husky.*

medium-length double coat is waterproof. The feet have large pads and the toes are thickly furred. Bushy tails curl over the back, or hang down in a wolf-like manner. When sleeping, this dog will often lie with its tail over its face for protection against the weather. Ears are small and triangular. This dog can withstand intense cold.

As pack animal, the Greenland Dog is very independent but will show affection towards an owner that it bonds with. Training can difficult but rewarding, as the animal still retains many wolf characteristics and may challenge its owner. Time, patience and experience will be needed. This is not a breed for the novice dog owner. It is inclined to roam and will need a large, well-fenced outdoor area.

◄ *The insulated double coat stands away from the body and is made up of guard hairs and dense underwool.*

Breed box
Size: 56–64cm (22–25in),
    30–33kg (66–70lb)
Grooming: Medium
Feeding: Moderate to demanding
Exercise: High
Temperament: Independent and
    dominant

Hovawart

Descriptions of Hovawart dogs can been found in medieval literature and legal papers. This German watch dog was bred by wealthy landowners in the Black Mountain region to guard their property and livestock. Later, the introduction of other working breeds, such as the German Shepherd Dog, resulted in a dramatic decline in Hovawart numbers. Just before World War I, work was undertaken to revive the breed by the zoologist Dr K. Konig. This resulted in the first litter to be registered by the German Kennel Club in 1922. However, World War II depleted numbers again, and many of these dogs were either lost or

▶ The black and gold colour gleams on this fit, athletic native of the Black Forest in Germany.

▲ This is an excellent watch dog, but is not recommended for the first-time dog owner.

▶ The Hovawart really needs a job to do; it excels at search and rescue work.

killed. Enthusiasts have worked hard to form a breeding programme, and numbers and popularity are once more increasing.

This is a very handsome medium-sized breed. There is a clear difference in both the size and appearance of dogs and bitches. The coat of both is long and water-resistant. Three colours are permitted: black, blonde, or black and blonde. The long tail hangs down when the dog is standing, but is raised over the back when moving or alert.

This a confident breed that has a strong working drive. It can be rather independent and learns better with the use of positive motivation.

▲ The face has a friendly look, and the breed enjoys human company.

Breed box
Size: 30–50kg (66–110lb);
male 63–73cm (25–29in);
female 58–65cm (23–26in)
Grooming: Medium
Feeding: Medium
Exercise: High
Temperament: Confident and courageous

Leonberger

Originally bred for use as a farm, watch and carting dog, the Leonberger has a strong work ethic. It derives from the town of Leonberg in Germany, and has traces of several large breeds in its ancestry. As could be expected from its bulk, it needs a great deal of feeding to sustain it.

▶ *These are powerful, self-confident dogs, but entirely good-natured.*

much of it. The colours range from reddish-brown through golden to a lighter yellow, but most specimens have a black mask on their cheerful face.

This dog's attitude to exercise reflects its attitude to life and people – it is accommodating and easy-going. It does not see much point in hurrying anywhere, preferring to amble amiably. It is also a good swimmer in any weather and, given its size, is best suited to country life. It is first and foremost an easy and genial companion.

▲ *The large size of this breed means that it is not suited to live in a small dwelling. Grooming is lengthy.*

It is a friendly dog, but it can give a good account of itself if asked to guard its home. Its coat is of medium length and is not difficult to groom, except for the fact that there is so

▲ *The closer you get to a Leonberger, the more you can see the kind expression in its face and dark eyes.*

▼ *Leonbergers move deliberately with a long-striding gait, and a great deal faster than their size might suggest.*

Breed box
Size: Male 72–80cm (28–32in), 54–77kg (120–170lb); female 65–75cm (25½–29½in), 45–61kg (100–135lb)
Grooming: Fairly demanding
Feeding: Demanding
Exercise: Medium
Temperament: Kindly

Mastiff

The Mastiff, also known as the English or Old English Mastiff, stands up to 76cm (30in) and is built on massive lines. Giant dogs such as this grow remarkably quickly and require care in feeding; they do eat a lot and can be expensive to rear. In addition, a dog that weighs as much as its owner

▶ *The Mastiff's hindlegs are not always well formed, so care has to be taken in selecting a sound puppy.*

Breed box
Size: 70–76cm (27½–30in);
male 68–113kg (150–250lb);
female 54–82kg (120–180lb)
Grooming: Simple
Feeding: Demanding
Exercise: Medium
Temperament: Steady

requires determination as well as ability to control it. Although the Mastiff is not demanding in its exercise requirements, it still needs an adequate amount of freedom.

This dog has a short-lying coat that is reasonably easy to keep in order.

The colour varies from apricot-fawn to a dark brindle-fawn, always combined with a black mask and ears. Fortunately, this breed has a calm temperament despite its massive jaws in a very solid head – if not, it would be a dangerous animal.

Neapolitan Mastiff

The Neapolitan Mastiff, also known as the Italian Mastiff or Mastino Neapolitano, has a square-shaped head and muzzle with loose skin around the jowls, lips and under the neck. This appears to make the head look larger than it is. The body is powerful and has strong limbs. The coat is short and can be black, blue-grey, mahogany, tawny or brindle. Skin on the body is tight-fitting.

This dog is courageous and protective of people and property. It can be stubborn and a little challenging to train. A prospective owner needs to be prepared for the fact that the Neapolitan, as with most mastiffs, eats a lot, snores and dribbles, all of which may prove offputting.

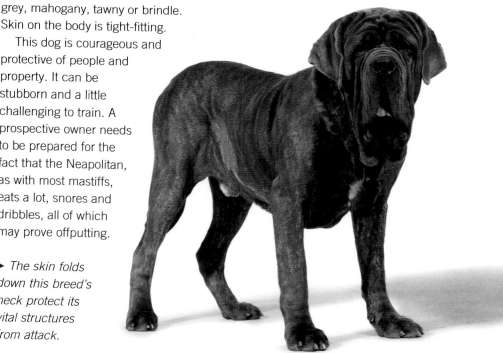

Breed box
Size: 65–75cm (25½–29in),
50–70kg (110–154lb)
Grooming: Undemanding
Feeding: Fairly demanding
Exercise: Medium
Temperament: Devoted guard
dog

▶ *The skin folds down this breed's neck protect its vital structures from attack.*

Newfoundland

▼ *The Newfoundland has immense charm and a sense of humour.*

The Newfoundland is a massive, cuddly bear of a dog, its large face radiating *bonhomie*. It is a water dog *par excellence* to the extent that its fanciers warn purchasers that if they do not want to be forcibly rescued from water, they should not go swimming with a Newfoundland! It is known colloquially as the 'Newfie'.

This breed can stand up to 71cm (28in) high, which is not particularly tall by some standards, but its body is built on generous lines, as are its legs. Its feet have webs between the toes, which help the dog to swim strongly at speed. It weighs up to 69kg (152lb) and eats to match.

Breed box
Size: Male 71cm (28in), 64–69kg
    (141–152lb); female 66cm
    (26in), 50–54.5kg (110–120lb)
Grooming: Fairly demanding
Feeding: Demanding
Exercise: Aquatically demanding
Temperament: Delightfully docile

▲ *The rather deep-set eyes give an expression of benign relaxation.*

◄ *The lung space is evident even in a front view of this master swimmer among dogs.*

It has an all-embracing coat which has a slightly oily feel to it. Not surprisingly, this renders the animal totally waterproof. The colour can be black, brown, or white with black markings, which is generally known as 'Landseer' (because Sir Edwin Landseer included Newfoundlands of this marking in many of his paintings).

In spite of being an aquatic dog, the Newfoundland has its own style of movement on the ground – it tends to roll in a charming, nautical fashion. It expects exercise, but prefers it to be in water. Then, when it gets back home, it has an engaging habit of shaking vigorously. This is a dog for the whole family, but not for the house-proud or the apartment-dweller.

▼ *A house needs plenty of room to accommodate a Newfie.*

Pinscher

The Pinscher, originally from Germany, is best described as a midway stage between the Dobermann and the tiny Miniature Pinscher. It wears the same short, dense coat in the same basic black-and-tan colour combination of the Dobermann, with the same alternatives of red, blue and fawn with tan.

It is a sharp-outlined dog with an alert-looking head and expression, and a neat, muscled body. It moves with nimble, athletic strides. As it stands up to 48cm (19in) tall, it is capable of accepting plenty of exercise and can make a splendid member of either a town or country family. It can be possessive.

▶ *The Pinscher is a very bright breed with clean-cut features and bright eyes.*

This breed needs minimal grooming to polish it into a glossy shine. It does not ask for excessive food, and it possesses a sharp voice and an intelligent mind, which make it a handy watch dog. It is territorial and not above following up a warning bark with a sharp nip. Owners need to ensure that they are the alpha member of this partnership. One breed club describes the Pinscher as 'energetic, watchful, agile, fearless and determined' – a good summary of this sharp, medium-sized dog which retains strong terrier-type characteristics.

Breed box
Size: 43–48cm (17–19in),
   11–20kg (25–45lb)
Grooming: Easy
Feeding: Undemanding
Exercise: Medium
Temperament: Active and confident

▲ *This red-coated version positively shines, indicating the dog's good health. Salt and pepper and harlequin-coloured dogs became extinct due to the decline in breeding and loss of dogs during the two World Wars.*

◀ *Although the Pinscher can be distrustful of strangers, it is responsive to training and makes a good family member. The breed originated as the German farmer's terrier and was recognized by the German Kennel Club in 1879. Popularity has been increasing in the United States due to its recognition by the AKC in 2003.*

Portuguese Water Dog

Also known as the Algarvian Water Dog or Portuguese Fishing Dog, this breed was used to herd fish into nets and carry messages from one boat to another or back to the shore. It was also trained to find and retrieve lost or damaged fishing tackle.

Not widely known outside its country of origin, the Portuguese Water Dog gained media attention when it was revealed that the US president Barack Obama owned two.

Breed box
Size: Male 50–57cm (20–22½in),
  19–25kg (42–55lb);
  female 43–52cm (17–20½in),
  16–22kg (35–48½lb)
Grooming: Demanding
Feeding: Medium
Exercise: Demanding
Temperament: Tireless and
  amenable

▼ *This breed has a powerful body and unusual tail carriage. This example is clipped in a 'lion clip', which shows the powerful, muscular hindquarters.*

Although similar in type to a Standard Poodle, the Portuguese Water Dog is more solidly built, with stouter legs and heavier bone. It has webbed toes to assist it when swimming. The non-shedding coat is curly or wavy, or a combination of these two types. The colour can be solid black, brown and white, or mixtures of these. This breed is slow to mature, both physically and mentally.

Active and intelligent, this dog makes a fine companion. It is good with children and other pets if brought up with them. The Portuguese Water Dog is very affectionate, but can be reserved towards strangers. It loves water and requires vigorous daily exercise. It can be destructive if bored, or if it does not have sufficient

▲ *This dog is similar to the Poodle, but without such a refined head.*

exercise. It excels in a range of canine sports, including obedience, flyball and agility or as a jogging dog, and is a tireless dog that is happy to join in with any activity. As this breed is non-shedding, it requires frequent clipping and styling in addition to daily grooming. The coat is high-maintenance and can be costly to keep in good order.

◄ *Among their devoted owners, the Portuguese Water Dog is affectionately known as a 'Portie'.*

Rottweiler

The Rottweiler comes from Germany, and is a handsome and striking breed. The male can stand as tall as 69cm (27in) and is solidly built of hard muscle, giving it immense strength.

Bred as a droving and carting dog, the Rottweiler's usefulness has evolved to encompass search and rescue work and use as a guide dog and police dog. Lack of socializing and training can turn this incredibly strong dog into a potentially dangerous animal. It is a breed that can be territorial and reactive, but with the correct care and in the right hands, the Rottweiler is calm and confident. It currently ranks in the top-ten pedigree breeds within the USA, but is not recommended for the first-time dog owner.

The coat is invariably of medium-short length, and black and tan in colour. Grooming is rewarding; the coat produces a magnificent shine very easily. Exercise is essential because of the muscular nature of the breed. It likes its food and expects plenty of it.

▼ An average-sized, strong and agile dog, the Rottweiler is not a suitable breed for the nervous owner or for a newcomer to dogs.

This is a breed for an experienced dog owner who will devote time and attention to the dog. The Rottweiler merits much of the enthusiasm it engenders, but needs good control.

Breed box
Size: Male 63–69cm (25–27½in), 50kg (110lb); female 58–63.5cm (23–25in), 38.5kg (85lb)
Grooming: Simple
Feeding: Demanding
Exercise: Medium to demanding
Temperament: Courageous and trainable

▲ The powerful muzzle shows why the breed has earned respect as a guard.

◄ The Rottweiler will respect the authority of an owner who merits it – both handler and dog need training.

Russian Black Terrier

Despite its name, the Russian Black, or Tchiorny, Terrier is not a true terrier, but a working, guarding and sporting dog. It is thought that numerous other breeds were used in its development, including the Giant Schnauzer, Rottweiler, Airedale and Newfoundland. Initially, this dog was only bred in the Russian state-owned Red Star Kennel in Moscow. In 1957 some puppies were sold to civilians, and the breed then spread to other parts of Russia and eventually worldwide.

The coat is double with a harsh guard hairs over a soft undercoat. Generally black in colour, some dogs may have a scattering of grey hairs mixed in with the black. Occasionally, puppies are born with wheat or sable coats, but these are non-standard colours. Presentation of the coat is important, and this breed should have

▼ *Highly prized in its native country, this breed is also popular in Italy.*

both beard and eyebrows. This is a strong, powerful dog with a broad skull and a long head. The body must be well proportioned and muscular.

It is a breed that needs firm leadership and clear guidelines. Early socialization is important, as it can be suspicious of strangers. Playful and enjoying human contact, it makes a good companion, providing the owner is prepared to put in the required training. Dominance can be an issue if, as with any breed, there is not a clearly defined human pack leader.

▲ *Underneath the eyebrows are dark eyes set well apart, with black almond-shaped rims. Light eyes are a fault.*

It is happy to live with children, other dogs and pets if correctly introduced. This breed is slow to mature, and will only bark if there is a reason to do so.

◄ *Also known as the Russian Bear Schnauzer, this dog has large, bear-like feet with very tough pads.*

Breed box
Size: Male 72–76cm (28–30in), 50–60kg (110–132lb); female 68–72cm (26–28in), 45–50kg (99–110lb)
Grooming: Moderate
Feeding: Medium to high
Exercise: High
Temperament: Intelligent and willing

Siberian Husky

The Siberian Husky is the racer of the sled-dog world. It may seem a harsh thing to say about what, in many ways, is a very charming dog indeed, but it lives only to pull a sled! It stands up to 60cm (23½in) tall at the withers, it is lean at its muscular best, and it has a head that is distinctly reminiscent of a wolf, but with a kinder look.

Its coat is fairly long and will keep the animal warm in the most bitter cold. It can come in virtually any colour or pattern of colours. Its eyes are the most remarkable feature of its face, as they too can vary in colour,

Breed box

Size: Male 60cm (23½in), 23.5kg (52lb); female 53.5cm (21in), 19.5kg (43lb)
Grooming: Medium
Feeding: Demanding
Exercise: Very demanding
Temperament: Friendly but reserved

even to the extent of one being brown and the other blue. If that was not odd enough, some dogs are found whose individual irises can show two halves of different hues.

This dog's attitude to people is of extreme tolerance, but to its own kind it can be very domineering, and there is a distinct pecking order in a racing

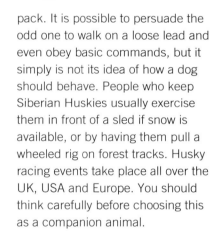

◄ This breed can jump a good height from a standstill.

pack. It is possible to persuade the odd one to walk on a loose lead and even obey basic commands, but it simply is not its idea of how a dog should behave. People who keep Siberian Huskies usually exercise them in front of a sled if snow is available, or by having them pull a wheeled rig on forest tracks. Husky racing events take place all over the UK, USA and Europe. You should think carefully before choosing this as a companion animal.

▲ The Siberian Husky rarely lowers its pricked ears.

◄ The legs are very strong, keeping racing Huskies on the move. The front legs are parallel and straight.

► Siberian Huskies were originally draught dogs with the Inuit people. Half a dozen dogs attached to a racing sled will give an exciting ride.

St Bernard

The enormous St Bernard is an instantly recognizable breed. It stands tall, but it is its massive frame that makes it so remarkable. It originated in the mountains of Switzerland, and is traditionally depicted with a miniature brandy barrel attached to its collar as it locates a traveller who has been stranded in deep snow.

▶ *This breed was first taken by monks to the famous hospice in the Swiss Alps, where it was used as a guard dog and companion in the 17th century.*

Breed box
Size: Maximum 91.5cm (36in);
   male 75kg (165½lb);
   female 68kg (150lb)
Grooming: Medium to demanding
Feeding: Demanding
Exercise: Medium
Temperament: Steady and
   benevolent

Everything about the modern St Bernard is huge, right down to its feet. It has a great breadth of skull and huge jaws. Its lower lip tends to droop at the outside corner, which means that it drools a fair amount.

Its limbs are big-boned, so rearing the young is expensive and needs to be well understood. Exercise in the puppy should be increased very slowly as it grows, to ensure that the minimum strain is put on tender tissues. Exercise in the adult is usually a gentle progression; a St Bernard pulling on its lead can be a struggle for the handler.

Grooming is not a problem, except there is a lot of coat to be dealt with. The coat is normally medium in length, but there is a short-coated St Bernard. The colour can be orange, red brindle or mahogany brindle with white markings, or white with any of the above as coloured patches.

Temperamentally, the breed is trustworthy and benign, which is just as well since the rare occasion when a St Bernard does erupt is awesome to behold. This is an attractive breed, but those who fall for it should consider carefully how well they can cope.

◀ *The St Bernards is a massive dog with truly powerful bones in the forelegs.*

▶ *It is all too easy to fall for the delightful charms of these dogs when they are still youngsters.*

Tibetan Mastiff

The Tibetan Mastiff is an unusual member of the mastiff world because it has a longish coat. It has a genial expression, but odd specimens can be touchy. On the whole, they are likeable creatures with coats of varying colours, ranging from black, through black and tan, to gold and grey.

It stands up to 66cm (26in) tall, which means it is not a giant, but its body is solidly made. It is also unusual for a mastiff in that it carries its tail high and over its back. It is a useful guard dog and enjoys its exercise, but those who choose it need to be prepared to handle a powerful dog.

◀ *Well suited to the rugged countries of Asia, this breed has a thick protective coat that requires regular grooming.*

▲ *A genial eye may belie a distrustful temperament – this is not a dog for the casual. It has a strong guard instinct.*

▶ *Originating from areas of Tibet, Syria and Arabia, this is a real mountain dog. It was used by nomadic tribes to protect livestock from leopards, tigers, bears and wolves. The Tibetan Mastiff guarded monasteries, palaces and villages too.*

Breed box
Size: 66cm (26in), 64–82kg (141–181lb)
Grooming: Fairly demanding
Feeding: Demanding
Exercise: Medium
Temperament: Aloof and protective

THE HERDING GROUP

This group is a collection of breeds that help people to move animals. The group is variable according to different kennel clubs. Some split them into sub-groups, while others use a different collective name such as the Pastoral Group. These dogs move or control animals such as cattle, sheep, pigs and even reindeer. This is done by a variety of methods: the Australian Cattle Dog and Welsh Corgi move stock by nipping at their heels; the Border Collie uses its 'eye' to gather flocks together and move them in the required direction; the Croatian Sheepdog runs over backs of the sheep to get where it needs to be; and the Catalan Sheepdog works independently with no instructions required from its owner. All of these breeds are high-energy dogs and require a lot of exercise. Most are responsive to training, but a strong herding instinct may mean that they try to round up people instead of animals.

◄ *Under its dense, shaggy coat, the Old English Sheepdog is an athletic worker that has helped farmers for generations by moving both sheep and cattle.*

Anatolian Shepherd Dog

The Anatolian Shepherd Dog comes from Turkey. It is known to its familiars as the Karabash ('Blackhead'), the Turkish term for its best-known feature. The dog is cream to fawn in colour, and sports a black mask and ears.

Many European and Asian countries use two distinct types of dog with their flocks of sheep, one for herding and another for guarding. The Anatolian Shepherd performs the latter duty, protecting flocks against marauding wolves and also marauding humans in the form of rustlers.

The Anatolian's height at 81cm (32in) puts it into the range of the awesome; it weighs accordingly, and therefore takes a good deal of feeding.

Its coat is short and dense, and not difficult to keep tidy. It likes its exercise, but because its ancestors were expected to amble about with the shepherd as the flocks moved from pasture to pasture, it is not often in a hurry.

This breed needs understanding; it makes a good family dog, but the family needs to make up its collective mind that their pet's sole purpose in life is to guard. A few generations of living a softer life has not obliterated the results of careful selective breeding since this mastiff type evolved.

▲ *This is a breed of ancient origin that is regarded as a national emblem in its Turkish homeland.*

▼ *This family group exhibits the prized black mask that gives the breed its popular name of Karabash.*

Breed box
Size: Male 74–81cm (29–32in),
50–64kg (110–141lb);
female 71–79cm (28–31in),
41–59kg (90½–130lb)
Grooming: Easy
Feeding: Demanding
Exercise: Demanding
Temperament: Bold and
independent

Australian Cattle Dog

This medium-sized dog has many names, including the Australian Heeler, Blue Heeler and Red Heeler. Bred to move stock over long distances, this dog possesses great stamina and endurance. It moves cattle by nipping at their heels, hence the name 'Heeler'. The breed has been in existence since the 1890s, and is believed to have the Dingo, Kelpie, Bull Terrier and Dalmatian in its ancestry.

Two colours of coat are acceptable, red or blue, although the coat can be mottled or speckled, and with or without black, white or tan markings. Regardless of colour, all puppies are born white, with the exception of any facial markings or solid-coloured patches. As the puppy matures, red or

▶ *This workaholic is used as a therapy dog and by the police for drug detection.*

black hair grows through the white coat, giving a blue or red ticking coloration. Dogs born with a 'star' on the forehead are said to have a 'Bentley Mark', so called because this pattern occurred on a legendary droving dog owned by a man named Tom Bentley.

Needing lots of exercise and a job to do, this dog is not suitable for an inactive owner. The breed can be wary of strangers, but early socialization will help. Since this dog herds by nipping at the ankles, it is only suitable for

families with older children. A Heeler forms a very strong bond with its owner and can become overly protective. It is not a dog for an inexperienced owner. It excels in cattle-herding trials, agility, Schutzhund, flyball, canicross, disc dog and as a hiking companion, and is also used as a police dog, drug-detection dog and for therapy work.

▼ *The Australian Cattle Dog is happy to join its owner in sporting activities.*

▲ *This dog is not overly tall, but is very thick-set and possesses powerful jaws and surprisingly large teeth.*

Breed box
Size: 43–51cm (17–20in),
  15–22kg (33–49lb)
Grooming: Easy
Feeding: Moderate
Exercise: High
Temperament: Protective and
  trainable

Australian Shepherd Dog

Despite the name, this dog does not come from Australia. It is thought to have originated from the French/Spanish Pyrenees. Basque shepherds exported flocks of Merino sheep to America and took dogs with them; these Spanish dogs would have crossed with native dogs and collie types, producing a versatile stock dog. This herding dog has been known as a Spanish Shepherd, Pastor Dog and Bobtail. It is uncertain why the breed is called an Australian Shepherd.

There is a pronounced difference between the size and build of male and female dogs. The medium-length double coat is weather-resistant, and can be red or blue merle, red, black or tricolour. Eye colour varies, and is generally related to coat colour. Dogs may have two different-coloured eyes; this is termed 'bicoloured eyes' and

▼ *This dog is capable of herding and guarding, and is good in obedience and agility competitions.*

does not affect the dog's sight. The tail is long and plumed, but some puppies are born with a natural bobtail.

This is a very glamorous and high-activity dog that is even-tempered and loving. It is suitable as a family companion, providing socialization

and training are ongoing. It can try to round up people and may be destructive if bored, so it needs long daily walks and loves human company. It is very loyal to its owner and develops a strong bond with those it includes in its family pack. The 'Aussie' is a good watch dog and will protect its property. It loves to work, and may enjoy taking part in obedience, working and herding trials, as well as flyball and agility.

Breed box
Size: 14–29kg (30–65lb);
  male 46–58cm (18–23in);
  female 46–53cm (18–21in)
Grooming: Medium to high
Feeding: Moderate
Exercise: High
Temperament: Energetic and easy-going

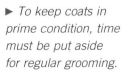

▶ *To keep coats in prime condition, time must be put aside for regular grooming.*

▲ *This breed is popular with ranchers in the United States who need a hard-working herding dog.*

Bearded Collie

The handsome Bearded Collie possesses bewitching eyes. It can make the toughest heart melt just by standing still and looking soft, hence its enormous popularity. Standing up to 56cm (22in) tall at its withers, it moves with athletic grace on legs and

▶ The Bearded Collie has pure Scottish ancestry and retains the basic instincts of a worker.

◀ Keen, observant eyes are one of the breed's most attractive features.

feet which, like its whole body, are covered with a harsh, shaggy coat underlaid by a soft, close undercoat.

The coat takes plenty of effort to groom, as it is capable of picking up a good deal of the countryside in which it prefers to spend its days. Colours range from all shades of grey, through black, blue and sandy, all with white

on the head, brisket and lower limbs; it is rounded off with the typical beard after which it takes its name.

The Bearded Collie looks what it is – a cheerful, fun-loving rogue – and has converted well from its original role as a farm worker to make a superb companion and family friend.

Breed box
Size: 18–27kg (39½–59½lb);
   male 53–56cm (21–22in);
   female 51–53cm (20–21in)
Grooming: Demanding
Feeding: Medium
Exercise: Demanding
Temperament: Lively and cheerful

▶ Quiet while lying waiting, these dogs will move like a flash when the order is given.

Belgian Shepherd

There are four varieties or breeds of Belgian Shepherd: Tervuren, Malinois, Groenendael and Laekenois. In some counties, including Belgium, they are regarded as being four variants of the same breed, while others consider some, or all, as separate breeds in their own right. All are large to medium in size, rather square in shape, and have erect ears. The only difference between types is the length and texture of the coat.

The Tervuren gets its name from a village in the province of Flemish Brabant. It has a medium-length double coat that is generally mahogany, but can also be sable, sand or grey. This breed or variant should have an overlay of black and a black mask. A small amount of white on the chest and tips of the toes is permissible. The coat on the chest and around the neck forms a mane. Potential puppy purchasers who wish to show their dog in the breed ring should consult the breed standard for their relevant kennel club, as there is a worldwide variation in permitted colours.

▶ *For many devotees, the most glamorous of all the Belgian Shepherds is the Tervuren.*

The Malinois has a short fawn, red or brown coat. The tips of the hair are black, forming a darker overlay. All colours have a black mask. Often confused with the German Shepherd Dog, the Malinois is smaller and squarer in shape, and has a lighter bone structure and finer chiselled head. This dog gets its name from a club that was set up in the city of Malines in 1898.

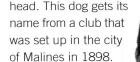

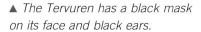

▲ *The Tervuren has a black mask on its face and black ears.*

◀ *The only smooth-coated Belgian Shepherd is the Malinois.*

Breed box
Size: 56–66cm (22–26in),
   20–30kg (44–66lb)
Grooming: Variable, depending
   on coat type
Feeding: Moderate
Exercise: High
Temperament: Loyal and intelligent

▼ *The Groenendael has a long, black coat, sometimes with frosting (white or grey hairs) around the muzzle.*

The aim of the club was to protect and promote this type of short-haired Belgian Shepherd.

The Groenendael has a profuse double coat that is similar in length and texture to the Tervuren. The colour is solid black, but a small amount of white is allowed on the chin, chest and the tips of the toes. The lips, nose and eye rims are black. Eyes are brown and almond-shaped. This is currently the most popular of the four types of Belgian Shepherd.

The Laekenois can be red, mahogany, fawn, red sable or fawn sable in colour. Black hairs may be mixed in with the underlying colour. The coat is medium in length, and rough and wiry. Facial fringing gives the head a rather shaggy look. The tail is thick and bushy. This is the rarest of the four Belgian Shepherd breeds. Originally bred to herd sheep, the Laekenois was also used to guard linen when it was put outside to dry after washing.

Belgian Shepherds are active herding dogs that require a good deal of exercise. The herding instinct is still strong in many animals, and they may try to herd up family members or chase cars and cyclists. With early socializing and obedience training, this trait can be corrected.

This is a loving breed that makes an excellent companion. It is a very loyal dog, forming a strong bond with its human family. It does not like being left alone for long periods, and can develop separation anxiety. If bored, it may become destructive. A trainable and very intelligent dog that needs mental as well as physical exercise, it can be trained for a variety of canine sports, including herding trials, competition obedience, agility,

▶ *A wiry-coated Laekenois looks very different from the other varieties of Belgian Shepherd.*

▲ *In Belgium, the four types of Belgian Shepherds are classified as separate breeds. In the USA, the Groenendael is the Belgian Sheepdog, and the Laekenois is not recognized.*

working trials and the breed show ring. The Belgian Shepherd is commonly used as a therapy or assistance dog, and is also used by military, police and service personnel for a range of activities, including search and rescue, crowd control, and drug and bomb detection.

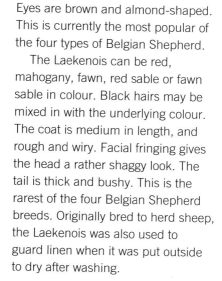

Bergamasco

The Bergamasco, or Cane da Pastore Bergamasco, is an ancient breed of herding dog that originated from the Italian Alps. It is still used by farmers in this region to herd cattle and sheep. It works independently, and can be sent out from the farm to collect and herd stock back home without any human intervention. It is such a good herding dog that shepherds kept the bloodlines a secret for many years.

Puppies are born with short hair that grows as the dog matures. The coat is very distinctive, consisting of three types of hair which mat or felt together over time to provide a thick, insulated covering. The mats start to form from the spine and grow longer each year until they reach the ground.

Breed box
Size: 54–62cm (21–24in);
male 32–38kg (71–84lb);
female 26–32kg (57–71lb)
Grooming: Medium
Feeding: Moderate
Exercise: High
Temperament: Patient and protective

▲ *The Bergamasco's coat, described as greasy to the touch, makes it appear unkempt, but also keeps the dog warm and dry. It tends to form loose mats, which are not brushed out.*

▶ *Grooming may be a problem with this breed.*

▶ *Coming from a cold and mountainous region, this dog is not suitable for hot countries.*

This can take up to six years. Long hair on the face falls over the eyes; this provides protection from the bright glare of snow.

This dog is heavy-boned and looks very chunky, but underneath the felted coat is an agile dog that requires exercise and a job to do. The breed is very good with children, with whom it forms a special bond. It accepts other dogs and, if introduced at a young age, tolerates cats and domestic pets. Like all herding dogs, it is happiest if it has a job to do.

▲ *Under all that hair, bright eyes watch its owner constantly.*

Berger Picard

A rustic-looking farm and herding dog from north-eastern France, the Berger Picard is also known as the Picardy Shepherd. It is thought to be the oldest of the French sheepdog breeds. This is a rare breed that almost became extinct after the two World Wars. In part, this was due to the fact that it came from the region in which

▶ *This sensitive and reserved breed requires socialization during the first two years of life.*

▲ *The Berger Picard is increasingly popular in a range of dog sports, including Schutzhund and flyball.*

trench warfare was taking place. The Berger Picard is often mistaken for a mixed-breed animal.

The fawn or brindle coat is harsh, rough and waterproof. It requires little attention other than a weekly brush through. The coat should look natural and slightly tousled. Although this

breed has eyebrows, the hair does not fall over its dark eyes. Ears are set high on the head and are erect. The tail is long, reaching down to the hock. This a medium-sized dog that is known for its smile.

As with all herding breeds, the Picard requires regular lengthy walks. Provided they have enough exercise,

they are calm and settled in the house, contentedly waiting for their next walk. The Picard may bark for attention if left alone for too long. Intelligent and trainable, but with a stubborn streak, this breed will make a good companion for an active owner. It is generally good with children and other dogs, but can be reserved towards strangers. Early and ongoing socialization is required to overcome this trait. Some Picards are fussy eaters, and time may be needed to find a suitable diet that the dog enjoys.

Breed box
Size: 55–66cm (21½–25½in),
23–32kg (50–70lb)
Grooming: Easy
Feeding: Moderate
Exercise: High
Temperament: Alert and reserved

▶ *Tousled but elegant, the Picard has a long tail that should reach to the hock. The tail is lifted higher when the dog is moving.*

Border Collie

The Border Collie is the classic farm dog. It is neat and agile, it thinks on its feet, and if its owner does not occupy its mind with useful training, it will get into mischief because its brain is always active.

Ideally, it stands some 53cm (21in) at its withers, although it may look lower to ground because when it travels at speed it takes on the posture of a permanent crouch. Its eyes show keen intelligence, and this type is the favourite for those who wish to compete at top-level obedience or agility competitions.

Breed box
Size: Male 53cm (21in), 23.5kg (52lb); female 51cm (20in), 19kg (42lb)
Grooming: Medium
Feeding: Medium
Exercise: Demanding
Temperament: Very alert and trainable

▲ The low-slung body of the Border Collie is essential for its super-agile performance at work.

The Border Collie's coat is usually moderately long, but it is relatively easy to groom as long as the tangles are dealt with on a regular basis. The coat comes in all kinds of colours together with white, but the most common base colour is black.

◄ A working dog from the Scottish borders, this breed needs to be occupied constantly if destructive behaviour is to be avoided.

▲ This is the sharp expression of what is, by common consent, the most trainable breed of them all.

This breed demands exercise for its muscles just as much as for its brain. It makes an ideal family dog for the grown family, but it is not best suited to be a nursemaid to the very young – although no doubt such heresy will raise a few protests. To put it bluntly, it does not suffer fools gladly, and it is not averse to taking a swift nip at those who do not understand its point, in the same way that it will liven the reactions of the sheep or cattle which are its natural flock.

Briard

The Briard is a farm dog from France with a Gallic charm about it, making it very captivating. It has a rugged appearance subtly combined with a slightly dapper look. At up to 68cm (27in) tall, it is a big dog, but underneath the long, wavy coat it is not a heavyweight.

The coat comes in black, slate grey or varying shades of fawn. It needs regular grooming, especially as the breed thoroughly enjoys exercise in town or country, and can bring the great outdoors back indoors on returning home. The Briard is one of a mere handful of breeds that is not only born with double hind dewclaws, but it should also retain them. This gives its feet a very hairy appearance, which adds to its tendency to act rather like a floor brush.

A Briard is trainable; all that is needed is determination and patience. The dog must have total confidence in its owner. When it plays, it plays rough. It is good with children but perhaps not with toddlers – they may get knocked over. This, of course, is true of many breeds, but it would be wise to remember that this handsome dog started off as a guard dog for flocks of nomadic sheep.

▲ This breed takes up a fair amount of space and needs a considerable degree of effort to keep it tidy.

▼ The Briard is a very impressive animal with a kindly disposition, but is also capable of being an effective guard dog. It is intelligent, loyal and faithful. In some countries, the breed is used by the police and military.

▲ In spite of all the hair around its eyes, a Briard is extremely sharp-eyed, making it a good watch dog.

Breed box

Size: Male 62–68cm (24½–27in), 38.5kg (85lb); female 56–64cm (22–25in), 34kg (75lb)
Grooming: Demanding
Feeding: Demanding
Exercise: Demanding
Temperament: Lively and intelligent

Catalan Sheepdog

The Catalan Sheepdog, also known as the Gos d'Atura Català or Perro de Pastor Catalán, comes from the Andorra region of Spain. It is used as a herding and guarding stock dog that will work with a shepherd or independently. Believed to date back to Roman times, this ancient breed comes in two variants: long- and short-coated. Short-coated dogs are extremely rare and thought to be on the brink of extinction.

▶ The Catalan Sheepdog was chosen as the mascot for the 1992 Olympic Games in Barcelona.

The coat is double with a rough topcoat and a thick undercoat. Unusually, the hair sheds at different times, with the front of the dog losing coat first, so for a short period it can seem as if the dog has two different types of coat. The hair is shades of fawn, grey and sable, and the coat can be flat or have a slight wave. Hair on the face forms a beard and moustache. Long hair falls over the eyes but does not obscure sight. Ears are triangular and covered with long fringing.

Easily trainable and quiet in the home, the Catalan is a good companion for an owner who is able to provide the exercise that it requires. It is a calm dog that likes children and gets on well with other animals. The breed is an instinctive guard dog and will protect family members by alerting them to any potential danger. Very intelligent and quick to learn, this dog is adaptable but requires a large garden and frequent walks. It enjoys having a task to do and excels at heel work to music, flyball, agility, obedience and herding trials.

◀ The lips and roof of the mouth are black, and the tongue may also have black patches.

▶ Although they are hard to see under the thick coat, this breed has double dewclaws.

Breed box
Size: 45–55cm (17–19in), 20–27kg (45–60lb)
Grooming: Extensive
Feeding: Moderate
Exercise: High
Temperament: Active and calm

Croatian Sheepdog

A description of this dog exists in a document written in 1374 by Petar, Bishop of Djakovo. The breed seems to have changed very little since then, other than being slightly taller in modern times. This is a brave herding dog that will work cattle or sheep. It is capable of turning a bull, and will run over the backs of sheep to get to where it wants to be.

With rounded cheeks, a lean muzzle and erect or semi-erect ears, this dog has a rather 'foxy' head. The coat on the head and legs is short, while the body is covered with longer, soft curly or wavy hair. The front legs and breeches are feathered. The coat is black, but a few white hairs are acceptable. Small white markings on the throat and chest are permitted. The Croatian Sheepdog has an economical long, striding, brisk trot that covers the ground effortlessly.

▲ Also known as Hrvatski Ovkar, this herding dog is mainly used to turn stock.

▲ The Croatian Sheepdog may look rather scruffy, but it has an extremely bright and busy brain.

This loyal dog will usually only obey the person it considers to be the pack leader. It is a highly energetic breed that can be noisy and destructive if it is not mentally stimulated and does not have enough exercise. The strong herding instinct means it may chase stock, cars and joggers. It is wary of strangers unless early socialization is undertaken, and it makes a good family companion, providing it is introduced to children at a young age. It excels at most dog sports, including tracking, hiking, flyball and agility.

▶ Not well known outside its country of origin, this breed nevertheless has a strong following in Japan.

Breed box
Size: 40–53cm (16–21in),
  13–20kg (29–43lb)
Grooming: Medium
Feeding: Moderate
Exercise: High
Temperament: Keen and energetic

Estrela Mountain Dog

The Estrela Mountain Dog is a sturdy, sizeable dog of the mastiff type, which comes from the mountainous regions of Portugal.

It is a well-mannered breed with a delightfully shambling way of going about. It regards people as friends and enjoys living with a family. It also enjoys exercise as befits its size, at a top level of 72cm (28½in) at its withers. It eats well but is not greedy.

Its coat is usually fairly long, and comes in fawn, brindle or wolf grey, but the general impression is of a large, benign dog with a dark muzzle. It has a moderate double coat that can be yellow, grey, fawn or brindle, and the mask should be dark. It is amenable to training but will seldom retrieve objects. It is a good watch dog and enjoys the company of children. The Estrela is becoming increasingly popular as a companion dog.

▲ The Estrela Mountain Dog looks what it is – massive and yet kindly. It requires a spacious home and a large garden or yard.

Breed box
Size: 30–50kg (66–110lb);
　　male 65–72cm (25½–28½in);
　　female 62–68cm (24½–27½in)
Grooming: Medium
Feeding: Medium
Exercise: Medium
Temperament: Loyal but stubborn

▲ The benign expression of eye is the key to this dog's personality.

◄ The Estrela is not a dog to delight in cramped accommodation; it needs a good amount of space.

Finnish Lapphund

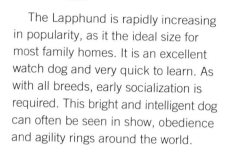

The Finnish Lapphund has herded reindeer for centuries, working in sub-zero temperatures on snow-covered tundra. Its survival was in doubt during World War II, when many dogs in this region were killed. Fortunately, dedicated breeders worked hard to conserve the breed.

The coat is thick and double, with a coarse outer layer of hair. This protection is needed to withstand extreme cold. All colours are permitted, as long as the main colour is dominant. Many Lapphunds have distinctive 'spectacle' markings around their eyes. The tail is carried over the back when the dog is moving, but may hang down when at rest.

The Lapphund is rapidly increasing in popularity, as it the ideal size for most family homes. It is an excellent watch dog and very quick to learn. As with all breeds, early socialization is required. This bright and intelligent dog can often be seen in show, obedience and agility rings around the world.

▲ *The Finnish Lapphund is a typical spitz-type dog, and was originally used to herd reindeer in the snow.*

▼ *This breed has become increasingly popular in recent years. It requires regular and thorough grooming to keep its thick coat neat and tidy.*

Breed box
Size: 46–52cm (18–20½in),
   20–21kg (44–46lb)
Grooming: Fairly demanding
Feeding: Medium
Exercise: Medium
Temperament: Calm and intelligent

◄ *The sharp, intense look on this dog's face befits the breed's character exactly.*

German Shepherd Dog

The German Shepherd used to be known by some as an Alsatian; with either name it is a very well-known breed. Its breeding and training have led to its renown as a herding sheepdog, a leader of the blind and as a police dog. Police forces, the armed services, prison officers, drug officers and private protection agencies all over the world employ the GSD.

There are considerable variations in what is regarded as the ideal shape for this multi-purpose dog. Traditionally,

Breed box

Size: Male 60–66cm
   (24–26in), 36.5kg (80½lb);
   female 55–60cm (22–24in),
   29.5kg (65lb)
Grooming: Medium
Feeding: Medium
Exercise: Demanding
Temperament: Steady and
   highly trainable

▶ *This is a handsome all-purpose dog that enjoys walking.*

▲ *The eyes show this breed's intelligence – the German Shepherd Dog does not miss a trick.*

the dog is a proud, powerful creature, standing an average of 63cm (25in) tall, with a body length slightly greater than its height. Coat lengths vary; some enthusiasts state that a medium-length coat is the only acceptable version, while others accept a long-haired type. Colours include black, black and tan, and sable. White and cream dogs do occur, but raise horrified protests

from many aficionados – something to bear in mind if your ultimate intention is to show your dog.

All such matters of taste aside, the fact remains that, at its best, the GSD is an intelligent, trainable dog with a pleasant and loyal disposition, and makes a first-class household member. It needs exercise and, on occasion, may need to be stimulated in that direction as it can be wilfully idle. On the other hand, most need to have their energies directed into useful pursuits, as the GSD, in common with many other breeds that were bred to work, originated as a shepherd dog and stock protector.

Hungarian Kuvasz

Predominantly a flock guardian, the Hungarian Kuvasz's ancestors are believed to have come from Tibet. It is uncertain whether the dogs came to Hungary with the Huns, or were brought by Turkish refugees fleeing from the Mongols. From medieval times, these dogs would accompany herdsman with their flocks, providing protection from wolves and deterring thieves. Like many breeds, the Kuvasz almost became extinct during World War II when kennels stopped breeding due to food shortages.

The Kuvasz has a dense white, water-resistant coat that is odourless and repels dirt. The hair can grow to

▶ This brilliant white dog never relaxes its guard. It is thought to have found its way to Hungary with nomadic Turkish shepherds sometime during the Middle Ages.

▲ The Kuvasz comes from a cold climate, hence its thick coat.

Breed box
Size: Male 70–76cm (28–30in), 45–52kg (100–115lb); female 65–70cm (26–28in), 32–41kg (70–90lb)
Grooming: Medium
Feeding: Demanding
Exercise: High
Temperament: Independent and protective

15cm (6in) in length. Some breed standards call for the coat to be straight, while others state that it should be wavy. Despite the white coat, skin pigmentation is dark and the nose leather is black. Eyes are almond-shaped and dark brown. This is a large, sturdy and muscular breed that is said to move in a wolf-like manner. It is a fit dog that can trot for 24km (15 miles) without ill effects.

Although loyal and patient, it can be challenging to train because it is very independent. It is not recommended for a first-time dog owner, but requires a person who understands and can enforce pack leadership. It will instinctively protect its owner and will bark at anything that is considered a threat. Care should be taken that children do not accidently get

knocked over by this big dog. While generally good with children within its own family group, it may consider a visiting child a threat.

▶ Early socialization and continued training is a must for this breed.

Hungarian Puli

The distinctive and eye-catching Hungarian Puli is a herding and livestock guardian dog similar in type to the Komondor. Its coat varies from black through grey and fawn to apricot. It grows massively into the

▶ *This breed has an unusual corded coat that swings like a loose rug as it goes on its energetic way.*

weather-resistant equivalent of an Eskimo's parka, withstanding both cold and wet.

As the dog matures, the coat tends to form into cords. These cords are not to be confused with the mats that are the sign of an idle owner. The coat takes a great deal of hard work to keep in order. The cords cover the dog completely from head to toe, including the face and tail. There is, indeed, very little visible of the dog beneath the coat. When the dog moves, the cords swing

en masse rather like a curtain. The Hungarian Puli is a fast-moving and energetic creature that loves exercise and people. It is a great barker and therefore an effective burglar alarm. This is a dog for the devotee.

Breed box
Size: Male 40–44cm (16–17½in), 13–15kg (28½–33lb); female 37–41cm (14½–16½in), 10–13kg (22–28½lb)
Grooming: Very demanding.
Feeding: Undemanding
Exercise: Medium
Temperament: Lively but reserved with strangers

Komondor

The Komondor is another dog from Hungary, where it guards flocks and farms. It has a huge corded coat that reaches the ground in the adult. It is

▶ *This is a dog for the wide, open spaces and an owner with plenty of time to maintain it.*

white immediately after the dog has been bathed and dried; drying it is a long, drawn-out process. Its whiteness tends to be rapidly compromised by contact with the countryside.

Its ancestry is as a farm dog; bringing such a dog into a town atmosphere is totally misguided. Its basic instinct is to guard, and to trifle with a dog of such dimensions is risky, to put it mildly. This is definitely a breed that is only for those who understand what they are taking on, and certainly not one for the first-time owner.

▲ *In spite of the thick coat over its eyes, the Komondor misses nothing.*

Breed box
Size: Male minimum 65cm (25½in), 50–51kg (110–112½lb); female minimum 60cm (23½in), 36–50kg (79½–110lb)
Grooming: Very demanding
Feeding: Medium
Exercise: Medium
Temperament: Wary and protective

Lancashire Heeler

The Lancashire Heeler is a stylish little dog. It stands a mere 30cm (12in) high, and is slightly longer than it is tall. Its forelegs tend to be slightly bowed, but this should not be excessive. As its name implies, this breed was used on farms to herd cattle by nipping at their heels, and it still does when required.

Its coat is not truly short, but it does not grow to any great length. It is always black and tan in colour, and a thorough, brisk grooming will have it shining in no time. It enjoys exercise, but does not make an issue of it. It makes a terrific household companion, and loves children and joining in games. It has a sharp bark, which is louder than one might expect from such a small package, it eats well and is highly biddable.

▼ Short legs carry a powerful little body; this breed of dog will clear the house of rats as a bonus.

Breed box
Size: 6.5kg (14lb); male 30cm (12in); female 25cm (10in)
Grooming: Easy
Feeding: Undemanding
Exercise: Medium
Temperament: Happy and affectionate

◄ This is a small and active dog that adapts easily from droving to being part of a household. The original Lancashire Heeler was used to drive cattle, much like the Welsh Corgi.

▲ The prick ears are a sign of the dog's readiness to join in any form of fun.

Maremma Sheepdog

The Maremma Sheepdog is Italy's version of the nomadic flock guardian. As such, this is a breed that has been derived from generations of working guard dogs. It stands as high as 73cm (29in), but it is not heavily built.

Originating from Italy, the popularity of this breed now sees it recognized by most of the world's major kennel clubs. It is used as a livestock guardian by farmers in Europe, Australia, the USA and Canada. The breed is renown for bonding with the animals that it is required to guard, if introduced to them when it

▼ *The expression on this breed's face suggests that it is not a fawning animal. It will take its time to admit strangers to the heart of its family.*

◄ ▼ *This dog's ancestry means that it requires plenty of exercise as well as discipline from its owner.*

is a puppy. It is an intelligent dog that requires calm constancy in training.

It carries a medium-length coat that fits it closely. The colour is white with a slight touch of fawn. The dog has an alert expression that denotes the watchfulness of its ancestry. It is a worker and requires regular exercise to maintain it as it the fit, muscular creature that its breeding has made it.

Breed box
Size: Male 65–73cm (25½–29in), 35–45kg (77–99lb); female 60–68cm (24–27½in), 30–40kg (66–88lb)
Grooming: Medium
Feeding: Medium
Exercise: Demanding
Temperament: Lively and active

Miniature American Shepherd

Work started in California, USA, in the late 1960s to produce a small herding dog with a strong working ethic. The foundation dogs used were thought to be small unregistered Australian Shepherds. Originally called a Miniature Australian Shepherd, this dog rapidly became popular as a multi-purpose sporting dog. In 2011, the AKC recognized it as a breed in its own right and gave it Foundation Stock Service status. This was followed in 2012 by allowing it to compete in the breed ring in the Miscellaneous class, followed by eligibility to compete in the AKC Herding Group from 2015.

The medium to long double coat can be black, red, blue merle or red merle. All colours may or may not have tan points and/ or white markings. Front legs and breeches are feathered. The tail is long, plumed and hangs down when at rest, lifting as the

▶ *This breed is very active, quick to learn tricks and loves to play.*

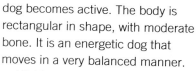

▼ *Ever watchful, this dog is waiting for its next command. Eye colour is dependent on coat colour, and ears should tip over at the top. This example is a red tri merle.*

dog becomes active. The body is rectangular in shape, with moderate bone. It is an energetic dog that moves in a very balanced manner.

Highly energetic outdoors but calm within the home, this breed makes an excellent companion for an active family. Time and training are needed to direct the strong herding and working instinct into suitable tasks. The dog is generally good with children and other dogs, and is devoted to its owner, as well as being trainable and very willing to learn. It is a sensitive breed that is reserved with strangers, but not shy. It excels in canine sports and activities, especially flyball, agility, obedience and disc dog.

▶ *The body of the Miniature American Shepherd should be longer than the height, and it should be powerful without looking stocky.*

Breed box
Size: Male 36–46cm (14–18in);
  female 33–43cm (13–17in);
  weight variable, dependent
  on height
Grooming: Medium
Feeding: Moderate
Exercise: High
Temperament: Intelligent and
  versatile

Mudi

The Mudi is a very rare dog from Hungary that would have faced extinction but for the diligence of the few owners of this breed. It is closely related to the Pumi and Hungarian Puli, and was only considered a separate breed in the 1930s. It is a very versatile dog that is capable of herding cattle, sheep and pigs, as well as acting as a flock guardian. It can work with very large flocks of up to 500 sheep. The Mudi is also used for hunting, and it will kill rodents.

Colours range through shades of black, brown, white, yellow and grey. Black, brown and grey merle are also acceptable. Hair is short on the legs and face, while the body is covered with a medium curly or wavy coat. The coat is glossy and forms tufts.

▶ A bored or lonely Mudi may suffer from stress, leading to destructive and excitable behaviour.

▼ Any potential owner needs to be keen on physical activity, because the Mudi has a high exercise requirement.

Ears are erect and set on a wedge-shaped head. This is a very powerful dog for its size, but many Mudi dogs are born without tails.

This breed is courageous and has a strong instinct to protect its family. It tends to bond with one person, but accepts children if it is brought up with them. Some are very reserved with strangers, so early socialization is required. It is friendly with other dogs and will tolerate cats if introduced to

▶ Once called the 'Driver Dog', the Mudi was featured on a Hungarian postage stamp in 2004.

them when it is a puppy. This breed has a tendency to bark, so neighbours need to be considered. Highly intelligent and trainable, it requires an active life and a job to do. It enjoys a variety of canine sports, including Schutzhund, rally, flyball and tracking.

Breed box
Size: 38–48cm (15–19in), 8.2–13.2kg (18–29lb)
Grooming: Moderate
Feeding: Medium
Exercise: High
Temperament: Courageous and intelligent

Norwegian Buhund

The Norwegian Buhund is a neatly shaped spitz. It has erect ears on an intelligent head and a lively attitude to life. It measures around 46cm (18in), so it is not an imposing dog, but it has an air of alertness about it that makes people pay attention.

Its coat is close and harsh. The most common colour is a wheaten

Breed box
Size: 41–46cm (16–18in), 24–26kg (53–57lb)
Grooming: Undemanding
Feeding: Undemanding
Exercise: Medium
Temperament: Energetic and fearless

◄ This dog's shape is the archetypal outline of a spitz – all neatness and expectancy. This breed was once used as a sled dog in its native country.

▲ The Norwegian Buhund is an easy dog to keep clean; it actually seems to dislike getting muddy.

◄ This is a breed of energetic dog that may initially be wary of strangers, but it fits family life well.

gold, but dogs with black and wolf-sable coats are seen. The coat is short enough to require no great skill or time to keep it well groomed.

This breed is a herder in its native Norway, and its good hearing allows it to react swiftly as a guard dog. It gets on well with its family, but is somewhat reserved with those it does not know. It thoroughly enjoys exercise and is relatively biddable, so its bustling style can be kept under control when let loose in field or park.

Old English Sheepdog

The Old English Sheepdog is instantly recognizable by those of a certain age as being the dog from the paint advertisement. It is one of those breeds that could be classified as distinctive the world over. It has evolved from a practical, working-style sheepdog into a stylized show dog; its use in commercial advertising has led to a growth in its popularity, sadly to the breed's overall detriment.

It stands around 61cm (24in) high, but its huge fluffed-up coat makes it look somewhat taller. The owners who exhibit their dogs have to put in hours of work in order to maintain them in

▶ *The Old English Sheepdog was previously known as the Bobtail, since its tail used to be customarily docked.*

show-ring style. Left ungroomed for any length of time, the harsh-textured coat can become matted to a degree that leaves little alternative but to clip.

This is a cheerful extrovert and makes a good family companion, provided the family is committed to

the dog's exercise and can cope with its occasonally explosive nature. It will join in every possible activity with enthusiasm. It is capable of being a first-class guard of its owner's property, with a highly distinctive bark to emphasize its presence.

▲ *This breed goes back at least 150 years, and possibly longer.*

Breed box

Size: Male minimum 61cm
  (24in), 36.5kg (80½lb);
  female minimum 56cm (22in),
  29.5kg (65lb)
Grooming: Very demanding
Feeding: Medium
Exercise: Medium
Temperament: Friendly and
  outgoing

▶ *The higher rump end is the result of grooming the hair upwards.*

Pumi

One of four Hungarian herding breeds (the others being the Hungarian Puli, Komondor and Mudi), the Pumi originated in the 17th century from inter-breeding French and German shepherding terriers with Puli types. As a farm dog, it works sheep, cattle and pigs, as well as killing rats and mice. Virtually unknown outside its country of origin until the 1970s, the Pumi is building a worldwide reputation as an excellent herding and sports dog.

The majority of Pumis are born black and turn grey around the age of 6–8 weeks. White, black and sable colouring is acceptable. Potential purchasers who wish to compete in

► *The Pumi is also known as the Hungarian Herding Terrier – a direct reference back to its early origins.*

▼ *This breed is nicknamed the 'clown dog' because its tufted ears give it a comical appearance.*

Breed box
Size: Male 41–47cm (16–18½in), 10–15kg (22–33lb); female 38–44cm (15–17½in), 8–13kg (17½–28½lb)
Grooming: Medium to high
Feeding: Medium
Exercise: High
Temperament: Alert and watchful

the breed show ring should consult the standard relevant to their country as to which colours constitute a fault. The double coat grows into corkscrew curls that do not cord but will require regular grooming and trimming. The head is long and narrow. The Pumi has very distinctive ears that are semi-erect; they tip forward and are covered with long hair.

The shaggy coat makes the Pumi look larger and heavier than it actually is. The breed is very vocal and, although an excellent watch dog, may not endear itself to close neighbours. It can be an aggressive dog and also shy with people, so it requires ongoing training and socialization. This is particularly important if there are children in the family. The Pumi is protective and will wander if it has the chance. It is a good ratter and should not be trusted with pet rodents. It would be best suited to an active owner who lives in a rural situation.

▼ *The Pumi's coat grows constantly with very little shedding, similar in appearance to that of a Poodle.*

Polish Lowland Sheepdog

The Polish name for this dog is
Polski Owczarek Nizinny, and this is
shortened to PON, a term used for the
breed worldwide. It is believed to be
the result of breeding the Hungarian
Puli with various other breeds,
including the Tibetan Mastiff, Tibetan
Terrier and the Lhasa Apso. In 1514,
several PONs travelled on a ship to
Scotland with a Polish merchant
named Kazimierz Grabski, who
intended to swap grain for some
Scottish sheep. The merchant also
exchanged three of his dogs for a ram.

▼ *This is a charming sheepdog from
Poland. Its friendly attitude has
brought it great popularity.*

▼ *The Polish Lowland Sheepdog is
usually born without a tail. Its long,
thick coat needs regular grooming.*

These dogs, crossed with Scottish
dogs, are thought to be the basis of
the Bearded Collie.

With a long and dense, shaggy,
wire-haired topcoat plus a very thick,
soft undercoat, the Polish Lowland
Sheepdog requires extensive
grooming. Colours range from white
or grey with black, grey, chocolate or
sand patches, to solid white or black
and black and tan. Colours fade as
the dog matures. This is a muscular,
medium-sized dog with facial hair that
forms a beard.

It is an independent breed that has
a very good memory. It is easy to train
but can be wilful if it thinks it can
control its owner. It is good with
children if raised with them from a
puppy. Like many of the Herding
Group, it may try to round people up,
chase joggers and nip at heels unless
trained not to. Some PONs are
dominant with other dogs, especially
those of the same sex, so socialization
is essential. Overall, it is a good watch
dog that requires both mental and
physical exercise.

Breed box
Size: 42–50cm (17–20in);
    male 18–22kg (40–50lb); female
    13.5–18kg (30–40lb)
Grooming: Extensive
Feeding: Medium to high
Exercise: High
Temperament: Lively and clever

▲ *Some dogs have blue
eyes, but this is not acceptable with
most kennel clubs for the show ring.*

Pyrenean Mountain Dog

The Pyrenean Mountain Dog, also known as the Great Pyrenees, is a solidly built animal measuring as much as 70cm (27½in) and weighing up to 60kg (132lb). It is one of the flock-guarding dogs of the European

▶ The Pyrenean Mountain Dog is massive and requires a firm handler. A steady-moving dog with very considerable dignity, it can be quite reserved with strangers.

nomad shepherd; with its coarse-textured white coat, it merges into the flock. As a domestic house dog, it requires regular grooming, and bathing it is no easy task.

The modern Pyrenean has more of the permitted badger coloration, especially on the head and ears, than it did during the 1960s. It is a breed that grows large double hind dewclaws, which help it in snow-covered terrain. It does not require excessive exercise, and normally moves at a dignified amble in a park or pasture. It makes a good household member, its basic temperament having become more gentle as a result of generations of selective breeding.

Breed box
Size: Male 70cm (27½in),
   50–60kg (119–132lb);
   female minimum 65cm (25½in),
   40kg (88lb)
Grooming: Demanding
Feeding: Demanding
Exercise: Medium
Temperament: Confident and genial

Pyrenean Sheepdog

Still relatively unknown by many people, this dog is beginning to be seen more frequently. There are two varieties: rough-faced and smooth-faced. The former has long hair all over the body, while the latter has a short coat with a ruff around the neck and some feathering on the tail, legs and belly. Coat colours include fawn, with or without a black mask, brindle, grey, black and merle. Solid colours are preferred, but some white is permitted on the head, feet and chest.

This breed is very energetic, and this characteristic, combined with its intelligence, makes it ideal for dog sports, including agility, flyball, tracking and obedience, as well as the breed show ring. It is ideal for an active family.

◀▲ This second breed from the Pyrenees is totally different in looks. Both breeds work with sheep, but they perform in contrasting styles.

Breed box
Size: 38–48cm (15–19in),
   8–15kg (18–33lb)
Grooming: Medium
Feeding: Undemanding
Exercise: Medium
Temperament: Alert and wary

Rough Collie

The Collie originates from the Highland region of Scotland. The name is thought to have come from the Anglo-Saxon word *coll* meaning 'black', and could be a reference to the Scottish black-faced sheep which this breed herded. A dog that was born in 1876, called 'Old Cockie', is considered to be one of the first Collies to look like the Rough Collie of today. She is credited with bringing the sable-coloured coat to the breed. The 'Lassie' films featured a Rough Collie in the starring role.

Nowadays, this attractive dog is bred more for looks and as a companion than for its working ability, although some lines retain their herding instinct. The long double coat can be sable and white, tricolour or

▼ *This is the breed known to the world as the 'Lassie' dog of film fame.*

Breed box
Size: 53–66cm (22–26in); some breed standards stipulate larger dogs; 25–47kg (55–105lb), depending on size
Grooming: Extensive
Feeding: Medium
Exercise: Medium
Temperament: Calm and loyal

▼ *Today's dogs are a lot bigger than the early specimens of the breed.*

blue merle. The AKC also accepts predominately white dogs. All Rough Collies should have white on parts of the collar and legs, plus a white tip to the tail. The head is similar to that of the Shetland Sheepdog. Ears are semi-erect and tip forwards.

This dog does not require as much exercise as most of the other herding breeds. It can be a little shy if not

▲ *This Rough Collie shows why the breed is known for its most attractive expression. They seem to smile.*

introduced to a variety of people, animals and experiences in the first months of its life. As it is good with children, it makes an ideal family companion. It will alarm-bark and does not always know when to stop unless trained to quieten. The Rough Collie will adapt to town or country living, and is calm within the home.

Samoyed

The Samoyed is the 'Laughing Cavalier' of dogdom, with its brilliant white colour and its typical spitz expression. It stands up to 56cm (22in) high, and it is very slightly

▲ The Samoyed has a smiling and cheerful expression. The nose leather can be black or brown, but the lips must be black.

▶ Under this dog's coat there is usually a muscular frame that fits well into a sled harness, given the opportunity. The breed originated with the Samoyeds, a nomadic tribe of northern Asia who roamed Siberia.

longer than it is tall. Its coat is harsh and stand-off in a basic white, but many of the breed carry varying amounts of biscuit, which is a light reddish-fawn.

Grooming is hard work, but the Samoyed is tolerant and will submit for hours, if necessary, to lying on its side while the owner brushes and combs it. The breed has a history as a sled dog, and has hairy, flat feet to enable it to cope with the surface ice that would otherwise pack into the spaces between its pads.

It enjoys exercise but needs human company; it is a super member of a family household, but still manages to be a great companion to those who live alone. In spite of its energetic

▲ This is a happy-go-lucky breed with never a nasty or negative thought – but plenty of mischievous ones.

lifestyle, it is not a huge eater. Its only real drawback is its tendency to bark noisily, especially when it is enjoying itself – which is most of the time.

Breed box
Size: Male 51–56cm (20–22in), 23kg (50½lb); female 46–51cm (18–20in), 18kg (39½lb)
Grooming: Very demanding
Feeding: Medium
Exercise: Medium
Temperament: Alert and smiling

Shetland Sheepdog

The Shetland Sheepdog is a diminutive version of the Rough Collie, although few companion dogs are genuinely as small as the official maximum height permitted for show dogs, which is around 37cm (14½in). In fact, this very attractive little dog has all the instincts that its name implies and, although today it tends to be very much a family dog, it is still quite capable of reacting as a worker.

It carries a long, straight topcoat that can be coloured sable, tricolour, blue merle, black and white, or even black and tan. The undercoat is thick, so it requires thorough grooming fairly frequently if it is not to become matted and impossible to cope with.

This is an alert dog and will take a great deal of exercise if it is offered, but can just as easily make a first-class companion for an elderly person. It is watchful and capable of following a scent when the occasion demands.

▶ *The slight tilt of the head, as if asking a question, is typical of the 'Sheltie'.*

▲ *This miniature version of the Rough Collie is a worker in its own right.*

Breed box
Size: 9kg (20lb); male 37cm
  (14½in); female 35.5cm (14in)
Grooming: Demanding
Feeding: Undemanding
Exercise: Medium
Temperament: Affectionate and
  responsive

▼ *Shelties are sturdy, cheerful and easy to train. They are also photogenic!*

Smooth Collie

In some countries, the Rough Collie and Smooth Collie are considered as two separate breeds, while in others they are regarded as variants of the same breed. The Collie became popular after Queen Victoria purchased some dogs from shepherds who were working on the Balmoral Estate. She was impressed with their looks, kind manner and working ability. It then quickly became fashionable to own a Smooth Collie.

This breed has a short double coat. Outer guard hairs are harsh and cover a dense, soft undercoat. Colours are similar to those of a Rough Collie. Merle dogs may have blue, merled or odd-coloured eyes, which, depending on the breed standard of the country, may be considered a fault in the conformation show ring. The head is wedge-shaped with a chiselled face. Both the Rough Collie and Smooth Collie should have a 'sweet expression'.

This dog is a non-aggressive breed that is good with children and is loving towards its family, however it will bark and needs to be trained as to when this is appropriate. It needs regular exercise but not as much as most of the herding breeds. The Smooth Collie is intelligent, sensitive and easily trained, as long as the owner is kind and consistent. It is a fastidious breed that is quick to house-train. This dog is eager to please and will made a loyal and faithful companion. As well as taking part in many dog sports, the breed is used as a therapy dog and as an assistance dog for the disabled.

Breed box
Size: 53–66cm (22–26in); some breed standards stipulate larger dogs; 25–47kg (55–105lb), depending on size
Grooming: Easy
Feeding: Medium
Exercise: Medium
Temperament: Faithful and intelligent

◄ *Rough and Smooth Collies used to be considered as one breed, and were called Scotch Collies.*

▲ *This dog has moderately large ears that are carried semi-erect when alert.*

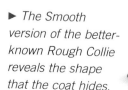

► *The Smooth version of the better-known Rough Collie reveals the shape that the coat hides.*

Swedish Lapphund

The Swedish Lapphund is built on very similar lines to the Finnish Lapphund. It may stand up to 51cm (20in) tall and is of typical spitz construction. Its coat is weather-resistant and of medium length; it is a mixture of black and brown, with an occasional touch of white on its chest or feet. It is not difficult to groom.

▶ *This stout-framed dog has a coat that is fit to withstand Scandinavian weather.*

▼ *The Swedish Lapphund has a gentle character.*

Breed box
Size: 44–51cm (20in),
  19.5–20.5kg (43–45lb)
Grooming: Medium
Feeding: Medium
Exercise: Medium
Temperament: Active and friendly

This breed is a friendly and intelligent dog, and its temperament would appeal to a family household, as it enjoys exercise and is not greedy. Good training is required to control its tendency to bark continuously.

Swedish Vallhund

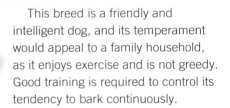

The Swedish Vallhund looks and acts very much like a grey or yellowish Corgi. It is built on similar lines, standing a mere 35cm (14in) tall, but is somewhat longer in body than height. Its coat is reasonably short, harsh and easy to keep in shape.

It comes in grey, greyish-brown and varying shades of yellow with reddish-brown thrown in.

Its job is to herd, and it does this, as do the Corgis, by nipping at the heels of cattle that are not as quick to move as required. It has sharply erect ears and is cheerful. The breed is steadily gaining in popularity, although it is not registered in the USA. It makes an excellent family companion, as it delights in exercise and human friendship.

▲ *If you are looking for real intelligence in a dog's expression, it is to be found in this charmer.*

Breed box
Size: 11.5–13kg (25½–28½lb);
  male 33–35cm (13–14in);
  female 31–33cm (12½–13in)
Grooming: Undemanding
Feeding: Undemanding
Exercise: Medium
Temperament: Friendly and eager

◀ *The Swedish Vallhund is a low-to-ground heeler type – agile, nimble and very biddable.*

Turkish Kangal Dog

The Kangal Dog is the national breed of Turkey, and as such has been declared a national treasure. Coming from the isolated region of Sivas Province in central Turkey, this dog has remained free from cross-breeding, therefore the animal is remarkably uniform in character and appearance. Used as a flock guardian, this powerful dog is capable of protecting its charges from bears, jackals and wolves. The export of true Kangal Dogs from Turkey is extremely difficult, and virtually forbidden.

Mastiff-like in appearance, the Turkish Kangal Dog is a large, powerful and heavy-boned dog. The coat is short and dense, with the undercoat providing insulation from both heat and extreme cold. The dog is pale fawn in colour, with a black mask, and black or shaded, velvety ears. The tail is long and curled over the back. There are great differences in the breed standards of various kennel clubs as to the markings and

▲ *This dog has the characteristic broad white chest blaze and white feet.*

size of this breed. Figures in the breed box should be used for guidance only.

Although this breed is loyal to its owner and generally good with children within its family group, it is not recommended for the first-time dog owner. It is territorial and defensive, so requires an experienced owner who has a sound understanding of dog behaviour and training. The Kangal is prone to wandering, so needs a well-fenced garden. It can be aggressive and has a very strong guarding instinct. This agile breed is also very fast, and can reach speeds of up to 48km/h (30mph).

▲ *In its county of origin the Turkish Kangal Dog is rarely kept as a pet, but is used solely as a working dog.*

▼ *The coat sheds heavily twice a year and needs vigorous grooming to remove all the dead hair.*

Breed box

Size: Male 77–86cm (30–32in),
50–66kg (110–145lb);
female 72–77cm (28–30in),
41–54kg (90–120lb)
Grooming: Easy
Feeding: High
Exercise: High
Temperament: Alert and protective

Welsh Corgi – Cardigan

The Welsh Corgi comes in two separate versions: the Cardigan and the Pembroke. The Cardigan Corgi stands ideally 30cm (12in) at the withers; it is relatively long-cast on sturdy, short legs. It is unlike its Pembroke cousin in that it carries a full tail, which is long and very well coated. This breed is not hard work to groom, nor is it greedy.

Colour-wise it can be almost any dog colour, although white should not predominate. It has large, erect ears and intelligent eyes. It does not bustle about very rapidly and is prepared to take life as it comes, but when working with cattle it has to be nimble enough to nip at their heels and avoid retaliatory kicks.

As a member of a household, it has a curiously benign attitude, but can raise the alarm vociferously if its territory is invaded.

▲ Cardigan Corgis come in a range of colour schemes and have large ears that are set well back on the head.

▲ A watchful expression is typical of this ancient yet fun-loving breed.

▲ Blue eyes only occur in blue merle dogs, but this don't indicate blindness.

Breed box
Size: 30cm (12in); male 11kg (24lb); female 10kg (22lb)
Grooming: Medium
Feeding: Undemanding
Exercise: Medium
Temperament: Alert and steady

◄ The Cardigan is solidly built on short, sturdy legs. This causes the body to look long and low slung. The tail is similar to that of a fox's brush.

Welsh Corgi – Pembroke

The Pembroke is the better-known version of the Welsh Corgi. The breed is favoured by the British royal family – Queen Elizabeth II has owned over 30 of them during her reign. The dog stands 30.5cm (12in) at the withers, and has a longish body. It is sturdily built with a sharp, bright expression and prick ears.

It has a straight, dense coat of medium length and is not difficult to

▲ The most common colour of the Pembroke Corgi is red and white.

groom once it has dried off after a country walk. Its colour is usually red with white markings, but it does come in sable, fawn, or even black and tan.

It is traditionally a cattle-drover, hence its occasional tendency to nip the heels of humans rather than cattle. The slightly doubtful temperament it may have had in past decades has improved since the 1980s.

It is a popular household dog with families who enjoy its brisk, energetic attitude to life, but it has a slight tendency to over-eat, and therefore needs rationing on occasion.

Breed box
Size: 25.5–30.5cm (10–12in);
    male 10–12kg (22–26½lb);
    female 10–11kg (22–24lb)
Grooming: Medium
Feeding: Medium
Exercise: Medium
Temperament: Workman-like
    and active

▲ This practical and adaptable breed is friendly and full of stamina.

▲ The fox-like head should show an intelligent and alert expression.

◀ This young dog displays all the charm of a breed whose purpose is to walk cattle, even if it isn't very big.

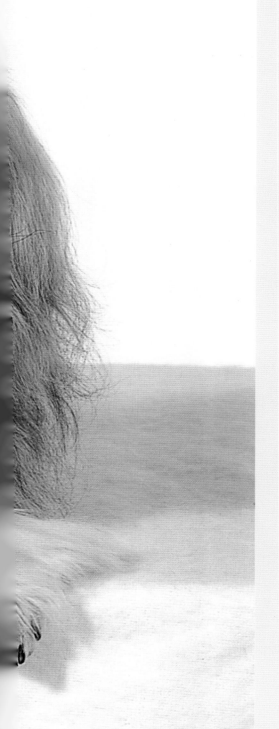

THE TOY GROUP

This group is made up of breeds that are among the smallest of all. The largest of these are the ever-popular Cavalier King Charles Spaniel, Chinese Crested and Löwchen, while at the other end of the scale are the Chihuahua and Pomeranian. Height measurements are not given in many of the Kennel Club's official breed standards; rather, these tend to give ideal weights or weight ranges. The name 'Toy' is in some ways misleading; admittedly some of the breeds tend to appear to be animated playthings, but their temperaments suggest that they are anything but. The breeds included here have some common factors, such as the ability to be picked up and carried easily, but they vary widely in size, type and behaviour. The misconception to be avoided is that they are all dear little creatures that behave impeccably and do not take any effort to look after. Many are feisty characters that are not afraid to nip.

◀ *Many dogs within the Toy Group will need extensive grooming and styling. This is so with the Löwchen, which has a very distinctive clip.*

Affenpinscher

The Affenpinscher, originally from Germany, is a dog that often makes people laugh. It is said to resemble a monkey facially, and certainly its twinkling eyes give its expression a thoroughly mischievous glint.

It has a coat that is harsh in texture and generally looks pretty untidy, so grooming it is not an over-serious business. This breed is game for fun, and is capable of taking part in family activities since its muzzle is not so exaggeratedly short as to interfere with its breathing to any real extent.

It is normally black all over, although a grey coloration does sometimes appear. As a house companion, it is one of the best choices because it is fearless and delights in confronting any intruder.

◄ *A sense of mischief prevails whenever two or more Affenpinschers are gathered together. You can see why they are also known as Monkey Terriers.*

Breed box
Size: 24–28cm (9½–11in), 3–4kg (6½–9lb)
Grooming: Medium
Feeding: Undemanding
Exercise: Medium
Temperament: Lively and self-confident

▼ *The coat is rough and of uneven length over the body – it is shaggy in some places and shorter in others. This example is a truly hairy specimen. Bred as ratters, the coat offers protection.*

▲ *The tail curls gently over the back when the dog is moving, and hangs relaxed at rest. This dog can be excitable.*

▲ *The greying effect produces a remarkable facial study. The Affen is a mischievous and loyal companion.*

Australian Silky Terrier

The Australian Silky Terrier, known variously as the Sydney Silky or just the Silky, is a mixture produced from cross-breeding the Australian Terrier and the Yorkshire Terrier. The result is a sharp-featured, silky-coated dog that stands some 23cm (9in) high at the withers and weighs 4kg (9lb).

◄ *A compact dog, the Australian Silky Terrier may have been bred primarily as a household companion, but it is also a pretty good rat-catcher.*

◄ *At times, the Silky can put on quite a serious expression, but this is not accurate evidence of its true temperament.*

▶ *Silkies should have small, cat-like feet, with no long hair on their legs.*

Breed box
Size: 23cm (9in), 4kg (9lb)
Grooming: Medium
Feeding: Undemanding
Exercise: Medium
Temperament: Alert and friendly

One would expect any animal produced by mating one from Australia with one from Yorkshire to be only too capable of holding its own, so the term 'silky' should never mislead anyone into thinking it denotes anything soft. Not a bit of it – this dog is full of character!

Its coat, which is fairly long and straight, comes in blue and tan, or greyish blue and tan, and it can become glossy with minimal brushing. This dog is intended as a household companion and does the job splendidly, but with a strong prey drive.

▶ *In silhouette, the essential sharpness of this dog's outline and its fixed gaze become obvious – it is a good mixture of toy and terrier.*

Bichon Frise

Believed to be a cross between Barbet Water Dogs and Poodles, there are many stories about the Bichon Frise, or Bichon Tenerife. It is known that this dog came from the Mediterranean area, and that they were admired by sailors who took them back to their home countries. Paintings and documents show that the breed was present in the court of Henry III, and was much loved by 15th-century Spanish Infantas. Its intelligence together with its good nature has gained it worldwide recognition.

This happy little dog has an arched neck and slightly rounded skull. Ears are dropped and covered with long hair. The nose is black, and eyes are dark in colour. Tails are well plumed and carried in a graceful curve over the back. The white, cream, apricot

▲ *This dog is a modern glamour star. With its coat trimmed like topiary, it is very stylish but hard work to maintain.*

or grey coat is curly and dense, with minimal shedding. Daily grooming and monthly trimming and bathing are needed to prevent matting and to keep the coat in good condition. Movement is balanced and effortless.

Bred as a companion dog, the Bichon is good with children and animals, making it an excellent family dog. It loves human company and is playful and affectionate. This dog can be difficult to house-train, so owners need to be diligent in this task.

◄ *A Bichon will enjoy learning tricks and taking part in canine sports.*

▲ *A white-coloured Bichon Frise is preferred in the show ring.*

Breed box
Size: 23–28cm (9–11in),
   3–6kg (6½–13lb)
Grooming: Demanding
Feeding: Medium
Exercise: Medium
Temperament: Friendly and
   extroverted

Bolognese

The Bolognese is a bichon type, and is closely related to the Bichon Frise, Havanese and Maltese. It is named after the Italian city of Bologna. This breed is known to have been in existence in the 1200s, and was favoured by the Italian nobility. Bolognese dogs feature in paintings by Goya and Titian. They have been owned by many famous personalities, including Catherine the Great of Russia and Marilyn Monroe.

The Bolognese is a small dog that has a square, compact and stocky body. It is white, with dark eyes and black eye rims, lips and nose. Apricot

▲ *Facial hair is often tied into a top-knot to avoid it falling into the eyes.*

▶ *This is a happy and joyful breed that is a real home-lover.*

▲ *The Bolognese is similar in type to the Bichon Frise, but the coat only requires brushing and bathing to keep it looking neat and tidy.*

shading is acceptable on the ears. It is a single long-coated breed and does not seasonally moult, but eventually loses and replaces individual hairs. The coat is woolly in texture and falls

Breed box
Size: 25–30cm (10–12in), 2.5–4kg (4½–9lb)
Grooming: Intensive
Feeding: Undemanding
Exercise: Low to medium
Temperament: Intelligent and easy-going

in loose, open ringlets. This dog is not normally trimmed, but requires daily brushing and monthly bathing.

More reserved than a Bichon Frise, the Bolognese is easy-going and intelligent. It is very responsive to obedience training but does not like repetitive tasks. This breed can be very stubborn if it does not get its own way. It is a non-aggressive family dog that is good with other dogs and children. It is not an incessant barker, but does make a good watch dog, barking only when there is good reason. It is not a high-energy breed, but still requires a daily walk. Enjoying the comforts of home, the Bolognese is suitable for town or country living.

Cavalier King Charles Spaniel

The Cavalier King Charles Spaniel, or Cavalier, is a very popular toy dog and a true favourite. Built on the lines of a small gundog, it has a charm for the elderly as well as the young family. It loves people, and it does not find fault with other dogs.

Its weight is 5.5–8kg (12–18lb), which is a wide enough range, but as a breed it does tend to get even heavier. The Cavalier's placid nature

▶ *This is a neat breed that is ideal for anyone who wants an active and cheerful companion. Like other spaniels, the Cavalier is a hunter. It will chase birds, small mammals and even butterflies if given the opportunity.*

▲ *The charm and affability of the Cavalier's expression is beautifully caught in this head study.*

and friendliness often induces people to give it injudicious titbits, but unfortunately this encourages obesity.

This breed has a good-looking head and a well-balanced body. It can appear in a series of colours, from ruby (red), black and tan, and tricolour (black and white with tan markings) to Blenheim, which is a mixture of rich chestnut and white, often with a lozenge of chestnut in the centre of a white patch down the middle of the head.

It enjoys exercise and is built on elegant, athletic lines; indeed, it needs good exercise in view of its hearty appetite. It is not difficult to groom, as its coat can be kept tidy with normal brush-and-comb techniques.

◀ *The Cavalier is in fact a miniature spaniel, combining all the qualities of dogs in the Toy and Gundog Groups.*

Breed box
Size: 32cm (13in), 5.5–8kg (12–18lb)
Grooming: Medium
Feeding: Medium
Exercise: Medium
Temperament: Very friendly

Chihuahua

◄ Three of a kind with two Smooths and a Long. This is an alert breed with a loud bark that can sound rather like a duck quacking.

The Chihuahua probably originated in South America, and is indeed named after a Mexican state. It comes in two versions, one of which is smooth-coated, the other long-coated. Apart from their coat, they are identical, tiny dogs of tremendous spirit. They weigh up to 3kg (6½lb), but lighter specimens are generally preferred in the show ring. The Smooth Coat has a soft, glossy covering of a coat, while the Long Coat is never coarse and is relatively easy to keep neat. The Chihuahua is very proud of its tail, which it carries high like a flag. This typifies the breed's personality. All colours are accepted, but fawn to red with white is the most frequently seen.

This is a brave dog, putting up with pain remarkably stoically, but not accepting cheek or insult from any dog that is vastly larger than itself.

It does not appreciate humans who invade its home without permission, yelling defiance and threatening mayhem as it races to defend its home and family.

Rearing a young Chihuahua puppy requires care in moving about; a high-stepping human can very easily trample on such a tiny creature, so Chihuahua breeders soon learn to use a shuffling method of walking. The breed, however, is not a weak or delicate one; in fact, the opposite is true. Both versions enjoy exercise and are extremely game, but families with young children must supervise all interaction between puppy and child carefully and constantly.

Breed box
Size: 15–23cm (6–9in), 1–3kg (2–6½lb)
Grooming: Medium
Feeding: Undemanding
Exercise: Undemanding
Temperament: Spirited and intelligent

◄ The Chihuahua is a well-proportioned little dog ready to take on anything.

▲ The large, round, bright eyes set wide apart are a hallmark of this spritely breed. Eye colour varies.

Chinese Crested

Despite its name, it is very unlikely that the Chinese Crested originated from China. The breed is believed to have come from Africa, and was originally called the African Hairless Terrier. Chinese traders brought these dogs home and the name was subsequently changed to Chinese Crested. There are two varieties, Hairless and Powderpuff, with both being produced in the same litter. Each type has equal recognition with most major kennel clubs.

The Hairless variety has long, single-coated hair on the head, extending down the neck and socks, and a plumed tail. The Powderpuff is covered in a long, silky double coat all over the body. Hair and skin can be any colour – solid, mixed or spotted. Both have almond-shaped eyes and

▶ *The Hairless version has a crest on the head and neck, a plume on the end of the tail, and thick hair on the feet and lower legs.*

elongated toes or 'hare feet'. The Hairless has primitive dentition with pointed teeth, and may have forward-pointing canines or 'tusks'. It suffers from tooth decay and tooth loss, while the Powderpuff does not. In both, the head is wedge-shaped and topped with large, erect ears.

These agile and alert dogs are very loving and do not do well in a kennel situation, as they need to be part of the family. They are suitable for town living but, despite their size and looks, need an active lifestyle. They are quite happy to go for long hikes and to

▲ *The Powderpuff has an undercoat topped with long, silky hair.*

take part in a range of canine sports. The Hairless needs a coat or jumper for warmth in colder climates, the Powderpuff requires daily grooming, and both types need regular baths. Hairless dogs also need to be given sunscreen and skin moisturizers.

▼ *The Chinese Crested Powderpuff, once seen as an outcast by breeders, is now recognized as essential to the future of a very unusual breed.*

Breed box
Size: 30cm (12in), 4.5kg (10lb)
Grooming: Moderate
Feeding: Undemanding
Exercise: Medium
Temperament: Loving and agile

Coton de Tulear

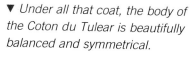

▼ The Coton de Tulear is similar in type to the Bichon Frise and the Bolognese. All have non-shedding coats.

Coming from Madagascar, this dog is relatively new to the American and European dog world. It is not believed to be a feral breed, but was developed via a cross between a bichon type – possibly the Bichon Tenerife – and native Madagascan dogs. It has been in existence for hundreds of years, but is still quite a rarity outside its home country. Also called the Royal Dog of Madagascar, it was at one time only owned by the Madagascan elite.

There is great variation from different kennel clubs as to the breed standard regarding height, weight and

▲ Once the favoured pet of the Madagascar upper classes, this dog has now become popular worldwide.

Breed box
Size: 22–30cm (8½–12in);
　　Tall Coton 38–43cm (15–17in);
　　3.5–6kg (7–13lb); both height
　　and weight rough guides only
Grooming: Extensive
Feeding: Undemanding
Exercise: Low to medium
Temperament: Playful and
　　affectionate

colour. Potential owners who wish to compete in breed shows should seek advice in their own country.

The Coton de Tulear has long, soft hair that feels like a cotton ball, and colours include pure white, black and white, and tricolour. Lemon or grey may be present on the ears. Normal litters can produce the rare Tall Coton version if the parents are carriers of the appropriate genes. In all cases, Cotons have a well-developed chest, slightly arched back and small arched feet.

This is a loyal companion that does not like being left alone for long. It can develop symptoms of separation anxiety. Early socialization is required, as it tends to bark at anything it considers unusual. This can become a problem if not addressed. Cotons are friendly, sociable and good with other dogs. The long coat requires daily grooming and regular washing. This breed is very trainable, but prefers to learn tricks as opposed to repeating obedience exercises.

▼ Under all that coat, the body of the Coton du Tulear is beautifully balanced and symmetrical.

English Toy Terrier

Formally called the Miniature Black and Tan Terrier, the English Toy Terrier is on the United Kennel Club's list of vulnerable native breeds. In an attempt to increase numbers, the UKC is allowing North America's Toy Manchester Terrier to be re-registered as an English Toy Terrier. Very popular in Victorian times, this dog was used as a ratter working in towns, on farms and on ships, controlling rodents. Competitions were held in taverns when dogs were put into rat pits to see which could kill the most rats in a given time. When this sport was made

▶ *Polishing the English Toy Terrier's coat with a piece of velvet or chamois leather will produce a glorious sheen.*

illegal, this dog's popularity continued in early dog shows, but numbers have since declined dramatically.

This elegant dog has a sleek and compact body. The head is long and narrow, with almond-shaped dark eyes. Pointed ears are set high on the skull and they face forwards. The ears are referred to as 'candle-flame' in shape. The coat is ebony black with

tan markings on the face, chest and legs. There should be a clear division between the colours. Movement is similar to that of an extended trot in horses.

This breed is alert but should not be nervous. Like many of the toy breeds, it does not like being left alone for long. It is good with children, but due to its fine bones it could get injured in rough play, so supervision is required. The short, shiny coat needs little attention. This dog can be slow to house-train, so its owner needs to be diligent and patient. This breed is not keen on going out in the rain.

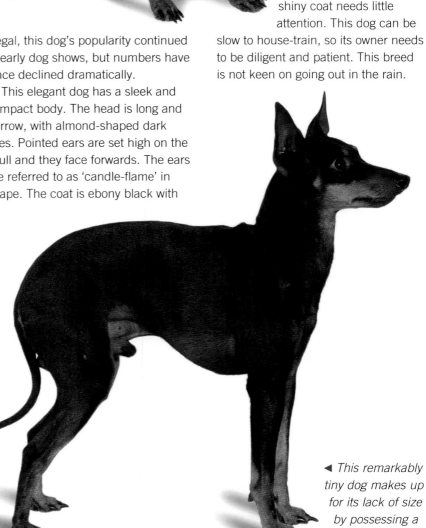

▲ *Don't be deceived – this elegant little dog is a true feisty terrier.*

Breed box
Size: 25–30cm (10–12in),
  2.7–3.6kg (6–8lb)
Grooming: Easy
Feeding: Undemanding
Exercise: Low to medium
Temperament: Intelligent and
  charming

◀ *This remarkably tiny dog makes up for its lack of size by possessing a mighty yap.*

Griffon Bruxellois

Named after the capital of Belgium, the Griffon Bruxellois, or Brussels Griffon, is one of the most delightful characters of the Toy Group. It is truly bright and cheerful. With a monkey-like expression and its usual harsh coat of red, it displays the equivalent of canine cheekiness. As well as the harsh-coated version, there is also a smooth-coated type, and this is an equally pert animal. Both kinds can come in other colours besides red.

It weighs anything from 2.2–4.9kg (5–11lb), but the middle of that range is the most common. It has a bit of the terrier about it, so it thoroughly enjoys exercising with a boisterous family, but it also makes a cheerful and fearless companion for those who live alone. It does not take much grooming, but occasional professional stripping in the rough-coated form is not a bad idea.

◄ *Originally bred as a street ratter, this dog still retains a prey drive. The rough-coated version sports a splendid walrus moustache and beard.*

► *Two of a kind, both harsh in coat, with the less common black colour in front.*

Breed box
Size: 18–20cm (7–8in),
2.2–4.9kg (5–11lb)
Grooming: Medium
Feeding: Undemanding
Exercise: Undemanding
Temperament: Lively and alert

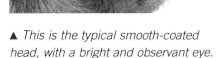

▲ *This is the typical smooth-coated head, with a bright and observant eye.*

◄ *The coat of the rough-coated Griffon Bruxellois is comprised of wiry, harsh hairs that stand away from the body. This breed featured in the 2001 British Academy Award-winning film 'Gosford Park'.*

► *The smooth-coated type has a solid body on neat legs, and is not too difficult to keep clean and tidy. Both types are very affectionate and loving.*

Havanese

The Havanese is a bichon type that is thought to have originated from the Bichon Tenerife. It is the national dog of Cuba, where it is called the Habanero, and it is also known as the Spanish Silk Poodle and the Havana Silk Dog. Very popular in the 1800s among the Cuban aristocracy, it was transported to other countries by sailors. Queen Victoria owned two Havaneses, and Charles Dickens had one that was adored by his children. The breed has changed remarkably little from those seen in paintings from this era.

Breed box

Size: 22–29cm (8½–11½in), 4.5–7.3kg (10–16lb)
Grooming: Intensive
Feeding: Undemanding
Exercise: Low to medium
Temperament: Spirited and curious

▼ *If you choose this breed, you must be prepared to spend some time each day grooming its long coat.*

This solid, sturdy dog has a fine, long and slightly wavy coat that acts as a heat insulator and helps to keep the dog cool. The coat can be any solid colour or combination of colours. The nose and eye rims are black, and eyes dark brown and almond-shaped. The dog is deep-chested and the topline rises from the shoulders to the base of the tail. The Havanese has a very flashy and distinctively springy gait.

▲ *The coat of a Havanese should have a rustic look, and not appear too sleek.*

It is a charming companion dog that is bright and spirited, and easy to train. It is loyal to its owner, but can develop separation anxiety if left on its own for too long. The non-shedding coat requires twice-weekly combing through to prevent tangles and mats. This breed is active and playful, and is very adaptable. It excels at agility, flyball, canine freestyle and obedience. It is used as a therapy and assistance dog, and some have been trained to detect mould and termites.

◄ *The popularity of this small, energetic breed has increased dramatically in recent years.*

Italian Greyhound

This ancient breed has been in existence for at least 2,000 years. Mummified dogs of similar type have been found in Egypt and in the lava flow at Pompeii. The name comes from a surge in this dog's popularity in Italy during the Renaissance period. It is the smallest of the gazehound dogs, and is classified as being in the Toy Group by the UK and US kennel clubs, but in the Sighthound Group by European kennel clubs.

The Italian Greyhound is very fast and agile, and has a high stepping gait when trotting. At the gallop, it is able to move with all four feet off the ground at the same time; this is called 'double suspension'. It is able to reach speeds of 40km/h (25mph), and with

▶ *The Italian Greyhound may be miniature in size, but still shows nicely balanced musculature in the hindquarters.*

its strong prey drive, exercise should be on lead unless in a safe, enclosed area. The very short, smooth coat can come in a range of solid or parti colours. Different kennel clubs accept

◀ *Early puppy socialization is important to avoid nervous, shy or timid adults. Sympathetic training is essential.*

▲ *This breed feels the cold and requires a coat when going outdoors in cold, damp climates.*

different colour combinations, and a potential owner who wishes to compete in breed shows is advised to study which colours are acceptable in their home country.

This is a beautiful companion animal that requires more exercise and entertainment than most of the other breeds in the Toy Group. Its slender build makes it rather fragile, and therefore it is unsuited to rough play with children. It is suitable for either town or country living, but does like to run and is active in the home.

Breed box
Size: 33–38cm (13–15in), 3.6–8.2kg (8–18lb)
Grooming: Easy
Feeding: Undemanding
Exercise: Medium
Temperament: Elegant and sensitive

Japanese Chin

The Japanese Chin, or Japanese Spaniel, is unlikely to have originated from Japan, but from either China or Korea. There is much speculation as to the early ancestors of this breed and how it made its way to Japan. It is known that the Chin was in the country around AD1000. Bred purely as a companion, ownership was restricted to Japanese royalty or high-ranking nobility. In part, this may account for differences in the breed, as each noble house bred these dogs to suit their own requirements. A pair was given to Queen Victoria in 1853, and the AKC recognized the breed in the late 19th century.

It has a large, broad head, wide and slightly protruding eyes, a short, broad muzzle and feathered ears. It has a

▲ *The first Japanese Chins brought to the Western world were smaller than those that we know today.*

bouncy gait and charming expression, and the single coat is white, with patches of either black, red, lemon, orange or sable, or tricolour markings. The coat can take up to two years to

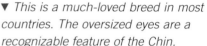

▼ *This is a much-loved breed in most countries. The oversized eyes are a recognizable feature of the Chin.*

grow to completion. This dog is very cat-like, and even uses its paws to clean its face.

This is a happy, lively breed that likes to be the centre of attention. It excels in learning tricks and is extremely devoted to its owner. As with many of the toy breeds, early socialization is needed. Although generally quiet, it will alarm-bark to warn of approaching strangers or unusual events. The Chin does not thrive in extremes of temperature, and is not suitable for outdoor living.

▼ *The Chin is easily mistaken for the better-known Pekingese, but has less prominent eyes which tend to show white in the inner corners.*

Breed box
Size: 18–28cm (7–11in),
   2–7kg (4–15lb)
Grooming: Moderate
Feeding: Undemanding
Exercise: Low to medium
Temperament: Devoted and
   intelligent

King Charles Spaniel

The King Charles Spaniel, also known as the English Toy Spaniel, is similar to the Cavalier King Charles Spaniel, but has a shorter nose and a more domed head. It has a long, silky coat, which comes in the same colour range as the Cavalier – black and tan, ruby, Blenheim and tricolour – and it is equally rewarding to groom.

This breed is more reserved than the Cavalier, but has the same kindly and intelligent disposition. It makes a genuine, devoted companion, and does not need too much exercise or food.

▲ The large, dark eyes and long, well-feathered ears give this breed an appealing look. It is a 'royal' spaniel with a regal appearance.

Breed box
Size: 3.6–6.3kg (8–14lb);
    male 25.5cm (10in);
    female 20.5cm (8in)
Grooming: Medium
Feeding: Medium
Exercise: Undemanding
Temperament: Gentle and
    affectionate

◄ This breed is easily mistaken for the better-known Cavalier King Charles Spaniel, but it has a slightly more snubbed nose. The Cavalier was developed from this breed.

▼ The well-feathered tail is carried low, and adds to the overall appeal of the King Charles Spaniel. Initially bred to hunt, the small size of this dog meant that it was not favoured.

Löwchen

It is unclear how the Löwchen, also known as the Petit Chien Dog or Little Lion Dog, originated. Bichon or Tibetan Terrier may be in its distant ancestry, but this cannot be proven. Dogs of similar shape and size, often with the distinctive lion clip, can be seen in European medieval art, tapestries and literature. Clearly these dogs were bred as companions, and appeared to be owned by the wealthy. By the end of the 19th century, the Löwchen had become extremely rare, and it was almost completely wiped out during the two World Wars. Numbers have steadily increased since then, and they are now recognized by most kennel clubs.

The coat is long, flowing and slightly wavy, and is made up of a mix of thick and fine hair. All colours or combinations are acceptable. Most dogs are presented in a 'lion clip', with the coat shaved over the haunches, back legs and front legs (retaining a bracelet of hair around the ankles), and part of the tail. The rest of the coat remains long, giving the impression of a little lion.

This breed is an excellent companion and family dog. It needs early socialization to prevent nervousness,

▲ The Löwchen needs clipping to maintain the characteristic leonine hind end and the trimmed tail.

as it can be a little timid. It is happy to live in town or country, but is unsuited to kennel living. It does not like being left alone, and needs to be part of the family. The Löwchen is capable of walking long distances, but is equally content with two short daily walks and a garden to play in.

▲ In the 1960s, the 'Guinness Book of Records' listed the Löwchen as the rarest domestic dog breed.

▶ A somewhat grave expression belies the fact that this dog can be a real live wire.

Breed box
Size: Male 30–35.6cm (12–14in), 5.4–8.1kg (12–18lb); female 28–33cm (11–13in), 4.5–6.8kg (10–15lb)
Grooming: Moderate
Feeding: Undemanding
Exercise: Low to medium
Temperament: Active and playful

Maltese

This companion breed has been in existence since Roman times. It was once called the 'Roman Ladies' Dog'. There are several surviving ancient tombs in Greece that were built to house and honour these little dogs. The breed was introduced to the UK in the reign of Henry VIII, and most stock in the USA can trace its British heritage. It nearly died out in the 17th and 18th centuries, when breeders tried to reduce the Maltese to the size of a squirrel. Fortunately,

▶ It is easy to see how this dog can become the star of the breed show ring. The Maltese often sports a 'top-knot', which is a practical way of keeping hair out of its eyes.

Breed box
Size: 18–30cm (7–10in),
    1.4–4.5kg (3–10lb)
Grooming: Extensive
Feeding: Undemanding
Exercise: Moderate
Temperament: Energetic and playful

enough healthy stock was found to build numbers and size back to the dog we know today.

This enchanting, long-coated, pure white dog has a rounded skull with a black nose and dark eyes. The compact body is square in shape, and the face is framed by pendulant ears. A jaunty flowing gait makes the Maltese look as if it is moving through a soft white cloud of hair. A dog in full show coat needs extensive grooming to prevent tangles and knots.

◀ The all-white coat and the round, dark eyes are features that breeders have striven to maintain for many centuries, but they have not made a softie of the dog in the process.

This dog remains active and playful into old age. It is a good watch dog, but may bark excessively if untrained or lacking in socialization. If allowed to be dominant or spoilt, it can become snappy, but as it is easily trained, this trait can be overcome with time.

▲ This is an excellent companion that is equally happy to take part in rally, obedience, agility and tracking.

Miniature Pinscher

The Miniature Pinscher, abbreviated to 'Min Pin', is the smallest version of the pinscher breeds. It stands up to 30cm (12in) high at its withers, and wears a hard, short coat that is easily groomed to shine. It comes in black, blue or chocolate with tan, and also various solid shades of red.

It carries its neat ears either pricked or half-dropped on a stylish head. It is sturdy in body and definite in its way of going, which is like that of a Hackney pony. It gives the impression that it loves being loose in a garden or park; it has quick reactions and makes a useful household watch dog.

▶ The large, erect ears are very striking in this red-coloured Miniature Pinscher which carries its tail at a jaunty angle.

◀ The black and tan coat is the one most often seen in this toy breed.

Breed box
Size: 25.5–30cm (10–12in), 3.5kg (7½lb)
Grooming: Easy
Feeding: Undemanding
Exercise: Medium
Temperament: Alert and courageous

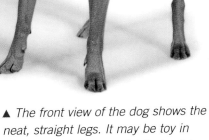

▲ The front view of the dog shows the neat, straight legs. It may be toy in stature, but it is very athletic in style.

◀ This ancient breed can trace its origins back to the 17th century.

Papillon

The Papillon, or Butterfly Dog, is a very attractive animal. It stands up to 28cm (11in) tall on neat, trim legs, and underneath its easily brushed long, silky coat it has a surprisingly strong body and fleet feet.

▲ *The tall, fringed ears represent the butterfly's wings. Puppies are born with folded ears, but these are normally erect by 8–12 weeks of age. Teething can affect ear carriage.*

The coat is a basic white with patches of a variety of colours, except liver. The traditional markings on its head and large, erect ears, with a neat white stripe down the centre of its skull and on to its nose, produce a combined effect resembling the body and open wings of a butterfly, which is how it was given its name.

It can be trained to a high level of obedience and delights in exercise with the members of its household, but is not suited to live with very young children in case it gets trodden on.

▶ *The whole dog is neatly covered with long, silky hair, but beneath all the glamour is a highly intelligent and trainable animal.*

Breed box
Size: 20–28cm (8–11in),
2–2.5kg (4½–5½lb)
Grooming: Medium
Feeding: Undemanding
Exercise: Medium
Temperament: Lively and very intelligent

▲ *The white line down the forehead is said to represent the body of a butterfly, from which the Papillon derives its name.*

Pekingese

The Pekingese has its roots in ancient China. Tradition tells us that it derives from the palaces of the Tang Dynasty, and this seems to be firmly engrained in its character, although it does show glimpses of a humorous nature on occasion. With a huge personality inside a relatively small body, it is a dog for the devotee.

It has an ideal weight of around 5kg (11lb), with the bitches tending to be heavier than the dogs. Inside an apparently small framework are heavily boned legs. The dog has a broad head and a very short muzzle, which can lead to severe breathing problems; careful selection is necessary to breed healthy 'Pekes', and there are no shortcuts to getting this right.

Exercise is a matter over which a Peke is not ecstatic. It tends to move with a dignified and leisurely roll;

consequently, country walks are not a good idea. The coat, which can be of virtually any hue except albino and liver, is long and profuse. It needs regular and dedicated attention to achieve a creditable result.

▶ *Modern Pekes have very pretty heads, and this photograph shows the true beauty of the Peke's expression with its lustrous, soft eyes.*

▼ *Pekingese dogs were at one time carried by ladies of the Chinese court, and were referred to as 'sleeve dogs'. Modern Pekes seem to be aware of their illustrious heritage!*

▲ *Many Pekes have huge coats, but no matter what the dog looks like, it is essential that it can walk freely.*

Breed box
Size: 18cm (7in); male
maximum 5kg (11lb);
female maximum 5.5kg (12lb)
Grooming: Demanding
Feeding: Demanding
Exercise: Undemanding
Temperament: Loyal and aloof

Pomeranian

The Pomeranian, or Zwergspitz, is the smallest of all the spitz-type dogs. It weighs up to a mere 2kg (4½lb), with the bitches being slightly heavier. Its abundant stand-off coat is normally a whole colour such as orange, black or cream, through to white. Regular grooming is necessary to achieve the overall look of a ball of fluff.

The margin between the sturdiness, which even this tiny breed should possess, and a shell-like delicateness is a fine one, and some breeders find this difficult to achieve. A 'Pom' exhibits a tremendous amount of energy, pirouetting gaily on the end of its lead. It is capable of producing a barrage of fairly shrill yapping, which may deter burglars – and interrupt conversation and gain attention!

▲ The Pomeranian can charm the hardest heart. This tiny character has all the courage of a lion in its eyes.

▼ This family trio is in the best of coats – but do not buy a Pom until you have tried grooming one yourself.

▲ A Pomeranian should have an expression of intelligence and complete confidence in its eyes.

Breed box
Size: 22–28cm (8½–11in),
   1.8–2kg (4–4½lb)
Grooming: Demanding
Feeding: Undemanding
Exercise: Undemanding
Temperament: Intelligent and
   extroverted

305

Pug

The Pug is a robust aimal weighing up to 8kg (17½lb) and packed tightly into a sturdy, compact frame. It wears a short and smoothly glossy coat, which most commonly comes in fawn, but can also appear in apricot, silver or black. It traditionally has a black mask. It is easily kept tidy.

The dog carries its tail tightly curled into a roll on the top of its back, and when it is in its most perky state of alertness, it gives the impression that

◄ An ancient breed of miniaturized mastiffs, Pugs were once the companions of Buddhist monks. They arrived in Europe with the Dutch East India Company, and became favoured dogs of the House of Orange.

Breed box
Size: 25–28cm (10–11in), 6.3–8kg (14–17½lb)
Grooming: Undemanding
Feeding: Medium
Exercise: Medium
Temperament: Lively and cheerful

it is leaning forward towards whatever its large, lustrous eyes are gazing at.

It is a dog who tends to make people smile when they see it, because it is so convinced of its own importance. For such a stocky dog it can move fast. Its slightly short nose sometimes causes it problems in hot weather as it restricts its breathing, but breeders tend to select for the wide nostrils, which will enable it to exercise as freely as it wishes.

▲ The stern expression of the Pug belies its real sense of fun.

► The tightly curled tail balances the snub nose exactly, to produce a very tidy little dog.

▲ The Pug is adaptable, sociable and good-natured, and makes a good family dog. It is a real charmer.

Toy Fox Terrier

The Toy Fox Terrier is both toy and terrier, and still retains a strong working instinct. This American breed, also known as the American Toy Terrier or Amertoy, was created in the 1930s and is directly descended from the Smooth Fox Terrier. Crosses with other small breeds, including Manchester Terriers, Italian Greyhounds, Miniature Pinschers and Chihuahuas, were introduced in order to decrease its size. It will hunt and chase rodents, squirrels and rabbits, but is equally happy to sleep on the sofa next to its owner.

The coat is very short, smooth, and predominately white with black, tan, chocolate or tricolour markings. Colours acceptable for the breed ring vary between kennel clubs. Potential owners who wish to show their dog should study the breed standard before choosing a puppy. Ears are erect and V-shaped,

◄ Without the correct training, the Toy Fox Terrier can be dominant, wilful and feisty.

▲ *Like all terriers, this breed is a digger and an escapologist, so it requires a well-fenced garden.*

▼ *Make no mistake – these cute little dogs are all terrier, with a high chase and prey drive, and all the other terrier characteristics.*

and eyes large and dark. This is a very striking and graceful dog that is both athletic and agile.

The Toy Fox Terrier is highly intelligent and very trainable, excelling at obedience, flyball and agility. It is a very loyal and loving breed, and a good companion. Although small, it is an active dog that requires daily walking and enjoys playing with toys. As its coat is less than 1cm (½in) long, it feels the cold and will need a coat or jumper when the temperature drops. As with all terriers, care should be taken to socialize and train correctly. This breed sometimes forgets its small size, and will challenge larger dogs.

Breed box
Size: 21.5–29.2cm (8½–11½in), 1.5–4.2kg (3.3–9lb)
Grooming: Easy
Feeding: Undemanding
Exercise: Moderate
Temperament: Loyal and athletic

Volpino Italiano

The Volpino Italiano, also known as the Italian Spitz, Florentine Spitz and Cane de Quirinale, is rare outside its home country of Italy, but it is gaining in popularity in both the UK and USA. Although similar in looks to a Pomeranian, it is a much older breed. It was originally used as a guard to alert a large Mastiff to the presence of an intruder. It subsequently became popular as a pet, and was often pictured wearing ivory collars and bracelets. It is said that Michelangelo

▶ *They may be small, but these dogs are true all-rounders, excelling in many canine sports.*

once owned a Volpino. The breed had almost died out in 1965 with only five dogs registered, so a recovery project was launched to save this historic Italian breed.

The spitz-like, long, dense coat is solid white, red or champagne, and stands away from the body. The head

◀ *'Volpe' is the Italian word for 'fox', and this breed is required to have a characteristic fox-like expression.*

is wedge-shaped with a pointed muzzle, giving the dog a 'foxy' look. The small triangular ears are erect. The tail is carried over a square, compact but agile body. The Volpino Italiano is similar in size and shape to the Pomeranian. It is very active and moves with a flowing gait.

Very loyal to its owner, this little dog makes a good family companion. As with all dogs, socialization is required because the breed can be wary of strangers. It is active and playful, and happy to join in with most activities. Excelling in obedience and agility, the Volpino can also be trained as a gundog. This affectionate breed is generally robust and long-lived, often reaching the age of 14–16 years.

◀ *The large, dark, round eyes, black nose, lips and eye rims stand out against the white coat of this toy dog.*

Breed box
Size: 25.4–33cm (10–13in), 4–5.5kg (9–12lb)
Grooming: Moderate
Feeding: Undemanding
Exercise: Medium
Temperament: Lively and loving

Yorkshire Terrier

The Yorkshire Terrier is a breed of two distinct types. The tiny version, seen immaculately groomed in the show ring, weighs up to 3.1kg (7lb), while the jaunty dog seen on a lead in the street or racing joyfully around the park is the same dog but often twice the size. The fact is that the long steel-blue and bright tan hair that bedecks the glamour star of the shows would break off and become short if the dog were to run loose. But the spirit of the true 'Yorkie' is the same inside, whatever the outward appearance.

▼ *This Yorkie has been groomed to perfection, as befits a top show dog.*

Grooming the household companion – a dog that is immensely popular throughout the world – is easily accomplished with ordinary brushing skills. As a home-loving animal, the Yorkie is tough, ready to play with children, or able to dispatch any rat unwise enough to invade its owner's dwelling.

Breed box
Size: Maximum 3.1kg (7lb);
 male 20.5cm (8in);
 female 18cm (7in)
Grooming: Demanding
Feeding: Undemanding
Exercise: Medium
Temperament: Alert and intelligent

▲ *Companion Yorkies wear their coats shorter than these show dogs, and do not require the same amount of artistry.*

◄ *This elegant display shows canine grooming at its most spectacular. Pet dogs are usually clipped to make coat care easier. This stops the hair falling into the dog's eyes and getting covered with food when eating. A dog coat may be required in cold weather.*

UNRECOGNIZED BREEDS AND HYBRIDS

The dogs featured in this section fall into three categories. Some, such as the Australian Kelpie and Patterdale Terrier, are breeds in their own right, producing offspring that are similar to the sire and dam. They were bred to do a job of work, and many breeders feel working ability is of prior importance and may be compromised by standardization. Often breed registers exist, but registrations are only available if the dog can pass an appropriate working test. Others dogs, including the Lurcher and Working Sheepdog, are a type. Body shape and working characteristics may have similarities, but size, weight and coats differ. Hybrids or first crosses form the third group, and these are often referred to as 'designer dogs'. They are not a breed, but rather a popular cross, with no certainty as to the look, size or temperament.

◄ *Jack Russell Terriers have many variants, including coat, size, conformation and ear carriage. Despite this, they are recognized worldwide and are often the first to come to mind when the word 'terrier' is mentioned.*

Australian Kelpie

▼ Some people believe that the Kelpie is a Dingo cross, but this assertion lacks any supporting data.

The Australian Kelpie is a herding dog that can control large numbers of animals and work for hours in intense heat. Brave and with amazing energy, it will jump up and run across the backs of a flock of sheep if that is the most efficient way of getting to where it wants to be.

The Kelpie is thought to have originated from the old form of British collie working dog, and may have some Dingo in its distant ancestry. Most kennel clubs do not recognize it as a breed, but the Australian and Canadian Kennel Clubs are the exception to this rule. There is a huge diversity in this animal. Show Kelpies look different from Working Kelpies, and coats and colours vary greatly between the two types.

▼ In many different countries around the world, the Australian Kelpie is variously employed to herd sheep, goats, cattle, chickens and even reindeer. It is a breed that lives to work.

The Working Kelpie has three coat types – smooth, rough and short – which can come in a wide range of colours. The Show Kelpie has a short, dense double coat that must be black, black and tan, red, red and tan, fawn, chocolate or smoke blue. This is a medium-sized dog that has a long tail that hangs down when at rest, but is raised when moving. Ears should be erect and set wide apart on the head.

▲ This is a breed that forms a strong bond with its owner, seconded only by its enthusiastic love of work.

This dog is almost inexhaustible – it is extremely agile, very intelligent, and has very high exercise requirements. A bored Kelpie can develop obsessive and destructive behaviour. It is a strong-willed and challenging animal to own, but can make a good companion if properly trained. It is not recommended for a first-time dog owner.

Breed box
Size: 39–51cm (15–20in),
 14–20kg (31–44lb)
Grooming: Easy
Feeding: Medium
Exercise: Very high
Temperament: Smart and energetic

Cavachon

The Cavachon is a hybrid, or first cross, between a Cavalier King Charles Spaniel and a Bichon Frise. This type is not a breed or a purebred dog, and if you are considering acquiring this type it is important to ensure that both parents are pedigree dogs, since this is often not the case. The introduction of 'designer dogs' has been an opportunity

▶ *The Cavachon will not come with any registration papers, since it is not a pedigree dog breed.*

for less than honest people to breed two dogs together and name the offspring whatever they like, often with no relevance to their parentage.

Provided the sire and dam are as stated, the resulting Cavachon is a small dog with a soft and slightly wavy, silky coat. Coat colours vary, but include solid white, or white with black or apricot markings, as well as white, black and tan. Often incorrectly sold as non-shedding, the Cavachon will moult, but not as much as some other dogs. The coat will require trimming regularly, and the cost of professional grooming should be factored into your budget.

This type of dog is active and requires moderate daily exercise. It enjoys playing and learning tricks, but like many small dogs, it can be slow

▲ *The Cavachon hybrid is believed to have been first produced in the United States in the mid-1990s.*

▶ *A Cavachon can have a curly coat like a Bichon, or a flatter coat similar to a Cavalier. It is impossible to tell which kind you will get when they are small puppies.*

to house-train. It is generally good with children, dogs and other domestic pets, and can adapt to apartment living. The Cavachon makes an affectionate family companion but requires early socialization and training, as with any dog. Potential owners should be aware that a Cavachon may possess the best traits of a Cavalier King Charles Spaniel and Bichon Frise, but it is equally likely that it will inherit the worst.

Breed box
Size: 30–35.5cm (12–14in),
　4.5–9kg (10–20lb)
Grooming: Moderate
Feeding: Undemanding
Exercise: Medium
Temperament: Affectionate
　and playful

Cockapoo

The Cockapoo is a cross between a Poodle and either an American Cocker Spaniel or an English Cocker Spaniel. In many cases, but not all, the Toy Poodle or Miniature Poodle is used. There can be a great variation in the size of this type of dog, which depends on the size of the Poodle parent. The Cockapoo is not a breed, but a hybrid or first cross, and as such is not recognized by any kennel club. Unfortunately, this dog is often bred by puppy farmers or backstreet breeders looking to make a fast profit. Potential owners should ensure that puppies are healthy, parentage is as stated, and that the breeders are

▼ Not all Cockapoos have curly coats; some are straight-haired, but all will require trimming every 6–8 weeks.

Breed box
Size: 25–43cm (10–17in),
5.5–15kg (12–34lb)
Grooming: Medium
Feeding: Moderate
Exercise: Medium
Temperament: Outgoing and friendly

genuine and caring people. Cockapoo Clubs will be able to advise on the whereabouts of reputable breeders.

As with any first cross, this dog may take characteristics from either parent. Generally, Poodle crosses require regular trimming and will shed less than some dogs, but it is incorrect to say that they are non-shedding. The coat can be solid, patched, spotted, merle, brindle or ticked, and comes in a wide range of colours.

▲ In Australia, this hybrid cross is known as a Cockerdoodle or Spoodle.

► This is a hybrid that is trainable, very agile and often enjoys swimming.

Weights and heights listed in the breed box are a rough guide only.

This is a moderately active and agile dog that requires regular exercise. It is loving and happy to join in with family activities, and it is good with children, other dogs and domestic pets, providing they have been brought up with them. The Cockapoo dislikes being left alone for long periods, and may suffer from separation anxiety.

Goldendoodle

This hybrid was obtained by crossing a Golden Retriever with a Poodle. As a mixed-breed or 'designer dog', the Goldendoodle is not a breed and is not recognized by any kennel club. It was originally bred in an attempt to create a dog that was suitable to use as a guide dog for visually impaired people with allergies. It was hoped that this cross would produce litters of puppies that were low-shedding.

As with all crosses, the resulting puppies may take after either parent, therefore coat type varies. Some Goldendoodles have a low-shedding Poodle-type coat, while others have a shedding coat that is closer to that of a Golden Retriever. Coats can be straight and flat, wavy or curly, all of which have different grooming requirements. Size is variable, depending on whether the Poodle was a Standard, Toy or Miniature.

The Goldendoodle is generally good with children and other dogs, and is affectionate, sociable and playful. This cross rarely has any guarding or watch-dog instinct. It makes a nice family companion, but does have a high exercise requirement. It is an intelligent dog that forms a strong bond with its family, and those that inherit Golden Retriever characteristics will work well to the gun. Potential

▲ *Note the diversity between this dog and the standing dog featured below. Both are first crosses between a Golden Retriever and a Poodle.*

puppy purchasers should view both parents so that they can assess the possible size their dog will be when it reaches adulthood. Since 2005, mainly in Australia and the USA, this animal has been used as search and rescue, guide and therapy dogs.

▼ *Smart and trainable, this is a cross breed that likes to retrieve.*

▼ *The Goldendoodle is a relatively long-lived hybrid, but unfortunately it can suffer from hip dysplasia.*

Breed box
Size: Variable
Grooming: Variable
Feeding: Variable
Exercise: Medium to high
Temperament: Social and trainable

Golden Labrador

The Golden Labrador is one of the few hybrids that is predictable in size, since both parents are large dogs. The name can be confusing, as it may seem to refer to a golden or 'yellow'-coloured Labrador Retriever, when in fact this is a first cross between a Golden Retriever and a Labrador Retriever. For this reason, it is sometimes referred to as a 'Goldador'. The two breeds were crossed to produce a working dog that had the Labrador tolerance and the sensitivity of a Retriever. It is not a breed and is not recognized by any kennel club.

The coat is similar to the double coat of a Labrador Retriever, and is generally yellow through to reddish-gold in colour. Occasionally, black puppies are born that have inherited the black gene from a Labrador parent. The Goldador is used with success as an assistance dog for the visually impaired and for people with autism. It is also trained as a detection dog, a therapy dog and is used for search and rescue.

▲ *Double-coated, the Goldador will shed hair and requires weekly brushing to keep in trim.*

This dog is good with children, but due to its size and enthusiasm for life, it may not be the best choice around toddlers. It does make an excellent companion, providing it gets enough exercise. Insufficient activity combined with its love of food can lead to an overweight animal. Early socialization with other dogs is recommended if the Goldador is the only dog in the household. It will adapt to town or country living, and can be trained to take part in a variety of canine sports.

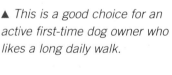

▲ *This is a good choice for an active first-time dog owner who likes a long daily walk.*

◄ *Inspect and clean the ears regularly, as the Golden Labrador is prone to ear infections.*

Breed box
Size: 56–61cm (22–24in), 27–36kg (60–80lb)
Grooming: Easy
Feeding: Moderate to high
Exercise: High
Temperament: Tolerant and sensitive

Huntaway

The Huntaway, or New Zealand Sheepdog, is a herding dog that drives sheep away from the shepherd. Unusually, it barks at the sheep to move them. The animal was developed to provide farmers with a strong dog that was capable of controlling large numbers of sheep and could work for days on end. It was recognized as a breed by the New Zealand Kennel

▼ A Huntaway may attempt to herd cats, other domestic animals and children.

Club in 2013, but the breed standard states that, "A Huntaway should never be shown, due to variance in colour, type and size and the inability to prove in the show ring their core (and only) task of working stock." This dog is not recognized by any other kennel club.

The coat can be smooth, rough or wiry, and is black, black and tan, white or brindle. Feet are sometimes webbed. The Huntaway is a large, deep-chested dog with enormous stamina. Statistics shown in the panel on this page are a generalization only, as the animal varies greatly in both height and weight.

This is a very intelligent and friendly dog with a strong working ethic. It is very energetic and is only suitable for an active owner. Its natural instinct is to bark, and this can cause problems, but it is possible to train a Huntaway to be quiet. This animal is not a good guard or watch dog, but it uses its voice only when working or excited. Primarily a one-person dog, this variety is gaining in popularity as a working dog in Australia and Japan.

▲ The average litter size of this gentle, loyal workaholic is usually between 4–7 puppies.

◀ This is a strongly built breed with drop ears and a long tail. Height can vary considerably, because working ability is favoured above conformity.

Breed box
Size: 56–66cm (22–26in), 25–40kg (55–88lb)
Grooming: Easy
Feeding: Medium to high
Exercise: High
Temperament: Intelligent and energetic

Jack Russell Terrier

Often confused with the Parson Russell Terrier, the Jack Russell Terrier originates from dogs bred by Reverend John Russell in the early 19th century. This small terrier is thought to trace its origins to the now-extinct English White Terrier. Bred to bolt foxes from holes, it is a feisty and diligent hunter. It is not generally recognized as a breed by most kennel clubs, as breeders and breed clubs consider their working ability more important than a standardized size and conformation.

This dog is generally white with patches of black, tan or black and tan. Brindle and black and tan colouring does occur, however this is rare. The coat can be rough or smooth. Almond-shaped eyes are dark, and the nose leather should be black. Ears are small and fold forwards close to the head. Both height and weight can vary.

This is an energetic, compact and muscular dog with a very high prey drive. It will chase rodents, cats and other small domestic or wild animals. This loving and intelligent dog is strong-willed and needs an experienced owner. It can be aggressive with other dogs, so early socialization is vital. Some are very good with children but others will snap if they feel that their space is invaded. A well-fenced garden is essential, as this little dog is capable of

jumping over 1.5m (5ft) high and is an industrious digger. It can be a persistent barker if bored. With the right owner and sufficient exercise, it is highly trainable and excels in canine sports such as flyball and agility.

◀ *Quick, sharp and with a strong prey drive, the Jack Russell Terrier is no lap dog.*

▼ *This bright-eyed dog has a wiry, rough or 'broken' coat.*

◀ *This group of Jack Russells display a range of ear carriages, coat types and colours.*

Breed box
Size: 25–38cm (10–15in), 5.5–9kg (13–18lb)
Grooming: Easy
Feeding: Undemanding
Exercise: High
Temperament: Feisty and fearless

Labradoodle

The best-known of the 'designer dogs', this hybrid is a first cross between a Labrador Retriever and a Poodle. It is not a breed, and is not recognized by any kennel club. The Labradoodle shot to fame after Australian breeder Wally Conron bred a litter for use by the Royal Guide Dog Association of Australia. He hoped to produce an assistance dog that was hypoallergenic. In fact, no dog is truly hypoallergenic, although some are low-shedding and produce less dander. Not all Labradoodles fall into this category. They are no longer used by the above association, but other groups use them as assistance, guide and therapy dogs.

Because this is a hybrid, puppies are not consistent in type or character. Coats vary and might be straight, wavy or curly, and the hair can be soft or wiry. Colours include chocolate, cream, gold, black and parti. Height

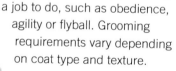

▶ *This hybrid has a high exercise requirement and needs an active owner who has plenty of time for long walks.*

is dependent on the size of the Poodle used in the cross. Potential puppy purchasers should always request to see both parents and be aware that there is no consistency in type either in first-cross Labrador Retriever to Poodle or Labradoodle bred to Labradoodle.

◀ *The Labradoodle will require trimming every 6–8 weeks. It tends to be styled with a lamb clip rather than the more elaborate cuts seen on pedigree Poodles.*

▶ *Ensure that you know the size of the Poodle used in the cross, as this will greatly affect the size of the adult hybrid. This picture illustrates the size difference in a Labradoodle dependent on the type of Poodle used in the cross.*

This dog is generally energetic and playful, and is good with children. It is intelligent and should be non-aggressive. As with all dogs, socialization and training are required to ensure a stable animal. The Labradoodle needs both physical and mental exercise and enjoys having a job to do, such as obedience, agility or flyball. Grooming requirements vary depending on coat type and texture.

Breed box
Size: Variable
Grooming: Variable
Feeding: Variable
Exercise: High
Temperament: Intelligent and
playful

Lurcher

▼ *Lurchers will work as a pack when hunting and chasing their prey.*

A Lurcher is a type of dog rather than a breed, and so is not recognized by any kennel club. It is a cross between a sighthound and either a herding or terrier breed. This hybrid dates back to the 17th century, and was bred by British and Irish travellers to produce a fast dog that hunted by sight. During this period sighthounds were only allowed to be owned by the nobility, whereas a cross breed was considered to have no worth and could be owned by commoners. The Lurcher was used to hunt hares and rabbits both for sport and the cooking pot.

Size and coat type varies depending on parentage. If you are considering buying a Lurcher puppy, you should view both parents to gain an idea of the size of the dog once it reaches adulthood. Any colour and texture of hair is possible. Most Lurchers have a tucked-up loin similar to that of a Greyhound or Whippet.

The Lurcher forms a strong bond with its family and is gentle and affectionate with children. This dog makes a loyal, loving companion, and is trainable if it can see some point in the required task. It is not to be trusted with cats and other domestic pets – a strong prey drive means it will take off after anything that it considers worth hunting. For this reason, exercise should be in a safe, enclosed area or on the lead. Providing it is well exercised, this dog is quiet and calm within the home.

Breed box
Size: Dependent on cross
Grooming: Easy
Feeding: Moderate
Exercise: High
Temperament: Affectionate and loyal

▼ *The name 'Lurcher' comes from a Romany word meaning 'to rob or plunder'. These are very fast dogs.*

▼ *This rough-coated dog has both Whippet and Bedlington Terrier in its parentage, so it is medium-sized.*

Patterdale Terrier

This terrier comes from the Lake District in northern England, and is also known as the Black Fell Terrier. Used to flush out foxes from their lairs, it differs from the Jack Russell Terrier in in its working method.

▲ *The ear leathers of this dog lift away from the head and fold forward, protecting the ear canal.*

Since its native environment is rocky, it is unable to dig out its quarry, but it has the ability to squeeze through crevices between rocks. It is recognized by the United Kennel Club in America and the American Rare Breed Association, but not by the majority of kennel clubs, including that of its home country.

This dog is bred for its working ability, but is fairly standard in type. The double coat is dense, harsh and waterproof, and can be either smooth, broken or rough. Colours include solid black, red, chocolate, liver and bronze. Some dogs have tan markings. A small amount of white on the chin, chest and feet is acceptable. The body is compact and must be balanced and flexible. The head is wedge-shaped and set on a strong neck.

▼ *The Patterdale has the ability to lie flat with the front legs stretched forward and back legs trailing behind.*

▲ *This dog will dig its way out of the garden if it is bored. Provide your Patterdale with plenty of toys.*

This confident and bold dog requires early socialization to prevent any dog-to-dog aggression. Providing it has enough exercise and is properly trained, it is good with children and makes an excellent family companion. A lack of exercise can lead to behavioural problems such as aggression, destructive activities and barking. The Patterdale is energetic and has a high prey drive, and is better suited to an owner with prior terrier experience. This robust dog likes to work, and enjoys taking part in obedience, flyball and agility.

Breed box
Size: 25.5–38cm (10–15in),
  7–13kg (15–30lb)
Grooming: Easy
Feeding: Undemanding
Exercise: High
Temperament: Bold and
  independent

Sprocker

Unlike most other hybrids, the Sprocker has been bred for over a hundred years, so it is not a modern-day 'designer dog'. Game keepers crossed the Cocker Spaniel with a Springer Spaniel to produce a working dog that would spring and flush game over varied terrain. The initial Sprockers are thought to have been bred on large Scottish estates. As with all first crosses, size and weight is not consistent, and the figures given in the panel are for guidance only.

Still retaining the Spaniel look and characteristics, the Sprocker is an elegant and intelligent dog. The coat

Breed box
Size: 35.5–51kg (14–20in),
14–20kg (31–44lb)
Grooming: Medium
Feeding: Moderate
Exercise: High
Temperament: Active and loyal

◄ Although not recognized by any kennel club, this dog is clearly a spaniel type. It excels on the hunting field and has a very loyal following.

◄ The Sprocker is known for its proud and sometimes arrogant expression. On rare occasions, an American Cocker is used in the cross instead of an English Cocker.

◄ The most popular Sprockers are those that have a Cocker as the sire and a Springer as the dam.

comes in a range of colours, and can be solid, roan, tricolour or with splashes of white. Males are generally taller and heavier than females. The Sprocker is widely used by the emergency services and as a detection dog.

This is an alert and intelligent dog that thrives in a family environment. It is good with children and loyal to its owner. Most will accept other dogs and domestic pets, especially if they have been brought up with them. This is an adaptable hybrid that is suitable for town or country living, but does need a lot of exercise. It is a high-energy dog that is ideal for active families, joggers and hikers, as well as hunters. Many Sprockers love water and enjoy romping in mud, so this might not be the best dog for a house-proud owner. Grooming requirements are similar to those of the Cocker Spaniel and Springer Spaniel.

Welsh Sheepdog and Working Sheepdog

There is a reluctance to standardize the confirmation and markings of British sheepdogs, to the possible detriment of their working ability. This is so in the case in the Welsh Sheepdog, also known as the Welsh Collie. This dog differs from the Border Collie in that it has a broader muzzle and chest, and is longer in the leg. It does not work by 'eye', but is mainly used as a droving dog. It is capable of working independently and can control a variety of stock, including pigs and horses. A concentrated effort is being made to maintain the Welsh Sheepdog as a distinct type.

The term 'Working Sheepdog' is used to describe any collie type of unknown or unregistered parentage,

► *The colours of the Welsh Sheepdog are similar to those seen in the Border Collie. This example is a red-and-white-coated dog.*

Breed box
Size: 46–60cm (18–24in), 16–24kg (35–53lb)
Grooming: Variable
Feeding: Medium
Exercise: High
Temperament: Intelligent and active

and is a descriptive term for farm dogs that herd stock and appear to come from Border Collie stock. It is also the terminology used by the Kennel Club when a Border Collie type that is not registered is placed on the Activity Register, enabling it to take part in licensed Kennel Club events such as obedience and agility.

Both the Welsh Sheepdog and the Working Sheepdog can have long or short double coats which are often black and white, red and white, merle or tricolour. These types retain the intelligence and energy of the Border Collie. Mental and physical exercise is essential, and a lack of either can lead to behavioural problems. These animals may try to herd anything that moves, including people and cars. They are generally accepting of children, dogs and domestic pets.

▼ *Working Sheepdogs are very intelligent and will problem-solve.*

► *Literally tens of thousands of Working Sheepdogs are used for herding stock on a daily basis.*

Wolf crosses

Wolf crosses, or 'Wolfdogs', are not a breed, but a hybrid formed by crossing a Wolf with a domestic dog. Many organizations, including the RSPCA, Dogs Trust and The Humane Society of the United States, condemn this practice and support a ban on owning, selling and breeding Wolf crosses. There are two exceptions to this, namely the Czechoslovakian Wolfdog and the Saarloos Wolfdog; these are now low in wolf content, and both are recognized by the FCI as breeds.

The Wolf is classified as a wild animal and is subject to legislation and licensing. The same rules tend to apply to first- and second-cross Wolfdogs. If considering one of these animals, potential owners should be aware of and abide by the laws in their country of residence concerning Wolf cross ownership. Many unscrupulous breeders advertise Wolfdogs for sale and command high prices, when their puppies are in fact crosses between a domestic dog and a Nordic breed. Not only is this fraud, but it also makes Wolfdogs appear easier to manage and train than they actually are.

A Wolf cross is not recommended for anyone but the most highly experienced dog owner, and it should never be trusted around children. Puppies will act in a dog-like manner until they are about 18 months old, and then Wolf characteristics and behaviour will become apparent. They will howl loudly, and need a minimum of an hour of fast exercise every day. Gardens must have high fences and be very secure. If this animal escapes, it will travel rapidly for great distances.

▲ *Wolves are not domesticated, but cunning and extremely intelligent. They are not submissive to humans, and it is usually illegal to own one.*

▼ *The Czechoslovakian Wolfdog originated from experimental crosses between the German Shepherd Dog and Carpathian Wolves.*

◄ *The Saarloos Wolfdog or Wolfhound contains some Grey Wolf DNA that has been greatly diluted by a mix of dog breeds, including the German Shepherd Dog.*

Breed box
Size: Variable
Grooming: Moderate
Feeding: High
Exercise: Very high
Temperament: Unstable and timid

Yorkie-chon

The Yorkie-chon is a first cross between a Yorkshire Terrier and a Bichon Frise, and is not a breed. It is listed under various other names, including Yorkie Bijon, Borkie and Yo-chon. It is often sold as a non-shedding dog, however this is untrue. All dogs shed, some more than others, and this cross may or may not be low-shedding. As with all cross breeds, it is advisable to see both

▼ *The Yorkie-chon is not recognized by any kennel club, and will therefore not come with registration papers.*

▲ *In theory, this feisty and playful hybrid should possess a blunt muzzle, dark eyes and a domed skull.*

parents to ensure that you are know what you are getting. 'Designer dogs' are a quick way for backstreet breeders to make money, and puppies can be described as any mix because no recognized registrations can be given to the new owners.

Coats may be long and wavy, or long and woolly. Colours include solid white, solid black, white with coloured patches, gold or fawn with dark or black markings and tricolour. The

Breed box
Size: 23–28cm (9–11in),
4.5–7kg (9–15lb)
Grooming: High
Feeding: Undemanding
Exercise: Medium
Temperament: Variable

coat will need regular grooming and trimming, as it will mat if left unattended. The services of a professional dog groomer may be required. Size and weight varies, even in the same litter of puppies.

Temperament depends on which parent the puppy takes after – the Yorkshire Terrier is feisty with a high prey drive, while the Bichon is a merry and playful animal. The Yorkie-chon is a small dog that makes a good watch dog, but it may bark persistently for attention if it gets bored. It is good with children if brought up with them. Most are easy to obedience-train, but can be slow to master toilet training. The Yorkie-chon will benefit from early and ongoing socialization.

▶ *Littermates – but what a difference! The puppy on the left closely favours the Bichon, while the right-hand puppy has a terrier head.*

TRAINING YOUR DOG

Every dog is capable of learning a great deal more than is generally recognized. Although it may take a special type of dog and a special type of owner to create a canine film star, home helper or agility champion, there is no reason why every dog should not achieve the essential basics of obedience and well-socialized behaviour. A well-trained dog is less likely to develop unwanted behaviour patterns, partly because dogs often adopt bad habits when they are bored. Dogs enjoy the stimulation of training, and most love to please their owners too. Trained dogs are able to become full members of the family and take part in many aspects of home life. They don't have to be shut away when strangers call or stay at home because they are too much trouble to walk. Training makes life equally better for dog and owner alike, and could be the start of a new and rewarding hobby.

◄ *Spending time training your dog will reap its own rewards. This Border Collie is waiting quietly for the next command from its owner, relaxed and eager to please. A trained dog is a joy to behold.*

The importance of training

Puppies learn from the day they are born. Long before they arrive at their new home, they will have learned a great many valuable lessons from their mother, siblings and the breeder. Such lessons include how to get food, play, bark and fight, as well as learning to cope with frustration when the mother stops feeding them and repeatedly walks away. What the puppies learn at this crucial time will help dictate their character, and whether they'll be confident with people and other dogs.

Another crucial aspect of early learning is a puppy's environment. If it is to be sociable and good with

people, it needs to be raised from the earliest days among people. Regular contact is vital, enabling it to experience the sights and sounds of a busy household. If the puppy is kept isolated in a barn, where it rarely sees its carers, it will find it relatively difficult at a later stage to adapt to life in a house, and it may be aggressive towards people. The quicker it gets used to people, the better.

The environment in which you live can also have a major effect. If you live in the countryside, it is possible that a dog will be less sociable than its urban counterpart, simply because there are fewer opportunities for socializing with other dogs and people. In contrast, the town dog will probably spend a lot of time in busy parks and walking the pavements to get to the parks, where it is impossible to ignore the scores of dog walkers. The young puppy quickly gets used to a wide range of dog behaviour, from aggression to a friendly hello.

▲ *Dogs need to spend time off lead, getting plenty of fresh air and exercise.*

THE IMPORTANCE OF TRAINING

In addition to these general influences, it is up to you to provide a specific training programme, the first two elements of which involve the food bowl and lead. If you can teach your puppy to wait nicely when you're preparing its dinner, rather than rushing around in a highly excitable frenzy, life will be much easier, as it will be if it it can sit calmly while

▼ *Mutual understanding goes a long way toward successful training.*

◄ *No breed is too small to learn. The same basic training principles apply to dogs in all their shapes and sizes.*

you put on its lead. Both lessons will also teach your dog that it will get what it wants when it behaves well rather than badly.

It is your job to teach your dog in the simplest way possible. Training is a two-way event: you need to understand your dog and it needs to understand you. You need to give unambiguous commands and make sure they are clearly understood. The more black and white your training programme, the quicker and easier it will be for your dog to understand exactly what you want – and the better the results.

REWARD GOOD BEHAVIOUR

Put simply, dogs like rewards. So, if your dog does what you want when instructed, reward it immediately. After several sessions it will have learned what's required. If it gives an inappropriate response, ignore it. Once it realizes that such behaviour has no benefit, it will stop doing it.

The onus is on you to make sure you don't reward inappropriate behaviour, because your dog will immediately think that's how you want it to behave. Don't send out the wrong signals. If your dog nudges you to stroke its head and you do so, it has

▶ *The bond you share with your dog will be deepened by the training procedure.*

learned how to get your attention and will do it again. If it manages to steal a tasty morsel from the worktop and is rewarded by eating what it has stolen, it will try it again. If it picks something up and you run after it to get it back, it knows how to get your attention and make you play with it.

Make sure you instil the right behaviour from the beginning. This involves both rewarding the right behaviour and ignoring or interrupting the wrong kind. Get this right and you will avoid a lot of future problems.

The key to such training is motivation. Motivation has a powerful effect on learning, so it's up to you to work out what best motivates your puppy from the beginning. If it has no interest in treats, toys or petting, then you've got a problem – and a very unusual puppy. All dogs are motivated by something; the secret is finding out what this is.

It's worth noting here that many terriers are classed as 'difficult to train' because they are not so easily motivated by food. For terriers, you can use toys or praise instead. Also note that

▲ *A well-trained, well-behaved dog will become a wonderful companion.*

what might seem like a perfectly good motivator to you can actually be a turn-off to your dog.

The best way to respond to any such difficulties is by not thinking of them as 'problems'. Some breeds are easy to train, some are tricky. But the latter are simply different, which means it's up to you to find a creative solution. If you're told that some dogs are stubborn, dominant, lazy or hard to train, don't listen. They've just been trained the wrong way. The problem doesn't necessarily lie with the dog; the owner just needs to take the time to find out what their dog likes.

ABOUT THIS SECTION

This section begins with an overview of responsible dog ownership, and guides you through the processes of welcoming a new puppy into your home. From house-training to playing tug-of-war, all the first steps are explained. There are instructions for training your dog to follow cues, such as 'sit', 'down', 'leave it', 'stay', 'wait' and 'settle down', and also solutions to problems you may encounter. The section aims to make training both easy and fun, and covers all the basic principles a first-time dog owner needs to know.

TRAINING PRINCIPLES

Training your dog will be the most important thing that you ever do with it. It builds up a trusting relationship, teaches you how your dog thinks and works, and will significantly improve your dog's behaviour. You should only carry out training when you are both in the mood for fun. If you are in a bad mood or your patience is low, stop immediately. Do the same if the training is going wrong; don't get frustrated with your dog if it does not seem to understand what you want. It's more likely to be your fault for not making your instructions clear. We often talk too much to our dogs, and during training this can cause confusion. That is not to say that you shouldn't talk to your dog, but during training you should keep it to a minimum to avoid causing any distraction. Also make sure that when different members of the household are training your dog, everyone is using the same commands.

◄ *Playing with your dog is an important part of training. It will keep it fit, as well as teaching it to behave well by responding to your cues.*

The effect of breed on training

There is nothing more disheartening than being placed next to a highly responsive Border Collie or Labrador in a training class, which obeys the same command again and again while your terrier is refusing to comply with anything you say, and looks totally, thoroughly bored.

One way around the problem is by being prepared. Knowing the traits of your particular breed means that you should know roughly what behavioural characteristics to expect and what kind of training programme to emphasize.

HERDING DOGS

Collies and Shepherds have to be taught to stop herding children and anything else that moves. One way of avoiding this problem is by giving the dog a tennis ball to play with – but use it wisely or your dog will become so fixated on the ball that it will be high

▼ The Collie's instinct is to chase, so ball games are good for this breed.

on adrenaline most of the time. If that's all it ever plays with, it will lose the ability to interact with other dogs.

HUNTING DOGS

Spaniels are hunting dogs and love using their nose to flush out game. (Labradors are slightly different, retrieving birds and bringing them back to the handler.) All Spaniel breeds tend to exclude the outside world when they're following a scent, and if yours wasn't well trained to return to a whistle as a puppy, you'll find that no amount of shouting will get it to return. It's not ignoring you; it's just so fixated on the scent that it can't hear you. The advantage of the whistle is that it has just the right pitch to break a dog's concentration.

Similarly, you can get one of the Hound Group, for example the Beagle and Basset, to come back even though they, too, follow a scent very readily. Again, you must start persistent training when they are young. When

▲ Huskies have been bred to be fast and to work under harsh conditions.

training sighthounds such as Whippets and Lurchers, note that they can be easily bored, so use frequent, brief training sessions lasting 5 minutes.

NORTHERN BREEDS

The Northern breeds – Huskies, Alaskan Malamutes and Northern Inuits – can also be tricky. All are bred to work independently from their owners, and they can be hard to motivate.

▼ Because they are bred to catch vermin, terriers excel at digging.

THE EFFECT OF BREED ON TRAINING

► *Greyhounds are known for their speed, and are often bred for racing.*

MATCHING TRAINING TO BREED

There are always exceptions to the rule, and your particular dog may actually train like a dream. Toy breeds, such as Toy Poodles, are intelligent and responsive. So, while each breed trains differently and some breeds have a reputation for stubbornness or being not too bright (Basset Hounds are often said to be lacking in brain power, for example), each breed can be trained to a high standard if you make the effort to find out what motivates it and whether the reward you are offering is high on that dog's treat list.

It is also a good idea to check that the reward won't annoy other dog owners who are trying to get their animals to concentrate at the same training session – so avoid noisy toys in a class situation. Squeaky toys may get your dog's attention, but will disturb the whole class. If your dog is easily distracted, make the training sessions short, fun and lively, so that the motivation levels stay high. Terriers, for example, are high-energy, highly active dogs, so avoid slow and tedious sessions for them.

The role of genes

A dog's genes play a significant role in how it behaves and learns: collies are renowned for herding and enjoy working hard; German Shepherds are herding dogs but also make good guard dogs; sighthounds excel at pursuing prey, keeping it in sight and using their great speed to bring it down; Labradors insist on retrieving things that you'd rather they didn't; and Spaniels love having their nose in the undergrowth, picking up a scent.

Knowing how your dog behaves naturally is vital, because then you'll know what it will be like to live with. Don't choose a breed if you can't supply its needs. For example, even though you might love the idea of a collie, don't choose this breed if you don't have the time to exercise it.

It is impossible to eradicate a dog's natural behaviour, but with the right training you can steer a dog towards honing its natural instincts to a more manageable level.

◄ *St Bernards were originally bred as working rescue dogs to find travellers lost in the snow.*

▶ *German Shepherds are intelligent and loyal, so they are well suited to working with handlers in army or police roles.*

Body language

Dogs communicate with each other and other species by using body language. If they are happy, sad, uncertain or about to bite, they will immediately communicate it. Being able to read the signals means that you can calm an anxious dog, for example, and avoid situations where it might bite. Being sensitive and alert to what a dog is trying to say also makes for a better relationship.

BODY

The dog uses its body posture to show submission or dominance. If it wants to appear dominant, it will make its body look larger by standing straight-legged and on its toes, with its head held high. In addition, a ridge of hair that runs down the back and lower neck – called the hackles – may stand erect. Some dogs will also put their heads across the back of a dog that they wish to dominate.

Submissive dogs, on the other hand, will do the complete opposite. They try to make themselves look as small as possible by keeping close to the ground and moving in a crouched manner, with their heads held low.

TAIL

There are three key points relating to a dog's tail. First, the tail is a barometer of the dog's emotional state. When looking at the tail, always remember how that particular breed holds it. Some breeds – such as Boxers, Dobermanns and Huskies – naturally hold the tail high, which can make it hard for other breeds to read any signals. Now that tail-docking is illegal in many countries (although the USA does still allow tail-docking and ear-cropping), it gives us more scope to read the emotional state of the Boxers, Dobermanns, Spaniels and Rottweilers that once went tailless.

▲ *Some breeds naturally hold their tail high.*

▲ *Other breeds naturally hold their tail low.*

▲ *A relaxed tail should be neither erect nor tucked under the body.*

▼ *A play bow is a signal that your dog wants to start a game.*

▲ *A full-on body posture can be very intimidating to both dogs and people.*

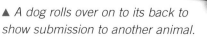

▲ *A dog rolls over on to its back to show submission to another animal.*

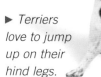

▶ *Terriers love to jump up on their hind legs.*

Second, note the natural position of your dog's tail so that you can read the signals when its emotional state changes. A confident dog will hold its tail high with just the tip giving a slow wag, and this usually happens when a male dog meets another male dog, usually adolescents. A happy, confident dog wags its tail from side to side, a frightened dog has a low tail, and a very scared dog might hold its tail so far between its legs that it may touch its stomach. If your dog's tail wags in a line from the end of the spine, from side to side and slowly, combined with lips pulled back, teeth bared, hackles raised and body stiffness, you are dealing with a state of aggression.

EARS

The position of your dog's ears needs to be read in conjunction with other visual signals. Some dogs hold their ears back and even flat against the head as a greeting gesture or in appeasement. If the ears are held back as a greeting, the mouth will usually be open and the tongue out. A dog that is afraid may have its ears held flat against its head, while a bold, alert dog usually has upright, forward-pointing ears.

▲ *An alert, interested dog will have its ears pricked up and pointing forward.*

EYES

In the absence of training, dogs generally do not regard direct eye contact as a pleasant experience; it is actually seen as a threat. In the past, some dog trainers used to give dogs a shake by the scruff and stared them down to make them submissive and comply with an order. But all that this achieved was to make the dogs even more wary of eye contact, possibly resulting in a bite as they defended themselves from further stress. It is therefore important to explain to children, who are at eye height with dogs, that they should not stare directly at their pet.

▲ *A dog that is unsure shows it is tense by holding back its ears.*

With training, however, it is possible to teach dogs eye contact, and this should be done right at the start of your training programme. When taught correctly, dogs can actually find it a rewarding experience, and it can help raise the confidence of a timid animal. It can also speed up the training process because your dog will learn to look you in the eye for further instructions, registering your pleasure when it gets something right.

If a dog is stressed, worried, frightened or overexcited, its pupils may dilate. You should learn to read these signals in conjunction with other aspects of its body language.

▼ *This relaxed, soft-eyed dog appears happy, trusting and confident.*

▼ *This Collie's eyes are fixated on any movement, ready to chase an object.*

▼ *The sideways, cautious look indicates that this dog is wary.*

▲ *With its mouth closed, this dog could be tentative and unsure.*

▲ *A yawn may signal that your dog is rather anxious or worried.*

▲ *Bared teeth indicates an aggressive threat and could result in a bite.*

MOUTH

If your dog has its mouth closed with the sides pulled back, it is rather unsure of itself, while a top lip curled to expose teeth is a warning signal. This remarkably effective threat is often used after more subtle signals have been ignored. If this signal is also ignored, the dog may increase the threat level by curling its lips to expose the major front teeth, with the mouth partly open and the nose area wrinkled. If you ignore that, it will curl its lips right back, exposing all the major teeth and the gums above the front teeth, with very noticeable wrinkling above the nose. Ignore that, and it will probably bite.

YAWNING

Sometimes mistaken for boredom, yawning is often displayed when a dog doesn't understand what you want it to do in a training session. If this happens, go back a couple of stages to help it. Yawning may also happen when the dog is in a situation that it cannot cope with – for example, if a child is invading its space.

SMILING

Various breeds, such as terriers, Dalmatians and Dobermanns, are known 'smilers'. Smiling can be a submissive gesture, but it is certainly not aggressive. Most owners find this natural action endearing and charming.

HACKLES

Often misunderstood, hackles can easily be mistaken as an aggressive display. They can be erect in one long line from the base of the neck all the way down to the tail, or just at the neckline. While hackles are a sign of arousal, the source can vary from playing with another dog to approaching a strange dog, usually two adolescent males, or visitors coming into the home.

INTERPRETING THE SIGNALS

You need to be adept at reading several body signals simultaneously. It is no good just reading the tail without seeing what the ears and eyes are doing. For example, if your dog is looking away from you, not making eye contact and possibly licking its lips, it is nervous. You can then ask yourself what has caused its anxiety. Have you inadvertently threatened it? Is your body language making it uneasy? To check what is happening, think about what you are doing at that moment, and try not to repeat it. Note that leaning over your dog can be threatening to a shy animal, and should always be avoided.

◄ *Barking may be either attention-seeking behaviour or just excitement. Once you learn to read your dog's body language, you'll be better able to understand the causes of it.*

One common problem that many dog owners make is in thinking that their dog really does know when it has done something wrong. But that is not necessarily the case. Dogs aren't human, and they don't share our moral code of right and wrong.

If you come home to find that your dog has raided the bin and scattered everything over the floor, for example, you might be tempted to shout at it. It will probably run away and hide. However, this behaviour is a direct response to your threatening body language and aggressive arm movements rather than its earlier bin-raiding behaviour. It is now trying to calm you down and defuse the situation by using body language. It is, in fact, being incredibly sensible. If you start imagining that dogs are human, you'll be very disappointed – which brings us on to stress.

▼ *Dogs will be dogs – there is no point in shouting after the event.*

Sensitivities to stress

Dogs vary in their ability to cope with stress, and the sensitive breeds start suffering more readily than the more robust kind. But also be aware of your own dog's particular personality. Keep an eye out for the following factors, all of which can cause stress:
• Lack of early socialization, making it difficult for your dog to cope with everyday events
• Inappropriate training methods
• Inconsistent treatment of your dog, with different family members sending out conflicting messages
• Showing frustration at your dog's behaviour
• Punishment
• Unrealistic expectations – don't forget, we're talking about a dog!

STRESS

A natural part of our daily lives, stress occurs to some degree whenever we learn anything new. In this respect, dogs are no different from people. Learning will actually be quicker and more effective if there is some degree of stress, provided that it energizes and doesn't badly affect those concerned. (Too much stress for your dog can increase blood pressure and heart rate, and breathing may become panting.)

If you ask your dog to do something it can't mentally cope with, it may become silly, jump up or bark and lunge at other dogs, or it may 'shut down' by lying down and looking bored. If it yawns and scratches when you ask it to do something, you shouldn't conclude that it is bored; it probably just can't cope with what you are asking.

▲ *Dogs can become withdrawn and even ill if they are feeling stressed.*

It's also worth pointing out while on the subject of stress that, in extreme cases, other parts of the dog's body might be affected. The digestive system is usually one of the first things to suffer, causing diarrhoea, or your dog may go off its food or vomit. Others can suffer from excessive coat moult that may only continue for a few hours. Some dogs might self-mutilate or lick walls, and some breeds revert to what is called 'breed-specific behaviour'. For example, Collies will round up children, cars or joggers; Pointers will point; and Labradors will carry items around in their mouth. In other cases, dogs may start chasing shadows or flies. If the immune system is affected, dogs become prone to illness and may get itchy skin or an allergy.

Avoiding stress

Always remember to finish a training session on a good note. If the session is going badly, then the best thing is to finish. It will not have a negative effect on your dog if you just stop and do something else.

Discipline without physical punishment

Unfortunately, physical punishment still plays a part in some people's dog training methods, with equipment such as rattle bottles, check chains, water sprays and spray collars at one extreme, and electric-shock collars at the other. Such devices are designed to cause pain in order to stop a dog from doing something. But not only are they obscene, they also fail to remedy the cause of the dog's behaviour, nor do they communicate to the dog what it should be doing.

NEGATIVE CONSEQUENCES OF PHYSICAL PUNISHMENT

Although you might get some results by smacking a dog when it's unruly, you'll get just as many instances of failure and psychological damage. Punishment always has a consequence, and you have to consider the possible side effects

▼ *If you need to punish your dog, calmly say "that's enough" and walk away.*

very carefully before striking a dog. Three possible consequences are: relationship problems; more behaviour problems; and subdued behaviour because the dog is too scared to behave in any other way in case it is punished for it.

One form of punishment that has persisted over the years is rubbing a dog's nose in the offending mess when it uses the house as a lavatory. But this simply tells the dog that its owner is not to be trusted, and that making a mess in front of it means trouble. This makes house-training even harder because the stressed dog is afraid to go to the toilet in front of you. What it doesn't do is teach your dog what it should be doing.

Punishment can also teach a dog that whatever was close to it when it was punished was the reason for the punishment, which means you could

▼ *If your dog raids the bin, move it away, then put the bin out of reach.*

▲ *If lots of children are running around, you could put your dog in a crate.*

end up with bigger problems than you started with. For example, if a child accidentally falls on and hurts a dog, which then growls – a perfectly natural response – followed by a telling-off from you, the dog will associate children with punishment. So, the next time a child goes near the dog, it will growl even louder. Again, you might shout and smack it, and eventually your dog is left with no choice but to bite the child to get them away.

The best way to avoid this problem is to move the dog out of the way when children are running around, and thus avoid a potential accident. This brings us to the crucial subject of how a dog should be punished.

THE IMPORTANCE OF TIMING

For punishment to work effectively, your timing has to be perfect. You need to make sure that the dog associates the punishment with the crime that it has committed. If you do use punishment, you should use it only once, and it has to stop the behaviour once and for all. However, it would be better to teach your dog what you would like it to do instead.

▲ *If carried out correctly, 'time out' is a quick and effective measure.*

Because owners don't really want to punish their dogs, they sometimes use a small amount of punishment first. Then, when that doesn't work, the level of punishment is increased, and so on, until it ends up with a vicious smack. This is not a good idea, because you are causing unnecessary stress to you dog, and you are also hardening it to your punishing methods. However, you should not give up and ignore your dog's bad behaviour. The dog won't stop; it will just become more practised at it.

Without using physical punishment, the question is: how do you teach your dog that it can't always do whatever it wants?

'TIME OUT'
Taking a quick break and walking away from your dog is a good way of stopping unwanted behaviour. Being a very mild form of punishment, it won't have any repercussions. If your timing is right, the dog will understand exactly what you don't want, and this method will sort out behavioural problems very quickly.

To use 'time out' effectively, you have to be quick and fair, either getting up quickly and walking away (not running) from your dog, or moving it to another room. Give your dog a cue to what's happening by saying firmly, "that's enough", without shouting. This isn't threatening or nagging, and it avoids the highly overused "no". So, when your dog begins to display unwanted behaviour, for example barking to get attention, say "that's enough" very calmly, take your dog out the nearest door and put it on a house line (a long thin lead that is attached to its collar at all times when you are in the house). Using a house line will mean that getting hold of your dog does not become a game of chase. Leave the dog out for 1 minute at the most, then let it back in. If it repeats the unwanted behaviour, repeat the action until it eventually realizes the connection between its behaviour and the consequences (separation from you).

BE CONSISTENT
If you are consistent and persistent, you'll remedy the problem within two weeks at the most. If your dog is exhibiting attention-seeking behaviour because you are too busy to spend time with it, you need to change your lifestyle. But attention-seeking behaviour does not just happen because you do not spend time with your dog. Sometimes it's quite the contrary. It doesn't matter how much time you spend with your dog, it may still learn to attention-seek.

The point to stress is that we can't control a dog's behaviour; we can only influence its behaviour by adjusting our actions. Make an effort to reward

Attention-seeking behaviour
If your dog's unwanted behaviour is attention-seeking, get up and walk out of the room immediately. Such behaviour includes:
• Mouthing, where your dog grabs at your wrists, hands or ankles
• Pawing
• Nudging you with its muzzle
• Begging
• Mounting inappropriate objects
• Stealing items and running away to initiate a game of chase
• Barking at you

the positive behaviour that you want. Don't fall into the trap of only noticing your dog when it behaves badly; that will simply make it repeat the bad behaviour to get your attention next time. Hence, chasing after a dog that is running around the garden with a towel is just a game to it, and won't make it stop.

▲ *With consistent training, your dog will settle when you want it to.*

Using rewards effectively

To get the best out of your dog when training it, you should reward good behaviour and the desired responses with either a small piece of food or by playing a game with it with its favourite toy, and with praise. As far as a dog is concerned, probably nothing beats the food reward, with praise at the bottom of the list.

Garlic sausage may work wonders because it has a strong smell and taste that most dogs enjoy. But not every dog likes food treats. Some dogs are fussy eaters, and you have to be quite creative to find the right reward. Others are so food-obsessed that they'll find it hard to think about anything else if they can see what you're holding in your hand. So keep treats out of sight, then give them with lightning speed so that your dog can't see what else you've got.

▼ *Use small, easily chewable treats as an incentive to repeat good behaviour.*

It's also sensible to carry out dog training after your dog has eaten, so that it's not too hungry. If you feel that it is getting too many rewards, you could always use smaller treats.

PHASING OUT FOOD TREATS
Some people argue against using food rewards because they think their dog will need such rewards all the time, but this is not true. Once your dog understands how it's supposed to respond to a command, it will instinctively do it and the reward system can be phased out. When it comes to commands such as 'fetch', the reward is your playing with it. That's all it needs. With you throwing a ball again and again, who needs food? That just slows things up!

▲ *Use tempting treats during training, such as pieces of cheese, cooked sausage and home-made liver cake.*

WHEN TO USE REWARDS
By using rewards effectively, you can teach your dog that the things it finds frightening are actually not a problem. So, a trip to the vet to have its claws cut can actually become a pleasurable experience, and instead of barking loudly every time the front doorbell rings, it will be able to sit quietly while

Food rewards
Tasty edible rewards include:
• Small pieces of cheese
• Frankfurters
• Carrots
• Chicken
• Liver cake
• Tuna cake
• Sausage
• Anything your children leave on their dinner plates
• Pieces of fruit, if your dog enjoys it

▼ *Most dogs can be motivated by the reward of playing with their toys.*

▶ *Choose exciting rewards that you know your dog really wants.*

you see who's there. If it pulls toward something while it's on the lead, take a couple of steps back and get it back to your side before you walk again; if it keeps the lead loose, it can have what it wants. It is also worth making sure that it sits nicely while you're putting its lead on, when it's at the door waiting to go outside and while you prepare its dinner.

VARY THE REWARDS
Finding out what your dog loves and what it sees as rewarding is initially guesswork. It is best to use more boring rewards in the home, and the most exciting kinds outside when you're competing for your dog's attention with playful dogs, children playing ball and puddles to splash in. Also try to vary the rewards. If your

dog keeps getting the same reward – even a tasty piece of sausage – it will eventually get bored with it. The reward won't be a "Wow!" anymore, but "Is that the best you can do?"

When using food treats, choose those that are soft and easily cut into small pieces, so that your dog can eat them quickly. Hard biscuits take time and make training sessions last longer.

◀ *Vary the types of rewards you use. Most dogs enjoy playing tug-of-war.*

▶ *Verbal praise for a job well done, together with a pat and a stroke, is a good alternative to using food treats and toys.*

341

Clicker training

One of the most effective ways to train a dog is to use a clicker. This is a small box that makes a 'click-click' sound, and is always used to mean 'you've just done the right thing'. The clicker doesn't have an off-day or sound cross, and can be used when your dog is some distance from you. Once your dog understands a clicker, the rest is easy.

To introduce the clicker to your dog, put a treat under its nose, lure it into the sit position and, when its bottom hits the floor, click and give it the treat. Then move a couple of steps away from it so that it has to stand and follow you, and then lure it into a sit position, click when its bottom hits the floor, click again and reward it. Again, move away and, when your dog follows you, show it the treat in your hand and then close it and wait to see if it sits. If it does, click and give it a few treats. Once it is going into position when you show it the treat, you can say "Sit" as its bottom hits the floor.

There are many benefits to using the clicker, and the moment your dog can reliably follow your commands, you can put it aside.

▼ *Use a clicker to show approval of your dog's behaviour.*

INTRODUCING THE CLICKER

1 To introduce the clicker, hold a small food treat under your dog's nose when it is standing up. Hold the clicker in your other hand.

2 Lure your dog into the sit position by slowly moving the hand with the food treat above your dog's head. As your hand moves up, your dog should sit.

3 When the dog's bottom hits the floor, click the clicker. You should not point the clicker directly at your dog, nor hold it too close to its ear.

4 As soon as you click the clicker, reward your dog with the food treat. It will begin to associate the clicker sound with doing the right thing.

5 Repeat the process two or three times more, moving a couple of steps away so that your dog follows you.

6 Show your dog the food treat, then close your hand and wait for it to offer a sit.

7 Be patient and wait the dog out; it may take a while. When its bottom hits the floor, immediately click the clicker.

8 The first time it gets it right on its own, reward it heavily with a food treat and plenty of praise.

HOW TO
BEGIN

You've scoured the Internet, reading everything on your chosen breed, and you know all about the behavioural characteristics and ultimate size of your dog. You know that your new puppy will fit perfectly into your lifestyle. You've also looked into the best training classes and bought all the equipment you need. Now it's time to learn the basics of dog training. It's up to you to find what motivates your dog, and to make sure it's given an appropriate reward that will ensure it does what it's told. With the right training, any problems can be put right. So, if your puppy does not come back when called, it's simply because the pleasure of playing with other dogs or foraging in the undergrowth outscores the reward it knows it will get from you. If you always give it a big treat, however, it will return quickly enough. It's up to you to be consistent in your training.

◀ *Training your dog when you are out and about will help to build a good relationship, and will give you the chance to praise and reward it.*

Bringing your puppy home

You've bought the lead, bowl, bed, toys, crate and how-to books. You've told the children not to pester your puppy, and you've taken a week off work to settle it in. You're ready. What next?

PUPPY-PROOFING

The first thing you need to do is look around each room in your house and think about safety. Making your home puppy-proof takes time and thought, and you need to conceal a number of dangerous objects. Start with wires and cables behind computers, televisions and telephones, because if chewed, they can be hazardous and could even kill your puppy. Then move everything that is at a low level in the house, including plants, shoes and children's toys. Look around the house and imagine you're a playful puppy. What can you destroy?

COLLECTING YOUR PUPPY

The best time to collect your puppy from the breeders is mid-morning. This will give it time to digest its breakfast, so that it's not sick in the car. Put it in a small dog basket or cardboard box lined with a blanket, and secure it. When it arrives home, it may be scared and refuse to eat, and if you have children, they may be overexcited. Your puppy may defecate on the carpet, but don't panic. It is under a great deal of stress, having just left its mother and siblings.

SETTLING IN

As soon as you get your puppy home, take it outside and let it get a feel for its surroundings, but stay with it at all times. If it goes to the toilet, praise it. If it doesn't, take it outside every 10 minutes until you get a result, then praise it.

▲ *It's exciting bringing a puppy home, but it can be stressful for the puppy.*

Help it settle in by keeping the house quiet and the children under control. Put its crate or bed in a quiet corner where it can be left in peace to sleep. Also, let it settle for a few days before letting friends see it. Don't be alarmed if it gets a runny tummy – this is likely to be part of the stress of settling in. Make sure it keeps to the diet provided by the breeder, otherwise you could inadvertently make things worse.

Have a selection of strong toys for your puppy to play with. But give it plenty of time to rest, because a young puppy needs lots of sleep. Make sure

◄ *Allow your puppy time to explore and get used to its new surroundings.*

▼ *Provide the new puppy with its own bed in a quiet corner of the kitchen.*

that children leave it alone when it's resting – a tired puppy will be a grumpy puppy.

Don't be in a rush to take your puppy to the vet for its first vaccination. Let it build a bond with you first, so that its first trip to the vet is minimally stressful.

PUPPY'S FIRST NIGHT
The first night could be a trying time if it isn't properly planned. Not only is the puppy's environment new, but it is almost certainly the first time the puppy has slept without its litter mates. Let your puppy go to the toilet, then put it in its crate, turn the light off and close the door. But what if it starts whining? Don't ignore it – it will be lonely and missing the familiar sounds, smell and warmth of its litter mates. For the first few nights, until it settles in, you could let it sleep in its crate next to your bed. If you don't like that arrangement, sleep on the sofa with the puppy beside you in its crate for a couple of nights.

Sleeping close to your new puppy also means that you'll hear it if it

wakes in the night needing the toilet, and you can take it out. This will greatly help with house-training. Puppies have very small bladders and need to go to the toilet much more often than you might think. It should take less than a week for it to sleep on its own in its crate in the kitchen.

If it still cries in the night, do not shout at it – this would cause stress and anxiety. Instead, put your fingers though the crate to soothe it back to sleep, or wrap a hot water bottle in a towel and put that in its bed.

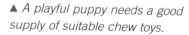
▲ A playful puppy needs a good supply of suitable chew toys.

You could also try turning on the radio. Soft music is very comforting. Silence can be frightening for a puppy if it is used to the snuffling and snores of the rest of the litter.

When it wakes up the next morning, take it straight outside again so that it can relieve itself. Carry the puppy outdoors in your arms, because walking that distance may encourage it to go inside the house.

◄ On its first night, put your puppy in its crate. If it cries in the night, soothe it back to sleep.

► Carry your puppy into the garden the next morning, so that it can begin house-training.

House-training

The the most crucial task with a new puppy is house-training. Hopefully the breeder will have begun taking the puppies into the garden to get them used to going to the toilet outside. What you shouldn't do is encourage your puppy to go inside, even on newspaper. You must also be alert to its signals, understanding when it needs to go, because when a puppy is desperate, it can't wait.

HOW OFTEN?

The frequency with which your puppy will need to go to the toilet depends on several factors, first its diet. If you use dried food, it will drink more water than when eating wet food, prompting more visits outside. Second, if you buy cheaper dog food with cheaper ingredients, it usually makes a great deal more waste and so, again, your puppy will need to go to the toilet more often. Third, the size of your puppy influences the number of visits to the toilet, with a small breed needing to go more often than a large dog, because the former has a smaller bladder.

◀ *Reward your puppy for being quiet in its crate – feed it small food treats for good behaviour. It is helpful if it learns to sleep in a crate, as it is unlikely to foul its sleeping place.*

HOUSE-TRAINING METHODS

Training your puppy not to go to the toilet in the house takes time, and there are bound to be some accidents along the way. It helps to get your puppy to sleep in a crate, because it won't want to foul its sleeping place. Introduce your puppy to the crate by feeding it in the crate, giving it treats there and lying it down in it when it's sleepy. Make sure that the moment it starts whining, you take it outside.

If your puppy does have an accident inside, do not punish it, because that will make it wary of going to the toilet in front of you, and house-training will then become very difficult. It will probably end up going where you can't see it – even in a handbag.

To begin with, take your puppy out soon after it has woken up, after it has eaten, after playtime, when it's excited and every 45 minutes. Make sure it knows which is its toilet area in the garden, especially if you have young children; you don't want your children wading through piles of faeces on the lawn. Fence off a

HOUSE-TRAINING USING A FENCED-OFF AREA

1 Take your puppy on its lead to an area designated as its toilet – ideally a fenced-off area of the garden.

2 Reward it with a small food treat as soon as it goes. It's important to do this the moment it has finished.

▲ *Buy a special cleaner from a pet shop for cleaning up after your puppy when it has toilet accidents.*

small toilet area and take your puppy there on the lead, rewarding it enthusiastically when it does what's expected. Give it a small treat, but remember that it is crucial that you get the timing right: reward it the moment it has finished going to the toilet.

Some puppies give signs that they are about to go, and they may begin sniffing the carpet or floor, circling or squatting. When this happens, clap your hands to get your puppy's attention, and encourage it to follow you out the door. If it really is about to go, pick it up and take it outside very quickly.

CLEANING UP

If your puppy does have an accident, treat the site with a cleaner specifically designed for the job. This will remove the scent of urine. If the odour is left, your puppy will think that's its toilet, and will be attracted there by the smell in future. Note that household

cleaners and disinfectants don't usually remove the scent, they just mask it, so you do need to use a special cleaner available from good pet shops.

OTHER OPTIONS

If you need to leave your puppy alone for long periods, you won't have any option but to use puppy pads, which are specifically designed to soak up urine, or sheets of newspaper on the floor, but at least make sure the puppy understands what the pads or paper are for. As with house-training, every time the puppy shows any inclination to go to the toilet, put it on the pads or newspaper. Dog flaps are not suitable because young puppies don't understand the concept of going out to the toilet and should not be unattended outside.

TRAINING A PUPPY TO RING A BELL

You could also teach your puppy to try to go on command, which is very useful if you are taking it out for the day or visiting friends, but you must use the command just as it's going to the toilet, so that it makes the correct association between the two events.

RINGING A BELL

If your puppy isn't very good at asking to go out, you can teach it to ring a bell. It's an easy little trick. All you need is a small, light bell. Hang it on a piece of string so that it is dangling at about nose height for your puppy. When you walk it to the door to let it out, ring the bell immediately before you open the door. It willl associate the door opening with the ringing bell. In future, the puppy should ring the bell it it wants to go. When you go on holiday, take the bell with you.

1 Attach a bell to a piece of string and hang it from the back door, making sure it is at nose height for your puppy.

2 Ring the bell before you open the door to let your puppy out. In time, it should ring it itself when it wants to go.

Socialization and habituation

Puppies need to be socialized so that they are happy meeting other puppies and adult dogs, people of both sexes, children, babies in pushchairs, older people and people in wheelchairs. The list is endless. It is important to note that the socialization window is only open for a short time – up to the age of 14 weeks – so you need to make the most of it to ensure your puppy doesn't have problems when it's an adult. Make all such encounters enjoyable, asking adults who are new to it to toss it a few treats.

SOCIALIZATION

Your breeder should already have begun the socialization process, with the puppy being handled regularly on a daily basis. If you have a busy household, your puppy will already have become used to household appliances, visitors and the hustle and bustle of day-to-day noise. If you have a quieter home, you will have to put more time and effort into exposing it to different experiences.

BEFORE 12 WEEKS

There are several things your puppy should be introduced to before it's 12 weeks old. First, when it has settled down, invite visitors of all ages to meet it. Keep it quiet when they arrive so that it learns to be calm when people are around. If you don't have children, ask friends who do have them to visit, but make sure they are well briefed and don't get your puppy overexcited.

Put something tasty in your puppy's food dish so that it gets used to people being around when it eats.

Groom and handle your puppy every day. Look in its ears, at its teeth and between its paw pads. Also get other people to handle your puppy, so that when it has to visit the vet, it isn't frightened. It needs to get used to wearing its collar too.

▲ *Children should be taught how to care for their dog's needs by grooming and handling them. Start the process before your puppy is 12 weeks old.*

HABITUATION

This is the name given to a natural process of learning by repetitive exposure to a stimulus. For example, a puppy may be frightened of the noise of a washing machine, but each time the machine is turned on, its reaction will diminish. Eventually, it will show no reaction to the noise at all, and it has become 'habituated' to it. Habituation to a wide range of items and experiences is vital for the young puppy, and the process will continue throughout its lifetime.

◄ *Cats and dogs can live in harmony, especially if they grow up together.*

▲ *Stay with your puppy when it is eating; it will get used to people around its food bowl.*

▲ *Giving your puppy a weekly health check will prepare it for its first visits to the vet or the groomer.*

▲ *Carrying your puppy everywhere you go will habituate it to the environment in which you live.*

Habituation can also be used as a training tool. If your puppy becomes overexcited when you pick up its lead, this is because it expects to go for a walk. But if you take the lead with you every time you leave the house, the puppy will soon come to realize that the act of picking up the lead is not a signal for walk time.

TOWN AND COUNTRY

Carry your puppy out to meet the postman, so that it won't bark at them. If you live in a town, try to take your puppy into the countryside, but keep it under strict control so that it learns to leave wildlife and livestock alone. Reward it for obeying your commands and staying with you. Never let it off the lead when around livestock. Remember that a farmer has the right to shoot your dog for worrying their animals, especially

▶ *If your puppy gets used to horses early, it will behave well around them.*

sheep around lambing time. If you live in the countryside, it is imperative that you carry your puppy around the nearest town to get it used to all the sights and sounds. Initially go when it is quiet, gradually building up to busier periods. Before its vaccinations, before it is around 12 weeks of age,

it is important that you don't let your puppy walk outside in parks and fields that are visited by other dogs – your puppy might get a fatal disease. However, you can carry it with you everywhere you go, and it can visit friends' houses whose dogs have been vaccinated.

Puppy classes and puppy parties

There are two main ways in which your local veterinary surgery can help when your puppy is ready to meet other animals and get used to going to the vet: puppy classes and puppy parties. The former provide professional advice and training for new puppies, with information about vaccinations and health, basic training and how to deal with common problems such as house-training and biting.

A puppy party, on the other hand, is an informal gathering of puppies and their owners at the local vet. The intention is a good one: to enable puppies to socialize with each other at the same time as getting used to the vet surgery. The idea is that puppies are put on the examination table, given a treat and are played with by the staff, all of which helps to ensure that future vet visits are relaxed. That is the theory, but unfortunately the reality can actually be a nightmare. Aspects of classes and parties can be combined.

▲ *If you reassure your puppy, the vet should not become a place to fear.*

PUPPY CLASSES

When looking for a good puppy class, ask your friends for recommendations, and ask the trainer if you can go along to watch first. Look for one that is run exclusively for puppies, with no more than eight puppies to a class, with one trainer and an assistant.

The class should be a mixture of advice and training, with the vet or the nurse giving a short talk on worming, vaccinations, diet, general care and other health-related matters. You should also have a chance to ask any niggling questions about puppy care and be able to talk to other owners.

The puppies should be let off the lead two at a time, the pairs being determined by temperament and size. Shy puppies should be twinned together, being praised when they are brave enough to greet and initiate play with their new friend. They must be given time, without fear of being ambushed by another puppy twice as big. Puppies that are not involved should sit on their owner's knees while they wait their turn.

▲ *Introduce your puppy to the vet so that it gets used to visiting the surgery.*

This is also an excellent time for you to learn about the small nuances of a dog's body language and dog-to-dog communication. The class should cover all the basics, showing you how

▼ *Staff at the vet will be more than happy to give puppies a cuddle. They also offer sound advice and reassurance.*

► *If you have litter mates, encourage them to play with you and not just with each other.*

to teach your dog to sit, lie, come when called and walk on a loose lead. The trainer should also be able to help you solve problems concerning house-training, biting, tantrums and diet.

OBEDIENCE TRAINING

Some puppy classes go one step further and concentrate on competition obedience, where they insist that your dog walks on a certain side, doing about-turns etc. If you want to take part in obedience competitions, that's fine, but in the real world it's not always easy to keep your dog on your inner side (if you are walking along the road it's natural to keep your dog on the side that's furthest away from the traffic). Good classes will offer flexibility to suit you.

▼ *Give your puppy small food treats as a reward for good behaviour and to encourage this to continue.*

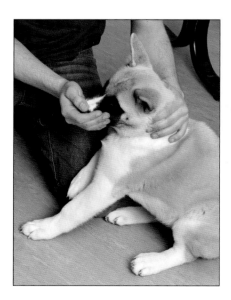

PUPPY PARTIES

Unfortunately, just like dog training, you don't need a qualification to hold a puppy party and, if the puppies aren't properly supervised, the event can easily become an off-putting experience. First, the average surgery waiting room is far too small for lots of puppies all off the lead together. Second, if there isn't adequate supervision, bullying can occur. Leaving the puppies to 'sort it out for themselves' is unfair, with the

▼ *It's important that your puppy learns to be relaxed with strangers. Ask other owners to handle it.*

bullied desperate to find a hiding place and the bullies getting a taste for it, while the shy animals simply have their shyness reinforced.

In these situations, puppies don't learn to become more confident – those that have had a bad experience won't relish meeting other dogs next time you're in the park. But it doesn't have to be like this. With good supervision, puppy parties can actually be positive for young dogs.

Some puppy parties are sponsored by well-known companies. Veterinary surgeries use the parties as an advertisement for their services. Therefore, it is in the best interests of both to ensure the parties are well run. In addition, a good number of vets offer staff courses as part of their team's professional development.

A good puppy party offers early socializing in a safe environment. Not only do the puppies see new sights and sounds, but advice is available on a range of veterinary and nutritional issues. It is an opportunity for puppies to interact with each other and for owners to discuss any issues that concern them. Puppy parties can offer a confidence-gaining experience to both owner and pet. Go and watch a puppy party first to make sure it is well run. Do this without your puppy.

Play is important

As well as being a great relationship-builder, playing with your puppy is also the perfect way to incorporate some training into its fun time. For example, tug-of-war, when played properly, is a great way of teaching your dog self-control, how to give things up easily and the consequences of accidentally getting hold of clothing or skin (which should immediately end the game). It's also a great way to build up teamwork, and if the weather is poor, you can get your puppy to expend some energy indoors. Even more importantly, it's a good way to practise your 'leave it' and 'drop it' commands, as well as 'sit' (if it gets overexcited) and 'wait'. To some breeds of dog, a game of tug will override any other reward. Terriers love it, which is why it should definitely become part of their training sessions.

TUG-OF-WAR

If your dog doesn't know how to play tug-of-war, it's very easy to teach it. Using a ragger, tempt your dog to chase it by wiggling it along the floor. When the dog chases and gets hold of it, praise it, then toss it away and let it

fetch it. Take hold of the other end and give it a gentle tug, then let go. If your dog runs away with the ragger, don't chase it. Let it have it. It will bring it back to you soon enough when it wants you to play some more.

Once your dog knows how to play tug, you can implement some rules and make it part of your training. If it gets overexcited when you get the tug toy out, hide it behind your back until it sits patiently, thus teaching it a bit of self-control. If it responds well when you get it out, hide it behind your back

▲ *Older children and dogs can enjoy playing tug-of-war together.*

and ask your dog to sit. When it sits, the ragger becomes the reward. Then give the command "take it" when it grabs it, have a good tug and then hold a treat right under its nose. When it lets go of the ragger to get the treat, say "drop it". After a few games, you should be able to make your dog drop the toy by holding a treat under its nose. If it accidentally grabs hold of clothing or skin by

◀ *Dogs enjoy playing with other dogs, but they need to be supervised at all times.*

▶ *Many dogs enjoy chasing and retrieving objects, and the game becomes an excellent bonding exercise.*

mistake, drop the ragger and walk away so that it realizes it has made an error.

CHOOSE SUITABLE GAMES

It is important that you don't win the game all the time; it's not much fun for the dog to keep losing. It used to be said that if a dog wins it will become dominant, but actually nothing could be further from the truth. The whole object of playing tug is that it is fun for both parties.

This explains why, in general, you shouldn't let young children play tug with your puppy – there's too much potential for accidents and overexcitement. The same applies to chasing games, and if you have any of the herding breeds (for example, a Collie or Shepherd), they may nip the children's ankles.

Wrestling games are also unsuitable, with puppies either becoming too rough, or if you try wrestling with a shy puppy, it might actually make it become even more timid.

TRAINING A PUPPY TO PLAY TUG-OF-WAR

1 Begin by wiggling a colourful ragger along the floor to get your puppy's attention, tempting it to start playing.

2 Your puppy should chase the ragger, jump on it and then start chewing it. Praise it for doing this.

3 Toss the ragger a short distance away for your puppy to chase. Encourage the dog to bring it back to you.

4 Let the dog play with the ragger without chasing it. When it brings it back, play with it and repeat the process.

5 Let your puppy win the tug-of-war game sometimes, allowing it time to chew the ragger on its own.

Building confidence in the shy dog

Puppies can be shy for all kinds of reasons, ranging from being genetically predisposed to shyness, being the runt of the litter, or a bad upbringing by an unsympathetic family and/or a spell in a rescue centre. But, whatever the reason, shyness needs to be dealt with promptly before it leads to problems of fear and aggression, such as lunging at whoever or whatever alarms the dog.

HOW YOU CAN HELP

If you have an older dog with a confidence problem, rehabilitation will take more time and patience, because you need to change its association of what is scary to what's acceptable or even fun. It is best to hire a dog trainer who can help you, and who will teach you its body language signals so that you'll know whether it is coping.

◄ *Some dogs are naturally shy, and may hide under the furniture until they feel more sure of their surroundings.*

▼ *Lack of early socialization will lead to shyness, but with time you can build confidence.*

▶ *Don't rush your shy puppy – let it investigate its surroundings and get to know family members at its own pace.*

The shy puppy can be helped by you, but each day you must go at its pace, never rushing it, gently coaxing it along and being ready to break off when it's clear it's had enough. Having friends who can help will be a big advantage, but they must follow your instructions and do exactly as you say. Nothing puts your training back so much as people who insist they are good with dogs, and who'll end up overwhelming your puppy by trying to stroke it and pick it up before it's ready. Don't let anyone force themselves on it. Further, don't overwhelm it by trying to force the pace, otherwise its fear could escalate into a phobia.

Tell your friends to sit down before you bring your puppy in, and let the animal investigate them rather than the other way around.

Let the puppy make all the moves. Praise it for any confident behaviour, but ignore it when it shows signs of fearfulness. If you punish it for its fearful behaviour, this will only escalate the problem. While it's human nature to comfort those who are upset, if you do that to the dog, it will think you are rewarding its

◄ *Reward and praise any brave behaviour shown by a shy dog.*

▼ *Introduce your puppy to as many people as possible while it is young.*

shyness. Working with a shy puppy takes time and patience, but the reward of seeing its increased confidence is worth the effort invested.

BUILDING CONFIDENCE OUTDOORS

Beware of strangers coming up to you when you are out with your shy puppy, wanting to say hello and give it a cuddle. It may well find this overwhelming and end up giving them a nasty bite. Instead, you could ask a friendly stranger to give your puppy a treat. Even if the puppy seems

reluctant, don't give up; keep trying. Eventually it will become increasingly at ease with new people.

While the shy dog may never become an extrovert, there are many things you can do to help it become more confident. Concentrate on rewarding any aspect of good behaviour, and it will boost your puppy's confidence.

SET REALISTIC GOALS

You need to be realistic when socializing your shy puppy. Nothing is more detrimental than swamping it

with too many potentially frightening experiences at once. Take small steps towards you goal, and build confidence gradually.

Progression should be made by first choosing a quiet place such as a bench in the park, and just sitting and watching. When your puppy is totally relaxed in this situation, try walking around the park. Next, walk down a quiet road, then choose a busier one, until finally over a period of days, weeks or months it is able to cope with a bustling environment.

◄ *Socialization is vitally important with a shy dog. Praise it when strangers are walking nearby.*

► *Using rewards will teach your puppy that there is no need to be scared of strange people.*

Teaching your puppy its name

When you are out with your dog, you need to be able to communicate with it when it is off the lead playing with other dogs or sniffing in the undergrowth. Calling out its name means you can get its attention, possibly giving it its next command like "come here, time to go home" or "leave it" if it is eating something unsavoury, chasing a jogger or pestering children playing football.

▼ *Once trained, your dog should look up at you when you say its name.*

WHY A NAME IS IMPORTANT

When you say your dog's name, you want it to look at you expectantly and wait for the next command. The importance of getting a puppy to respond to its name cannot be stressed enough. If something scares it and it flees, it might dash toward a main road; getting it to return promptly could save its life.

It's no surprise that most puppies think their name is 'No' by the time they are 4 months old; it's one of the most over-used words with puppies and dogs. It's far better to teach your puppy to respond to its name and then give a command, rather than just shouting "no".

At the other extreme, children often excitedly say their puppy's name over and over again when trying to get his attention, but this becomes so over-used that it means nothing to the puppy and just becomes background noise. So, when you do call your puppy by name, make it a rewarding experience. Don't call it to tell it off because it is having a good chew on your shoes or to make it do something it will hate, like having a bath, or it will associate the sound of its name with trouble and run away.

TEACHING A NAME

Several times a day, take the time to teach your puppy its name, using a handful of treats or a toy that it loves. Put it on the lead so that it can't wander off. Toss a small treat on the floor just a short distance away from you and let it eat it. Just as it has finished, say its name. If it looks up at you, praise it and tell it that it's a good dog.

▲ *Teaching a puppy its name means you can always get its attention, even in a distracting place such as a park.*

If it ignores you, don't say its name. The object of the exercise is to get your puppy to look at you the first time you say its name.

If it does not respond to the sound of its name the first time you say it, that's probably because it doesn't understand what its name means. You need to get its attention another way, either by clapping your hands, slapping the floor or tapping it on the bottom. As soon as it turns to look at you, tell it that it's a good dog and reward it. Four or five times, toss a treat or toy away from you, get your dog to look somewhere else and then see if it will look at you when you say its name. Go through this three or four times a day, and eventually it should immediately respond to its name every time.

The same method is used if you're re-naming an older dog. Some people think you can't change a dog's name, but this is untrue. A name is only a sound to a dog; it doesn't understand the actual word. Rescue dogs may have had several names before gaining a permanent home. You can ensure they respond to their new name by following the three training steps on this page.

Once your puppy really understands the sound of its name, don't ruin it by trying words like 'biscuit', especially if it's slow to respond. Why? Because this teaches it that its name means nothing, whereas the word 'biscuit' is significant. You need to reinforce the fact that its name really does mean something.

ADDING DISTRACTIONS

The next stage is to add distractions to your training so that when your puppy is busy doing something else, it will still respond to your call. Distract it by inviting people to your house, letting it play with children, allowing it to run around the garden and giving it new toys. When it is

able to respond to its name in every situation, it's time to use its name when it is a short distance away in the park, when it is sniffing a tree or when it has just said hello to someone.

You need to teach your puppy that whatever it is doing when you say its name, it must respond. Always follow

▲ *Reward your puppy with a game when it responds to its name.*

up with a command. Just watch in the park and see how many owners use the dog's name and expect it to understand that it actually means 'come here'. You need to be very clear to your dog what you want it to do.

TEACHING YOUR PUPPY ITS NAME

1 Toss a small food treat on to the floor a short distance away from you, keeping your puppy on a lead.

2 Allow your puppy to reach the treat and let it eat it. Just as it finishes eating the treat, say its name.

3 If it looks at you, praise it. If it ignores you, do not reward it; repeat the process until it does look at you.

Adolescent dogs

It is no surprise that the majority of dogs in rescue centres are adolescents, between the ages of six months and two years. Like humans, dogs are at their most challenging during adolescence, when they're bombarded by hormones.

THE URGE TO CHEW

Your cute puppy will suddenly become gangly as it goes through a rapid growth stage, possibly accompanied by growing pains. To make matters worse, it will have a strong urge to chew things as its adult teeth bed down in the gums. So, just when you thought you'd got through the puppy chewing stage, it starts all over again, only this time the teeth are bigger and capable of doing more serious damage. For this reason, you can't have too many chew toys. Buy new ones if those it had as a puppy are now outgrown.

▼ *Adolescent dogs need to chew, and they also love playing with other dogs.*

HORMONAL CHANGES

Sex also comes high on the agenda as bitches head towards their first season, and a male's testosterone begins to reach new heights. The adolescent male has more testosterone than an adult dog, and your obedient puppy will be replaced by a sex-mad, hormonal teenager. He may chase after bitches and fight males, or become fearful of dogs that he once played with nicely. Worse, he may ignore your commands. It's not surprising that some owners give up and hand their adolescent dogs into rescue centres, because the problems can seem insurmountable.

It is very tempting to put your dog back on the lead at this stage, but it's important to still let it play with other dogs. You'll quickly notice that your growing, confident dog charges towards other dogs with tail high, shoulders back and a swagger, whereas before it may have approached with its tail down and its head low. However, while older dogs will tolerate a great deal of raucous puppy behaviour,

▲ *During adolescence, puppies start to become more confident.*

they are less likely to tolerate rude adolescent behaviour, and you may find that your dog is being reprimanded by other dogs.

SOCIAL SKILLS

One way of maintaining your adolescent dog's social skills is by taking it to new places where it can meet new dogs. Most owners get into a fixed routine with their dogs too easily, taking the same route through the same parks, and meeting the same people with the same dogs. But an adolescent dog's social skills will quickly deteriorate if they don't get any variety.

It's worth adding that we sometimes expect too much of our dogs, and think they'll become instant best friends with every dog they meet. Certainly during adolescence there will be dog fights, sometimes over a bitch, but they are usually not serious – more a case of 'teeth and noise'. Fights tend to look worse than they are.

MALE ADOLESCENTS

Your adolescent male dog may begin to leave scent marks in great quantities over upright objects, including every lamp post and tree.

▼ *Male adolescent dogs urinate frequently to mark their scent.*

He may even disgrace himself and leave scent marks indoors or in a friend's house. Don't panic if he does; just re-train him by giving rewards when he goes to the toilet where you want him to. He may also become sexually aware and find mounting people's legs irresistible and very exciting. You might consider having him castrated, which can help.

FEMALE ADOLESCENTS

Bitches can be equally troublesome. When in season, they may become withdrawn and moody, get snappy with males that want to sniff their rear, and go off their food. If you own more than one bitch, keep an eye on them, because fights may develop.

A bitch's season can start at any time after 6 months, and the smaller the breed, the earlier the season begins. A bitch usually loses blood for 10 days, and it is then that she will

▼ *Developing males may try to mate by mounting a person's leg.*

want to mate with any available passing male. It is unfair to continue walking bitches in parks during this time, because they'll cause fights between male dogs.

Not only will your bitch be a bit tetchy when on heat, but she may well have a phantom pregnancy. She'll act like she's having puppies, may become grumpy, go off her food and carry around a particular toy as if it were a puppy. This can be very

distressing both for the bitch and the owner. Having your female puppy spayed after her first season will remedy this problem. If your bitch is really out of sorts, the vet can administer something to help, and if you plan to breed her but want to wait until she is more mature, see how her first season progresses, then decide.

▼ *Adolescents often sniff each other in the park. Watch out for fights.*

TRAINING BASIC COMMANDS

The simplest command to get your dog to obey is 'sit'. Get it to obey immediately and you'll avoid having an overexcited, yapping, leaping hooligan every time you have a visitor. If it can sit on cue and be calm, you can take it anywhere and it won't pester you for attention. When training your dog, it's best to start indoors in one room, then move to another room, then to the garden, and finish off by the roadside. But note that when you teach a dog to sit in one particular place, you may have to repeat the entire lesson to get it to sit in another room or outside. The length of each training session often depends on which breed of dog you have, with sighthounds and terriers benefiting from frequent, short sessions, while Border Collies and Labradors perform better with relatively long (and fewer) sessions.

◄ *With patience, you can train your dog to enjoy responding to your cues. It is best to train little and often, gradually building up your dog's skills over time.*

Sit

▶ *Teaching your puppy to sit when it is off the lead is important.*

Teaching a dog to sit is relatively easy. You need to get your dog to do it on command, at a time when it might be interested in doing something much more interesting, such as snuffling through the undergrowth following some weird, enticing scent.

Have a handful of small treats. Hold one in front of your dog's nose, and move it upward and slightly backward towards its tail slowly, so that your dog's head moves up to follow the treat. You'll quickly see that as its head moves up, its bottom will go down. As soon as its bottom hits the floor, reward it and say "good boy" or "good girl". If your dog begins jumping up at your hand, you are holding the treat too far away from the front of its nose; put your hand behind your back until it settles down. When you start again, make sure the treat is right at the end of its nose.

Repeat this three or four times with a small treat, then let it have a rest. This stage needs to be repeated three or four times a day, and can easily be fitted in between television programmes and meals. The second time you try teaching a sit, if your dog's bottom hits the floor consistently, keep the treat in your hand behind your back and use your other hand to give the signals, moving it upward and backward towards its tail. Say "good boy/girl" as its bottom hits the floor and reward it with the treat from your other hand.

The next stage is to make sure you say the word 'sit' as it is going into the sitting position – not a second before. Follow this up by checking that it understands what you are asking it. Hide the treat behind your back and tell it to sit. Does it do it the first time? If it stands looking at you, it doesn't understand, in which case you should go back to saying "sit" as it's going into the sitting position. Only proceed to the next stage when it sits immediately every time, on command.

You'll soon note that once you've said "good boy/girl" or given it a treat, it stands up again. To get it to stay in the sitting position, initially withhold the treat for a couple of seconds, gradually making this period longer by several seconds before it gets its reward. Don't be too hard on your dog; make this an achievable feat.

The final stage of the lesson is getting your dog to sit by the roadside while you are talking to someone. If it ever hesitates, however, it is important to resist the urge to push down on its back. There are a couple of reasons for this: first, you may damage its developing bone structure; and second, the dog will usually offer some resistance, pushing back, which causes you to push harder and harder every time you want it to obey.

TRAINING A DOG TO SIT

1 Have a few small food treats ready. Hold one in front of your dog's nose and move it upward and backward.

2 As you move the treat towards your dog's tail, its head will move up and its bottom will move down. Say "sit".

3 As soon as your dog sits, reward it with the food treat. Repeat, gradually increasing the time before the reward.

Down

▶ *Once your dog has learned to sit, it is easy to train it to lie down.*

Teaching your dog to lie down on cue is another essential command, especially when you're in a friend's garden or sitting in an outdoor café. Like sitting, teaching it to lie down isn't usually difficult because it's such a natural movement, although some breeds (such as Border Collies) find it easier to do on command than others (such as sighthounds and Whippets).

First, get your dog to sit in front of you, then hold a treat under its nose and move it in a straight line from under its nose to its paws on the floor. As soon as the dog's chest hits the floor, reward and praise it. Only practise this about four or five times in each session, to keep it interested.

If you have a terrier, who finds it easier to go straight down from the

standing position, again have the treat right under its nose and lure it down and slightly backward. If it goes down with its nose and front legs but leaves its rear in the air, resist the urge to push down on its bottom. Just hold the treat on the floor between your finger and thumb and wait, and it will eventually lie down or get up and walk away. If it does walk away, repeat the exercise but reward it for each stage that it completes successfully. So, if you reward your dog for putting its front end down first, it may well put its front end down and its chest, and before long it will be lying down. Be patient.

If you have a small dog or puppy that is having real trouble lying down, sit on the floor with your legs outstretched in front of you, bend one leg up and lure your dog under the crook of your knee. This works particularly well with terriers.

The time to introduce the word 'down' is just as your dog is going into the correct position. Gradually increase the amount of time before you reward it. After that, try getting it to lie down where there are minor distractions, for example in the back garden. The rule to apply is that the harder the task, the better the reward.

Never use force; this will get you into a wrestling match that you will invariably lose, or alternatively your dog will become suspicious and will immediately shy away from you.

TRAINING A DOG TO LIE DOWN

1 Ask your dog to sit in front of you. When it is in the sit position, hold a small food treat under its nose.

2 Slowly lower the treat down in a straight line from its nose to its paws. While doing this, say "down".

3 As soon as your dog's chest hits the floor, give it the treat and praise it. Repeat the lesson four or five times.

Leave it

▶ 'Leave it' is an essential command if you want your dog to ignore an object.

There will be many times in your dog's life when you'll want it to leave something or someone alone, such as an object it has picked up in the street, children's toys, joggers, cyclists or children playing in the park. A 'leave it' command covers all the items and people that you would rather your dog didn't touch, eat or chase. When teaching a 'leave it' command, let your dog decide what

position it wants to go in. You shouldn't suddenly ask it to obey two commands at once, for example 'leave it' followed by 'down'.

Get five or six high-value treats and put them to one side. Put a dog biscuit in the palm of your hand, show it to your dog, close your hand and hold your closed hand under its nose. Let your dog sniff, paw and lick your hand, but don't say anything. Your

dog will eventually back off, confused, but as soon as it moves its face away from your hand, say "leave it" and give it one of the treats. You're teaching your dog that it won't get the object you've told it to leave. At the end of the exercise, put the dog biscuit away and don't give it to it. As you teach the 'leave it' command, your dog should begin to back off faster and sit patiently, and you can then hold your hand open for a couple of seconds before you praise and reward it.

When the dog is consistently leaving treats in the palm of your hand, start making the exercise more difficult. Try higher-value rewards for the dog to leave, and roll a biscuit along the floor, being prepared to put your hand over it to begin with until the dog understands it has to leave it.

When it has mastered all these 'leave it' commands, put your dog on the lead and let it see you put some food away. Tether it to something or ask someone to hold it while you do this. The food should be about 3m (10ft) away from you. Walk towards it and, as soon as your dog begins to pull towards the treat, walk backward until your dog stops pulling towards the treat and looks at you. Then reward and praise it for looking at you.

Once your dog has realized that looking at you gets it a reward, it should be easier to get it closer and closer to the treat on the floor, until it will eventually walk past.

TRAINING A DOG TO LEAVE AN ITEM ALONE

1 Hold a treat in the palm of your hand under your dog's nose, then close your hand. Don't say anything.

2 Let your dog sniff, paw and lick. It will eventually back off. When it does, say "leave it" and give it the treat.

3 Next, make the exercise more difficult: put a few treats on the floor and ask your dog to "leave it".

4 If your dog sits patiently, reward it with a treat. Over time it will wait and look at you whenever you say "leave it".

Stay

▶ *Teaching your dog the 'stay' cue will help to keep it out of danger.*

The 'stay' command means 'stay where you are until I get back to you'. So, if your dog accidentally escapes out the front door and runs across a road, the wisest course of action is to tell it to stay where it is until you can get to it. Your dog will also need to master the 'stay' command if you want it to enter dog competitions.

There are two aspects of the exercise to work on: duration and distance. Gradually increase the amount of time your dog stays, while you move further and further away. It needs to have the confidence to stay where it is. In fact, this is much harder for a dog than you realize, so never get angry if it can't stay for long and comes bounding up to you. After all, the training you have done with it previously has been right in front of it, with a reward just seconds away. If you do get angry, the dog will get stressed, which will make it even more likely to get up and follow you. If it does break a 'stay', take it back to where it was, put it back in position and go back a few steps so that it understands what you want.

First, tell it to sit but don't move away yet. Say "stay" while holding up the flat of your hand (this visual command will reinforce the verbal cue). Then count to five and reward it. When it can sit and stay for 1 minute, you can begin to move away from it. Do this very slowly, taking one step back, then move back and reward your dog, adding plenty of verbal praise.

The next time you do this, take two steps back before going back to it with a reward, and so on. If it gets up to follow you when you move back, it does not understand what you want.

In that case, go back a few stages and start all over again. Continue to increase the duration and distance in small stages, making it as easy as possible for your dog to succeed.

When you are confident that your dog understands the word 'stay' and you can move a few steps away, start to train in a safe area with distractions. This could be in a quiet area of your

local park. Again, gradually build up time and distance, and always praise it when it gets it right.

TRAINING A DOG TO STAY

1 Begin by teaching your dog to remain still. Say "stay" while holding up the flat of your hand.

2 Count slowly to five, and if your dog has not moved away, reward it with a small food treat.

3 When it can stay still for 1 minute by your side, begin moving away. Very slowly, take one step back.

4 Return and give it a reward, then gradually increase the number of steps. Always return and reward it.

Wait

▶ *Teaching your dog to wait will help it with patience and good manners.*

There is a subtle difference between 'stay' and 'wait' commands. 'Stay' means 'stay where you are until I get back to you' and is usually used from a safety point of view when it is essential that a dog doesn't move, for example when it might have slipped out of its lead while standing beside a busy main road. In contrast, 'wait' means 'we are going to do something else' and is more a case of good manners when you want your dog to keep quiet and behave, for example while waiting for its dinner or waiting on the lead to cross a road. You could also ask your dog to wait while you open the front door, so that it learns to leave the house in an orderly fashion, instead of barging past you in its hurry to get to the park. Similarly, asking your dog to wait while you open the car door is a good habit to get into.

TRAINING A DOG TO WAIT

1 Hold on to your dog's collar while you put a treat just out of its reach. Don't say anything at this stage.

2 Allow it to pull towards the treat while you hold its collar. When it relaxes and looks at you, say "wait".

3 Let go of its collar and allow it to go and get the treat. Praise it for having waited patiently.

4 Practise the exercise until your dog can successfully wait without you having to hold on to its collar.

To teach a dog to wait, take a small treat and hold your dog by the collar. Roll the treat away from you, just out of reach of your dog. Don't say anything to it yet, but let it pull towards the treat while you hold on to its collar. It will eventually relax, sit and possibly look at you. Say "wait" and then let it get the treat.

Next, teach your dog to wait at the front door. Put it on a lead, get it to sit next to you and ask it to wait. Open the front door a bit and, if it gets up to charge out, close it immediately, making sure you don't trap its nose. Drop the lead, walk away, wait a few seconds, then try again. It may take six or seven attempts before your dog sits nicely while you open the door, and don't forget to reward it on each occasion. Teaching it this self-control will make going out for a walk a much calmer experience.

When in the park, practise asking your dog to wait while on a flexi-lead or long line first – not when your dog is running, which is too dangerous. Wait until there are other dogs or people around. Let your dog get slightly ahead of you, then ask it to wait. Put the brake on the flexi-lead or hold on to the line and, when it stops to look at you, praise and reward it. Only do this when it is walking slowly; it may hurt its neck if it is running.

Eye contact

▶ *A dog should enjoy eye contact. It will improve a shy dog's confidence.*

Teaching your dog to make eye contact with you should be one of the most rewarding things you do with it. Once learned, it's a good exercise that you can use again and again, for example when you want to keep your dog's attention so that it doesn't go dashing off after a group of dogs in the park. It's also very useful if you have a shy dog. Teaching it eye contact is actually a good game to play, and will help build its confidence.

It used to be thought that you should never look a dog in the eye. However, this only applies to staring a dog down when it's wrong, in which case it will associate eye contact with punishment. Because children are about head-height with dogs, they will almost always look dogs in the eye. If a pet has not been trained to make

eye contact, there is a risk of being bitten in the face by an apprehensive pet. By teaching a dog that eye contact is a rewarding experience, it will not fear being looked at; in fact the dog will positively look forward to it.

Start in a room without any distractions, holding a handful of treats, with your dog off the lead. Show it the treats, then close your hand and hold it out to the side. The dog will try to jump up to get the treats, but if you wait, it will eventually sit down and glance at you. Tell it it's a good dog as soon as it looks you in the eye, and reward it by tossing the treat away from you to encourage it to move away. What you are hoping is that it will come back and sit in front of you again, offering more eye contact. After about five or

six attempts, your dog should sit in front of you and look at you when you hold out your hand. When it is looking you in the eye consistently, you can begin to say "watch me" so that it understands the command.

If your dog is particularly shy, it may find it difficult to make eye contact, but persevere with the task, rewarding even a glance in your direction. Proceed at your dog's pace.

TRAINING A DOG TO MAKE EYE CONTACT

1 Begin with your dog off the lead. Show it a handful of treats, then hold them out to your side.

2 Be patient while your dog watches your hand and tries to get the treats. Eventually it will look up at you.

3 When it looks you in the eye, toss a treat away from you. After eating it, it should return for more eye contact.

Recalling your dog

Of all the commands that you will teach your dog, a recall is one of the most important. If your dog does not come back when called, it will always have to be kept on a lead. This will reduce its social skills with other dogs and people, as it will not be free to interact. Being on the lead all the time would also mean that it couldn't have as much fun following weird and wonderful scents, snuffling away through the undergrowth.

There are many reasons why a dog does not come back when called, the most obvious being that it has never been trained. Owners can be lulled into a false sense of security when their dogs are puppies, because they rarely go off, instead tending to stay by their side. However, a dog may suddenly realize it's not so bad being away from its owner, and when you shout "come back", you might as well be yodelling in another language.

Some dog owners think that just calling a dog by its name when it's off playing with other dogs will get an instant result. It won't. Calling like this

▼ Be enthusiastic and reward your dog keenly when it comes to you.

means that when you use its name in future, it will associate that with the end of its fun and the end of the walk, making it less likely to return.

So it's important when training your dog to come back that you use a suitable reward – one that compensates it well for being told to stop chasing other dogs. Ordinary dog biscuits will not be enough. Instead, try one of the home-made treats shown earlier in this book. With recall training it is important to put a firm foundation down before you move on to the next level. Always set your dog up for success.

The secret to getting your dog to obey is time, work and plenty of patience. Once your dog has learned to return to you, you can safely let it off the lead so that it can have some fun on its own. Training a recall is all about conditioning your dog so that when it hears the 'come' command, it will automatically turn and come charging back to you.

SIMPLE RECALL

Start teaching your dog in a place where there are no distractions. Carry a handful of treats and your dog's

▲ Once your dog is trained to come to you, it will be free to play off the lead.

favourite toy. Feed it a few treats from your hand to get its attention, then toss a small treat away from you. If necessary, show it where the treat has gone and, just as it is eating the treat, back away a few steps from the dog and call its name. When it looks towards you, praise it just for looking up and paying attention. As it comes back to you, get really excited that it is coming in your direction – give it a round of applause. Dog owners can be reticent about praising their dogs, but getting a recall is a situation in which you should go overboard with praise. Make its tail wag with happiness.

When your dog gets back to you, give it a treat immediately and let it play with its favourite toy. Don't tell it to sit before giving it the reward; this would incorrectly reward the sit rather than the recall.

Then toss another treat out and, again, just when the dog has eaten the treat, call it by name. As it is coming towards you, say "come". Only do this five or six times, then finish. If you carry out short training sessions four or five times a day, your dog will stay alert and happy. You can practise recalls in the kitchen when the kettle is boiling, tossing treats up and down the room when the advertisements are on the television – in fact, during any spare couple of minutes that you have.

TRAINING A DOG TO COME BACK

1 In a place with no distractions, feed your dog some tasty treats by hand, to get its attention.

2 Toss one small treat a short distance away from you, showing the dog where you want it to go.

3 While your dog is busy finding and eating its food treat, walk a few steps away from it.

4 When the dog has finished eating, call it. Praise it for looking up. In later repetitions, say "come" at this point.

5 When the dog begins to run back to you, get really excited – smile, give it a round of applause and praise it.

6 As soon as the dog reaches you, reward it with a food treat and/or a favourite toy, then repeat the process.

◀ *Use extra-tasty treats for rewarding recalls in places with distractions.*

RECALLING WITH DISTRACTIONS

The next stage is to try this training in the garden, where there are plenty of distractions. Use a highly visible reward such as a chunk of red cheese that can be seen in the grass (this will give hunting breeds plenty of stimulation). Let your dog use its sense of smell to hunt down the treat. To create even more excitement, throw the cheese behind you when your dog is running towards you, so that it has to fly past you to get the reward. This makes recall a really exciting game for your dog.

After about a week of this training, choose a time when your dog is in the garden and you are indoors, watching it through the window. Call your dog by name and give the cue 'come'. If it comes charging into the house, give it a really high-value reward and praise it until it wags its tail. It now understands what 'come' means.

Having achieved this result, take your training to the next level. This requires a willing volunteer, some boring dog biscuits and a handful of really tasty treats. Place your dog by the volunteer and tell them to hold an ordinary dog biscuit right under the dog's nose. Stand about 3.6m (12ft) away, then call your dog. Repeat the command until it comes. Initially you'll have to call it five or six times but, eventually, it will respond more quickly. Always give it a special reward so that it knows it's worth responding. Give it better treats for better responses, until you eventually give it a handful of chicken.

If you practise a little and often, you will quickly reach this stage. The secret is to add the command 'come' after you call your dog's name and it runs towards you.. This ensures that it's second nature for the dog to come whenever you ask it to.

▼ *Begin recall training indoors, using a treat such as a piece of cheese.*

For the final stage, you need a volunteer who knows your dog. Stand about 12m (40ft) away from your volunteer, get them to call your dog and, as it obeys and goes off, call it back when it is halfway there. Then try calling it back from playing with a friend's dog and even from strange dogs. Never forget how good it has been to obey you – make sure it gets an excellent treat for every recall. Having a good recall is the most important command that you teach your dog. A life on the lead is not good and, with that in mind, never stop rewarding successful recalls.

WHISTLE RECALLS

There are a number of benefits to teaching your dog to respond to a whistle, not least because a whistle is much louder than your voice and can easily cut through a blasting winter wind. If you have a quiet voice and don't like shouting, a whistle is ideal.

▼ *Instead of food, playing a game is also a good reward for coming back.*

Another advantage is that the sound is always the same, whether you walk the dog yourself, use dog walkers or if different members of your family walk the dog. It is a clear, distinct sound that will cut through any distractions or the sound of people talking. It is used for one command only – 'come here' – and should not be confused with anything else.

There are many different whistles on the market, and a loud one is best. The range includes specialist gundog whistles and a referee's whistle, and you might also like to try a silent dog whistle. It doesn't matter which one you use, provided you stick to it.

Like recall training, whistle training is all about repetition, so that the dog instinctively associates the sound with the command 'come here'. When training your dog, carry out the above procedure but exchange the 'come' command for a blow on the whistle. You can also make the association between the whistle and good news at meal times: hold a bowl of food, blow the whistle, then give your dog its dinner. If you do that for a week at every meal when it is a puppy (three times a day), it will quickly make the connection. If your dog will retrieve a ball, try blowing the whistle as it comes towards you. This will strengthen the association between the whistle and the 'come' command. Finally, if you take your dog on a walk with a friend, practise whistle recalls between the two of you, increasing the distance as its reliability increases. Always take rewards out with you.

From a safety point of view, your dog needs a strong recall; continuing to reward it intermittently will keep the recall response strong.

TRAINING A WHISTLE RECALL

1 Throw a treat a short distance away from you, making sure your dog sees where you want it to go.

2 After your dog has found the treat and eaten it, blow a whistle. Praise it for looking at you.

3 When the dog comes running back to you, smile and encourage it, stroke it and give it a food treat.

4 Take the time to praise your dog, and always use very tasty treats when training a recall with distractions.

Lead-walking

▶ Reward your dog when it obeys your command to 'walk close'.

Teaching your dog to walk on a loose lead is one of the hardest things you'll have to do. Roads and parks are full of fascinating smells, the scents of other dogs and the aroma of dropped food, all of which entice your dog to pull away and investigate. When it becomes an adolescent, the urge to scent-mark over those smells will be very strong, and there'll be an extra need to pull you in all kinds of directions. In addition, most dogs quickly realize that if they pull when they are keen to get to the park, their owner tends to walk faster.

Most dog owners do not want obedience-style heelwork; all they want is to keep their arm in its socket and to have a pleasant walk! Dog-training classes often teach you to walk a dog on your left, simply because obedience competitions demand it, but for the average dog owner it really doesn't matter which side it walks on. If you are walking along a main road, it is usually safest to have your dog walking on the inside, away from the traffic.

Lead-walking can be difficult in terms of being consistent. If you are pushed for time and have to get home to leave for work after the morning walk, there isn't always time to stop every time your dog pulls. If so, unfortunately your dog's pulling behaviour will be reinforced.

There are many training aids to facilitate lead-walking. If you have a strong dog, a harness is a great help, and a head collar will give you more control, provided your dog will accept wearing one over its nose. Try out a few different ones to see which type your dog is most comfortable with.

Start by training your dog to walk by your side without its lead on. If your dog cannot do this without being distracted, it will not be able to walk on a loose lead. Begin by sitting it by your side, feeding it a few treats to get its attention. Pat the side of your leg as you step off to signal where you would like it to be, then reward it after a couple of steps. In fact, you cannot reward your dog too much in the early stages of teaching it to walk on a lead. Every couple of steps, offer another reward. Eventually, however, you'll want it to learn to walk calmly by your side with its head up, taking in a wide range of sights and smells; it would

▼ If your dog likes to pull hard, a harness will give you more control.

be unnatural for it to trot along while fixated on your hands and a possible reward. Until it reaches this stage, reward it when it's walking by your side, but don't stop to make it sit for its reward, otherwise it will think it's being rewarded for the act of sitting.

If your dog pulls ahead, resist the urge to yank it back on the lead – this is a sure way to damage its neck and hurt your shoulder. Instead, stop walking and take a couple of steps back until your dog is by your side. Get it to sit, gain its attention, then start again. Do not praise and reward your dog for just being by your side; save that for when it's walking calmly by your side on a loose lead.

Continue using vocal praise when the dog is positioned exactly where you want it to be, and always use the words 'walk close' when it is in the right position – not when it is pulling. Also reward your dog when it obeys you, especially when it stays by your side while walking past a distraction. The more encouragement you give it, the more it will learn not to pull and try to investigate everything. When it consistently and automatically responds to your commands, you can dispense with the food treats.

TRAINING A DOG TO WALK ON A LOOSE LEAD

1 Begin by rewarding your dog for being at your side without a lead. Feed it a small treat to get its attention.

2 As you step forward, pat the side of your leg. This is to let your dog know where you want it to be.

3 When your dog stands up and walks by your side, reward it with another food treat. Repeat this every few steps.

4 Once your dog can successfully walk by your side, carry out the same training procedure with a lead.

5 Pat your leg to show your dog where you want it. Do not pull on the lead; let your dog walk forward on its own.

6 Do not reward the dog for sitting. Wait until it walks calmly by your side with a loose lead, then give it a treat.

Settle down

▶ *Your dog should be able to settle down quietly and happily when asked.*

Having a dog that is able to settle down means that it won't be a pest when you are trying to eat a meal, that it will lie beside you when you have visitors, and that it will happily curl up next to you when you are reading. In many households there's already enough noise and confusion. You don't need to add to it by having an agitated dog, and it would be a shame to have to isolate it by putting it in a crate, locking it in another room or shutting it behind a baby gate. The command 'settle down' will allow calm to reign over the chaos.

When your dog is lying down of its own accord, reward it with a small treat, tell it it's a good dog and stress the word 'settle'. The more you reward a dog's natural behaviour, the more it will be able to do it, and the delight of this command is that it doesn't involve one fixed position. The dog can flop over on its side, curl up, roll or stretch. It can do anything, as long as it is settled. Unfortunately we often ignore dogs (and children) when they are quiet, not realizing that such behaviour should be actively encouraged. The more you reward a particular behaviour, the more often your dog will do it.

When you teach your dog to settle, make sure it is tired, for example after an evening meal or its walk. Put it on a long, loose lead so that it can sit, lie or stand while you watch television. Ignore it, and while it may find this (and being tethered) rather odd and get restless, it will eventually settle down. Don't say anything (no 'down' or 'sit' cues); just wait it out until it settles. The hardest part is getting it to settle down for the first time, and thereafter your dog should find this easier and easier. Don't go overboard with praise, because this will just make the dog jump straight back up again. Gently stroke its head, slip it a treat and say "settle down". The more you practise, the easier it will get, and the longer amount of time your dog will remain settled.

TRAINING A DOG TO SETTLE DOWN

1 Choose a time when your dog is tired, such as after a meal or a walk. Put it on a long lead and sit quietly.

2 Ignore it for a while. Do not say anything; wait it out. Eventually the dog should lie down by your side.

3 When the dog settles, reward it quietly by gently stroking its head. Give it a food treat and say "settle down".

Retrieve

▶ *Repeating your retrieval training will keep your dog well exercised.*

Some dog breeds love to retrieve more than others, with Collies and Labradors being high up on the list. Other dogs find retrieving a pointless exercise, but although it might take them a while to be trained, it can be done. One of the advantages of training a dog to retrieve is that you don't have to take it on a long walk to get it fully exercised. If you're feeling tired but it's bursting with adrenaline, you've only got to throw a ball. It's also a great bonding exercise for both of you.

Dogs that are not natural retrievers need short training sessions or they'll quickly get bored, and this particularly applies to puppies. Begin in a place where there are few distractions, and don't be surprised if your dog initially picks up the toy that you have thrown and runs off in the opposite direction. Whatever you do, don't run after the dog, or it will think you're instigating a game of chase.

The easiest way to teach a dog to retrieve is by first teaching it to pick up an object. Have some small, tasty treats and a toy. Offer the dog the toy, and if it takes it in its mouth, praise it wildly and offer it a treat. This will teach the dog to drop the object into your hand.

Pick up the toy again and play with it on the floor, get the dog interested in chasing it, then toss it a short distance away from you. As soon as the dog puts it in its mouth, praise it again and offer a treat. It may spit the toy out and come to you for the treat, but don't worry – this is only the beginning of the game.

If your dog doesn't seem interested in picking up the toy, play a fun game of hide-and-seek with it – showing it the object, then hiding it behind your back. When you eventually get the dog's interest, throw the toy away. If the dog chases the toy and picks it up, praise and reward it. If it really has no interest, go further back in the sequence and reward it for just sniffing the toy a couple of times.

By doing the training a little and often, and putting the toy away after each game, your dog's retrieval skills should gradually build up over a couple of sessions.

TRAINING A DOG TO RETRIEVE AN ITEM

1 Have some tasty treats handy. Offer your dog a toy, but keep it just out of its reach; this should get it excited.

2 Let the dog hold the toy. Put a treat under its nose. When it lets go of the toy, praise it and give it the treat.

3 Once it has learned that dropping the toy gets it a reward, toss the toy a short distance away from you.

4 Praise your dog for picking up the toy, and give it a treat when it brings it back to you. Do not chase the dog.

Drop it

There will be times when your pet picks up something it shouldn't, and teaching your dog to 'drop it' means you can retrieve your possessions without it becoming a battle of wills. From a safety point of view, it is important that your dog is able to give things up willingly on command.

It is best to teach this is in stages. Use a favourite toy that can be used for tug, and some very tasty treats – the smellier the better. Offer your dog the toy and initiate a game of tug. Soon after, put a treat right under the dog's nose, at which point it should drop the toy and take the treat. It may take a couple of seconds to think about it, but bear with it. The crucial point is to say "drop it" at the moment it drops the toy. Then show it the toy again and have another game.

Play this game of tug a few times each day, always putting a treat under its nose and saying "drop it" at the appropriate moment. After a few days,

try saying "drop it" before you offer the treat and, if the dog drops the toy, give it a handful of treats as the jackpot.

Your dog should learn to give things up as a young puppy, and whenever you take something away from it, always swap it with something equally rewarding. Don't take bones and other prized objects away from your dog just because you think you should, because this is the fastest way to teach a dog to guard its possessions. If it does tend to guard bones, food or toys, get specialist help from a behaviour counsellor.

When your dog has mastered the 'drop it' command, this will open up the possibility of playing a whole range of interactive games. Most dogs love fetching a ball, but nothing can be more frustrating for an owner than having to hunt all over the house for a dropped toy. Because your dog has learned that it can exchange a toy for a treat, it will now bring the ball back

▲ *Teaching your dog to drop an object will make games of fetch fun.*

to you to gain its reward. You could also try hiding a toy and getting your dog to seek it out and return it to you. These games will help to keep your dog's mind and body well exercised.

Some formal obedience tests involve retrieving and returning an item, and dogs working to the gun must seek and return fallen birds. For all these disciplines, a well-taught 'drop it' command is a very good basis on which to build.

TRAINING A DOG TO DROP AN OBJECT

1 Offer your dog one end of a tugger toy and initiate a game of tug-of-war, pulling the toy away from the dog.

2 Let go of the tugger and take a treat out of your pocket. Hold the treat right under the dog's nose.

3 Allow the dog time to decide what to do. Say "drop it" as soon as it drops the toy, give it the treat and praise it.

Phasing out the reward

The ultimate aim of training your dog is to get it to obey your commands whether you provide a reward or not. When your dog is a puppy you need to reward and bribe it, but that state shouldn't exist forever. You can't keep stashing away rewards that will excite it (which soon becomes a practical problem), just to make sure it's obedient. The use of food becomes bad psychologically: there's a very real danger that your dog will become too reliant on rewards and bribes, and will never obey a command without food. In addition, rewards can become boring over time, and the behaviour you want to encourage will gradually diminish. But at what point should you start phasing out food treats? The answer is as soon as your dog understands a command and can respond correctly with a treat.

Put your treats somewhere that you can reach them but your puppy cannot, such as in your pocket or in a treat bag. Using the same hand movement that you used with the food lure, ask your dog to sit. When it does, praise it profusely. Repeat the request several times, sometimes giving your dog a treat when it sits and sometimes not. There may be some confusion on your puppy's part when you first dispense with the food lure, but bear with it. You may need to ask it twice to begin with.

When your puppy manages to sit successfully without the food in your hand, you can now go on to rewarding the best responses. Make the rewards intermittent, only rewarding the very best responses and ignoring those that aren't as good. Use different rewards, such as a game of tug or throwing a ball, combined with verbal praise.

Improving training is all about getting the best out of your dog, so now is the time to ask more of it. Ask your dog to follow a few commands before you praise it – maybe a 'sit' and then a 'down'. Next, ask it to sit, walk ten paces away from it, then return and praise it. Then try asking it to sit, lie down and sit again, and then reward it. Don't be too predictable with your training; ask for cues in different combinations and reward your dog at different times.

Delay the time your dog follows a cue and gets its reward. Ask it to sit, count to ten, then reward it. Next time, ask it to lie down, count to five and then give it its reward. You will get the best out of your dog if you keep it guessing. If your training is boring and predictable, the dog will also find it boring and predictable, and you won't get the behaviour you deserve for all your hard work.

▲ *Eventually, praise, strokes and games can replace food rewards.*

When you begin asking more of your dog, it may break its positions – the dog is used to being rewarded immediately, but you are changing the conditions. Don't panic; just put the dog back in position and try an easier task. If you were trying for a 10-second sit and your dog gets up, put it back calmly and count to five instead. In time it will get it right, and its confidence will grow accordingly.

PHASING OUT FOOD REWARDS

1 Hide some treats in a bag. Ask your dog to sit, using the hand movements you used before, but without any food.

2 When the dog sits, praise it. On some occasions give it a food treat; at other times, reward it with a game.

Household manners

Just as children have to be taught basic manners, so do puppies. One of the first things we teach our children is to be polite and say "please" when they want something, but we miss many opportunities to teach our dogs the same thing on a daily basis.

Using everyday life rewards is a great way to practise all the exercises that you have trained your dog to do in the context that you want it to do them. For example, if it wants to go out to the garden to go to the toilet, ask it to sit for a moment, thus training it to hold its bladder. Concentrate on life rewards such as going outdoors, walks and games, and you will get good results.

It's best to give your dog only one cue; don't nag it. When asking it to sit before going out to the garden,

if it doesn't sit the first time you ask, calmly walk away from the back door for a moment, without saying anything. Then go back and try again. After about the third or fourth time, the dog should understand.

As another example, ask your dog to sit so that you can put its lead on to go for a walk. If it begins leaping and running around in its excitement to get out the door, calmly drop the lead and walk away. After 30 seconds, go back and pick up the lead. At this stage its excitement will probably be even greater, so drop the lead again and walk away. You may want to put the kettle on and make a cup of tea when you are teaching this skill – with some dogs it will take a while before they learn that it's actually what they are doing that is responsible for your

▲ *The door is a place of excitement, so your dog needs good manners.*

actions. When you have the lead on and your dog is sitting calmly, put your hand on the door handle. Here, if it begins to jump around and tries to push through the door, close the door, drop the lead and walk away. Continue the process until the dog is able to stay calm while you're preparing for its walk.

TRAINING A DOG TO SIT CALMLY BEFORE GOING FOR A WALK

1 When it's time for a walk, pick up your dog's lead and go to the door. It may get very excited and jump up.

2 If the dog doesn't sit the first time you ask, drop the lead, turn around and walk away without saying anything.

3 You may have to do this a few times before it gets the message. Once it has learned to sit nicely, put its lead on.

Sitting when visitors call

Some dogs greet visitors so enthusiastically that it can be embarrassing – or worse, your dog may cover your visitors' clean clothes with muddy paws. Most dogs jump up to get attention, so you need to avoid giving them attention such as shouting "get down", grabbing their collar to pull them away or smacking them, because even negative attention inadvertently reinforces the jumping-up behaviour.

Even if visitors tell you, "I don't mind; I love dogs", this doesn't mean your dog should be allowed to jump up on them. If it jumps up on children or on the elderly, it may knock them over, with serious consequences. Your dog will not be able to discriminate between who it can and can't jump on, so you must be consistent with all household visitors.

The secret is not to let jumping up become a habit in the first place. When your puppy jumps up on you, take a step back so that its feet land on the floor, then kneel down to its level to say hello. This means there will be no reason for it to jump. It's important to teach children to do the same thing, because it's usually children who shout when the puppy is jumping up, which only gets the puppy more excited.

If jumping up is already an established habit, it will take a bit longer to teach your dog an alternative behaviour. You need a willing volunteer to help you. Have your dog on the lead when your volunteer calls. Ask the visitor to stand beyond the reach of your dog. Let your dog pull towards the visitor, but ignore the dog's behaviour – don't shout at it, push it into a sit position or yank it back on the lead. The idea is that you are teaching your dog the consequences of its behaviour.

When the lead has gone loose and your dog has settled down, reward it. Don't ask your visitors to reward it, however, because there is going to be

▲ *It is important for your dog to learn to be calm around visitors.*

a time when you'll have a guest that is not keen on dogs; you'll want your dog to sit quietly by your side when they are visiting. Conversely, if someone were to come in and provide a reward, your dog would begin to expect rewards from everyone it comes across – in the park and in the street.

Note that you don't always have to use food as a reward. Instead, you could have a quick game of tug for sitting quietly when visitors call.

TRAINING A DOG TO SIT WHEN VISITORS CALL

1 Find a willing volunteer to help you. Have your dog on a lead and ask your visitor to come into the room.

2 Allow your dog to pull towards the visitor. Do not try to stop your dog – do not shout at it or pull the lead.

3 Eventually your dog will sit down. As soon as it does, praise it and reward it with a food treat.

Distance, duration and distractions

We need our dogs to follow commands, whether they are on or off the lead, in a park full of dogs or walking along the road, and for the length of time that we require. Many owners become dismayed that their dogs follow all their commands in the house and in training classes, but as soon as they're outside it seems as if they'd never been to a training class before.

When you're ready to train your dog to obey you at a distance, it's best to keep distractions to a minimum to begin with, and increase the duration of the exercises a little at a time. Note that you will have to increase the number of rewards when you make the exercises more difficult.

Once your dog is performing well in your usual training environment, begin training in the park where you take it for a walk. The difficulty in this is that your dog probably only associates the park with playing with other dogs, and it may be more keen to run off rather than complete your obedience exercises. But if you're patient, you will see results. Note that if you increase the value of the reward, it's a good idea to make sure any other dogs are as far away as possible.

DISTANCE

When you begin training in a park where you have never done distance exercises before, don't try a difficult 1-minute 'stay' right at the beginning of the session. Instead, ask for several short sessions of 'sit' while you walk a couple of steps away from your dog, then come straight back to it. Don't start off with long distances; it is better to make it easy at the beginning, and gradually build up your dog's confidence. Use the environment as a reward. For example, if the dog is on a long lead, you could let it walk towards a tree for a good sniff. If it pulls towards something it wants without sitting first, take a couple of steps back as a penalty, then try again. When it gets it right, use rewards that your dog enjoys. Once it can sit successfully, stay and watch, let it off the lead and continue the training.

DURATION

As well as increasing the distance between you and your dog, you can also begin to increase the amount of time between the desired behaviour and the reward. This training works best when you're unpredictable. For example, vary the length of time that you stand back from your dog during a 'stay' command. On the first occasion,

WORKING WITH DISTANCE, DURATION AND DISTRACTIONS

1 When training your dog to 'stay' while outdoors, gradually increase the distance between you and your dog.

2 Also try increasing the duration of time between your dog's desirable behaviour and the reward.

3 Finally, add distractions to your training. For example, ask your dog to sit, then make a telephone call.

CHECKING THAT A DOG UNDERSTANDS A CUE

1 To test if your dog understands 'walk close', take its lead off in the garden. Say its name to get its attention.

2 Take a few steps back and say "walk close". If your dog understands, it will make eye contact and approach.

3 When it walks by your side, reward it with a handful of food treats and praise it enthusiastically.

reward it after 25 seconds, the next time 5 seconds, then 10 seconds. Similarly, when teaching your dog to walk on a lead, reward it after a couple of steps, then 10, 5 and 20 steps. This will keep your dog guessing and, more importantly, it will make it try harder to get you to reward it.

DISTRACTIONS

It is important to hold training sessions not just in classes but in the real world, which is packed with distractions, because that's where your dog needs to obey you. Make sure it can walk on a loose lead without pulling forward when it sees a family member approaching. You don't want it dashing across a road and causing an accident. Can it leave a toy on the floor when it walks past it, and sit while you talk on the telephone? Adding distractions is challenging, but make sure that whenever you increase the pressure to follow commands, you always initially increase the reward.

DOES YOUR DOG UNDERSTAND?

When you take your training 'out on the road', you will soon find out whether it has worked. Does your dog really understand that 'sit' means 'sit', wherever you are, in different environments and with distractions? Similarly, does it understand that 'walk close' means it needs to keep close to your leg whether it is on or off the lead? Most dogs learn to walk on a loose lead because we use the lead to control where they are – they know they are tethered to us, but do not necessarily understand the command. However, if your dog is off the lead and you need it by your side, understanding the cue is important so that it can come quickly and walk with you.

Test your dog out in the garden, when it is not distracted. Start walking, then say your dog's name followed by the cue 'walk close' (or whatever cue you use). If it comes and walks by your side, give it a handful of treats.

The secret to teaching the cue properly is to name the behaviour at the exact time the dog is doing it. For example, say "sit" just as the dog's bottom hits the floor, not before or after. This will make the dog associate the action with the cue. If you get this right, it will sit the first time you ask. Training is a two-way process: you have to learn the dog's language and it has to learn yours. You must teach it which actions match the sounds you make.

▼ *Your dog should still listen to you even when there are other distractions.*

Essential training reminders

To help you remember the key points when training your dog to follow basic commands, here is a quick summary.

TRAIN RIGHT AWAY

The more a dog behaves in a certain way, the more ingrained this behaviour becomes. This applies to both acceptable and unacceptable behaviours. So, it's your responsibility to start training your puppy as soon as you can after the age of 12 weeks, to make sure it is behaving the way you want it to, and doesn't completely disrupt your life.

HAVE A PLAN

Avoid the temptation to be exclusively negative, and don't fixate on what you don't want your dog to do. Decide what you would like it to do. Have a series of goals. Imagine it in, say, three years' time. How would you like it to behave then? Make sure you teach it what's required.

STAY CALM

It's unfair to both you and your dog to undertake training when either of you is angry, grumpy, stressed or just not in the mood. It's far better to wait until you're both happy, alert and responsive, which will give

◄ Use a variety of rewards, particularly your dog's favourite toy.

your dog a much better chance of learning its lessons. If you do train it when you're in a bad mood, it may well pick up your stress, and you're more likely to snap and be over-critical when what it really needs is encouragement and kindness.

BE CONSISTENT

It's all too easy to confuse a dog by using the same words to mean different things. For example, the word 'down' is often used in very different contexts: when your dog is jumping up on a person; when you want it to get off the sofa; when you want it to lie down; and when it is snuffling scraps on the breakfast table. It is no surprise that your dog might look confused or completely ignore you. For this reason, it is important to make sure the whole family uses the same set of commands.

◄ Stay calm and consistently praise and reward your puppy whenever it does something good.

► Be relaxed in your training and your dog will respond better. It is best to train when you're in a good mood.

LEARN BODY LANGUAGE

If you can read your dog's body language, you'll be able to help it out of situations when it's not coping. For example, understanding that a dog's yawn is actually a stress signal – not a sign that it's tired or bored with training – means that you need to put more effort into helping it, instead of giving up because you think it has had enough.

CARRY TREATS IN YOUR POCKET

You never know when you will have a chance to reinforce your dog's good behaviour, so always carry treats.

◄ *Crates keep your dog safe and are also a good aid for house-training.*

▲ *Training will often reap its own rewards.*

TELL YOUR PET IT'S A GOOD DOG

As with children, it's very easy to focus on bad behaviour and ignore the good, taking the latter for granted. But don't do it. To reinforce your dog's behaviour when it's being good, go out of your way to praise it. Conversely, ignore it when it's bad. It will feel deprived when it isn't being regularly praised, and will soon learn that good behaviour is worth learning because it brings happiness, games and treats. Remember to tell it it's a good dog just for lying quietly beside you, and give it a stroke when it sits at your side while you're having a conversation. The more you reward such behaviour, the more often your dog will display it.

MANAGE THE ENVIRONMENT

If your dog raids the bin, steals food off the worktop or jumps up on visitors, manage the environment until you can train your dog to do otherwise. Put the bin out of reach, put food away and put the dog in the kitchen with some treats when visitors arrive. Also teach your children to keep their toys tidy so that the dog can't run away with them. If your dog pulls when on the lead, use a head collar or harness. By managing the environment, you'll reduce tension between you and your dog.

USE CRATES

When used correctly, the crate is a brilliant idea. It's a place the dog can call its own, and where you can safely put it when it's going through the chewing phase and can't be supervised. It also makes a good holding pen if you are having a children's party and don't want it jumping up, giving nips and bites, with the children getting it overexcited. If you take your dog on holiday, let it sleep in a crate so that it has to whine to wake you up when it wants to go to the toilet. If it does have an accident in it, it won't stain the carpet.

REMEMBER, IT IS JUST A DOG

All the behaviour that your dog displays is dog behaviour. Don't forget it. We may not live comfortably with biting, barking, digging and fighting, but remember that they are all perfectly natural to a dog. What we can do is influence a dog's basic behaviour, and make it more acceptable. Don't leave things to chance; dogs have to be trained. If you sometimes think your dog is being naughty, try making a list of what you did as a child, and as an adult. Who was worse?

ABOVE ALL, HAVE FUN

Training shouldn't be stressful. It needs to be relaxed and fun. The happier and more confident your dog is, the quicker it will respond to your commands. So if the training is going wrong, take a rest and have a rethink. What are you doing wrong?

▼ *Training should be an enjoyable experience for both you and your dog.*

HOW TO SOLVE COMMON PROBLEMS

There will be many times during the first few months of owning a puppy that you might wonder if you have taken on more than you can cope with. Biting, chewing, digging, stealing and attention-seeking behaviour can stretch your patience to the limit. Some behaviours that puppies engage in are specific to their breed. For example, nipping children's ankles is common with the herding breeds (the collies and shepherds); digging can be a speciality of the terriers; and retrievers like carrying things. Such genetic behaviour can never be eradicated completely, but it can be redirected in a more useful way. Everybody would like a perfect dog, but these do not come ready-made. As soon as possible, owners need to identify behaviour that could lead to problems. With kindness, understanding and consistency, and occasionally the help of experts, most problems can be solved.

◄ *Puppies will play with anything that is left around, such as electric cables, mobile phones and shoes. You can minimize this by providing chew toys.*

Biting

Like a baby, a puppy explores texture and taste by taking objects into its mouth and biting on them. However, a puppy learns naturally from a very young age that its teeth can hurt, and that its biting behaviour has negative consequences. For example, when it begins hurting its mother while suckling, she will get up and walk away, thus initiating weaning it on to solid food. It also learns that its siblings have teeth that can hurt, usually ending in a fight or one puppy refusing to play after a particularly painful nip.

Unfortunately, a puppy can be persistent in its biting, and if it bites children, their cries and squeals could send it into a biting frenzy. The more noise, the more biting; and the more you push the dog away, the more it throws itself back at you. Such puppies are usually overstimulated or over-tired, or terriers, and the best way to respond is by calmly getting up and ending

▶ Biting is natural puppy behaviour, but rough games should be discouraged.

the game. If the puppy comes after you to bite your trouser leg, then put it behind a baby gate for a 'time out' period, and you will usually find that it lies down and falls asleep. If you respond with your own freneticism, you'll simply encourage more of the same. Don't forget that dogs only have one form of defence when it comes to self-preservation, and that is their teeth. This does not make them bad – they're just being dogs.

To help your puppy learn to have a 'soft mouth', and ultimately never to use its teeth at all on human skin, you have to act like its litter mate. If you receive a painful nip from your puppy, give a high-pitched squeal and turn your back on it. It should back off,

possibly returning to lick you. Also make sure that you give it plenty of acceptable items to chew, including raggers, rawhide chews and cardboard tubes from kitchen rolls.

However, note that this method becomes less effective as your puppy grows up. An older animal is more likely to come at you with renewed vigour when you squeal. To avoid this, finish the game, get up and move away. If your dog persistently follows you, again put it calmly behind a baby gate. It is important that everyone in the house responds in the same way, discouraging all rough games. Also, don't forget that children should be supervised at all times when playing with a puppy.

TRAINING A PUPPY NOT TO BITE

1 Puppies tend to bite anything that moves and catches their attention, including trouser legs and skirts.

2 When your puppy bites your leg or clothing, turn your back on it, ignore it and walk away.

3 If you can't ignore the dog, give it something it is allowed to bite, such as a rawhide chew.

Chewing

An activity that all puppies and adolescent dogs enjoy, chewing usually begins during the teething stages: 4 months old for puppies, and about 8 months old for adolescents. During the teething phase, puppies explore absolutely everything with their mouth; it's their main tool when investigating the world. It is up to you to teach your puppy which objects are acceptable for it to chew, and which are not.

To a dog, all of your possessions can seem like a steady stream of chew toys. Some items are obviously dangerous, such as electric and telephone cables, television remote controls, mobile phones and poisonous plants (including many bulbs, which dogs can easily dig up). Discarded shoes and clothing can be very tempting for your dog, as can children's toys. Maybe this is a good time to train everyone in your household to put their belongings away! You should also check that

▶ Chewing is normal when teething. Provide your puppy with a good selection of chew toys.

cupboard doors – especially kitchen units – close correctly, so that items can be put out of harm's way.

You can never eradicate your puppy's natural need to chew, but you can make sure that it chews safely. Good pet shops sell many types of virtually indestructible chew toys, while butchers can provide raw beef shin bones. Note that you should never give your puppy chicken, pork or lamb bones. These splinter easily and the shards of bone, once swallowed, could damage the stomach and intestine, resulting in the need for veterinary treatment. Similarly, you should never give your dog plastic toys. These are dangerous because they can easily be broken into small

pieces that get stuck in a dog's throat or stomach, sometimes causing tearing and bleeding when the dog passes a stool.

Have a good look around the house and see what your puppy might be tempted by, and put all inappropriate items away. Provide it with a good selection of safe chew toys and hide chews. Ensure that all toys, either for play or chewing, are large enough so that your puppy cannot swallow them.

When teething, a knotted tea towel soaked in water and frozen will ease your puppy's sore gums. Some pet shops stock puppy teething toys that can be either frozen or chilled in the refrigerator. These are clean, dry and safe to use, even on a carpeted floor.

TRAINING A PUPPY NOT TO CHEW ITEMS

1 Keep clutter such as electric cables, mobile phones, remote controls and plants out of your puppy's reach.

2 Have a good selection of chew toys available, offering your puppy alternative, safe objects to play with.

3 Cold toys – such as an old tea towel with knots tied in it, soaked in water and frozen – will ease painful gums.

Digging

Does your garden look like the archaeologists have just left? Do you have large craters on the lawn? Are your flowerbeds shredded? You have a puppy! Most dogs will do some digging at some time, whether they're burying a toy or just for the fun of it.

The best way to control this tendency is not by trying to eradicate it, but by fencing it off – literally. Trellis off part of the garden so that there is a clearly defined area where your dog can dig. Hide a few of your dog's favourite toys or biscuits under the soil. Teach it that this is its special digging place by allowing it to dig them up, and let it enjoy itself in its special area.

If your dog is digging in another part of the garden, don't chase it away or you will simply teach it a new game – next time it wants to play, it will start digging so that you come running after it. If you don't want it to dig in any part of the garden, buy it a child's sandpit, fill it with builder's

▶ *Digging is second nature to a dog, so it needs a special area of its own in the garden. Make sure it is never left alone for long periods of time.*

sand and bury your dog's toys or some biscuits in it. Cover the sandpit at night so that the neighbourhood cats don't use it as a toilet.

Some dogs will try to dig under the garden fence in an attempt to escape. This will be very dangerous if they succeed, so immediate action must be taken. Placing large rocks or boulders in the area where your dog is digging will put it off, but it may just move its tunnelling activities to another part of the boundary. In the short term, the best course of action is to fix strong wire mesh to the bottom of the fence

and to bury it at least 60cm (2ft) under the ground. Ensure that there are no sharp edges to the fencing so that your dog will not hurt its paws.

In the long term, try to work out why your dog feels the need to escape. Does it have enough exercise, or could it be bored? Is there anything in the garden that it is afraid of? Watch it for a period of time and see if you can work out the reason. Increasing exercise, providing mental stimulation and ensuring the dog is not left alone for long periods will go a long way towards solving this problem.

TRAINING A DOG TO DIG IN A SPECIAL AREA

1 Fence off a small part of the garden where it is acceptable for your dog to dig. This can be achieved with a trellis.

2 While your dog watches, bury a few toys and/or biscuits in the special fenced-off part of the garden.

3 Encourage your dog to dig in the special area, and praise it when it finds its buried treasure.

Jumping up

Particularly if you have a large breed of dog, jumping up can be a serious problem. It can be downright dangerous when a dog jumps up on children or the elderly, and although smaller dogs are not as dangerous, they can certainly be a nuisance with a prodigious spring and muddy paws. The problem is that when puppies are young, we inadvertently teach them to jump up to say hello so that we don't have to bend down to reach them. But a puppy's growth rate is so fast that within 3 months you will already have created a problem.

Training your dog not to jump up at people is extremely important, as this problem can have very serious consequences. A stranger may mistake your dog's over-enthusiastic greeting for an attack and be very frightened. This could result in an official complaint against your dog, and pleading a lack of training is not a very good defence! It's always your responsibility to control your dog.

To convert jumping up to sitting down for a greeting, ask your friends and family to help. Put your puppy on a lead and ask someone to approach it, but they must stop as soon as the dog strains on the lead to jump up. Ignore the puppy until it calms down, then reward it with a treat and get your friend to back off and approach again. It should only take four or five attempts to get your dog to understand that sitting for a greeting is the acceptable way to act. Practise on all family members, especially children. You, the owner, should always be the one to reward the dog, otherwise the dog will assume that everyone carries treats around, making its jumping-up behaviour even worse.

If your dog jumps up on you at other times – not just when you have visitors or when you open the front door – this is probably attention-seeking behaviour. If so, you need to walk away from it as soon as the unwanted behaviour begins.

▲ *Jumping up is a nuisance and can become a dangerous habit.*

It may take time and patience to re-model the jumping-up behaviour, but you must persevere. Your dog may have been allowed to jump up as a way of greeting for a considerable part of its life. If so, this has become a habit. It may remember how it was rewarded for this action with affection and praise when it was a puppy.

TRAINING A DOG NOT TO JUMP UP

1 Get a willing volunteer to help you. Ask them to approach your dog while you have it on a lead.

2 Ask your volunteer to stand just out of reach so that when your dog jumps up, it is unsuccessful.

3 When your dog sits, reward it with a small food treat while your volunteer remains where they are.

Barking

It is natural for dogs to bark, but persistent barking can be a big problem, bringing trouble from neighbours and the authorities. If your dog barks when left alone, there could be several reasons for this. It could be bored, it could be guarding its home, or it might be suffering from separation anxiety. Puppies often feel anxious when their owners go out, and rescue dogs in particular can suffer from separation anxiety when they are left alone – and when anxious, they bark. But it's possible to overcome the problem.

First, you need to find out what the problem is. Perhaps your dog is being left alone for too long without adequate exercise and a chance to go to the toilet (dogs hate going inside

▶ *Barking is always a nuisance, but once you have determined its cause, it can be controlled.*

the house). If this is the case, employ a dog walker. Also try taking your dog for a walk before you go to work, and leave it a good selection of toys to play with while you're out. If it barks when people walk past the window, close the door to that room so that it so that it can't see out. It may be that your dog is alarm-barking because it can hear your next-door neighbours or noise from outside the home. If you think this is the case, try leaving a

radio on when you go out. This will help to muffle any noise and make your dog feel more secure, so that it is less likely to feel it has to be on guard duty. Some dogs will also bark at cats or birds in the garden, in which case closing the curtains may help.

It is up to you to find out why your dog is barking – observe what is happening when it barks, make a checklist, and then do something to change the situation.

TRAINING A DOG NOT TO BARK

1 Dogs can start to bark when you leave the house, and may suffer from separation anxiety when left alone.

2 Before you go out, leave a selection of toys with your dog to keep it occupied while it is on its own.

3 If your dog needs to be left alone for a long time, employ a dog walker to take it out for some exercise.

Stealing items

In the wild, dogs need to be opportunists, so if they see something they want, they will invariably try to take it, even if it involves fighting. This is part of the principle of 'survival of the fittest', and ensures that they have enough for their needs. Although it is a natural instinct, it is not one that we want occurring in our homes. Fortunately, wild dog behaviour has changed somewhat since dogs have become domesticated. Modern pets no longer have such a strong need to possess, and the reason for stealing has also changed slightly.

A domestic dog steals for one very good reason – to get attention. The first time it did it, its owner might've yelled, got up and ran after it, trying to get the stolen item back. Far from

▶ Dogs steal items because they enjoy the consequence of being chased. Train them to 'leave it'.

being a negative consequence, as far as the dog was concerned, it had simply asked for attention and been rewarded with a good game of chase. So what does it do? Pick up another object and wait for its owner to come running.

To teach your dog not to take items, you need to ignore its stealing behaviour. However, if it takes something you can't ignore, use the commands 'leave it' or 'drop it'. If the dog doesn't respond, distract

it by ringing the doorbell. It should gallop away to see who has arrived at the door. Alternatively, scatter some treats over the floor. It should drop the stolen item in favour of the treats. Never chase your dog into a corner, though. This may scare it and cause it to growl, and you will have taught it that whenever it acquires something, it needs to guard it. By ensuring your dog has plenty of its own toys, it is less likely steal your possessions.

TRAINING A DOG NOT TO STEAL ITEMS

1 Do not ignore your dog if it takes something important that you really need, such as a tea towel.

2 Scatter some small treats on the floor to distract the dog, and ask it to 'leave it' or 'drop it'.

3 Praise your dog when it picks up the treats, and then retrieve your important possession.

Stealing food and begging at the table

Understandably, dogs can be a nuisance when there's food about. Some dog owners advocate the use of punishment and setting up booby traps, but the reward of food is usually so good that most dogs are prepared to take the risk. It's actually very simple to stop a dog from stealing food: never leave it unattended where your dog can reach it.

Similarly, if raiding the bin is becoming a nightmare, keep it out of reach. As much as anything else, this is important for health reasons. There may well be dangerous items in the rubbish bin, such as broken glass, empty cans or sharp chicken bones, which can cause your dog a bad injury, or even poisonous items. Don't risk it. Some dogs are very clever and can open refrigerator doors. Remedy this by fitting a child-proof catch.

It is also important that you are not taken in by those imploring, pleading, 'feed-me' eyes when your dog is looking up at you while you're eating at the table. If you give in and feed your dog a juicy sausage, it will begin a lifetime of hoping that you'll do it again next time. Eventually the pleading will become more animated, and it will begin to paw at you, whine and bark at every mealtime.

Be aware that dogs are very good at manipulating young children and are more than happy to act as dustbins for any food the child dislikes. It does not take long for a dog to learn to steal from a small child, whether the child wants to feed the dog or not. So it is important that children, too, understand the reasons why their pet should never be fed at the dinner table.

▲ *A begging dog can become a problem, and should not be indulged.*

If you do want to give your dog a treat, give it some food out of its own bowl. While you are eating, keep your dog happy by giving it a hide chew on its bed or in its crate.

TRAINING A DOG NOT TO STEAL FOOD OR BEG AT THE TABLE

1 Keep worktops free of food, putting tempting items out of sight and making sure kitchen surfaces are kept clean.

2 Put the rubbish bin out of your dog's reach, for example into a cupboard under the sink, where it can't see it.

3 When you are eating, put a hide chew in your dog's bed or crate. This will keep it busy during mealtimes.

Jumping on the sofa

You might never want your dog to jump on the sofa, you might want to move it out the way when you sit down because it takes up so much room, or you might not want it leaving muddy marks on the furniture. What can you do? What you must not do is react with haste, grabbing your dog by the collar and yanking it off the sofa, accompanied by shouting at it. The next time that happens, the dog will growl at you, which will only make the situation worse.

The best way to get your dog off the sofa is by using a training game, first teaching it to get on – yes, ON – the sofa. With a handful of treats, encourage the dog to jump on the sofa. You may want to cover the surface with an old sheet first. Reward it when it jumps up, then hold a treat near the floor to encourage it to jump off. Just as

▶ *To train your dog to stay off the sofa, you must first teach it to jump on the sofa. Having achieved this, reward it for jumping off.*

it is getting down, say "off" (this is preferable to 'down', which can be confused with 'lie down'). Go through the process several times. Once your dog has learned the command, you should be able to get it to jump down whenever you want it off the sofa.

If you let your dog into the bedroom, you can use the same 'off' command to teach it to get off the bed. The 'jump up' command can also be used to train it to jump into the car.

As mentioned, some dogs can growl when asked to get off the sofa or bed. This is usually a learned response: the first time the owner wanted to get their dog down they may have yanked it off by the collar and hurt it. If this is the case, the next time the dog is asked, it may become defensive and give a warning growl. Further, the dog may have an ear infection, in which case grabbing the collar will also hurt it.

TRAINING A DOG NOT TO JUMP ON THE SOFA

1 To teach your dog 'on' and 'off', first offer it a treat while encouraging it to jump up to retrieve it.

2 Lure your dog on to the sofa and give the cue 'on' (or 'up'). Reward it when it jumps up and eats the treat.

3 Hold a treat near the floor to lure your dog off. Give the cue 'off' and reward your dog when it jumps down.

Attention-seeking behaviour

Dogs have a large repertoire of attention-seeking behaviour, such as barking, stealing items, pawing, nudging, tail-chasing, light-chasing, chewing, jumping up, dropping toys on your lap and mounting your leg. Such behaviour is best ignored, but this is not always possible. In the case of mounting, for example, nothing tends to get attention more quickly than a dog trying to mount a child or a visitor's leg.

There is a wide variety of reasons why dogs resort to attention-seeking actions. It is always worth trying to address the possible causes as well as correcting the unwanted behaviour. Is it possible your dog has been left alone for too long or has not had sufficient exercise? If so, increase the length and frequency of walks. See if you can make some lifestyle adjustments so that the dog is not left alone as much. Do you think your dog is bored or lacks mental stimulation? If so, how about taking it to obedience or agility training classes? Also try

providing it with some reward-based puzzle toys. A lot can be done to make your dog's environment more satisfying and rewarding, thus decreasing attention-seeking behaviour.

You need to think carefully about the response you give when your dog is looking for attention. For example, if you shout at your dog when you are trying to speak on the telephone, you are actually giving it the attention it is seeking. Further, running around after it when it steals a tea towel is also giving it an attention reward.

The way to change the behaviour is to make sure you don't give it what it wants – your attention. As soon as it starts pestering you, get up quickly and walk out of the room, closing the door between you and the dog. Don't stay out for long – 1 minute is enough – then go back in. At this point the dog will probably try even harder to get your attention. Get up and walk out of the room again. If you are consistent, the problem should be eliminated within 5 days.

▲ *Dogs often demand attention when you are busy doing something else.*

It is important to involve the whole family in the training, because your dog will experiment with each family member to see which one will give it the attention it wants. Throughout the process, don't forget to reward your dog when it is doing what you do want, such as lying quietly by your side.

DEALING WITH ATTENTION-SEEKING BEHAVIOUR

1 When you are sitting on the sofa, your dog may pester you for attention by bringing you a toy and jumping up.

2 If it does this, ignore its behaviour, get up and walk away from it. Do not give the dog the attention it is seeking.

3 At a later time, reward your dog for good, calm behaviour. Stroke it when it lies down quietly on the floor.

Problem behaviour in the older dog

If you have an older dog displaying problems that have not been covered in this book, it is best to get specialist help. In particular, aggression towards people or other dogs really needs professional help. Other problems might have an underlying medical cause that can be picked up by a vet or qualified behaviour counsellor.

Think about your dog's genetic history, training, diet and the circumstances that provoke or are associated with its bad behaviour. Keep an eye on it and keep a diary, noting down what it does, when, for how long, and what external factors might have been the cause, then consult a vet. If you try to guess why problems occur and attempt to cure them yourself in a haphazard way, you might actually exacerbate the bad behaviour, with the dog eventually ending up in a rescue centre.

If you need specialist help, don't be afraid to seek it. Ask your vet or friends to recommend a good dog trainer and/or behaviour counsellor.

► *Older dogs may have problems that can take a long time to diagnose and sort out. Do not be afraid to seek specialist help from a professional, especially when dealing with aggression towards people or other dogs.*

If your vet refers you directly to a behaviourist, it is worth looking at the small print in your insurance documents to see whether you are covered for this and could make a claim. Specialist help can be costly, but it is well worth the expense if a satisfactory outcome can be achieved.

Take the diary that you have written regarding your dog's behaviour when you have your first appointment with your chosen trainer/behaviourist, as it will help them to get a clear picture of the problem. They will be able to advise you of any changes that you should make in your dog's lifestyle and help you put a remedial training programme in place. Do not expect an instant fix, but with patience and consistency most issues can usually be dealt with or, at the very least, the severity of the problem lessened.

SEEKING SPECIALIST HELP FOR AGGRESSION

1 Aggressive behaviour towards people or other dogs is not acceptable, and may require specialist help.

2 A good trainer will observe your dog and help you understand why the aggressive behaviour is happening.

3 Once the cause is understood, the trainer will then help you to manage your dog's unwanted aggression.

CANINE SPORTS AND ACTIVITIES

Most dogs were bred to do a specific job, but in more recent times that job is to be a companion. Gone are the days when gundogs worked to a gun or herding breeds moved flocks of sheep, but dogs still retain the instinct to please their owners and the need to use their brains. The term 'canine sports' can be rather misleading. It seems to imply super-fit people with highly active dogs rushing about and competing against each other. This is true in some cases, such as agility, but in many sports the activity is much more sedate and may not have a competitive element. All sports are fun for you and your pet: dogs learn new skills and training while gaining confidence and exercise; and owners meet like-minded people, set a training goal to work towards, and have the opportunity to strengthen the human-canine bond.

◄ *There is a wide range of dog sports, all providing a degree of physical and mental exercise. This terrier is competing in the high-performance sport of agility, which is against the clock – so every second counts.*

Breed shows

A breed show is a formal method of showing a kennel club-registered purebred dog. Think of it as a beauty contest. Each recognized dog breed has a 'standard' which outlines the ideal conformation and characteristics of the breed. A judge compares each dog with the standard to find the dog that best represents the ideal picture of the breed. This sport is time-consuming and can be very expensive.

Early socialization is important, because your dog must be used to crowds of people and the hustle and bustle of the breed ring. It must be happy to move with other dogs in front and behind it and to be felt all over, including having its teeth inspected, by a judge. A specialist ringcraft club will help you to train your dog so that it is used to being inspected by a stranger. You will be shown how to present your dog to its best advantage both while standing still and on the move.

Training requires time and patience, and is much harder than it looks. A dog that is jumping about or having to be dragged around the ring will gain the judges attention for all the wrong reasons. The handler should be familiar with their chosen

breed's standard, and also needs to learn ring etiquette.

Breed shows are held at different levels, and those new to the sport will gain experience by starting at the lower levels and progressing upwards. Some shows, such as Crufts, can only be entered if the dog has qualified by winning or being placed at a qualifying show. The kennel club for each country will provide information on the types of show available and the

requirements for progression or qualifying for entry to the top show in that country.

Grooming and presentation of the dog is vital. Study the top dogs in your breed to gain an overall picture of how the dog should be trimmed and presented. Your breeder will also be able to give you advice on this. Dental hygiene is also important, as many standards require that the judge inspects the dog's teeth placement.

◀ The judge checks that body conformation and dentition conform to the breed standard.

▶ A steward notes down the number of the winning dog.

Competition obedience

We all aim to have an obedient dog, but to be able to enter a competition obedience class, training needs to be more intensive. Most dog training clubs will have an advanced class that you and your dog can work towards. Any breed or cross-breed dog can take part in obedience training and competitions. A few minutes' work each day practising the exercises that you have been taught in your training club or class will help to teach the dog new elements and to polish your overall performance ready for the ring.

Competition obedience or obedience trials take the form of a series of exercises to test the training of the dog. Usually the classes are progressive, with a wins entitling the dog to enter into a class of higher standard and difficulty. Companion shows may run informal obedience competitions which are an excellent method of entry into this sport. More formal competitions of a higher standard are regulated by the kennel club of each country.

▼ Dogs can be tested on the stay exercises as a group – unless the class is just for fun, that is.

▲ This dog and handler are perfectly in tune with each other during a heelwork exercise.

Exercises that the dogs are tested on are varied according to the level of the competition, but in each case they will include some heelwork, either on or off the lead, a recall, and sit and down stays. More advanced classes may include send away, retrieve, scent discrimination, distance control

▲ In this test of obedience, the dog is required to retrieve a dumb-bell and then present it to the handler.

and stays out of sight. In many levels of competition, the dogs are collectively tested on the stay element of the class.

When dog and handler have entered the ring, instructions are given to them by the steward who then works them through the elements of the test according to the judge's direction. The judge looks for a good partnership between the dog and its handler, producing acute completion of each element of the class. Points are deducted for faults and any mistakes made. The judge then enters the fault marks and any relevant comments on to a score sheet.

Most judges will let entrants look at their score sheet at the end of each competition, so that they are able to assess areas they might need to work on before their next show.

Companion shows

A companion show is an informal breed or beauty show that often includes novelty classes. This type of show is normally organized as a fundraiser for a charity or the local community, and may be part of a bigger event. There is great flexibility in the classes available. Some have pedigree classes where dogs from breed groups, as apposed separate breeds, are judged together. The pedigree dogs do not have to be registered with a kennel club, but are still judged on the same lines as in a breed show. Classes are available for all dogs regardless of their breeding, for example 'Prettiest Bitch', 'Most Handsome Dog' and even 'Fastest Sausage Eater'. This type of class is referred to as a novelty class, and is judged at the judge's own discretion.

▼ *These handlers may not be as skilled as those in the breed show ring, but they are just as proud of their dogs.*

Entries are normally taken on the day and are inexpensive. Child handlers are encouraged making this type of show a family event. Rosettes and prizes are awarded, with the possibility of some classes being sponsored by businesses. The judge may have dog showing experience or be a local vet or even a celebrity guest. Often the day is concluded

◄ *This little chap seems to be enjoying his moment in the limelight, dressed as a bee.*

▼ *'Best Dressed' or 'Fancy Dress' classes are always popular with owners and audience alike.*

with a class for all the dogs that have not won a prize, to try to ensure that most owners go home with an award.

Presentation of the dog is an important feature. A clean, groomed and well-behaved dog is more likely to catch the judge's eye. Companion shows can be used to help train dogs looking to compete in breed shows, as they enable handlers to get their charges used to a ring situation. Although the high standard of training as seen in the breed ring is not expected at companion shows, any dogs that are aggressive or unsocial will be asked to leave.

Since companion shows take place in a relaxed atmosphere, they are ideal for socializing dogs, but owners should always read the schedule to find out the minimum age of puppies for entry. These events also provide an excellent opportunity to introduce children to the world of dog shows and dog handling. Although not a condition of entry, owners should ensure their pet's vaccinations are up to date, as with all dog events.

Rally obedience

The sport of rally obedience or Rally-O is best described as an obstacle course made up of obedience elements. The course is set by a judge who lays out a route in which the competitor follows signs that tell them what must be done. The signs, called stations, each have a simple instruction written on them. There are over 40 different stations for the judge to choose from when they design their course.

The instructions vary, and may include commands such as 'turn left', 'turn right', 'sit', 'down', 'go over a jump', 'serpentine', 'stay' or 'halt'. Exhibitors are given a course map and are allowed to walk the course before their class starts.

Each handler and dog is referred to as a 'team', and the winning team is the one that has had least marks

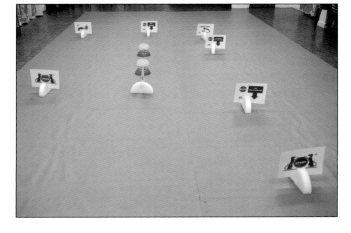

▶ *Markers and obstacles laid out on a non-slip floor covering, ready for an indoor rally competition. The team completes the course in a brisk manner, with no pause between the obstacles unless this is requested.*

deducted for faults. Points are taken away for a variety of reasons, including incorrectly completed or missed stations, tugging the lead, or touching the dog. The team is required to move from station to station with the dog in the heel position.

The judge looks for a team following instructions close to the stations and in a smooth manner as they follow the course. Each team is timed as they complete the course, and in the event of two teams having the same finishing score, the fastest time determines the winner. In some countries, exhibitors are encouraged to compete against their own scores rather than other teams. At many levels of rally obedience the handler is allowed to use verbal praise, so this event is more encouraging than the more silent sport of competiton obedience.

Rally obedience is relatively new to the world of canine sports, but it is recognized by several kennel clubs, including those in the UK, USA, Canada, Italy and Switzerland. Rules, deduction of points and progression routes vary according to each governing body. Owners who wish to try this sport are advised to join

a rally training club in their area, who will be able to explain the applicable rules. It is a more relaxed sport than competition obedience and does not require the judge to handle the dogs, making it a suitable alterative for more nervous dogs.

▼ *The look of love between pet and owner at the end of a rally obedience test – job well done!*

▼ *This dog and handler are concentrating on weaving in and out of the coloured cones.*

Sheepdog trials

Also known as stock dog trials or herding events, sheepdog trials are competitive dog sports where herding breeds move sheep around a course, through gates and into enclosures following their handler's instructions. These events take place in farming communities all over the world. It is thought that the first sheepdog trial took place in New Zealand in 1867. Although originally devised to demonstrate the skill of the dog at its natural work, trials are now also used to prove that breed lines have not lost their herding ability.

Tests vary around the world, but include the dog leaving the handler, fetching and controlling a small number of sheep, and then returning them to the handler following a set route. The dog must also be able to demonstrate that it can move the sheep away from the handler. Working as a team, the dog and handler also have to confine the sheep within an enclosed area or pen. There are a range of other elements that may be

included in a test, depending on the standard of the trial. 'Shedding', for example, involves splitting several marked sheep from the flock, while 'singling' requires the dog and handler to remove just one marked sheep from the flock. These activities are done within a set area on the field called the 'shedding ring'. A 'double lift' may be

▲ *A blue merle Border Collie 'eying' the sheep, totally absorbed in its work during a sheepdog trial.*

included; this requires the dog to fetch one flock of sheep, return them to the handler, then leave to find a second flock in a different area of the field.

Modern yard dog trials are now becoming very popular. These can include elements of traditional trials, plus requiring dogs to move animals through several yards and into and out of trucks.

Judges award marks for each element of the test, and are looking for a dog that is able to work in a controlled and efficient manner which causes the sheep the minimum of stress. Any sign of aggression is penalized, and a dog that bites the stock could be eliminated.

◄ *Having 'gathered' the sheep, the dog now 'drives' the flock through the gates that mark the route that the judge has set for this trial.*

Tracking

Dogs are born with the ability to use their noses to track a scent. Selective breeding has produced some breeds that excel at this task, but any dog can be trained to track to varying degrees of difficulty.

There are various reasons why a dog may be trained to track. The police might use dogs to hunt down criminals, find articles that may be involved in a crime scene, and to locate explosives and drugs. Search and rescue dogs track to find missing people and corpses. Hunters use dogs to track down injured or fallen animals. Dogs are also trained to compete in sports such as tracking.

The basic training for tracking is the same regardless of the reason. The dog is encouraged to use its nose to sniff a scent, and then to follow the trail until it has found its quarry. Dogs either follow a scent that is left on the ground or sniff the air to pick up the trail. Search and rescue dogs are

▲ *This German Shepherd is waiting to start its tracking task with an evident sense of enjoyment and anticipation.*

trained to use both methods of scenting, so they are still able to pick up a trail even if other people have walked over it.

Tracking harnesses must fit comfortably and not restrict the dog's movement. A long tracking line is attached to the harness, which allows the dog to move forward freely but gives the handler some control over the speed of the dog. Tracking lines are available in a range of materials, including leather, fabric and cord. The line should be comfortable for the handler to hold, and not too heavy so that it impedes the dog's progress. Training is progressive, starting with

a short, straight track to a reward, and building up to more advanced tasks. Well-trained, experienced dogs are able to track a scent that may be several days old, cover a long distance, and involve changes of direction and terrain.

Specialist clubs can help with training methods and progression. They will also be able to give advice on rules and regulations for tracking trials, as these vary greatly from country to country.

▼ *Nose to the ground, this dog has found the scent and is moving with the handler to follow the scent trail.*

▲ *A neatly coiled cord lightweight tracking line (left), and a leather tracking harness (right).*

Schutzhund

From the German word meaning 'protection hound', Schutzhund was devised as a series of tests, dating back to the early 1900s, to prove that the German Shepherd had the necessary traits to be a proper working dog. Nowadays, any breed or mix of dog is able to compete for a Schutzhund title.

Prior to competing, all dogs must pass a B or BH test that ensures they have basic obedience, are safe around strange people and dogs, and are not afraid of loud noises. If a dog fails this test, it is not allowed to take part in the Schutzhund.

There are three Schutzhund titles – 1, 2 and 3 – each more challenging than the previous. They are designed to test a dog's trainability, agility, strength, temperament, courage,

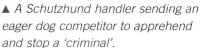

▲ *A Schutzhund handler sending an eager dog competitor to apprehend and stop a 'criminal'.*

▼ *The dog makes contact with the padded arm protector, but at a given command must release it immediately.*

sense of smell, and bond to the trainer by undertaking a range of set tasks. There are three phases to each test: tracking, obedience and protection.

The tracking phase involves the dog following a trail made by a track layer and finding articles that have been dropped on the way. At each article, the dog must signal its find, usually

by lying down. The dog is scored according to how careful and accurate it is in completing the task.

Obedience is tested in a large outside area. Dogs work in pairs, with one sitting quietly at the edge of the field while another works, and then they exchange roles. Exercises include heelwork, retrieves, send-outs, recalls, agility and steadiness to gunshot. The dog must show enthusiasm in all tasks.

The protection aspect requires the dog to find a hidden helper, who will be wearing a padded arm protector, and prevent them from moving. At some point during the test, the helper either tries to run away or attack the dog. The dog must stop the attack or escape by biting the padded arm until told to stop by the trainer. At command, the dog must stop biting, and it is severely penalized if it does not. In this phase, the judge is looking for both control and courage.

Agility

The fastest growing of all the dog sports, agility is very popular with spectators. It was first seen as a demonstration at Crufts in the 1970s. Classes are available for dogs of different sizes, and the dog does not have to be purebred to take part. The handler is required to direct the off-lead dog around a course of obstacles, in the order laid out by the judge, with accuracy and speed being measured. A round with no faults – called a clear or clean round – in the fastest time dictates the winner.

A range of obstacles may be present in each agility course, dependent on the class. These can include a variety of jumps or hurdles, tunnels (both open and flat), a tyre, weave poles, and also contact equipment such as an 'A' frame, dog walk and seesaw (teeter-totter). A course is laid out in an area of set size, with a time limit for the dog's completion set by the judge.

▶ *There are classes for all heights of dog, but regardless of size, all must be able to negotiate the weave poles correctly.*

Toys and treats are not allowed in the ring, with the dog responding solely to the handler's voice and body movements. The handler may have to direct the dog from some distance away' often with other obstacles between them.

Prior to the start of each class, handlers are allowed to 'walk the course' to learn the order in which the obstacles must be completed. Handlers will also work out where they should move so that they are in the best position to be able to direct the dog over each part of the course. Faults are allotted for any deviation

of the course, and for mistakes such as knocking poles down, negotiating obstacles incorrectly, and exceeding the course time. Dogs are eliminated from the class if any of the competition rules are broken.

Agility training clubs are available to provide instruction, and they can be very social for both handler and dog. Training at home can be challenging due to the cost of the equipment required to form a full course. Agility is a fun activity for dog and owner, but if you wish to compete at this fast and furious sport, a level of physical fitness will be required by both of you.

▲ *A very balanced dog completing the 'A' frame part of the agility course, with all four feet on the contact area.*

▶ *Obstacles for jumping over are varied, and could include a brightly coloured 'brick' wall such as this one.*

Flyball

The sport of flyball is a knockout competition involving teams of four handlers, their dogs, some reserves and a 'box loader'. It started in Southern California in the early 1970s, and the first flyball tournament was held in 1983 in the USA. It is now seen in other parts of the world, including the UK, many European countries, Canada, Australia and South Africa.

Two teams compete at the same time, with the aim of getting each dog to jump four hurdles set in a straight line and then trigger a mechanism to release a tennis ball that they must carry back over the fences. The winning team is the first to have the fourth dog cross the finish line with all runs correctly completed.

Most competitions require the teams to run three times against each other, with the team with the most wins going forward to the next heat. A dog that crosses the start line before it should, or who drops the ball, will occur penalty points for the team.

Any dog can take part in this sport; animals do not have to be purebred. Speed and a strong drive to retrieve are the main criteria. The hurdle or jump height is dictated by the smallest animal in the team, so that any size of dog can compete on an equal footing. Different controlling organizations have varying rules as to the required jump height. Teams are usually 'seeded', depending on their times and wins. This makes for an exciting contest, as each team is of a similar capability. Electronic timers are mainly used to record times, as these can be literally 'split-second'. Competition is

▲ *Two excited dogs, almost neck to neck, racing up the lane of hurdles towards the flyball box.*

fierce, with teams working hard to improve their overall times so that they can progress to a higher level.

Specialist flyball training clubs can offer detailed information and training, while some obedience or agility clubs also provide basic training classes for this sport. Flyball is a true spectator sport, with easy-to-understand goals and rules, although it can be very noisy – dogs become highly excited as they wait for their turn to run.

▲ *The loader has placed the ball in the flyball box, ready for the dog to retrieve it without dropping it.*

◄ *After retrieving the ball from the box, the dog must turn quickly and race back over the hurdles again.*

Canicross

The sport known as canicross or CaniX is cross-country running with your dog. It was developed in Europe from skijoring (where a dog pulls a person who is on skis) and off-season training for mushing. Originally, canicross dogs were spitz breeds or sledging dogs, but now all types of dog are welcome. The sport can be competitive or just a way for a runner and dog to increasing their fitness levels and enjoy the countryside.

Although no special equipment is required, most canicross dogs wear a harness. This encourages them to throw their weight forward and pull out in front of the runner. Many dogs are trained not to pull when wearing a collar and lead, so the introduction of a harness acts as a signal that pulling is required. If a dog pulls when wearing a collar, this can cause damage to its neck. The runner wears a canicross belt around their waist.

A line is then clipped from the belt to the harness. This allows the runner's hands to be free and by their sides, so they can run properly. Most runners use a line that is similar to a bungee. This acts as a shock-absorber and provides protection to both dog and runner from any sudden jarring.

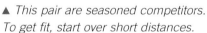

▲ *This pair are seasoned competitors. To get fit, start over short distances.*

Training is simple. A second person, in front of the dog, encourages the dog to pull out in front of its owner. When the dog does this, the owner praises it. You should start with short runs and always finish when the dog is still keen to pull forward. Distances can be increased as the dog's and your fitness levels improve.

Events, either for fun or competition, are held during autumn through to spring. Running during the summer months, unless early in the morning, should be avoided, as the dog may become too hot. Canicross is suitable for all sizes of dog, from small terriers to large mastiffs, and some people run with up to three dogs at the same time. All ages of runner can take part, including children. The sport is suitable for runners with sight disabilities, as the dogs follow a clear trail.

▼ *Eagerly waiting to start their canicross event, with dog and runner wearing correct and safe equipment.*

Heelwork to music

Evolving in the early 1990s, heelwork to music is thought to have started with a demonstration by Mary Ray and her Border Collies in the main arena at Crufts, causing a canine sensation. This was followed by Tina Martin and her Golden Retriever 'Cognac', who performed at the Pacific Canine Showcase at Vancouver. Tina's routine was adapted from a dressage test, as she was a Grand Prix dressage rider.

The discipline has continued ever since, both delighting viewers who love to watch 'dancing dogs', and also challenging trainers to develop new skills. But training is only part of this event, as each handler has to choreograph a routine for themselves and their dog that suits a piece of music of their choice. The music can be for up to 4 minutes in duration. The handler normally designs a costume to wear during the performance, and props can also be used.

Both pedigree and crossbred dogs can take part in heelwork to music

▲ *Two dogs and handlers working in perfect harmony as a team.*

▲ *A Cocker Spaniel weaving between the handler's legs as she walks forward.*

competitions. Training is done mainly by motivation and reward. Most dogs love this form of training, and will often go through a series of moves to gain praise and attention even when they are not in the ring. Your dog should be

well-socialized and trained in basic obedience prior to learning to take part in these events. Handlers must be aware that this sport is undertaken off-lead. Specialist training clubs are available, and details of a club in your

▼ *This spectacular trick requires total trust between dog and owner.*

▼ *Great agility is required to jump up and then do a complete somersault.*

▼ *A little dog riding confidently on the back of a larger friend.*

▲ *In some classes, handlers are encouraged to dress in a manner suited to their music and routine.*

▲ *Both dog and handler look elegant and graceful here. They are clearly working well together as a team.*

▲ *Regular training is needed for both the handler and the dog to produce this level of precision and style.*

area can be found on the Internet or by contacting your local kennel club.

Heelwork to music is the generic term for the sport, but it is split into two divisions: heelwork to music (HTM), and freestyle. In the former, the principal element consists of the dog, off-lead, performing exercises with the dog's shoulder approximately level and close to the handler's leg. The dog can be on the left- or right-hand side, in front of or behind the handler, and facing forward or backward. A minimum of two-thirds of a heelwork to music routine must consist of heelwork, except in the USA where the whole routine must consist of heelwork positions.

Freestyle or musical freestyle is also performed off-lead, but includes movements with the dog in any position, with a maximum of one-third

of the routine consisting of the dog in the heel position. Combinations of obedience and tricks make up each performance. Dogs are taught to jump, spin, wave their paws and roll over, and even leap into their handler's arms or on to their hander's back.

Competition classes are available in HTM and freestyle for single animals, pairs, or teams of dogs and handlers. In all cases, the way the routine reflects the music and the rhythm of dog and handler form an important part of the sport.

There is some variation around the world in competition rules and regulations. In some countries, a panel of judges are required, while others run the competitions using just one judge. Some variation in scoring can be seen worldwide, but competitors are usually awarded a

maximum of 30 marks divided into 10 marks each for three sections. The first set of marks is awarded for the variety of different moves the dog has been taught to perform. The next set of marks is given for accuracy and execution of the moves. The judge is looking for an accurate performance, with each move flowing smoothly into the next. The final set of marks is awarded for choreography and interpretation of the music.

This sport can be enjoyed by any age of dog and handler, although a good level of fitness is required from both. No particular breed or cross-breed has been seen to be better than any other, making heelwork to music truly an event for everyone to take take pleasure from. It is a great way to build up a real partnership between you and your dog.

Mushing

The art of getting sled dogs to pull a person or a load on some form of transportation is known as 'mushing'. Traditionally, teams of sled dogs would pull a loaded flat-bottomed sled over snow while being controlled by the musher. This is a form of transport for supplies, mail deliveries and at times is the only way people can travel. Sled dogs still run across snowy terrain just as they have done for centuries, but more often for sport than a necessary job of work. As the ownership of sled dogs has spread across the world, the sport known as mushing has evolved. Mushing can now be undertaken in any country, weather or terrain.

▼ *A team of three dogs taking part in a bikejoring event. You do not have to use three animals – this bicycle sport can be carried out with one or two.*

The introduction of dryland mushing means that sled dog racing can be enjoyed regardless of the lack of snow. Wheeled vehicles can be used rather than a flat-bottomed sled, and there are different variations of the sport. Dog scootering, for example, involves one or more dogs pulling a kick scooter controlled by the musher. A dog pulling a person

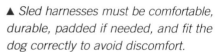

▲ *Sled harnesses must be comfortable, durable, padded if needed, and fit the dog correctly to avoid discomfort.*

mounted on a bicycle is called bikejoring. Skijoring refers to a dog or dogs pulling a skier. In countries devoid of snow, teams of dogs race pulling three- or four-wheeled rigs with a musher sitting or standing on the back. The variations of sled substitutes are great and ingenious, and mushing now takes place in countries as diverse as Jamaica and Canada.

Just as the sled has changed, so have the dog teams. Initially, dogs were purpose-bred to pull sleds and withstand extreme cold, ice and snow. They included breeds such as the Alaskan Malamute, Canadian Eskimo Dog and Greenland Dog. Urban or dryland mushing opens the sport to all. Any breed or mix of dog, regardless of type, can take part, as they do not have to cope with extreme weather conditions. In all cases, dogs respond to the musher's voice for direction and are motivated by their desire to run.

Advice on training and equipment should be sought from experienced mushers or local dog sled clubs. The Internet lists clubs, race meetings and sled dog fun days in all areas.

Carting

Dogs have been used to pull carts for hundreds of years. In fact, many breeds have evolved with this purpose in mind. The Bernese Mountain Dog and Greater Swiss Mountain Dog, for example, were trained to pull carts loaded with milk churns and other farm produce over rough mountainous terrain that was not suitable for or practical to use a horse. These dogs were an important part of the farming community and were always lovingly cared for by their owners.

Large breeds are mainly used for carting, with the Swiss Mountain breeds most commonly seen. Carts are two- or four-wheeled and, in the case of the Swiss breeds, often beautifully decorated with handlers in traditional costume. These dogs and carts can be seen at many public or charity events and fetes, where they always delight the audience.

Carting is not a sport to be undertaken without expert advice and training. Dogs need to be both physically fit and of good, calm temperament. Many of the Swiss Mountain Dog breed clubs have experienced carters who can give advice, not just on the methods of training but also on the best type of cart for the dog. Great care should be taken that the cart is not too

▲ The Bernese has strength, a gentle nature and a willingness to please, making it an ideal carting breed.

heavy for your dog and that the harness is correctly fitting. Handlers and owners are advised to check regulations and laws for their own country, as it is illegal to allow a dog to pull a cart on the public highway in some parts of the world.

▼ These owners, dogs and carts are all superbly presented in this spectacular display of carting.

▲ Even when standing at rest, this dog is eagerly looking towards its owner for the next command.

Dogs pulling laden carts, especially in towns, were a familiar sight worldwide over a century ago. Dogs that were even as small as terriers were used as a cheaper alternative to the horse. Sadly, many of these animals were subjected to extreme cruelty by being forced to haul loads that were much too heavy, and for long periods of time. Gradually, many countries made the commercial use of carting dogs illegal. But carting has a place as a sport where training and the dog's enjoyment – and not financial gain – are the incentive.

Greyhound and sighthound racing

Hounds split into two main types: there are those that hunt using their noses to scent their prey, and those that hunt by sight alone. The latter group are known as 'sighthounds' or 'gazehounds', and include breeds such as the Greyhound, Afghan, Saluki, Sloughi, Whippet, Scottish Deerhound and Borzoi.

Although sighthounds may differ in size and coat type, they all are long-boned with streamlined bodies and excellent eyesight. These dogs are built to chase. Some are sprint runners, such as the Greyhound and Whippet, while others, such as Salukis and Sloughis, can run all day.

Sighthounds have been used for hunting or coursing prey for thousands of years. Coursing is now illegal in many parts of the world, and pet dogs no longer have the opportunity to hunt. This gives rise to an increased interest in dog racing with a range of sighthounds, not just the well-known 'king of the track', the Greyhound.

▼ *Afghan hounds exiting the starting traps and starting to race on a sand track – elegance at high speed.*

Greyhound racing is well-regulated and routinely held at designated tracks or stadiums. These are mainly commercial ventures, with the dogs professionally trained. Legalized gambling is available at these meetings, and there is an official racing code. Other sighthound racing is generally held at smaller venues.

The basic procedure is the same for all. The dogs wear brightly coloured jackets that identify them. Greyhounds are muzzled, not because they are an aggressive breed, but to prevent them from nipping other competitors through excitement. The dogs are placed in a trap, and at the starters

▲ *These Greyhounds are racing at a professional night meeting in a large well-lit stadium packed with spectators.*

▼ *Even when wearing a racing jacket, it is easy to see how fit and well-muscled this Greyhound is.*

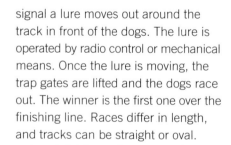

signal a lure moves out around the track in front of the dogs. The lure is operated by radio control or mechanical means. Once the lure is moving, the trap gates are lifted and the dogs race out. The winner is the first one over the finishing line. Races differ in length, and tracks can be straight or oval.

Local sighthound races can be found advertised on the Internet and in the press. Amateur racing clubs exist, and will give helpful advice on training and racing. Dogs must be extremely fit to take part in this sport.

Terrier racing

For hundreds of years, farmers have tried to stop uninvited animals from eating their grain supplies. Small dogs with high prey and chase drive were bred to produce animals that could chase and kill rodents. This was the evolution of the many breeds of terrier.

Terrier racing involves dogs chasing and trying to 'kill' a lure. There is no set distance for a terrier race, but the tracks are generally fenced off from the public. A lure, usually a piece of animal pelt, is attached to a cord the length of the track. The other end of the cord is fastened to some type of winding mechanism. At one end of the track are starting boxes called 'traps', and at the other is a solid wall built of straw bales with a hole large enough for the lure to pass through.

At the start of a race, the terriers are placed in the traps and are able to see the lure through the mesh at the

▲ *Excited dogs need to be gently encouraged to enter the correctly numbered racing trap.*

front. The lure is then moved about to get the dogs attention. The dogs will become highly excited, and bark and whine. At a given signal, the lure is wound in rapidly to the end of the track, and the traps are opened. The terriers will try to catch the lure, and

if one does, the race must be re-run. The winning dog is the first animal through the hole in the straw wall still chasing the lure.

Races take the form of heats, with the heat winners racing against each other in a knockout system to determine the overall winner. This sport is mainly seen at country events, with experienced dogs often travelling long distances to take part. Working dogs have the edge over pet dogs, as they chase vermin on a daily basis. Nevertheless, if you own a terrier it can normally take part, but it is unlikely to win unless it has a strong chase instinct. This is a fun canine sport with spectators cheering on the dog that they would like to see win.

▼ *A diverse group of terriers exiting the racing trap with only one aim: to try to catch the speeding lure.*

Gundog and retriever trials

Classes, rules, regulations and outcomes for gundog and retriever events vary enormously between different governing bodies and kennel clubs worldwide. Therefore, the information given here is an overview only. Owners interested in taking part in this sport should consult their national kennel club and breed societies for clear guidelines.

Gundog, retriever, field, working tests, hunt dog and shooting dog trials are all tests to evaluate the skill of dogs in a hunting situation. These events are undertaken off-lead. All dogs are expected to be steady with the sound of gunfire. They must not retrieve until instructed to do so by the handler. When asked, the dogs should move directly to the fallen game or retrieve an article. Handlers are allowed to direct their dogs, but a higher mark is achieved by dogs that do not need direction.

Judges look for a smooth, clean pick-up with the retrieved item held in a balanced manner in the dog's

▼ At the end of the working day, this Springer Spaniel shows no sign of tiring.

▲ Talking to other sportsmen is the best way of getting practical advice on training a gundog.

mouth. Retrieved game is checked by the judge to ensure it has not been crushed or bitten by the dog. Dogs that damage game in this manner are said to have a 'hard mouth', and are severely penalized. All gundogs and retrievers should have 'soft mouths' and return game that has only been damaged by the shot or fall. Dogs are required to work in situations that they are bred for. This may involve working in undergrowth or retrieving from water.

There is a wide range of events in which gundogs can take part, as long as they have the required training. Game or country fairs run fun classes where dogs retrieve dummies. This is a good starting point for those who are interested in the sport. Kennel clubs and breed clubs organize trials that mirror the activities undertaken in the field. Dogs can gain award titles at these formal events.

▼ A selection of gundog training dummies, a slip lead and a whistle on a leather lanyard.

Training differs depending on the type of breed that you have. Retrieving, flushing and pointing dogs all work in a different manner. Breeders can give advice and may know of suitable gundog and retriever training classes. There are many specialist publications that feature training articles and list venues and dates of gundog and retriever events.

Disc dog

Also known as frisbee dog, disc dog can either be a fun way to exercise and entertain your dog, or alternatively a competitive sport. All that is needed is a flat area of grass and a flying disc or flat ring. Traditionally, and in competition, a disc similar in shape to a flying saucer is used. There is some evidence that this type of disc may cause damage to the teeth, so a softer flat ring may be chosen instead.

Simple training is required, as not all dogs will chase and catch a flying object. To begin, encourage your dog to stand a short distance away, watching you. Throw the disc straight at the dog, ensuring it is easy for the animal to catch. When the dog is happy doing this, start to throw the disc over the animal's head. This will encourage the dog to turn and chase prior to catching. Gradually increase both the distance and height.

▼ *For the owner, disc dog may be a great way to increase a dog's fitness, but for the dog it is just pure joy.*

▲ *Taking off almost vertically each time, this Jack Russell leaps many times its own height to catch the ring in acrobatic fashion in a freestyle disc dog event.*

It is thought that over that over a million dogs in the USA play disc dog daily, but only a very small percentage of those animals take part in competitions. It is a safer game then catching a ball, as there is no risk of the dog being able to swallow the ring or disc. This exercise is best undertaken on soft ground to minimize concussion damage from jumping repeatedly.

There are various classes in disc dog competition, including both

▲ *This dog is retrieving a solid type of frisbee and racing back to its owner.*

long- and short-distance throwing, as well as freestyle. Points are awarded for the distance thrown and the style in which the dog catches the disc. Extra points are gained for catching the disc in mid-air, and catches made when the dog has all four feet off the ground are highly valued. Some dogs are able to do amazing flips and turns in the air when jumping for the disc.

All types of dogs are able to take part in the sport of disc dog. A level of fitness is required from the dog, but none from the owner. Care should be taken not to let the dog do too much of this vigorous exercise at any one time, to avoid muscle strain.

Dock jumping

▶ A water-loving dog taking part in a dock jumping competition for leaping the longest distance.

The exciting modern dog sport of dock jumping, also called splash and dash, draws crowds of competitors and spectators whenever it is staged. The aim is to get the dog to jump from a dock into a body of water. There are two types of competition: ultimate air looks for a long-distance jump, while ultimate vertical measures the height that the dog achieves.

Training for either event involves getting a dog used to jumping into water and retrieving a floating toy. Start by introducing your dog to shallow water. Then ask the dog to retrieve a toy from the water. When the dog is comfortable with this task, increase the length of throw so that the dog has to swim to fetch the article. Gradually work so the dog runs and leaps into deep water to retrieve.

Handlers employ differing methods to achieve long-distance jumps in

▼ Gundog breeds excel at this, as most were bred to retrieve from water.

ultimate air. Some will run forward with the dog, throwing the toy across the water at the last moment. Others leave the dog in a wait and stand at the dock edge before calling their pet and asking it to retrieve. In either case, the speed of run has a direct bearing on the length of jump. Any size or type of dog can take part, and classes are graded by the length of jump. The real athletes in this sport regularly achieve distances of over 7.6m (25ft).

Ultimate vertical involves dogs leaping upward at the end of the dock to grab a toy suspended over the water. This is a knockout competition, with the toy being lifted 5cm (2in) higher

after each retrieve. Top dogs can jump over 2m (7ft) high. Jumping into water is much safer than on dry land, as the water cushions the dog's body and avoids impact injuries on landing.

Many dock jumping organizations run training days. These are an excellent way to gain advice and to teach your dog to use a ramp to exit the pool. They also enable the dog to get used to jumping into clear water, which is harder to see than the murky surfaces of lakes, rivers and the sea.

▼ This sport is a real crowd pleaser – the audience are both enthralled and also at times very wet!

Hiking and trekking

Walking your dog is an excellent way for both you and your pet to improve your fitness levels. Hiking and trekking are the next step. If you only walk your pet for 10 minutes a day, you cannot expect it to complete a 16km (10-mile) hike without suffering some after effects. As with all canine sports, fitness levels need to be increased gradually.

Not all terrains are suitable for all dogs. A toy dog may struggle to climb up a steep hill, while a fit working dog will not even notice it. Plan your route according to you and your dog's capability and fitness. Before setting out, prepare for your day. Ensure mobile phones are charged and that you have the numbers of your own vet and a vet in the area that you are hiking. A basic first aid kit is essential. Carry water for you and your dog. If your dog will not drink from a bottle,

invest in a collapsible bowl. A snack for both of you will help lift energy levels. Items can be packed in a rucksack, leaving your arms free. If trained, the dog can carry its own requirements in a canine rucksack, as long as the bag is well-fitting, evenly balanced and not too heavy.

▼ *Panniers must fit comfortably, and the weight of their contents should be balanced equally on each side.*

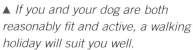

▲ *If you and your dog are both reasonably fit and active, a walking holiday will suit you well.*

Marked trails can be found in most areas, and information on their length and difficulty can be obtained from local authorities. Avoid walking during the hottest part of the day. Remember that not every walker is a dog lover, so give them and animals a wide berth. Many places specify that dogs remain on the lead, but even if this is not the case, it can be the safest option. Stay on the marked path and do not trespass on to privately owned land. Always bag your dog's faeces and dispose of them appropriately. Observe all aspects of the country code, shutting gates behind you and taking litter home. Barking dogs disturb humans and animals alike, so train your dog to walk quietly.

At the end of the trek, thoroughly check the dog for ticks, cut pads and grazes or abrasions. These should be treated appropriately, and if concerned, visit the vet for advice and treatment.

HEALTH CARE

The ultimate responsibility for a dog's welfare rests with the owner. This includes first aid, veterinary attention and pain relief. All dogs should be registered with a veterinary practice before they become ill. This saves time and means that prompt attention may prevent a problem from becoming a major incident. First aid cannot be considered a substitute for veterinary attention, but can be vital in stabilizing an injured or sick dog prior to transporting it to a veterinary clinic. It is useful in treating minor injuries such as stings and small wounds. Many education centres run canine first aid courses, and these are a worthwhile investment. Holistic medicine treats symptoms and looks for underlying causes. It covers both physical and emotional aspects of health, and can be used with veterinary treatment or on its own. All dog owners need to be aware of the signs of good and ill health, as this will assist them in making a judgement regarding treatment.

◄ *Regular veterinary checks are important. The vet may pick up the early symptoms of illness and be able to treat it before it becomes a major problem.*

Good health in dogs

A fit and healthy dog in the prime of life is a wonderful animal. Like humans, a dog's life proceeds through several stages. First, there is the 'infant' or puppy, dependent upon its mother. It has to be weaned and taught how to live in a social group. Very quickly, the puppy grows and becomes an extremely active 'adolescent', or young adult dog. Mature adulthood follows, and gradually the dog becomes old. In time, it will follow natural laws and die.

The basic physical needs of a dog remain the same throughout its life. The fine details vary according to the stage of development that the dog has reached, and the life that both the dog and its owner lead. Young and active dogs need a lot more exercise and a different food ration from that of a more elderly dog, for example.

Humans have had a direct impact on dogs as a species. Selective breeding over the centuries has led to the production of hundreds of

▼ *Fit puppies are very active. They need robust toys to help the development of their teeth and jaws, and to divert their destructive impulses.*

▲ *The more elderly dog is often content to sit in peace and comfort in a quiet corner of the garden, enjoying the warmth of the sun and simply watching the world go by.*

different dog breeds, each with its own preferred conformation. Each breed has its own basic requirements, and these can be very specific. For example, accommodation that is suitable for a very small dog, such as a Dachshund, is obviously wrong for a larger breed, such as a St Bernard. The two breeds also have different dietary requirements, mainly in the amount of food they need to eat every day, but also in the food's composition.

Fit, healthy dogs of all breeds and ages share certain characteristics. Their coats are in good condition and do not smell. Their eyes are bright and there are no stains on their faces from tear overspill. There is no discharge from their ears or nose, and no smell from their ears. They move freely and easily, and do not limp. They can enjoy strenuous exercise without physical distress at normal temperatures for a time commensurate with their breed and age.

Unfortunately, the breeding patterns that have emphasized the characteristics of many of today's

breeds have sometimes inadvertently encouraged susceptibility to specific diseases. Genetically programmed susceptibility to disease cannot be eliminated unless there is a change in the criteria for selecting breeding stock, although there are screening programmes currently in place to identify those animals that are susceptible to inherited disease, in order to minimize the risks.

While conventional veterinary medicine is used to treat the physical symptoms of a sick animal, holistic care is interested in the whole dog, and in preventing disease from occuring. Providing a dog with a lifestyle suited to its physical and emotional needs will stimulate its body's ability to heal itself – optimum health is always the best possible protection against disease.

Holistic medicine

Modern science tends to concentrate on understanding the world by looking at each of its components in great detail. This approach has been taken up by the medical professions, and medical and veterinary specialists concentrate their attention on the minutiae of their patients' physical symptoms, sometimes to the exclusion of everything else. Drugs are chosen for their effect on the system or the tissue thought to be the source of the illness. Problems caused by the drugs appearing in other parts of the body are seen as inevitable side effects which have to be tolerated. All patients are expected to respond to treatment in the same way, and there is little allowance made for individuality.

Holistic medicine, both human and veterinary, takes a much wider view of the patient and their disease. In holistic medicine, the three components that make up the individual – the spiritual, mental and physical – are all considered to have a bearing on the development of disease, and are taken into account

▲ Physiotherapy can help control pain and speed healing in injured tissues, and is an important part of both conventional and holistic care.

▲ Essential oils, such as lavender, are used by aroma therapists to treat a range of conditions. Consult your vet first before using any of these oils.

when planning the treatment. The patient is very much an individual, and the treatment must take account of their unique needs. This is often expressed as 'treating the patient and not the disease'. There are difficulties involved in holistic care for dogs, in that the vet is not able to discuss emotions and moral concepts with the patient. However, in the same way

that a doctor looks to the parent for information when treating a young child, so the vet will seek imput from the dog's owner.

Because no one therapy is 100 per cent effective in all cases, more than one therapy or more than one therapist may be needed. It is imperative that the vet and all therapists involved explain their own therapy, and how it is expected to interact with others – aromatherapy can inhibit the action of homeopathic remedies, for example, while massage is compatible with all therapies.

Holistic medicine does not aim to ignore conventional science, but to work alongside it in a supportive role. Complementary treatments can promote well-being in a fit and healthy dog and can help to alleviate the distress of illness, but if modern drugs are needed for acute cases of disease, then they are given. The prime concern with any form of veterinary care is always how it will affect the quality of the dog's life.

► Hydrotherapy can be used in post-operative recovery and as an aid in the treatment of some chronic conditions, as well as being a great form of exercise for your dog. It is often used in conjunction with veterinary treatment and may require a vet referral. Many veterinary insurances cover the cost of this therapy, but it is wise to check with your provider first.

VETERINARY CARE AND FIRST AID

In order to recognize when a dog is ill, you must know the signs of good health. A healthy dog is alert and lively, and takes a great interest in its environment, although young puppies will normally be rushing about one minute and sound asleep the next. There should be no discharges from the eyes or nose. The nose is usually moist and shiny, but this will depend on what the dog has been doing – people are often concerned that their dog's nose is dry, when it has just been digging for its favourite bone! The ears should be clean and free of visible wax. The coat should be free of dandruff and shiny. The skin should be free from sores or spots. The dog should move soundly, without favouring one leg over another, and it should move freely. A healthy dog should have a good appetite, and it should eat its food with relish.

◄ *Never think that you can take the place of a vet. If you have any concerns about the health of your dog, always seek expert, professional advice.*

Introducing your dog to the veterinary surgeon

Ideally, if you have not previously owned an animal, you should make the acquaintance of your local veterinary surgeon before you acquire the dog. How you choose a vet is a matter of personal preference. You may be guided by friends, or the convenience of the surgery, but there is no substitute for a personal interview to get an idea of how the practice runs, its surgery times and facilities, all of which the veterinary surgeon will be pleased to discuss with you.

Within 24 hours you and your family are going to have grown very attached to your puppy. That is just the way it happens. It is important that, if the veterinary examination discovers anything that indicates the puppy should be returned to the seller, you should know immediately before this bonding has taken place.

▼ *Minimum restraint is important in encouraging your dog to relax at the veterinary surgery.*

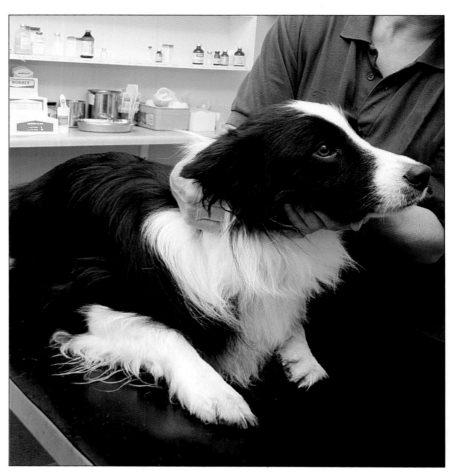

So you must arrange for the puppy's examination to take place on the day you collect it.

The veterinary surgeon will repeat the superficial health checks that you will already have carried out before buying the dog, but will go into greater detail, with a check on the puppy's heart and lungs, its ears and skin, its legs and feet and its genito-urinary system as far as possible.

This examination should not alarm the puppy. The veterinary surgeon will spend time getting to know your new dog with a little friendly fussing to give it confidence, before making the more detailed examination.

▲ *Most dogs, if handled with confidence, will not require heavy restraint during veterinary procedures.*

Unless it has already received its first inoculation, it will be given it now. This should not alarm the puppy, and many don't even notice the injection. At worst there may be a squeak, followed by some more comforting. The whole event should be very low key. The vet will also probably advise on worming and anti-flea regimes, and tell you how long it must be before the puppy meets other dogs in order to give the vaccine a chance to develop the dog's immunity to infections.

The inoculation regime

The dog's inoculations cover a core of four major diseases: distemper, which includes hardpad; leptospirosis, a liver and kidney infection; hepatitis, caused by a liver virus; and parvovirus. Kennel cough vaccine may also be included at a puppy's primary vaccination stage.

The first component of the vaccination course is usually given at seven to eight weeks old, although in circumstances where there has been a perceived risk in the breeder's kennels, much earlier protection may be given against certain diseases. Such very early vaccinations are usually disregarded for the purposes of routine protection.

The second injection is given at around 12 weeks of age. The interval between vaccinations is necessary to allow the puppy's immune system to react properly to the first dose of vaccine; the second dose then boosts the level of immunity to such an extent that the dog is protected for a prolonged period.

The vaccines are repeated annually, a process known as 'boosters'. Owners are inclined to be lax in their response to booster reminders as the dog gets older. Don't! Although some elements of the dog vaccination programme may confer a solid immunity for life, this cannot be relied upon, and other elements definitely need boosting annually.

LIFELONG IMMUNIZATION

Some infections in dogs are unlikely to strike the dog more than once in its lifetime. Vaccination against these diseases may confer a lifelong immunity. The virus hepatitis of the dog is one of these diseases.

BOOSTER INOCULATIONS

Unfortunately, other infections, although again unlikely to affect the dog more than once, do not confer such a solid immunity for life, although the immunity that they do confer is excellent for as long as it lasts. Typical of this group is distemper and hardpad (which is caused by the same virus). Distemper vaccinations must be boosted about every second year to maintain a high level of immunity.

There is a third group of infections that may recur and to which the immunity offered by vaccination is relatively short-lived. It is still worthwhile to use the vaccine because of the dangerous nature of the illness. Such a disease is leptospirosis, transmitted usually by foxes or other dogs, but occasionally, in the case of one type of the disease, by rats.

Not all diseases to which dogs are susceptible can be avoided by vaccination, but the commonest killers certainly can.

KENNEL COUGH

A particular problem for which there is no total preventive control is kennel cough, an infectious inflammation of the larynx and trachea. Kennel cough may be an unfair description. The disease is transmitted by droplets coughed into the air by dogs actively suffering from the illness. Fairly close contact between dogs is necessary for its transmission, such as a nose-to-nose greeting through the wire by dogs in kennels. At least as common a cause is dogs meeting at shows, competitions or training classes.

Kennel cough is caused by a mixture of infectious agents. The most effective vaccine is given as a nasal spray. Most kennels advise owners to make sure their dogs have had a kennel cough vaccination shortly before going into kennels. Some insist on this before accepting the dog.

▼ *Inoculations are not usually painful to dogs, particularly if the animal is relaxed.*

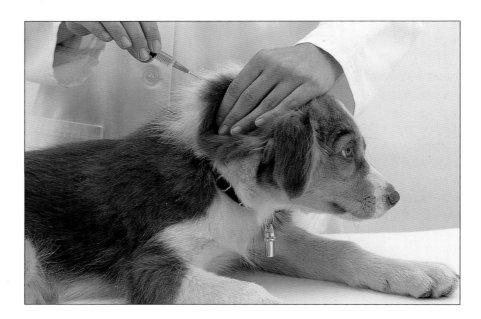

Worm control

Dogs are prone to both internal and external parasitic infestations. There are two common worms in dogs: the tapeworm and the roundworm.

TAPEWORMS

These may affect dogs at any age, although they are less common in young puppies than in older dogs. The tapeworm has a life cycle that depends on two different host species, in the case of the most frequently seen worm, the dog and the dog's fleas, although in another species they are transmitted through sheep.

Tapeworms may be recognizable as 'rice grains' in the faeces, but the dog may give you an indication by undue attention to its anal region.

Control of the tapeworm in the dog is simple; modern treatments are straightforward, requiring no fasting before dosing, and highly effective, with very little in the way of side effects (occasional vomiting).

It is a good idea to treat your dog routinely against tapeworms every six months. However, prevention of re-infection depends on control of the flea population in your house.

ROUNDWORMS

These are practically universal in puppies. They may be transmitted directly from dog to dog by faecal contamination, which is almost impossible to avoid. A high proportion of puppies are actually born infected with roundworms, transmitted via the uterus of the mother. Worms that had lain dormant in the tissues of the dam are activated by the hormones produced during pregnancy, circulate in the mother's bloodstream and pass into the unborn pups. There are

▲ *Any tablet needs to be given right to the back of the dog's mouth. Wrap it in something pleasant to distract the animal from spitting it out.*

control regimes that depend on using a safe anthelmintic early in pregnancy to destroy the maternal worm load, but this treatment is by no means universal.

A proper rearing regime includes dosing the litter when it is three or four weeks old, and perhaps again before leaving the kennels. Once home, the puppy should be treated regularly, every three to four weeks until it is six months old.

Adult dogs build up a level of immunity to the effects of roundworm infestations, and after six months do not need such regular treatment. Keep a constant look-out, although roundworms are not always easy to detect in a dog's faeces.

▶ *All dogs will lick and clean their anal region, but frequent licking is a sign that veterinary attention is needed.*

▲ *A dog will eat grass when its stomach is upset, but many dogs simply enjoy a little grazing. Some grass is an irritant and may induce vomiting.*

WORM TREATMENTS

Some drug treatments are effective against tapeworms and roundworms in one dose. The ascarid roundworm may be the cause of a very rare eye condition in children. If the dog is regularly wormed, the risk is eliminated. With this exception, the worms of dogs and of humans are not transmissible. Other species of worms, including the hookworm, may occur in dogs. Treatment is not difficult, but diagnosis may not be straightforward. Consult your veterinary surgeon. In the USA, heartworm is a common problem. A preventive medicine is given orally; treatment can be costly, and dangerous for the dog.

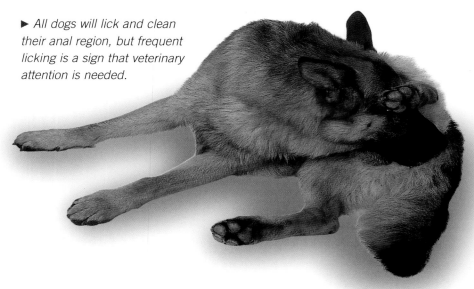

External parasites

Fleas, ticks, lice and mites are all external parasites. They affect the dog in a variety of ways. Some can cause serious skin disorders or even carry life-threatening diseases.

FLEAS

Start by assuming that your dog has fleas! They are by far the commonest external parasite of the dog, and many skin problems may be caused by fleas.

Fleas thrive in the warm and cosy environment of a centrally heated house, and there is no longer a flea season in summer followed by a flea-free winter. Treatment should be continued all through the year.

Fleas are often difficult to diagnose. They are small, move rapidly and are able to hop considerable distances. They are not very easy to see on the dog, but they never live alone. If you see one flea, it is safe to assume that there are plenty more. If you see none at all, they are probably still around.

A useful home test is to scrape hair detritus on to newspaper, and then to dampen the paper. If red smears appear, it is a certain indication that the dog does have fleas. The detritus may look like coal dust, but it is flea excreta.

Once you have convinced yourself that even your dog may have fleas, treatment is straightforward, although control is anything but. There are several effective sprays and washes available that will kill fleas safely (but some for which care is necessary), and most have some residual effect. But re-infestation is very difficult to prevent. If protection is, say, for three months, in practice the effectiveness is likely to decline well within that time. So some fleas come back.

Recent advances have been made with non-toxic preparations to be given to the dog monthly in tablet form. These do not kill adult fleas, but act by breaking the flea's breeding cycle. All flea treatments are demanding in that they must be given regularly if they are to work.

The important thing to remember is that fleas leave the host to reproduce, and that for every flea you find on the

▶ *Scratching is normal, but persistent scratching demands attention. In nine out of ten cases it will be something as simple as fleas. The most effective method to deal with the problem is to use a 'drop-on' preparation combined with a household spray. Your vet will advise on this.*

▲ *Dogs will lick and occasionally chew their paws, but if your dog does this persistently, examine its feet. Grass seeds are a common irritant.*

dog, there are literally thousands in your dog's bed, in the nooks and crannies in the floor, in the carpets, between the cushions on the sofa, all breeding away like mad.

There are a number of preparations on the market that provide effective flea protection around the house. Thorough vacuuming of the carpets helps, but will not overcome the problem. Flea eggs, laid in their thousands, are able to survive for long periods in a warm environment. Disturbance causes the eggs to hatch, in itself a reason for regular vacuum cleaning, as the eggs in their shells are resistant to insecticides.

TICKS

These tend to be a country dog problem. The tick's usual host is the sheep. In the United States, Australia, South Africa and the tropics, ticks transmit certain rapidly fatal diseases to dogs, and the dogs are routinely dipped or sprayed against infestation, often on a weekly basis. This is not necessary in Europe, where tick-borne disease is uncommon in the dog.

Ticks engorge on the blood of their host; the engorged tick is sometimes mistaken for a wart on the dog's skin.

Dogs will occasionally pick up a solitary tick, but may sometimes be seen to have several. Adult female ticks lay groups of eggs, which hatch at more or less the same time to form a colony of young ticks attached to grass stems waiting to find a host. If a dog comes by, several of the 'seed ticks' may attach themselves to it.

The ticks are usually removed individually. Do not try to pick them off. That's rarely successful, and there are various substances that will kill them. Ear drops that are intended to destroy parasites are useful as is methylated spirit, or even gin! The tick will not fall off immediately, but it should have disappeared 12 hours

after application. Most anti-flea preparations will also kill them. In the USA, Lyme disease is transmitted by ticks that live on deer and mice, and is a serious threat to dogs. Fortunately, a vaccine is available.

LICE

Fortunately, lice are now uncommon parasites of the dog. They are detectable by the presence of just visible groups of eggs attached to the hair, often of the ears or head of the dog.

Lice are small and they are not mobile. They tend to occur in large numbers, but do not seem to be as itchy to the dog as fleas.

Lice are transmitted directly from dog to dog by contact. They are not transmitted to humans or to other animals. They may be controlled by the use of insecticidal shampoos.

▼ *The Elizabethan collar is extremely useful to prevent self-mutilation around the head. The cause of the inflammation must be determined.*

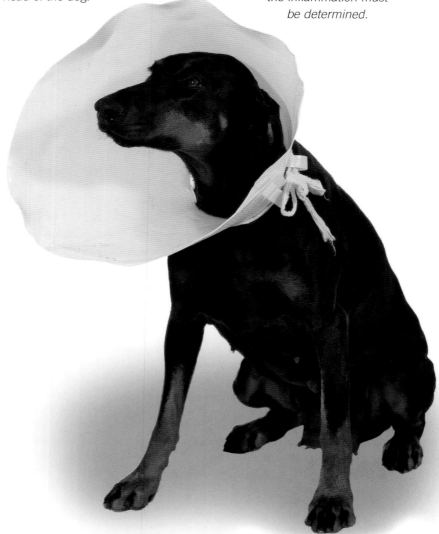

Signs of illness

One of the first signs that a dog is ill is if it refuses its food. Most fussy dogs will at least smell the food on offer, but a sick dog may have no appetite and simply not approach its food. The dog will tend to become duller than usual, although many sick dogs will still respond to their owner's enthusiasm for a game or a walk.

Signs of acute illness

Each of the following conditions needs immediate attention from your veterinary surgeon.
• Tense, swollen stomach. A drum-like swelling of the abdomen an hour or two after feeding, accompanied by obvious distress with panting and salivation may indicate that the dog has bloat. This is an emergency.
• Vomiting several times, particularly if it persists for more than 12 hours. Vomiting once or twice is common, and a normal reaction to eating something unsuitable. Some dogs eat grass, appearing to do it to make themselves sick. If this happens occasionally, there is probably nothing to worry about. However, persistent vomiting after eating grass may suggest an acute problem that needs attention.
• Diarrhoea persisting for 24 hours or longer. Diarrhoea will often accompany vomiting. If the faeces are bloodstained, treatment may be needed urgently.
• Difficulty breathing, gasping, coughing or choking.
• Loss of consciousness or fits.
• Serious uncontrollable bleeding.

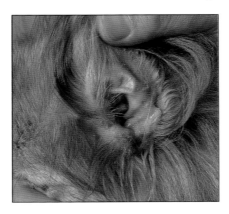

▲ *The ear is an extremely sensitive organ. Any inflammation demands immediate attention from the veterinary surgeon.*

ACUTE ILLNESS

The term 'acute' does not necessarily mean a serious illness. When your veterinary surgeon refers to an acute illness, they simply mean one that has come on rapidly, whereas a 'chronic' illness is one that is long-lasting and has appeared gradually.

Young puppies are occasionally subject to fits, from which they usually recover quickly. Observe the fit carefully so that you can describe it when you get to the vet's. Did the dog just collapse silently, did it squeal or howl, did it paddle its legs, did it urinate or defecate during the fit? Once a dog has recovered from a fit, it may be very difficult for the veterinary surgeon to be precise about the cause; there may be nothing to see.

Other signs of acute illness include serious bleeding or bleeding from any orifice; obvious pain indicated by noise (squealing, crying, yelping on movement), lameness or tenderness to touch; straining to pass faeces or inability to pass urine; any obvious severe injury or swelling on the body;

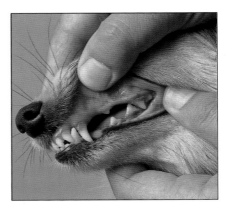

▲ *Dogs on modern diets are inclined to acquire tartar on their teeth, which needs attention if it is not to lead on to more serious problems.*

a closed eye or inflammation with excessive tears; and violent scratching or rubbing, particularly around the ears or head.

CHRONIC ILLNESS

The signs of chronic illness appear gradually and are likely to be more subtle and difficult to recognize.

Loss of weight, persisting over a period of weeks, is a common indicator of chronic disease. This may be accompanied by a normal or reduced appetite. Gradually developing swellings may indicate the growth of superficial tumours, often not cancerous but usually needing attention.

Other signs include hair loss, with or without sore skin or itching and scratching; slowly developing lameness; and excessive drinking, with or without an unpleasant odour from the mouth or body. Occasional vomiting may indicate an internal problem, although many healthy dogs may also vomit. In the normal course of events, bitches may frequently regurgitate food for their puppies.

First aid for your dog

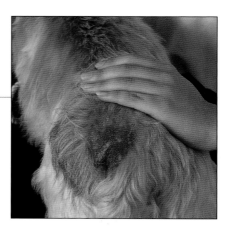

First-aid treatments may be divided into problems that you can deal with yourself, and treatments to carry out to keep the problem to a minimum before you take the dog to the veterinary surgeon.

SORES AND RASHES

A dog may get a sore place or a rash through chewing itself. Many dogs will chew their skin raw if there is an itch. The dog may get a rash from insect bites – typically flea bites, from skin contact with irritants such as nettles, or as an allergic response to an external or internal substance. It is often difficult to tell to what extent the sore area is caused by the irritant or is self-inflicted as a result of the irritation. The object of treatment, whether your

own first aid or your veterinary surgeon's, is to eliminate the cause before attempting to cure the effect.

If a dog has been scratching itself a little more than usual, the commonest cause is the presence of fleas. Fleas never come singly. If you see a flea, there will be others. One or two may be sufficient to start the itch cycle. The answer is to treat the fleas, and the problem will usually disappear. If it doesn't, a soothing cream, such as rescue cream, will be sufficient.

CUTS AND SCRATCHES

Treatment depends on how large and how deep the cut or scratch is. A dog's skin does not usually bleed profusely, and it is easy to miss even quite a large cut because there may

▲ *Sores and rashes may develop beneath a long coat for some time before they become obvious.*

be very little bleeding and the dog's fur covers the site. If there is any sign of blood on the dog, look carefully and once you have located the cut, clip sufficient hair around it to expose the wound. If the cut looks deep, or longer than about 1cm (½in), it will need attention and probably a stitch or two at the veterinary surgery. If you decide

First-aid kit

The most important item in your first-aid kit should be your veterinary surgeon's name and telephone number. Even though you may have it elsewhere, it doesn't harm to duplicate it.
• Absorbent cotton wool
• Adhesive and gauze bandages, 5cm (2in) and 10cm (4in)
• Gauze swabs and sterile wraps
• Cotton buds
• Sharp-pointed scissors
• Thermometer
• Medium forceps with blunt points
• Plastic syringe, 20ml (½fl oz)
• Eye drops
• Cleansing ear drops
• Antiseptic or antibiotic ointment
• Antiseptic powder and wash
• Rescue cream
• Medicinal liquid paraffin

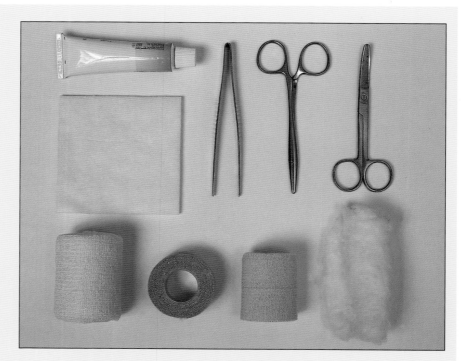

▲ *The forceps in a first-aid kit should never be used for probing around. You must always be able to see whatever it is you are attempting to remove.*

to take the dog to the vet, do nothing with the wound, unless it is bleeding profusely. The nurse is likely to take longer cleaning your dressing off the wound than the stitching itself. A minor scratch that does not penetrate the skin will usually need very little treatment. Soothing cream will be sufficient. Similarly, a small cut needs no particular attention once you have trimmed the hair away, other than to keep the wound clean with a mild antiseptic solution, and to keep an eye out for any swelling. Swelling may indicate that an infection has set in.

TAKING TEMPERATURE

1 First, shake the thermometer so that the level of mercury is well below the expected temperature of the dog.

2 Slide the lubricated thermometer carefully into the dog's anus and press lightly against the side of the rectum.

3 The thermometer should be held in place for at least 60 seconds before reading.

BANDAGING A PAW

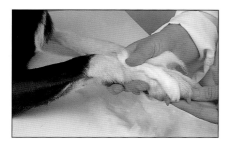

1 First, pad the leg with cotton-wool strips between the toes.

2 Place a generous amount of further padding over the end of the foot to cushion it before starting to bandage.

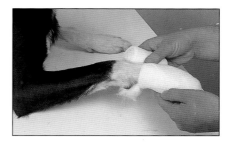

3 The bandage must always include the foot and be extended above the wound.

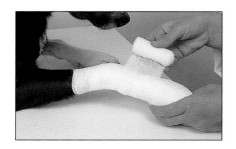

4 Bandage the leg firmly, but take care that the bandage is not so tight that circulation is restricted.

5 Tie the bandage off well above the site of the wound.

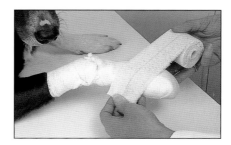

6 Cover the bandage in an adhesive dressing, firmly but not tightly, and secure it at the back of the dog's leg.

BITES

Dog bites will often become infected. This is particularly the case when the bite causes a puncture wound. Unless the wounds are multiple or very large, there is no emergency, but the dog should be taken to the veterinary surgery within 24 hours to allow the vet to assess whether antibiotic injections are needed. Prior to that, the wound may be cleansed with antiseptic lotion.

BLEEDING

Treatment will depend on how heavily the wound is bleeding. Skin wounds may only need cleansing, followed by the application of a little antiseptic cream and a careful monitoring of the progress of the wound. The bleeding will probably stop in a short time.

Profuse bleeding is an emergency, usually indicating a wound that is sufficiently deep to need urgent veterinary attention. Steps to control the bleeding while on the way to the surgery are worthwhile, and may be life-saving. Tourniquets are no longer used, so do not attempt to make one. Instead, use a pressure bandage over the wound.

The rare need for a pressure bandage is one reason for the cotton wool and bandages in your first-aid kit.

▲ *On warm days, even with a window open, a car will rapidly become an oven. Don't cook your dog.*

BANDAGING AN EAR

1 Ears are often damaged in dog fights. Clean the wound, then place an absorbent pad behind the ear.

2 Carefully fold the ear back on to the pad. Place the pad over the folded back ear.

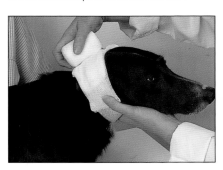

3 Start bandaging around the neck from behind the ear and work forwards, enclosing the ear, but not too tightly.

4 The unaffected ear should not be included in the bandaging.

When needed, take a large wad of cotton wool – as large as is available in your kit. Place it directly over the wound, and bandage firmly. If the wound is on a limb, bandage right down to the foot and include the entire leg below the wound in your bandage. Make sure the site over the wound is firmly bandaged, and then take the dog to the veterinary surgery.

HEAT EXHAUSTION

Some breeds of dog are more prone to heat exhaustion than others – Chow Chows and Bulldogs come to mind, but several other short-nosed breeds can also be affected.

The most common reason for heat exhaustion is human error. Dogs are too often left inside cars in summer without adequate ventilation. The owner is usually just thoughtless, or caught out by a change in the weather during a longer-than-expected shopping trip. The temperature inside a closed car in summer in even a temperate climate can kill a dog.

Many animals have died in this way. The signs of heat stress are obvious distress, heavy panting and an inability to breathe deeply enough, indicated by a half-strangled noise coming from the dog's throat. The dog's tongue looks swollen and blue.

Treat heat stroke as an immediate emergency, and do not attempt to take the dog to the vet until you have started its resuscitation. Plenty of cool (not cold) water and shade is the first-aid treatment. First, move the dog to a shaded area, with a breeze if possible, or use an electric fan. Apply plenty of cool water, especially to the head and neck. Continue with this treatment until breathing becomes easier, but avoid cooling the dog to an extent that it starts to shiver. Then take it to the vet. The vet may put the dog on to an oxygen air flow, and will probably give it an injection to reduce the swelling in its throat, but unless the vet happens to be at hand, for example if the animal is at a dog show, this life-saving treatment needs to have been given before the dog gets to the surgery.

BANDAGING A TAIL

1 Successful tail bandaging is fraught with difficulty. First, enclose the tail lengthways in a bandage.

2 Lay strips of bandage along the length of the tail.

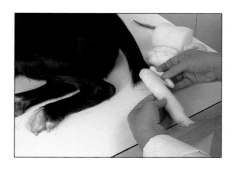

3 Bandage the tail around its length, whenever possible including some of the dog's tail hair within the turns of the bandage.

4 Cover the bandage with an adhesive dressing. Take the adhesive dressing well above the end of the bandage, and include strands of hair within each turn.

TREATING HEAT STROKE

1 The first signs of heat stroke in your dog are obvious distress and incessant heaving panting. This is a serious condition that needs quick treatment.

2 Cool the dog down immediately by sponging or spraying with cool (not cold) water, ensuring the head and neck are wet.

3 Allow the dog to drink a small amount of water. A wet towel, frequently changed, will help to cool the dog down, and may prevent heat stroke.

◀ Sick dogs may be encouraged to eat but never force-fed. They should always have easy access to water.

SNAKE BITES, AND STINGS FROM OTHER VENOMOUS CREATURES

These are often difficult to recognize unless the bite is witnessed. The degree of urgency depends on the type of venomous creature, where on its body the dog was bitten, and the age of the dog. Small puppies are obviously more at risk than older, larger animals.

The only venomous British snake is the adder. The risk is greater in areas with certain types of soil – sandy downs seem to harbour more adders than most other areas. In the USA, Australia and Africa, the most common snake bites in dogs are from the viperine snakes. Poisonous North American snakes include rattlesnakes and coral snakes. Snakes are often more likely to bite when they come out to sun themselves on a warm spring day and the dog goes to investigate. So the dog is most likely to be bitten on the face, head or neck.

If the dog's face starts to swell up while you are out on a walk, the chance of a snake bite must be considered. Unless the swelling starts to cause obvious breathing distress,

TREATING EYES

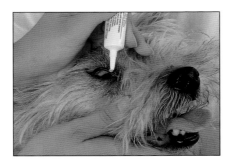

1 Take great care when administering eye drops or ointment. It is important to hold the dog's eyelids open so that the medication actually goes into the eyes.

2 After the drops have been put in, the eyelids must be gently massaged over the surface of the eye to encourage the spread of the medication.

BRUSHING TEETH

1 Regular brushing will slow up the formation of plaque and tartar.

2 Some dogs will resent the use of a brush, but toothpaste on the end of a finger can be almost as effective.

3 Specially made dog toothbrushes are often well tolerated.

▶ *Disturb an injured dog as little as possible, although be prepared to lift it carefully and take it to a vet.*

treatment is urgent, but this is not a life-threatening emergency. You can afford to walk back to the car – no need to run – but make sure the dog walks quietly. Exercise should be minimal. Carry a small dog. Take the dog straight to the veterinary surgery. Very few dogs in Britain die from the effects of adder venom, but many each year have distressing abscesses caused by a combination of the venom and infection. In the USA, Eastern diamondback and coral snakes are the cause of 20 per cent of dog fatalities from snake bites.

Bites from non-venomous snakes should be thoroughly cleaned, as the snake's teeth may be carrying bacteria, which could cause infection.

The only reason to include snake bites in the first-aid section is that there is a belief that the venom of a snake should be 'sucked out' of the wound. Do not attempt to do so.

Bee and wasp stings carry a similar risk of death to snake bites – generally, they are only likely to be lethal if the swelling from the bite blocks the dog's airway. The exception to this is the case of multiple stings, the shock of which can cause the death of the dog. However, such events are rare.

Venomous spiders are unknown in the United Kingdom and uncommon in the United States, although they do occur there. The Australian funnel-web spider, however, is an extremely venomous arachnid.

A single swelling from a bee or wasp sting does not usually require veterinary treatment, but home attention with a soothing cream will speed the dog's recovery, and possibly stop the 'sore scratch' cycle.

CHOKING

Some dogs are inveterate pickers-up of sticks and stones, or ball chasers. All carry the risk of getting an object stuck in the mouth or throat. A half-swallowed ball may be an emergency by reason of a blocked airway. First aid may be a two-handed job, as you could get bitten. If the dog seems to be choking, look in its mouth with care. A block of wood to prevent it closing its teeth over your fingers can help, with one person holding the dog's head while the other looks into its mouth. If there is a ball in the dog's throat, try to lever it out with a fine rod rather than with your hand.

A frequent occurrence is that a piece of wood becomes wedged across the teeth, or between the back teeth. Treat removal with similar caution, using some sort of lever to remove it. This type of incident not infrequently requires a trip to the vet and sedation to remove the object.

ROAD ACCIDENT

It is virtually certain that a dog involved in a road accident will not be under control. The first step, even before looking to see what may be

wrong, is to leash the dog with whatever comes to hand. But you must do this without risk to yourself.

A noose needs to be made and slipped over the dog's head without actually touching the dog. The noose may be easily made from your own dog's lead or any other line, or even a piece of string.

▼ *Many road accidents and injuries to dogs may be avoided if the owner exercises the dog sensibly by restraining it with a lead.*

▶ *Large injured dogs may be carried with one arm at the front of their chest, under the neck, and the other looped through to allow the back legs to hang. A muzzle may be necessary.*

The next step, unless the dog is unconscious, is to muzzle the dog. Any dog that has been involved in a road accident is likely to be in shock, and even the most friendly can bite whoever is attending it, through pain or fear. You are unlikely to be carrying a proper muzzle with you. A cord, a dog lead or a bandage can be used. Only once the dog is secure, and you are unlikely to be bitten, should you try to examine the dog.

If the dog is not conscious, do not try to resuscitate it – get it to the vet as quickly as possible. If other people are there, ask someone to phone ahead to the surgery to warn them that you are coming.

A coat or blankets may be used as a makeshift stretcher, but only a dog that is so badly injured that it is unaware of its surroundings is likely to tolerate being carried in this way.

If the dog is bleeding heavily, use whatever is available to make a pressure pad; bind the wound and take the dog to the veterinary surgery immediately.

If the dog is carrying a leg, or is limping, there may be a fracture. Despite the first-aid warning about not moving an injured person, you are better to take the dog straightaway to the veterinary surgery than to wait while someone phones around to find a vet who can leave the surgery to attend the accident. There is no organized emergency ambulance service for animals.

Once the dog's mouth is bound and it cannot bite, it is almost always safe to carry the dog. If possible, let the affected leg hang free – you will avoid further damage and pain.

Dogs in road accidents will often run away, despite serious injury. If you see this happen, warn the police, who will at least be able to inform anyone who enquires about their missing dog. Sometimes the police will accept responsibility for the care of dogs involved in road accidents. If they are informed and are able to attend the scene, they will usually know the local veterinary surgeons and be able to advise on their phone numbers.

MUZZLING AN INJURED DOG

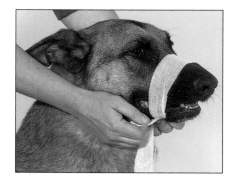

1 An improvised muzzle may be made with a bandage or almost any material. Make a loop, pass it over the dog's muzzle and under its chin.

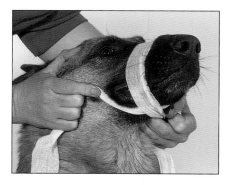

2 Take the ends of the material behind the dog's ears.

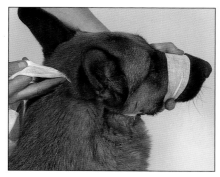

3 Tie the muzzle firmly behind the dog's head. An improvised muzzle must be tied tightly. It will not choke the dog.

POISONING AND COMMON POISONS

The poisons likely to be encountered by a dog are almost always those found around the house and garden. They include tablets and medicines intended for human consumption, or those not for internal use at all – household chemicals such as bleach or detergents, and garden chemicals.

Puppies will try anything. You must keep all potentially dangerous materials out of their reach, preferably in a locked cupboard.

If an accident does occur, and you think your dog has eaten something that could be poisonous, there are two things to do.

1 Make the dog sick. If this is to be of any help, it must be done before the poisonous substance has had a chance to be absorbed from the stomach, so do it before contacting

▲ *Cigarettes are toxic to dogs and may cause nicotine poisoning. Fortunately, however, few dogs will actually eat cigarettes.*

your veterinary surgeon. But if you know your vet is immediately available for advice, and you are certain what the dog has eaten, do not make the dog sick until you have spoken to the vet.

The most effective substance to use to make the dog sick is washing soda. Put two small crystals on to the back of the dog's tongue, and make the animal swallow them by holding its

▲ *If poisoning is suspected, take the container and, if possible, some of its contents to the veterinary surgeon with the dog.*

mouth shut and stroking its throat. Vomiting will take place within minutes, so be prepared with old newspapers to hand.

2 Contact your veterinary surgeon. Retain some of the poisonous substance, or at least its wrapping, to show them. There may be no ill effect, or immediate further treatment may be necessary.

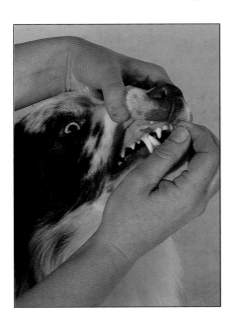

▲ *Do not make the dog vomit if the toxic substance is already being absorbed, which occurs within 30 or so minutes of ingestion.*

Some common poisons

• Rat poisons – all rat poisons are coloured to indicate the active substance. They are of low toxicity to dogs when used properly, but dogs may get hold of bulk quantities.
Blue: Anticoagulants
Brown: Calciferol
Green: Alphachloralose
Pink or grey: Gamma-HCH (Lindane)

If rat poisoning is suspected, the package or some of the suspect material must be retained for examination by the veterinary surgeon.
• Barbiturates – human sleeping pills
• Sodium chlorate – weed killer
• Detergents – usually safe, but

if concentrated may cause external lesions, or vomiting if swallowed
• Antifreeze – Ethylene glycol
• Lead – old paint chewed by dogs
• Slug bait – Metaldehydrate, attractive to dogs; some brands now have an anti-dog component
• Cigar and cigarette ends – nicotine
• Organochlorine, Organo-phosphorus compounds – flea and lice killers
• Paraquat – herbicide
• Aspirin – if taken in large quantity
• Strychnine – vermin killer; dogs may get at carcasses
• Toad – from mouthing the toad; exotic toads are more venomous
• Tranquillizers

Inherited diseases

An inherited disease is one that may be passed from generation to generation through affected genes of the sire or the dam, or sometimes a combination of both. Genetics, the study of inheritance, is a highly complicated science, becoming increasingly so the more we learn of the subject.

There are two main problems in the control of inherited diseases in dogs. Some diseases are partly inherited, and partly occur as a result of some environmental influence, which is often difficult to determine precisely. The inherited element may depend on several inherited factors rather than a single gene.

Typical of this type of disease is hip dysplasia, probably the most widely known of all inherited diseases of the dog. It is a hind-leg lameness, caused by severe erosion and damage to the hip joint. It is generally considered that inheritance accounts for about 50 per cent of the clinical signs of hip dysplasia, and that the remainder is caused by some environmental circumstance – the dog's weight, exercise, diet perhaps – but precisely what is not known. In these circumstances, attempts at control are slow at best, depending on diagnosis of the disease and the avoidance of affected dogs in breeding. This may sound simple, but it is not.

The condition affects many breeds, mostly the larger ones, including the German Shepherd. Largely due to the efforts of German Shepherd breeders, control schemes have been operating

▲ *The breeder carries a heavy burden of responsibility to produce a healthy, keen-to-please dog such as this German Shepherd.*

in several countries for many years. Progress has been real but is slow, and sometimes heartbreaking for breeders, who may have used a dog and a bitch that both have excellent 'hip scores', only to find that the offspring are seriously affected.

The second problem is that the disease may not show itself until the affected animal is mature. The dog or bitch may well have been used in a breeding programme before any signs that it has the condition are seen. To some extent, this may be overcome by control schemes that do not give certificates of freedom from the disease until the dogs in the scheme are old enough for the particular

◄ *This Irish Setter is free from the distressing condition of Progressive Retinal Atrophy (PRA), which responsible breeders are doing a great deal to eliminate in the breed.*

▲ *Until a specific gene test becomes practicable, it is important that not only this pregnant Dalmatian bitch but also the sire have been certified healthy.*

disease to have shown itself. Hip dysplasia is again an example: hip scoring is by an expert panel who examine x-rays of submitted dogs. These x-rays may not be taken until the dog is 12 months old.

There are several diseases that are known to be inherited in a straightforward way and are present at birth. These diseases can be controlled, depending for the success of the control scheme on the co-operation of the breeders, and their recognition that animals that show signs of the disease are actually afflicted, rather than the subject of mysterious accidents that merely mimic the condition.

The most outstanding example of breeder co-operation in the control of inherited disease must be the experience of Progressive Retinal Atrophy – night blindness – in Irish Setters. By the involvement of nearly all the breeders, and with recognition that the disease had a straightforward inheritance pattern, this condition has been virtually eliminated from the breed.

Up-and-coming schemes include one to control deafness in Dalmatians. For many years, a proportion of Dalmatian puppies have been born deaf or partially deaf, but breeders were generally only able to recognize stone-deaf puppies, which were routinely put to sleep soon after birth.

Scientific testing, developed for use in people, has now enabled breeders to have their puppies examined before

sale, not only for total deafness, but for partial deafness in one or both ears. There is evidence that partially deaf dogs can pass on partial or complete deafness to their offspring, and the numbers of dogs being tested are increasing rapidly in several countries. The test for dogs originated in the United States, which is probably leading the world in this area.

Almost certainly, present studies of the 'genome' or genetic make-up of all species will result in a revolution in the study and control of genetic diseases. Once the precise positions of inherited diseases on the DNA molecule are known, specific action may be taken to eliminate the problem. This approach is no longer 'pie in the sky'. Within a few years, DNA testing will become routine.

▼ *Dalmatians may be tested scientifically for deafness before they are six weeks old.*

441

Neutering, spaying and breeding

Being a responsible dog owner means that you will not increase the number of unwanted dogs being sent to rescue centres. Every year, thousands of dogs are put down because they are unwanted, but having your dogs neutered and spayed will stop unwanted pregnancies, and also provide health benefits. Such treatment can substantially lower the risk of prostate problems and testicular cancers in male dogs later in their life, and mammary cancers and pyometra (a life-threatening disease of the womb) in bitches. Neutering and spaying is the responsible, practical approach to dog ownership.

NEUTERING AND SPAYING

It is often thought that castration will cure any problem with an adolescent dog, including jumping up and overexcitement, but in fact castration only helps with problems directly related to testosterone (and definitely not those caused by attention-

▼ *Veterinary checks of bitches are important to ensure healthy puppies.*

seeking). If testosterone levels are high, then roaming the neighbourhood looking for bitches (with the risk of getting run over and causing accidents), scent-marking, mounting inappropriate objects and people, and male-to-male aggression may be remedied, but extra training sessions will also be required. However, contrary to a popular misconception, neutering and spaying does not alter the personality of the dog, nor does it make the dog fat (this is usually caused by a lack of exercise). Both operations will, however, make a dog a more content, happier member of the family.

Spaying bitches will also halt phantom pregnancies, which can be upsetting for both the bitches

▲ *Bitches can have as many as 12 puppies in a single litter.*

and their owners watching them go through this phase. A bitch having a phantom pregnancy may carry a toy around in her mouth as a substitute for a puppy, become aggressive towards other bitches or dogs and become withdrawn and moody, and may stop eating.

People can have strong feelings for and against getting dogs and bitches neutered and spayed, but it's important not to confuse a human's response with what's best for your dog. As for the ideal age, the best advice is to wait until your dog has matured emotionally and physically, although if your male dog is beginning to show behavioural problems caused by high testosterone levels, you should castrate sooner rather than later, before it becomes a permanent problem.

TO BREED OR NOT TO BREED

If you do decide to let a bitch have a litter, it's best to research all the options beforehand. This is a responsible, time-consuming job. Your bitch will

Health checks for different breeds

Even before breeding, it's a busy time. There are health checks for certain breeds of dog: Labradors, Border Collies and Golden Retrievers are prone to hip problems, and the parents should be hip-scored. Hips can only be x-rayed when the dogs are 12 months old. The x-rays are examined by the vet and given a score on nine points of the hip joints. The lower the score, the better the hip joint (a perfect score is 0/0 and the worst is 53/53). Border Collies and Tibetan Rerriers need eye checks; Dalmatians are prone to deafness, and Cavaliers and Boxers are prone to heart problems and need checks before they are mated. In addition, the stud also needs to be checked for potential problems, and both dog and bitch need to have a good temperament with no aggression.

Cavalier King Charles Spaniel

Labrador

Border Collie

Boxer

Golden Retriever

Dalmatian

need a quiet room away from the hustle and bustle of the house in the first weeks. If you think you can make a quick profit, nothing could be further from the truth, because breeding is an expensive business.

The first job is to check whether a Caesarean operation is likely, and to make sure you know what to do if there are any problems during whelping. The size of the litter can be anything from 1–12 puppies, with larger dogs producing larger litters – and they all need to be cared for. You will have to start house-training them, oversee the first inoculation, let them socialize and keep them for eight weeks until they are ready to go to their new homes.

You'll also need to be sufficiently knowledgeable about dogs to impart all the relevant information to the new owners, covering everything from diet and worming to socialization and training – and that's before you have to field their emergency phone calls.

If you do decide to breed from your bitch, check the suitability of prospective new owners by visiting them in their home. Finally, be prepared to take any of the puppies back into your care should anything go wrong along the way.

Dogs and human health

There are some diseases that may affect both dogs and humans. The technical term for such a disease is 'zoonosis'. The most feared of these diseases is undoubtedly rabies, the reason for long-standing quarantine laws between the UK and all other countries, which have only recently been changed. The laws throughout the EU countries have now been dramatically relaxed for many domestic pets. It is now possible to acquire a 'pet passport', which allows owners to bring their pet into Britain without them spending six months in quarantine kennels, as the old laws used to require.

The passport requirements are very stringent and include a full health check by a vet, which includes up-to-date immunizations against rabies and many other diseases. Animals must also have an identification chip inserted, a photo, current certificates and pet insurance.

When travelling in an area that is not rabies-free, consult a doctor immediately if you are bitten by a dog or any other animal.

Fleas, common on dogs (but most frequently actually the cat flea) will bite humans. It is unlikely that dog or cat fleas can survive on humans, so a few intensely itchy bites are the only likely problem. The presence of flea bites on you or your children is a timely reminder that flea control on your dog has, perhaps, not been as effective as you thought.

Rabbit mites frequently cause a skin rash in dogs. They are capable of biting humans, and may cause an itchy rash on the forearms from contact with the affected dog, however the rash is unlikely to spread.

Ringworm is not a common disease in dogs but, when it does occur, precautions should be taken to avoid its spread to human members of the family. It is a true zoonosis and can establish itself on the human skin. Affected areas are again likely to be those of contact – the hands and forearms in particular.

Toxocara, the most frequently encountered roundworm in puppies, and indeed almost universal in very young puppies, has been implicated in a rare specific type of eye disease in children. Roundworms that are ingested by a species other than their

◀ *The many benefits of association between children and dogs far outweigh the risk of cross-transmission of diseases. Sensible hygiene will almost always overcome the risks.*

◀ *Dogs should never be permitted to run freely where children may play, because of the risk that the animals may deposit faeces.*

▼ *Many local authorities provide dog litter bins. They are to be encouraged.*

normal host may encyst and settle in almost any part of the body, but are known to invade the eye. These cysts have been known to cause blindness. Such an occurence is extremely rare but, of course, a tragedy for the child and their parents if it happens.

Good hygiene and vigilance should prevent any child from coming into contact with dog faeces. Puppies must be wormed regularly, every three weeks until they are six months old. Their faeces must be collected, at home as well as on the street, and the puppy should be taught to defecate in a prescribed spot in the garden, not in a public place. If an accident does happen while you are out with your dog, scoop it up. Always go prepared. Legislation now covers fouling by dogs in public places, and 'poop scoop' laws are in force in many areas.

Simple hygiene for children must be practised: they should always wash their hands after playing with the dog. But children should not be discouraged – there is so much to be gained from a happy association between child and dog that, provided risks are minimized by adopting sensible precautions, their close companionship should be encouraged. Remember, the dog is our oldest friend.

▲ *Owners must always collect faeces deposited by their dogs.*

▶ *Dogs should be discouraged from playing with the baby's toys.*

HOLISTIC
CARE

Holistic medicine is based on the concept that there is a link between physical health and more general wellbeing. A classic example would be a dog mutilating itself because it is stressed. Although its wounds can be treated, the problem will reoccur unless the dog's lifestyle is altered or the reason for its stress is resolved. There is a direct link between the two. Dogs with behavioural problems, emotional issues, chronic ill health, unexplained fear and aggression may all benefit from a holistic approach. Holistic care works well alongside more traditional veterinary treatments, but always talk to your vet first before embarking on a course of action. *"Many times an illness begins when one is unaware of an imbalance that has subtly begun. Do not forget that the myriad things of the universe have an intimate relationship with one another"* – 'The Yellow Emperor's Classic of Medicine', 250BC.

◀ *Hydrotherapy improves mobility and increases fitness. Check with your vet that your dog is fit enough to undertake this therapy before booking an appointment.*

Holistic therapies

The basic philosophy underlying holistic medicine is a concern for the living totality of the patient. Its aim is to treat the patient as a whole, and not the disease in isolation.

If you wish to use to use holistic therapies on your dog, discuss the matter with your vet first. Ensure that essential conventional medical care is given before a complementary treatment plan is worked out between you and your veterinary practitioner.

Holistic treatment is not aimed at the cause of the infection or the suppression of symptoms, but at all aspects of the patient's life. This

▼ *Good dog health is a question of mental, emotional and physical balance; food and water alone can only ensure survival.*

includes the patient's mental and emotional state, any co-existing physical complaints, lifestyle, stresses and nutritional status. While Western medicine looks at the true name of the disease (the diagnosis) and the correct treatment to cure the patient, holistic medicine looks at the whole picture. It recognizes that a range of treatments may be necessary, from simple lifestyle changes to surgery and conventional medicines. It also

◄ *Just like us, dogs suffer from stress, and they need emotional comfort and support from their owners.*

accepts that therapies which cannot be explained by science can affect the whole being, and are often helpful if a true cure is to be achieved. Some holistic treatments are physically manipulative, while others concentrate of the flow of energy around or within the body and restoring balance to this system.

In human medicine there are holistic clinics where patients are treated by teams of therapists under the supervision of a doctor. The patient's response to treatment is closely monitored and varied accordingly. In the veterinary field this is not so common. There are a growing number of veterinary practices worldwide offering alterative or complimentary healthcare, but the range services available in some areas is still very limited.

There are various legal restrictions in the use of holistic practice for animals. The law recognizes that humans understand the risks involved in seeking non-medically qualified treatment. An animal is incapable of assessing risk, so the treatment of disease in animals is restricted to veterinary surgeons only.

Vets may, however, work with or refer patients to suitably qualified physiotherapists who practise manipulative therapies. This includes the use of osteopaths, chiropractors and those trained in the use of hydrotherapy for animal health and wellbeing. Therapies that have a physical basis such as these are generally more accepted by vets.

▲ *Lemon balm has a strong anti-inflammatory action, and is used to treat hot spots, burns and stings.*

▲ *Holistic care such as massage can help to reduce pain while providing comfort and support for your dog.*

▲ *Amethyst is reputed to calm hyperactive behaviour, as well as easing painful joints and arthritis.*

Treatment in the form of acupuncture or homeopathy can only be given to animals by a veterinary surgeon who has an additional qualification covering these therapies. It is illegal for non-veterinary surgeons, however well qualified in the human field, to treat animals. If your veterinary practice does not have a vet qualified in these therapies, they could refer your dog to another vet who is.

Reiki, any type of 'laying on of hands' or faith healing is a difficult area. Legally, in many countries, this treatment should have the consent of a veterinary surgeon. It is undecided whether reiki falls into the group of therapies regarded as manipulative and therefore needs veterinary referral before treatment can commence. It would be wise to discuss this with your vet prior to seeking a practitioner.

For hundreds of years, herbalism and aromatherapy have been used on animals and humans alike, often with great benefit. It is worth remembering that these therapies actually form the early basis of pharmaceuticals. But just as you would not give your dog a random selection of pills, these therapies should not be used without proper advice.

The owner of an animal is allowed to treat their animal themselves, providing the treatment does not include invasion of the body. The therapies that fall within this non-invasive group include massage, TTouch, Bach flower remedies and crystal therapy. Courses and books are available to learn how to practise each of these holistic treatments.

Treating your dog in a holistic manner can benefit both its physical and mental wellbeing, but should only be undertaken with the correct consent, qualification and knowledge.

▼ *If your dog appears to be unaccountably out of sorts, always have it examined by a vet.*

Pharmaceuticals

Even when adopting a holistic approach to health, conventional Western medicine does not need to be abandoned altogether. Acupuncture, herbalism and homeopathy are complete systems of medicine in their own right, but this does not necessarily mean that these systems are equally effective 100 per cent of the time. Each individual is unique, with their own unique response to treatment. Every dog will respond in a different way to the same treatment. Complementary treatments can and do work, and sometimes they are enough in themselves to effect a complete cure. There are also times, however, when modern medicines are needed. They may not be needed as the sole medication, but they can form part of an approach using a combination of several therapies.

Modern Western medicine is based on an accurate diagnosis. After the illness has been correctly identified and named, the aim is to find and administer the one, true medicine that will cure the condition. This medicine is the 'magic bullet' that will kill the disease. It is a beautiful idea, but unfortunately medicines have more than one simple action in the body. Unwanted actions are the side effects of the drug. When medicines are given in short courses of small doses, the body is able to correct any damage which has been done inadvertently by the medicine while it heals the disease it was sent to cure. In chronic disease, where medicines are given over longer periods of time, the side effects can overcome the body's ability to deal with them. The original natural disease can then be overtaken and made worse by medicine-induced disease. It might be argued that chronic disease is itself an indication that the medicine has not cured but has simply suppressed the symptoms, giving a false impression of a cure.

Many modern medicines are derived by isolating the active ingredient found in herbal medicines. Having isolated and identified the chemical structure of the active ingredient, attempts are then made to

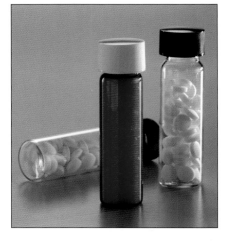

▲ *It is important to balance the pros and cons of giving long-term pharmaceuticals. Your veterinary surgeon will advise you on this.*

synthesize medicines that have a similar structure and a stronger action. These tend to have stronger side effects as well. The first antibiotic, penicillin, was isolated from a fungal culture. Since then, other natural antibiotics have been found, and synthetics based on the chemical structure of these natural products have been manufactured. However, the side effects of synthetic drugs usually become more serious as each new generation of antibiotics is developed. Scientists have also

◄ *Pharmaceutical preparations come in many forms. They are all standardized to ensure that every dose has the same effect on every patient. Never give your dog drugs that have not been prescribed for it.*

manufactured synthetic hormones and vitamins, but some of these have proved to be less effective than the natural product.

Modern medicine is at its best in cases where the patient has a mineral deficiency, for example when a bitch develops milk fever after whelping. Injection of a calcium salt solution will remove the symptoms, but it must be followed by dietary changes, preferably backed up with further support from appropriate homeopathic medicines.

In the case of hormone deficiencies, for example in conditions such as diabetes and the under-activity of the thyroid gland (hypothyroidism), replacement with insulin or thyroid extract is beneficial. Properly supported by an appropriate complementary therapy, the amount of the replacement can be reduced, and sometimes the need for replacement therapy disappears altogether.

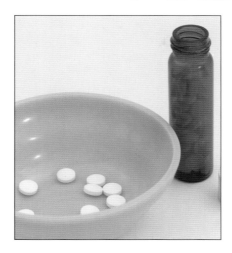

▲ Tablets must be stored correctly. Some require refrigeration, while others must be kept away from light.

In acute bacterial infections, antibiotics are of great value, but good complementary medicine used alongside antibiotics will allow the use of smaller courses of milder antibiotics than would otherwise be needed. Such a holistic approach will reduce

▲ Some medication is produced in granular form that can be added to dog food, making it easier to administer.

the number and the severity of the side effects experienced by the dog. It will speed convalescence and correct the weakness that enabled the infection to occur in the first place. Steroids are useful when your dog has severe inflammatory conditions (they should only be used in short courses), but complementary support used with antibiotics can provide similar benefits without the need for steroids. With certain forms of cancer, chemotherapy is a valid treatment, although the painful and very distressing side effects of the therapy can be substantially reduced with a sensible holistic treatment plan used in support.

Modern medicine has a genuine place in the treatment of disease. However, used ideally, it should form only one part of a holistic approach to your dog's overall health.

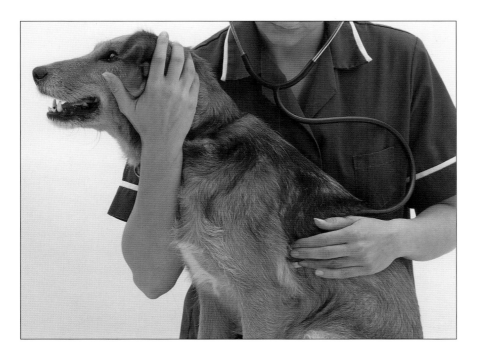

◄ The scientific approach of modern Western medicine can provide an accurate diagnosis, and the dog may then be treated holistically.

Treating your dog

The pleasure of keeping a dog brings with it the responsibility of ensuring the dog's lifestyle is as good as it can be. If the dog becomes ill, it is your responsibility to see that it receives the best possible treatment.

As the owner, you have the legal right to treat your dog yourself, although the law insists that the diagnosis and treatment of dogs must be done by, or under the supervision of, a qualified vet. This means that you can treat your dog yourself provided that you discuss the treatment first with a vet. This is particularly important if there is chronic disease and the dog is suffering.

In mild cases, some of the therapies discussed in this book are suitable for home treatment. The use

▼ *The power of touch alone can alleviate all kinds of hurts and upsets.*

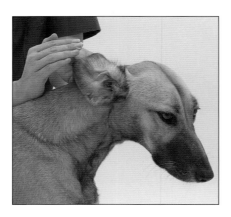

▲ *TTouch recognizes a link between posture and behaviour. Aggressive dogs often have neck and spine tension.*

of modern pharmaceuticals is restricted by law to medically trained professionals. Likewise, the practice of acupuncture, osteopathy and chiropractic must be left to qualified therapists. Herbalism is a borderline case. Simple Western herbalism is

▲ *Bach flower remedies may help to alleviate stress, excitable behaviour and travel-sickness problems.*

a home therapy using proprietary veterinary remedies available from health-food shops and some pet shops. Traditional Chinese herbalism, on the other hand, must be left to trained practitioners. As with self-help treatments for use on humans, the basic rule has to be: if you are in any doubt, consult a trained professional.

The remaining therapies can be used at home with a self-taught knowledge of the therapy. Introductory courses in TTeam and TTouch are held, as are courses in homeopathy and the veterinary use of Bach Flower remedies. Courses for using massage, Reiki or crystal therapy on dogs can be difficult to find. However, the therapies are energetically based, and they can be adapted from use on humans with a little common sense.

If your dog displays mood swings, emotional problems or signs of behavioural problems, try the therapy with which you are most familiar. If the dog shows mild physical symptoms, such as diarrhoea and vomiting, a cough or muscular stiffness, home treatment can be tried. If, however,

▶ *Give your dog time to acclimatize to anything new and don't bombard it with ointments and oils too quickly. Sometimes giving an animal its own space can be just as beneficial.*

there is severe pain, blood in any of the bodily discharges, or if the dog does not respond to treatment, you should see a vet. You should also see a vet if your dog is suffering from the same complaint repeatedly. The vet will then check for a more serious underlying cause; this is one of the reasons why conventional medicine is a necessary part of holistic care.

Some injuries need surgical repair, but after the surgery, holistic support will speed healing. Conditions such as diabetes and hypothyroidism respond quickly to medical veterinary treatment, but complementary support can reduce the amount of medicine needed, and may even effect a complete cure.

When you next visit your vet, make a point of asking what the treatment being provided for your dog is designed to do, and ask about possible side effects. Discuss your

▼ *All breeds make suitable patients for holistic care, although the character of the dog may affect its response.*

interest in complementary medicine and ask about any available therapies that could help in your dog's case.

Relatively few vets have practical experience of complementary therapies. This is not a comment on the success of holistic medicine, and you should not let it deter you. For a long time, conventional vets all over the world have shown an interest

in holistic practice, but the veterinary profession as a whole is still relatively poorly informed on the subject. The aim of both conventional and complementary medicine is essentially the same: to promote and maintain good health, to restore balance that has been lost and, at the end of life, to help smooth the transition from this world to the next.

Holistic first aid

Accidents will happen in the best-run households. It is valid for an owner to give first aid, but any dog involved in a serious accident must always be checked by a vet. Complementary medicines are well suited for first aid use in the home.

ARTIFICIAL RESPIRATION
The routine for attending to injured dogs is essentially the same as for a human. If it is not moving, check to see if it is conscious by pinching the web between its toes; a conscious dog will pull its foot back. If it doesn't, watch to see if the chest is moving. If it is, the dog is breathing; if it isn't, make sure that there is no blood, mucus or other material obstructing the throat and nose. If the dog does not start to breathe, hold its mouth closed and blow gently down its nose and watch its chest rise as air enters the lungs. Keep the lungs inflated for the count of three, then let the air out naturally. Repeat this at 5–10 second intervals. In between puffs,

▼ *Small bites can be bathed with diluted Hypercal tincture before they are dressed. If the wound is gaping, stitches will be needed.*

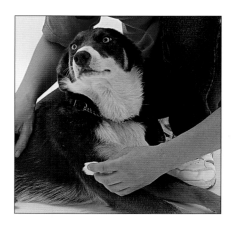

feel for a heartbeat with your fingers on the ribs just behind the elbow. If there is no beat, cardiac massage can be given by squeezing the chest vigorously between the fingers and thumb of one hand once or twice a second. Alternate the breathing and squeezing, changing every 15–20 seconds. If there is no heartbeat in 4 minutes, the heart is unlikely to restart. Artificial respiration can be kept up for 20 minutes if there is a heartbeat.

BLEEDING
If there is serious bleeding, put a layer of wadding (batting) material over the wound and apply a firm bandage. A conscious dog may object to being handled and it may be necessary to tie a piece of bandage, such as a tie or scarf, around its mouth to stop it biting you. If the vet hasn't been told before, tell them now and arrange to take the dog to the surgery. The treatment for shock that accompanies any accident is either to give two drops of the Bach Flower *Rescue Remedy*, or a tablet of homeopathic *Aconite 6C* or *30C*. These medicines can be given to unconscious dogs, because they will be absorbed through the mouth lining.

▲ *If your dog is bitten by another dog, let your vet know before rushing to the surgery. The injury will need urgent attention, but if they are on a visit it might be quicker for them to come to you.*

WOUNDS
Cuts and bruises result from many causes. If necessary, treat for shock and bleeding, as above. In addition, homeopathic *Arnica* is the ideal medicine for all cuts and bruises, although if the bruising is severe, change from *Arnica* to *Bellis Perennis* after a couple of days. *Hypericum* helps for crush injuries to the legs and tail, and *Calendula* is good for minor cuts and grazes. If the bleeding persists, give *Phosphorus* or *Ipecacuana* to stop it, and *Hamamelis* stops dark-coloured oozing from badly bruised wounds. Use the *6C* potency of all homeopathic remedies.

Acupuncture can help relieve severe pains. The tissue salt *Ferrum Phosphoricum* can stop bleeding if a powdered tablet is sprinkled on the wound, and can also be given by mouth afterwards. Minor wounds can be cleaned with *Hypercal* tincture diluted 1:10 and *Hypercal* cream used

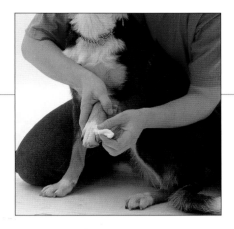

as a dressing. Essential oils of *Lavender* or *Terebinth* may be massaged around wounds, but must not be put on them directly. Serious wounds must always receive professional help.

BURNS AND SCALDS

These are caused by dry and moist heat respectively, and can be very painful. Do not apply grease, but bathe them with cold water. Bach Flower *Rescue Remedy* and homeopathic *Aconite* can be given as for bleeding, and *Cantharis* will help, particularly if there is blistering. The surrounding area can be massaged with essential oils of *Lavender* and *Rosemary*.

BITES AND STINGS

Rescue Remedy and *Aconite* can be given if shock is suspected. Aromatic *Lavender* oil can be massaged around but not on animal bites. Homeopathic remedies used are: *Arnica 6C* for dog bites that tear the skin and muscles; *Ledum 6C* for cat bites causing deep penetrating wounds which are more

painful than they look; *Apis Mellifica 6C* for insect stings that are swollen, red and better for cold bathing, while *Urtica urens 6C* works on stings that are better for warmth. These can be given every 10 minutes if needed.

HEAT-STROKE

This is usually seen in summer in dogs that have been left in cars or fallen asleep in bright sunshine, and it kills many dogs each year. The Bach Flower essence *Rescue Remedy* can be given initially. Among the homeopathic remedies, *Belladonna 6C* given every 5 minutes will help dogs that can still stand and whose pupils are widely dilated; *Glenoine 6C* is more helpful if the dog has collapsed with an unnaturally high temperature. Contact your vet for conventional support, which includes fluid therapy and oxygen. Do not cool the dog too quickly, as this can cause shock and make things worse. Cool the dog gently using tepid water on its ears and limbs.

▲ *Wounds between the toes and on the sole need to be dressed. They will gape as the dog walks, allowing dirt to enter.*

POISONING

If poisoning is suspected, you must seek veterinary help immediately. If the dog has swallowed human tablets, let the vet know the name and quantity of the tablets swallowed. Do not try to make the dog vomit unless advised to do so by the vet. You can begin by giving the Bach Flower *Rescue Remedy*, followed by *Crab Apple* for detoxification. Homeopathic *Nux Vomica* also helps detoxification, and *Veratrum Album* can be given if the dog is cold and collapsed, especially if it also has diarrhoea.

TREATING WOUNDS

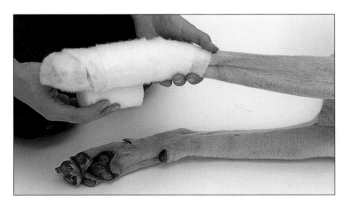

1 Having removed any objects from the wound and after cleaning it, apply a bandage to cover it, using a non-stick dressing and a soft cotton bandage. It may need two people: one to comfort the dog, and the other to treat it.

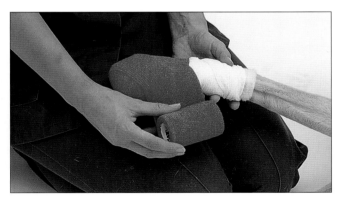

2 In an emergency, masking tape or adhesive tape may be used instead of elastoplast to hold the dressing in place. Take the adhesive bandage 3cm (1in) up the fur to prevent it from slipping off.

The eyes

A dog's eyes should be clear and bright, the pupils black and round, and the membrane that lines the lids (conjunctiva) should be a pleasant salmon-pink colour. The dog has a third eyelid that moves across the eye from the inside to the outside corner. It is barely visible when the eye is fully open, but becomes more apparent if the eye is painful, or if the pad of fat behind the eye disappears. If the third eyelid becomes and remains visible in the absence of inflammation or discharge, see a vet in case it is the first sign of a chronic wasting disease.

▼ *There should be no discharges from the eyes, no nodules on the lids, and the conjunctiva should be a healthy salmon-pink colour, as seen here.*

DISCHARGES, SWELLING AND INFLAMMATION

If discharges gather in the corners of the dog's eye, or on the lids, and there is no inflammation, bathe the eye with cold, boiled salt water using 5ml (1 tsp) of salt in 300ml (½ pint) of water.

If inflammation occurs and the eye begins to look angry and red, the eye can be bathed in homeopathic *Euphrasia* tincture diluted 1:10 with cold boiled water, or with a herbal infusion of *Golden Seal* made fresh each day. If the eye has not improved after 6 hours, you should go to the vet.

If the eyelids are swollen and red but there are no discharges, bathe the eyes as for inflammation and give homeopathic *Apis mell. 6C* every

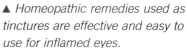

▲ *Homeopathic remedies used as tinctures are effective and easy to use for inflamed eyes.*

2 hours until the eyes look better. If there are discharges present, bathe the eyes in a saline solution, as before, and try one of the following homeopathic medicines hourly until an improvement is seen, then gradually reduce the dose: *Arsen. alb. 6C* if the discharge is watery and scalds the hair off the face; *Pulsatilla 6C* if the discharge is bland and creamy, especially if the dog is gentle; or *Kali bich. 6C* if the discharge is thick, green and stringy.

Should the condition not improve, or if it keeps returning, have your vet check the dog for a more serious underlying cause. If none is found, a homeopath may be able to prescribe a constitutional remedy to help the dog, or a tissue salt can be given to restore

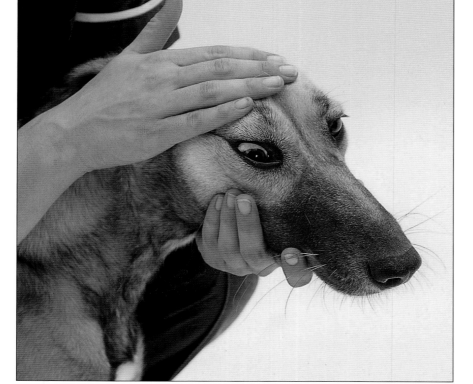

▲ *Homeopathic tablets should be handled with care. Store them in the phials in which they were bought, and discard any that are spilt.*

▶ *The eyes can be cleaned with golden seal infusion, or diluted tincture of Euphrasia. Use separate pieces of cotton wool or cotton balls for each eye.*

▲ *Golden seal has been shown to have antibiotic properties. It is a traditional remedy for eye infections when used as an infusion.*

balance. The following tissue salts may be helpful: *Ferrum phos.* if there are no discharges; *Kali mur.* if there is a white discharge; or *Natrum phos.* if the discharge is sticky and yellow.

STYES

These are infections of the glands in the edge of the eyelid, and are very uncomfortable. They can be helped with homeopathic *Silicia 6C* given hourly in most dogs, but *Pulsatilla* may be more successful for gentle, affectionate dogs. If the dog may be harbouring resentment, *Staphysagria* can be very good. Again, bathing the eye twice a day with diluted *Euphrasia* tincture or a *Golden Seal* infusion will support the main medicine prescribed by the vet.

CORNEAL ULCERS AND GLAUCOMA

If the eye goes cloudy, there could be either an ulceration of the cornea (the transparent front of the eyeball) or

swelling of the eyeball due to impeded drainage of the eye itself, a condition known as glaucoma. If an ulcer is left untreated, it can deepen and may eventually rupture, leading to a loss of fluid from the eyeball; the eyeball will then collapse and vision will be lost.

Glaucoma in a dog usually results from a congenital deformity of the eye's drainage apparatus. Inflammation or infection of the inner structures can also interfere with the drainage mechanism. The increase in pressure within the eye results in damage to the retina and loss of vision.

These two conditions are painful and serious, and should be seen by a vet as soon as possible. Homeopathic remedies can be used to support conventional treatment. For ulcers, the following may be tried: *Argent. nit. 6C* if the dog is anxious; *Acid nit. 6C* if the dog is irritable or aggressive; *Merc. cor. 6C* if the eye is very sore, the dog dislikes the light and the discharge is green; and *Silicia 30C* used twice daily to help the last stages of healing.

Support the treatment by bathing with *Euphrasia* or *Golden Seal*, as before. For glaucoma, help the dog with *Phosphorus 6C* if it is normally very active and dislikes thunder, or *Spigelia 6C* if the eye is very painful. In all cases, give the tablets hourly to begin with, and reduce the dosage if there are signs of improvement.

▼ *The Bach Flower mustard, given orally, can help lift a dog from a state of melancholy brought on by the pain of an infected eye.*

DRY EYE

Occasionally, the eye stops producing tears, becomes dry and loses its moist appearance, and a thick glutinous mucus gathers over the surface. This condition appears to affect Westies more than any other breed. It can be due to a malfunction of the immune system, an injury to the eye and its surrounding tissues, or a side effect of some drugs, particularly *Salizopyrin*. Your vet can test the rate of tear production. If it is low, they can prescribe artificial tears to lubricate the eyes. Bathing with cold tea may soothe the eye before the drops are administered, and cod liver oil has been used successfully as a lubricant in mild cases. Homeopathic *Zincum met.* or *Silicia 6C*, used twice daily, has helped, but not cured, some cases.

CATARACTS

These are opacities in the eye lens which obstruct light from entering the eye, causing blurred vision. They can

▼ *Cold tea can be used to clean dry eyes before three drops (2.5ml/½ tsp) of cod liver oil are instilled to lubricate them. This Westie, like most dogs, does not mind having its eyes bathed.*

▲ *Homeopathic Arnica is known to have a beneficial action in support of cataract surgery.*

be present at birth (congenital) or they may develop later in life (acquired). Congenital cataracts do not normally increase in size. Acquired ones come with age or may be associated with diabetes. This type grow slowly and will eventually cause total blindness.

Modern laser treatment is very efficient but it is expensive and should be carried out sooner rather than later, unlike the older surgical method which required the cataract to have ripened before surgery was

contemplated. Any surgery should be supported with homeopathic *Arnica 6C* given as needed, or *Staphysagria 6C* given four times a day if the dog is prone to resentment. Should surgery be declined on the grounds of the dog's age or the cost, bathing the affected eye with a homeopathic *Cineraria* tincture diluted as for *Golden Seal* may help the dog if daily treatment is maintained for at least three months.

The following homeopathic tablets may help the dog on a constitutional basis. Use the *30C* potency, twice daily, once a week; *Calc. carb.* for elderly, overweight dogs; *Causticum* for withered dogs with lots of warts; or *Silicia* for deeper-chested and thin-limbed dogs, such as Whippets. The tissue salt form of *Silicia* can slow the development of cataracts if given daily, as can herbal infusions of *Greater Celandine* by mouth. Dietary supplements of *Selenium* and *Vitamin E* can also help.

DISTRICHIASIS

Some dogs have two rows of eyelashes, a condition known as districhiasis. The inner row rubs against the front of the eye, causing

▲ *Infusions of greater celandine will help to soothe inflamed eyes, and have been used internally for cataracts.*

▲ *Raspberry leaf is used for the female reproductive organs, and it also has a beneficial effect on inflamed eyes.*

watering and then ulceration. The surgical treatment given for the condition tends to create scarring which can be just as irritating to the eye. Homeopathic *Borax 6C*, given twice daily, has been known to pull the lashes away from the eye.

ENTROPION

Some dogs, especially gundogs, have eyelids that turn inwards so that the eyelashes rub against the eye. This condition is known as entropion, and conventional treatment is not usually recommended for use on very young dogs. Applying the homeopathic remedy *Borax 6C*, as for districhiasis, can delay the need for surgery in puppies until the body is fully grown, and the impact on the adult dog can be properly assessed. In some cases, this can prevent the need for any surgery. A herbal infusion of *Rosemary*, given orally twice daily, helps over a long period.

TEARDUCTS

These can become blocked by frequent heavy discharges, although some very small dogs are born without them. The

▲ *Entropion is common in gundogs, such as this Golden Retriever. Corrective surgery should be delayed until the dog is fully grown. Borax or rosemary may help to delay the problem and keep the dog's discomfort to a minimum.*

▶ *The facial skin of some dogs is so loose that facelifts are needed to correct drooping eyelids. The St Bernard is a classic example.*

result is that tears spill over the lower lid, run down the face and stain the cheek. A vet will test the tearducts by putting a dye into the eye, which should drain into the nose and appear at the nostrils. If it doesn't, the duct is either missing or blocked. If it is missing, nothing can be done except to bathe the eye with *Euphrasia* or *Golden Seal*. Conventionally, a blockage is removed under anaesthetic, but the following may also be tried: *Silicia 200C* given twice daily for five days, then weekly, to unblock the duct. The tissue salt *Natrum mur.* can help in long-standing cases.

The ears

Contrary to conventional thought, most ear conditions are an expression of an internal problem. The size, shape and hairiness of the ear are minor factors in most cases of ear disease.

The glands in the lining of the ear can excrete mineral salts and other toxins if these build up to an excessive amount in the body. If too much toxic material is excreted, the microclimate inside the ear changes, and this in turn will allow parasites and other micro-organisms to colonize the ear. The overgrowth of disease-causing organisms then produces an abnormal discharge.

A healthy ear, of whatever shape or size, will have a pale pink colour to the lining and a clean, healthy smell. The proprietary Indian herbal cream *Canador* is useful when there are mild disturbances. *Echinacea 6X*, or a herbal infusion, can be used to aid ear detoxification. Other non-specific ear cleaners are homeopathic and herbal

▶ *Rosemary has been prized since ancient times for its antiseptic properties. Used as an infusion, it can help clear the ear of mites.*

preparations, such as *Hypercal* tincture (an equal mixture of *Hypericum* and *Calendula*) diluted 1:10 in water, two drops of lemon juice in 5ml (1 tsp) of almond oil, or three parts of *Rosemary* infusion with one part of witch hazel lotion. If the dog's constitutional homeopathic remedy is known, it will help to correct the underlying disorder.

The presence of dark, dry, crumbly wax in the ear often indicates the presence of canker mites. If these are suspected, use one part each of *Rosemary*, *Rue* and *Thyme* infusion mixed with three parts of olive oil to clean the ear.

In any case, if the ears are very sore or if there is a profuse discharge, consult your vet, and support their conventional treatment with an appropriate remedy. Alternative treatments include the use of homeopathic *Graphites 6C* four times daily if the discharge is very sticky (similar to glue ear in children), or *Hepar sulph. 30C* every two hours if the ear is very painful and sensitive. At a deeper level of treatment, *Sulphur 30C* often helps dogs that are itchy and like to be cool, while *Psorinum*

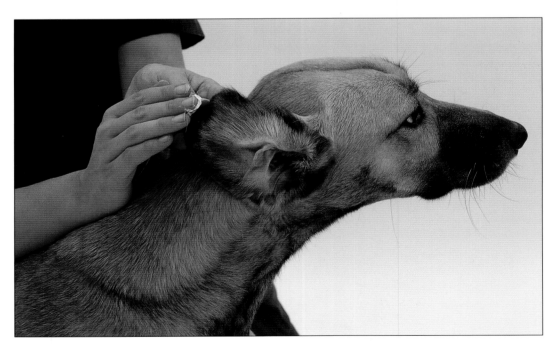

◀ *Check the ears daily for abnormal smells and discharges. In summer, also check for the presence of grass awns. Applying the homeopathic Pulsatilla cream will help alleviate irritations and minor sores in the ears.*

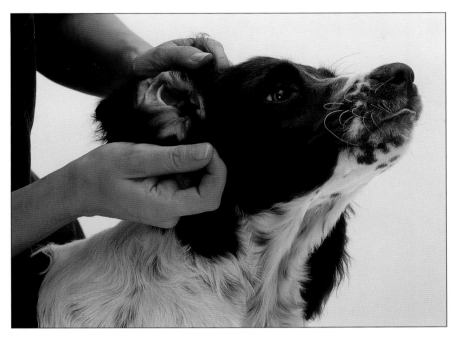

▲ *The hair growing inside the dog's ear canal should be gently plucked regularly, and excess hair removed from the inner surface of the ear to allow good ventilation.*

30C is useful for itchy dogs that like to be warm. Dogs that need either of the last two remedies tend to be scruffy, dirty-looking animals.

AURAL HAEMATOMA

A dog's ear flap is essentially a bag of skin attached to an inner sheet of cartilage. The blood vessels that serve the ear lie on the inner side of the cartilage. If these vessels bleed, the blood fills and distends the bag in a condition known as aural haematoma, the same as happens in humans when boxers get cauliflower ears. This type of bleeding results from blows to the dog's ear or from a malfunction of the immune system.

Conventional veterinary treatment for aural haematoma involves cutting the inner surface of the ear to release the build-up of blood, then sewing the two surfaces together like a mattress. This stops it refilling while the cut heals. Alternatively, the blood is drained using a wide-bore needle and a small dose of steroid injected into the ear using the same needle.

If the condition is caught in the very early stages, homeopathic *Arnica 6C* four times a day for two days, then *Hamamelis 12C* twice daily may reverse the process. Hamamelis cream or lotion can be applied to the ear flap. *Pulsatilla 6C* can be used instead of *Hamamelis* in gentle, affectionate dogs, and *Phosphorus 6C* often works in dogs that are sensitive to thunder. The tissue salt *Ferrum phos.* can be used if there is a tendency for the condition to recur.

MIDDLE AND INNER EAR INFECTIONS

Severe or neglected ear infections can spread to the middle and inner ear, causing a head-tilt towards the affected side or a complete loss of balance. At this stage, the dog should certainly be taken to the vet. Dogs with recurrent ear infections should be referred to a holistic vet who will treat the underlying causes and will prescribe holistic support for any antibiotics given by the conventional vet. They will also treat any mineral imbalances or stress factors that may be involved. The dog's own homeopathic constitutional remedy can be supported by aromatherapy or a Bach Flower remedy at this time, if stress factors are involved.

▶ *The aromatherapy oil Roman chamomile, used in a burner, will soothe a dog who is suffering stress as an unseen cause of infection.*

◀ *Lemon juice has anti-inflammatory properties and can be used, when diluted with spring water, to clean healthy ears.*

The nose

Nasal discharges are uncommon in dogs. They do occur, however, in canine distemper, a viral disease which is potentially fatal. If the dog is also coughing, vomiting and suffering from diarrhoea, it should be seen by a vet as soon as possible. (Canine distemper will be discussed more fully under the nervous system.)

Sometimes nasal discharges can be the result of a foreign body, such as a grass awn, getting stuck in the nose. Generally, these foreign bodies need to be removed under a general anaesthetic, but try homeopathic *Silicia 200C* twice daily for five days. This may help to loosen the obstruction so that it comes out naturally.

Discharges can also result from fungal infections and tumours. A vet will need to carry out x-rays and blood tests to identify which is involved. Conventional treatment can be supported with a herbal infusion of *Golden Seal*, which reduces mucoid discharges, or homeopathic remedies: *Allium cepa 6C* four times a day if the discharge is thin and burns the nose;

Pulsatilla 6C four times a day if it is bland and creamy; and *Hydrastis 6C* four times a day if it is thick and white. If the x-rays show signs of bone destruction, you can try *Acid nit.* if there is no smell, or *Aurum* if the discharge is foul-smelling, both at the 6C potency, four times a day. Herbal *Garlic* infusions or tablets benefit the immune system and help to fight infections, but they can interfere with the action of homeopathic remedies.

▼ *Homeopathic Aconite given in a low potency every 5 minutes can help to thicken blood and slow a nose bleed.*

▼ *The dog's nose is as important as our eyes are to us. All discharges are therefore of great significance.*

▲ *A damp towel placed over your dog's snout will help to stop the flow of blood if your dog has a nose bleed.*

Nose bleeds can occur for a variety of reasons. They can follow blows, be caused by ulceration of the lining of the nose during infections, or be present where there are tumours or more serious diseases. Persistent or recurrent nose bleeds should always be checked by a vet. One-off cases can be treated by finger pressure on the nose, if the dog will allow it. Otherwise, homeopathic remedies can be tried as follows: *Aconite 30C* every 5 minutes until the blood thickens and the flow slows down; if caused by a blow, *Arnica 6C* every 15 minutes reducing the dosage as the flow slows down; *Phosphorus 6C* every 15 minutes in active dogs which seek heat and fear thunder; and *Mellilotus 6C* every 10 minutes if the bleeding is bright and flowing. The tissue salt *Ferrum phos.* will stop bleeding if sprinkled on to a wound; given twice daily it can help prevent the recurrence of bleeding.

The throat and neck

Inflammation of the tonsils, other glands in the throat and of the larynx can result in coughs. If the cough is mild, there is no reason why home treatments cannot be tried. Homeopathic remedies include: *Calc. carb. 6C* four times a day in heavy, sluggish dogs with glandular enlargement; *Phytolacca 6C* four times a day where the throat looks a bluish/purple colour; or *Rhus tox. 6C* if the throat is an angry red colour and the glands are swollen. The tissue salt *Silicia* helps glandular function generally and is useful in chronic troubles. A herbal infusion of *Sage*, *Thyme* and *Liquorice* is also beneficial for coughs and glands.

Coughs that start after the dog has been exposed to dry, cold winds (typically the bitter, easterly winter winds) respond well to *Aconite*, while coughs that begin after exposure to damp, cold air in the evening following a mild day (as often occurs in autumn

▼ *Splinters from sticks picked up outdoors can easily become lodged in the back of a dog's throat, causing tonsillitis and coughs.*

and winter, for example) respond well to *Dulcamara*. Use the *6C* potency four times a day.

KENNEL COUGH
This is a bacterial or viral infection. The main organism responsible is usually related to the one responsible for whooping cough in humans. The cough is a harsh, dry, booming one, and tends to be worse at night. The dog can be made to cough by gently putting pressure on its windpipe and larynx.

Kennel cough is often seen in dogs that have been away from home at kennels. The incubation period is about ten days, so it often appears just after the dog comes home. Conventional veterinary treatment usually involves an antibiotic.

Because of the kennelling aspect, it is likely that there are emotional factors involved in the disease, and so support with the Bach Flower remedies can be tried: *Heather* for loneliness; *Honeysuckle* for homesickness; and *Walnut* for

▼ *Coughs and colds caused by infections respond well to homeopathic remedies.*

▶ *Throat problems with underlying emotional causes may need the help of a Flower Remedy.*

difficulty in adapting to new circumstances. Of the homeopathic remedies, *Arsen. alb. 6C* can help dogs whose cough is worse in the early part of the night, and *Drosera 6C* for those who are worse around 3am. Give both remedies four times a day.

◀ ▲ *Honeysuckle and walnut make a suitable combination for treating kennel cough.*

The chest

The chest contains two major organs: the lungs and the heart. Disease of either of these can result in coughing. Persistent coughs should always be checked by a vet.

LUNGS

Inflammation of the lungs may start in the airways – bronchitis – and spread to the lung tissue itself – pneumonia. This is normally caused by a bacterial or viral infection, but can also be due to a tumour. If there is not a quick response to either conventional or complementary treatment, x-rays are essential. Conventional treatment is by antibiotics, often with steroids to suppress the inflammation. Short courses of steroid treatment are acceptable, but if long courses are prescribed, seek a holistic referral.

In mild cases, inhalations of aromatic oils can provide useful support: *Eucalyptus* if there is a lot of mucus on the chest; and *Tea Tree* or *Thyme* where infections are suspected. Homeopathic *Aconite 6C* can be given in frequent doses if you catch the cough at the early stage

▲ *Dandelion is a diuretic. Herbal infusions can reduce the build-up of fluid in the lungs in the first stage of heart disease.*

where the temperature is starting to rise. Follow this with *Belladonna 6C* also given in frequent doses as the fever peaks. Once the initial stages have passed, give support with one of the following remedies: *Bryonia 6C* if the dog resents moving, does not want to be touched and drinks a lot at long intervals; *Phosphorus* if there is blood in the sputum; *Kali carb.* if the

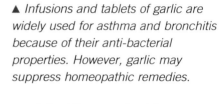

▲ *Infusions and tablets of garlic are widely used for asthma and bronchitis because of their anti-bacterial properties. However, garlic may suppress homeopathic remedies.*

cough is at its worst about 3am; *Rumex crisp* if the cough is worse by day; *Spongia* if the cough is at its worse at night; and *Antimon. tart.* if the respiration sounds rattling. Give these four times daily.

Tissue salts can also help. Give *Ferrum phos.* for harsh, dry coughs, *Kali sulph.* when yellow phlegm is coughed up, and *Kali mur.* for white phlegm. Herbal infusions of *Mullein* are good for night-time coughs; *Thyme* and *Liquorice* help coughs generally. *Garlic* helps the immune system fight infections, but it may act as an unwitting antidote to homeopathic remedies.

HEART

Heart-coughs are usually dry and brought on by exercise. As the heart function deteriorates, body fluids seep into the body tissues, where they

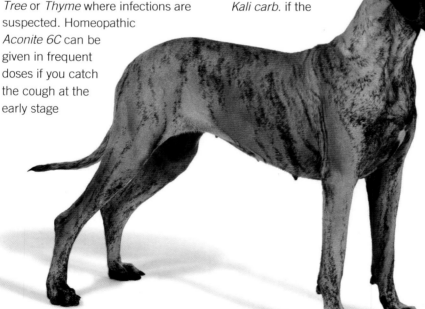

◀ *Coughs may be caused by heart problems as well as lung infections. Persistent coughing that does not show signs of abating should always be checked by a vet.*

▲ *Symptoms of heart disfunction include the dog's unwillingness to exercise, and a soft dry cough when it does start moving about.*

cause swellings or oedema, and into the body cavities where they cause dropsy. As the lungs fill with fluid, the cough worsens becoming soft and moist. Dropsy can also result from liver troubles and tumours, so it is worth having the dog checked if symptoms appear.

Conventional veterinary treatment for heart-coughs is to use diuretics, to remove water from the body, and circulatory stimulants. Complementary remedies can be very successful and could mean that conventional treatment can be delayed or reduced.

Ask yourself first if there may be any underlying emotional cause to the cough: think along the lines of a broken heart. If so, the Bach Flower remedies *Heather* for loneliness, *Star of Bethlehem* for emotional shock and *Walnut* for difficulty in coping with change can be considered.

Homeopathic low-potency herbals are effective in well-chosen cases, but these have to be prescribed by a homeopathic vet for accuracy. As well as treating the cough, the vet may also prescribe a constitutional prescription which will help treat the underlying causes. Remedies that help are *Spongia 6C* for coughs that are worse at night, and *Rumex 6C* if they are worse by day. Give them four times a day. Sometimes these are more effective when given in higher potencies, but the vet will be able to advise on this. *Digitalis 30C* helps when the pulse is very slow, and

Carbo veg. 30C when there is a great desire for fresh air as well as a slow pulse. Give these twice daily. *Cactus grandiflora 6C* can be given up to four times daily if there appears to be a great deal of pain in the chest.

If swellings develop in the limbs, *Apis mell. 6C* four times a day can help. If the dog is restless and its cough is worse around midnight, try *Arsenicum*, but if the cough is at its worst around 4am and 4pm, try *Lycopodium*. The tissue salts *Calc. fluor.* given twice daily can help to strengthen the heart muscles, and *Kali phos.* can help if the dog's heartbeat is abnormal. Herbal infusions of either *Dandelion* or *Hawthorn* can also help.

Dietary advice is to give the dog a low-salt diet – proprietary heart diets are lower in salt than normal ones. Conventional diuretics can result in the loss of phosphorus from the body; if your vet recommends a phosphorus supplement, try seaweed powder, which is rich in minerals and vitamins, or the tissue salt *Kali phos.* Reduce exercise to a steady level to avoid undue distress to the animal.

▲ *Eucalyptus oil has antiseptic and expectorant properties, and works well for dogs when used in a diffuser.*

The abdomen

The abdomen contains the stomach, intestines, liver, pancreas, kidneys, bladder and the sex organs – the ovaries and uterus of the female, and the prostate of the male.

Disease of these organs is accompanied by severe pains and can cause vomiting and/or diarrhoea. If the pain is behind the ribs, it is probably related to a liver problem. Pain in the triangle between the ribs and the back muscles can relate to the kidneys or ovaries. General abdominal pains indicate intestinal trouble, and pain in the rear abdomen points to the bladder or prostate.

VOMITING AND/OR DIARRHOEA

These may be the result of a either a primary or a secondary stomach inflammation. A primary inflammation can be caused by food and other poisoning, eating too much rich food, and swallowing foreign bodies – such as stones and children's toys – but is rarely due to tumours. A secondary inflammation results from a primary and more serious disease in the liver, kidney or pancreas. If blood is present or if symptoms persist for more than 24 hours, you should see the vet. They may wish to x-ray for foreign bodies,

▼ Children's toys hold a fascination for dogs, who can easily swallow them, often with disastrous results.

especially if there is vomiting first thing in the morning, or take blood samples to look for underlying causes.

In all cases, treatment will either be by antibiotics for infections, anti-inflammatory steroids to control inflammation, anabolic steroids when there is loss of body weight, insulin when diabetes is present, and fluid replacement if there is concern about dehydration. Dietary changes, such as vitamin and mineral supplements, and medical diets may also be suggested.

Complementary support does help acute conditions, and can reduce dose levels in chronic cases. An immediate first-aid step is to stop feeding the dog and to give a little salt if it is vomiting, or bicarbonate of soda if it has diarrhoea. If stress is implicated, try the Bach Flowers: *Aspen* for fear; *Chicory* for separation anxiety and attention-seeking; and *Impatiens* for the irritability associated with Irritable Bowel Syndrome. *Rescue Remedy* may help severe pains and ease the dog's distress.

Of the homeopathic remedies used for vomiting and diarrhoea, *Arsen. alb.* helps if the dog is restless and gets worse around midnight and thirsts for a little water very often. *Phosphorus* can be tried if the dog is very thirsty for large quantities, yet vomits 15–20 minutes after drinking; blood may be present. *Ipecacuana* is for persistent vomiting and diarrhoea, often with

▲ Rosemary oil vapour is inhaled for its anti-inflammatory properties. Use with mint to ease acute liver problems, and with wild marjoram for chronic ones.

bloody mucus; this may follow eating indigestible food. Alternatively, try *Nux vom.* for vomiting after rich food, *Aloes* for diarrhoea with flatulence, *Podophyllum* for watery stools, *Chamomilla* for teething pups if the stools are green, and *Capsicum* for light-coloured recurrent diarrhoea in rehomed pups. In all cases, give the *6C* potency frequently, reducing the time between doses as the condition improves.

Herbal infusions of *Gentian*, *St John's Wort* and *Peppermint* ease the stomach, while *Slippery Elm* and *Arrowroot* help to soothe the intestines.

Tissue salts can help. If the dog is vomiting undigested food, try *Ferrum phos.*, *Kali mur.* for thick mucus, *Nat phos.* for sour, acid vomit, and *Natrum*

► *Tarragon oil has an anti-spasmodic and calming action when used by inhalation.*

sulph. for yellowy green bile. For diarrhoea from anxiety, use *Kali phos.* or *Natrum mur.* if it alternates with constipation. As the dog improves, slowly reintroduce a bland diet, such as fish or chicken (off the bone) with rice or pasta.

Bloating is a distension of the abdomen with gas, caused by excessive fermentation of the stomach contents, and is very painful. If the dog can pass wind or belch, *Carbo veg.* *6C* every 15 minutes helps. However, if the dog is doubled up in pain, this is an emergency and you must call the vet at once. While you are waiting, use *Colchicum* if the dog lies still, and *Colocynth* if it rolls in agony.

LIVER AND KIDNEYS

Liver disease causes the vomiting of bile, pain behind the ribs, loss of appetite and eventually jaundice. Kidney problems may be indicated either by thirstlessness or an extreme thirst with vomiting. Chronic kidney problems lead to increased urination, loss of appetite, high thirst and vomiting, weight loss and dehydration.

For severe liver and kidney trouble, the Bach Flower *Crab Apple* helps to detoxify the body. Homeopathic *Lycopodium* helps liver symptoms that worsen around 4pm, *Chelidonium* for early jaundice with vomiting and/or diarrhoea, and *Carduus marianus* for dropsy, jaundice and hard, dry stools. Kidney problems with intense thirst, weight loss and greasy hair respond to homeopathic *Natrum mur. Merc. sol.* helps if there is a lot of saliva

► *The Bach Flower remedies are useful in stress-related bowel problems in dogs.*

present and ulcers start to form in the mouth, and *Kali chlor.* if the breath is putrid and the ulcers greyish.

Herbal infusions of *Dandelion* helps the liver, *Bearberry* helps the kidneys, and *Barberry* helps both liver and kidney problems. The aromatic oil of *Rosemary* can help liver problems, while *Juniper* helps those of the kidney and bladder.

PANCREAS

Both acute and chronic conditions of the pancreas should be diagnosed by a vet. Homeopathic *Iris ver.* is useful if the dog is restless and vomits mainly at night. The tissue salts *Natrum phos.* and *Ferrum phos.* can help with acute problems, as can herbal infusions of *Gentian*.

BLADDER

Bladder problems can be due to infections or to the sedimentation of crystals and stones in the urine. These may arise through kidney problems, or because the dog is not drinking enough water, or because its urine is too alkaline. Crystals can lump together to form stones. Both crystals and stones can cause mechanical obstructions. Signs of bladder

problems include frequent attempts to urinate, straining to urinate, blood-stained urine, or the involuntary passing of urine. In most cases, abdominal pain will be present and you should see the vet.

Complementary therapies will help, particularly in chronic disorders. Sudden onset of straining to pass small amounts of bloody urine often responds to twice-hourly homeopathic *Cantharis 6C* or *Merc. sol. 6C* if there is a lot of mucus present as well. *Causticum 6C* twice daily is helpful in chronic, recurrent cases. If the vet says there are a lot of crystals present, *Thlaspi bursa 6C* can be very helpful. *Equisetum*, which is both a herbal and a homeopathic remedy, can help frequency when large amounts of urine are passed painfully a few drops at a time. Herbal infusions of *Buchu* can help to dissolve any gravel-like deposits that may be present in the bladder.

Incontinence in dogs can be treated with homeopathic *Causticum* in elderly, warty dogs, and *Staphysagria* in recently kennelled ones. The Bach Flower remedies *Aspen* for emotional stress and *Olive* for emotional weakness can also help.

The skin

The skin is the largest organ of the body. It protects against the elements, helps to control body temperature, and excretes waste via sweat and sebum produced in the sebaceous glands. The skin is the body's barrier against the outside world, and it is on the skin that many underlying problems will first be seen.

In disease, body metabolism is disturbed, and this results in abnormal secretions from the sebaceous glands, which change the skin's microclimate and lead to the development of skin infections or skin disease. Conventional treatment is excellent at reducing pain and inflammation in acute conditions, but it is not able to remedy the underlying defect in metabolism.

Prolonged or frequently repeated skin treatment leads to suppression of symptoms, which in turn can lead to the establishment of chronic and sometimes drug-induced disease. Chronic skin diseases are based upon malnutrition, hormonal imbalances and emotional problems that stress the immune system, opening the way for bacterial and fungal infections and parasitic infestations. All chronic skin problems will benefit from the support of holistic treatment, no matter what their conventional categorization.

PARASITIC SKIN DISEASE

External parasites include fleas, lice, ticks, harvest mites and Cheyletiella mites. Fleas are reddish-brown in colour and move quickly; lice are grey, slow-moving and are often found on the ears; ticks look like warts and are removed using special hooks available from your vet. Harvest mites are orange or red, and are found between the toes; Cheyletiella are whitish in colour, slow-moving and are known as 'walking dandruff'.

◄ *The evergreen citrus tree Neroli is native to China. Its floral essential oil works well for anxiety and stress-related skin conditions.*

Conventional treatment for external parasites involves strong chemicals to kill the insects. Complementary treatments repel the insects rather than kill them. A herbal treatment, *Xenex*, has been shown to repel fleas for up to 40 days. Herbal *Garlic* will repel them, as will homeopathic *Sulphur* given weekly, or three drops of one of the essential oils of *Cedarwood*, *Eucalyptus*, *Lavender*, *Lemon*, *Mint*, *Rosemary* or *Terebinth* added to 150ml (¼ pint) of water and brushed into the coat.

Two species of mite live on the skin. The Sarcoptic mite affects humans and dogs, and causes red spots that itch uncontrollably in both species. The Demodex mite is only a problem if there is a defect in the immune system. First signs may be a spectacle-like balding, which starts around the eyes and spreads over the body. Strong conventional washes are needed to kill both mites.

As complementary support therapies, homeopathic *Sulphur* can help dogs that dislike being warm, and *Psorinum* those who want to be as warm as possible. *Garlic* tablets help, but they may interfere with homeopathic treatments. The tissue salt *Calc. sulph.* is beneficial but not a complete cure, while the essential oil

◄ *A daily spoonful of fish oils makes a tasty treat, and the extra minerals it adds to the diet will help to soothe any dry and inflamed skin.*

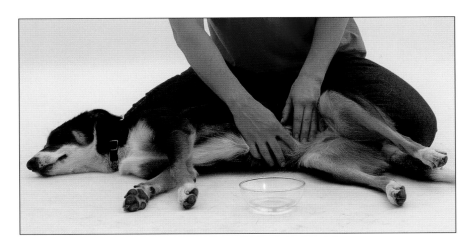

◄ *Check the underside of your dog. Many skin conditions first appear in the armpit and groin areas.*

matches the remedy; *Lycopodium* can help old, lean dogs that are prematurely grey if they lose their hair, and *Thallium* is good for general hair growth. Use the *30C* potency weekly until signs of regrowth are seen.

of *Lavender*, *Lemon* or *Wild Marjoram* can be used in diluted form in the same way as for parasites.

ECZEMA AND DERMATITIS

These conditions need a holistic consultation to get a cure. If stress is implicated, the Bach Flowers are helpful: *Agrimony* helps skin irritation due to anxiety; and *Crab Apple* if the dog is toxic, the skin is dirty-looking, the hair is matted and secondary skin infections are present. *Holly* aids allergic conditions, especially in malicious dogs. Aromatherapy using *Rosemary* and *Lavender*, or *Lavender*, *Pine* and *Terebinth* to massage unaffected areas of the body does help. Homeopathic treatments include *Hypercal* tincture diluted 1:10 to cleanse the skin, tablets of *Sulphur* if the skin is hot, dry and itchy and the dog dislikes heat, and *Psorinum* for dirty-looking, itchy, smelly dogs that want to be warm. Use *Apis mel.* for allergies where the skin is shiny, red, dry, and better if cold, or *Urtica* if these symptoms are eased by warmth. *Lycopodium* is useful where there is an underlying liver problem, and *Natrum mur.* if there is long-standing grief. In acute cases, use *6C* potency several times a day; in chronic cases, use *30C* potency twice daily. Herbal

infusions of *Oak Bark* or a decoction of *Mallow* can be used as compresses, and *Aloe Vera* gel is useful on dry, inflamed skins. Nutritional support with *Evening Primrose* and fish oils will help in long-standing cases.

HAIR LOSS

If this is the result of skin disease, it is treated as above. If it is bilaterally symmetrical, there may be an underlying hormonal imbalance. The Bach Flower *Scleranthus* helps to restore balance. One of the following combinations of essential oils is helpful in massage: *Calamus* and *Lavender*; *Pine* and *Terebinth*; *Cedar* and *Thyme*. Homeopathic *Sepia* or *Pulsatilla* will balance a bitch's hormones if the animal's constitution

WARTS

These are common in old age, and are difficult to treat by any therapy. Surgery is best avoided unless the warts are causing trouble. Homeopathic *Thuja* tincture can be painted on the wart twice daily for up to three months, *Causticum 6C* twice daily helps old, stiff dogs with warts, and *Nitric acid 6C* twice daily helps if the warts are close to the eyes, ears, mouth or anus. A piece of banana skin taped over the wart and replaced fresh each day has been known to work, as have the tissue salts *Kali mur.* and *Natrum mur.*

▼ *Dogs are more sensitive than humans to the toxic effects of massage oils, so they must be well diluted with a suitable carrier oil.*

The female system

The ovaries and uterus are the organs responsible for reproduction in the female. The ovaries do not normally cause primary trouble. Cystic ovaries lead to hormonal imbalances, but the symptoms are produced elsewhere in the body. Serious problems may occur, however, in the uterus.

The uterus may become infected following an abortion or after giving birth (metritis), and can usually be treated by antibiotics. Sometimes the contents of the uterus build up and distend it (pyometritis); this is often a sequel to recurrent false pregnancies or repeated contraceptive treatments. If the cervix is open, profuse discharges occur, and if it remains closed, pressure in the uterus causes pain and collapse. In both cases, a toxaemia occurs that can be fatal. Pyometritis usually needs an emergency ovario-hysterectomy.

Complementary care may eliminate the need for surgery if the condition is caught early enough. Homeopathic remedies using *30C* potencies up to four times a day are beneficial. Use *Sepia* if the bitch is dull and irritable, has a high thirst and a brownish discharge; *Caulophyllum* if the discharge is chocolate-brown in

▶ *Inhaling lavender oil will help relax a bitch who is stressed by hormonal imbalance. Give her a momentary sniff of the bottle – the canine sense of smell is extremely keen.*

colour; *Hydrastis* if the discharge is white mucus; but use *Pulsatilla* in the more unusual case where the thirst is low and the discharge creamy yellow. If the discharge is bloody, use *Sabina*. Herbal *Golden Seal* can help catarrhal discharges, and *Myrrh* foul ones.

MISCARRIAGES

Bitches may fail to carry pups to full-term due to infections, hormonal imbalances or poor nutrition. Early abortions may result only in a catarrhal vaginal discharge; in late pregnancy dead foetuses are expelled along with some pus. Discharges should be treated as for metritis. Bitches with a tendency to abort repeatedly can be given homeopathic *Viburnum Opulis 30C* weekly for the first month of pregnancy and *Caulophyllum* weekly for the last five weeks. The tissue salt *Calc. phos.* helps to maintain a healthy uterus during pregnancy.

FALSE PREGNANCY

Bitches may act as if they are pregnant, nest and come into milk after a season, even though they have not been mated. In the wild, bitches may be needed to act as foster mothers to

abandoned or orphaned pups, but in the family setting the behaviours that accompany false pregnancies can be distressing. Homeopathic treatment is much more successful than conventional in this case. *Sepia* aids grumpy bitches with high thirsts, *Pulsatilla* helps affectionate thirstless ones, and *Clematis* those whose milk is dropping from them. Use a *30C* tablet up to four times a day.

◀ *An infusion of sage helps if there is pain when the bitch is in heat.*

▼ *Scleranthus can restore stability to bitches with any type of hormonal imbalance.*

◀ *Infusions of golden seal or myrrh are useful in early cases of pyrometritis.*

The male tract

The reproductive system of the male is far simpler than that of the bitch. Its function is constant, not cyclic, and there is less that can go wrong.

PENIS
This is not usually affected, other than by trauma following the misjudgement of a jump. Treatment should be according to the injury. However, the penis is very vascular: cuts can bleed for some time and often need to be stitched.

PROSTATE GLAND
This is a small gland that surrounds the first part of the urethra, and lies just in front of the pelvic brim. Normally it cannot be felt, but if it enlarges due to infection or tumours, or in old age, it can be felt by a vet

▼ *Sabal Serrulata is helpful in the case of senile prostatic hypertrophy. It is used as a low-potency liquid.*

during an internal examination. When enlarged, the prostate puts pressure on the urethra, restricting the flow of urine and causing pain, and blood will appear in the urine. If the prostate swells enough, it can move backwards into the pelvis where it acts as a blockage, restricting the passage of faeces. The dog then produces thin, watery stools which bypass the obstruction. There is an apparent constipation as stools do not pass the obstruction, but the pain will cause the dog to walk with its back arched and as if it were knock-kneed. Conventional treatment with anti-male hormones shrinks the prostate to its normal size. If it becomes a recurrent problem, castration is advised. This removes the source of male hormones and the prostate withers away.

Complementary medicine is effective. The Bach Flower *Scleranthus* can help to restore balance to the male hormone system.

▲ *Puppies may experience difficulty in urination due to juvenile hormone problems. Homeopathic Clematis will help relieve the problem.*

Homeopathic remedies also help. *Sabal Serrulata 3X*, three drops given three times a day, acts directly on the prostate in the majority of dogs. *Pulsatilla 30C* twice daily is helpful in affectionate but jealous dogs; *Ipecacuana 6C* given hourly will stop profuse bleeding due to ulceration of the urethra; *Clematis 6C* given four times daily aids young dogs with upset hormones; *Agnus* castus helps old dogs with shrivelled testes; and *Digitalis 6C* given every two hours helps if the problem is sudden and painful. The tissue salt *Silicia* can help the older dog with prostate troubles.

TESTICLES
These sperm-producing organs rarely cause disease. The main problem associated with the testicles is tumours in old age. These are best treated by surgical removal. Castration is also recommended for hypersexuality, but it only works effectively if there is an overactive prostate gland.

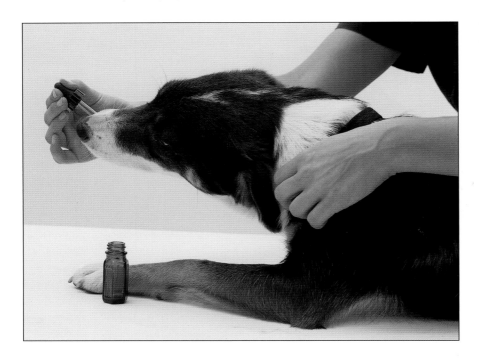

The hormone system

The endocrine glands produce hormones that are carried around the body in the blood to other organs and tissues whose function they help to control. There are three endocrine glands: the pituitary, adrenal and ovaries, and between them they control the female reproductive cycle and pregnancy. The thyroid controls the body's metabolic rate, and the pancreas controls the glucose metabolism. The adrenal gland produces cortisone and other steroids which control many functions.

An over-production of cortisone, or Cushing's disease, may be due to tumours of the pituitary gland or of the adrenal gland itself. An underproduction of cortisone, or Addison's disease, can result from the gland's capacity being suppressed by prolonged use or over-dosage of cortisone-type drugs, or tumours of the adrenal gland.

All these diseases will lead to weakness and lethargy. A high thirst is common to diabetes, Cushing's and

▼ *Homeopathic sarcodes help restore function to endocrine glands for a return to health. Use only with veterinary supervision.*

▲ *The diuretic effect of a parsley infusion can help to control the dropsy seen in both Cushing's and Addison's disease.*

Addison's disease, and hair loss is seen in hypothyroidism and Cushing's. If your dog shows symptoms of any one of these diseases, you must see your vet immediately. They will make a diagnosis based on blood and urine tests, and will prescribe an appropriate course of treatment.

In general, hormone deficiencies are best treated by conventional replacement therapy, such as insulin for diabetes, or thyroid extract for hypothyroidism. Holistic treatment can help to reduce the amount required

▼ *Haricot beans mixed into the dog's food will have a beneficial effect on the pancreas, and can be used in both acute and chronic pancreatitis.*

and give a better quality of life. If alternative support is given, the hormone levels should be carefully monitored by the vet so that drug overdoses are not given.

The Bach Flower *Scleranthus* will help stabilize any endocrine organ. Homeopathic preparations made from normal glands (sarcodes) can help if given in the *30C* potency weekly; *Pancreatinum* for diabetes, *Thyroidinum* for hypothyroidism, *Cortisone 30C* for the adrenal gland, and *Pituitrin* if the pituitary gland is involved. In addition, *Iris ver.* will aid the pancreas generally. *Syzygium 6C* will stimulate the body's natural insulin production, while *Thyroidinum 6X* acts as a replacement for thyroid extract. *Natrum mur.* as a tissue salt can help any type of hormonal problem, and in homeopathic form can be used as a constitutional remedy. Herbal *Seaweed* tablets and *Garlic* are used for hypo-thyroidism, and *Dandelion*, *Nettle* and *Parsley* infusion for adrenal problems.

The nervous system

The nervous system consists of the brain, spinal cord and peripheral nerves. Physical trauma to the spine can injure the spinal cord, causing paralysis, but this will be considered under the locomotor system.

Convulsions, or fits, can result from viral infections such as canine distemper, metabolic diseases such as diabetes and milk fever, poisons – particularly lead, slug-bait and anti-freeze – and tumours of the brain. Sometimes no known cause is found. Fits are not painful to the dog. The animal should be left in a quiet, dark, cool place to come round before it is taken to the vet, unless the fits become continuous. This is an emergency, and the dog should be seen at once.

Inflammation of the nerves is known as neuritis. This is extremely painful and may result from mechanical injury to the nerve or pressure on it from a tumour or other swelling. Inflammation of the brain itself is called encephalitis, while

▼ *Neuralgias respond very well to homeopathic chamomile if given every 15 minutes. This is particularly useful for teething pains.*

meningitis is inflammation of the surrounding brain membranes. Both of these can be caused by bacterial and viral infections and tumours. The symptoms can be behavioural changes, head-pressing, swaying, falling and severe convulsions. Chorea is uncontrollable twitching. It is usually a long-term effect of canine distemper, but poisons and brain tumours can also be to blame.

Conventional treatment for all of these conditions is based on anti-convulsants plus antibiotics if bacterial

▶ *Lavender oil calms and sedates the nervous system, and can be used as an inhalation in all nerve conditions.*

◀ *Distemper is the most common cause of fits and chorea. Vaccination does give protection but also has more side effects than is often recognized. If side effects are suspected, complementary treatment for your dog is essential.*

infections are suspected. Complementary support is very valuable. The Bach Flowers can be used: *Crab Apple* helps in any case of poisoning; *Holly* can restore balance if the onset of symptoms is very quick; and *Cherry Plum* calms uncontrollable behaviour and fits. The homeopathic remedy *Belladonna* is good for dogs whose pupils remain widely dilated after fits, and *Strammonium* for dogs which stagger just before the start of a fit and fall to the left. *Cocculus 6C* given daily for one month, then in the *30C* potency weekly for three months may prevent the recurrence of fits. *Agaricus* helps twitching associated with convulsions, and *Cuprum* or *Zinc* for twitching only. Give both remedies as a *6C* twice daily. Aromatic oil of *Lavender* by diffuser calms and sedates the nervous system, as do herbal infusions of *Skullcap* and *Valerian*.

Nerve pain resulting from a heavy blow will respond to homeopathic *Hypericum*. *Chamomilla* helps if the pain makes the dog snappy, while *Spigelia* helps facial neuralgia, *Colocynth* left-sided neuralgia, and *Mag. phos.* right-sided pains. Herbal infusions of *Oats* or *Passiflora* also help neuralgias.

The locomotor system

The locomotor system consists of the muscles, bones and joints of the body, and disease is usually accompanied by pain.

Severe, sudden-onset pain is normally caused by accidents and acute infections; chronic low-grade pain is usually due to rheumatism (muscle-based) or arthritis (bony changes in the joints). All dogs involved in accidents that cause great pain, lameness or unconciousness should be seen as quickly as possible by a vet. Low-grade stiffness that lasts for more than five days should also be checked so that x-rays can be taken. Fractures and dislocations will need surgical treatment. Antibiotics are usually given if infection is suspected. Pain relief is normally with non-steroidal anti-inflammatory drugs, but steroids may be used for serious back pains.

Severe back pain can arise from partial dislocation or misalignment of the veterbrae, intervertebral disc disease and arthritis of the intervertebral joints (spondylitis). Two other painful conditions are inflammation of muscles (myositis) and inflammation of bone (osteitis). Both are due to infection or bruising. There are also developmental diseases which occur in dogs. Hip dysplasia, in which the hip joint fails to develop normally, results in early chronic arthritis. There is also osteochondritis dessicans (OCD) in which the cartilaginous surfaces in the joints of large-breed dogs degenerate between 6 and 12 months of age.

All these conditions are extremely suitable for complementary treatment or support. The Bach Flower *Rescue Remedy* or homeopathic *Aconite 6C* should be given as soon as possible after any accident. These can be followed by homeopathic *Arnica 6C* as often as needed. If there is no fracture or dislocation, back pain can be treated by acupuncture, chiropractic or osteopathy. Limb pains can be treated by one of the massage therapies. Aromatherapy massage with *Rosemary* or *Birch* oils can also help. Where there is no major injury but the dog is reluctant to use its leg, homeopathic *Bryonia* is used instead of *Arnica*; this is followed by *Ruta grav.* and finally *Rhus tox*. Use the *6C* potency four times a day for all remedies. If infection is present, *Hepar sulph. 30C* can be used for muscles and joints, but *Hepar*

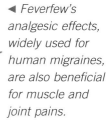

◀ *Infusions of mallow will speed the healing of sprains and strains, especially if used in conjunction with a TTouch massage.*

◀ *Feverfew's analgesic effects, widely used for human migraines, are also beneficial for muscle and joint pains.*

sulph. 200C may be tried if there is a bone infection. If this does not help, use *Calc. fluor. 6C* until the pus finds a way to the surface, then change to *Calc. sulph.*

All bone and joint surgery should be supported by *Arnica* at the time of the operation, and *Arnica* or *Bryonia* for 24 hours afterwards, the choice being made as above. Further support with weekly doses of homeopathic *Calc. phos. 30C* to balance calcium metabolism and *Symphytum 12C* to stimulate the cells that repair the bones can be given. If the dog is a large breed, *Calc. carb.* can be used instead of *Calc. phos.*

RHEUMATISM

This can be helped by acupuncture, physiotherapy and massage therapies. The Bach Flowers can also be helpful: *Beech* can help dogs that are rigid and stiff with pain; try *Impatiens* for those that become irritable; and *Rock Water* can restore physical flexibility to dogs that are mentally as well as physically worn and need a fixed routine. Homeopathic *Rhus tox.* helps

▼ *5ml (1 tsp) cider vinegar in 600ml (1 pint) water, along with vitamin supplements and royal jelly, will help to keep muscle pains away.*

classical rheumatism, which is worse in cold, damp weather and is better for gentle exercise in restless dogs, and *Causticum* helps the stiff, prematurely ageing, warty dog, *Caulophyllum* helps where the knee, hock and other small joints are involved, and *Calc. fluor.* given weekly can help to dissolve bony changes. Dietary supplements of *Evening Primrose*, *Cod Liver Oil* and *Royal Jelly* help, as do *Vitamins B, C* and *E. Chondroitin sulphate* and *Green-lipped Mussel* extract help where there are cartilaginous defects and changes. These supplements are also useful in OCD.

HIP DYSPLASIA

This condition can be helped but not cured. The same treatments for arthritis can be given with the same nutritional support as for rheumatism. Breeds that are more

▼ *Acupuncture is becoming more popular as a treatment for limb and back pain in dogs.*

◄ *Most dogs with strains and pains will benefit from having an intensely cold compress pressed against the affected limb. A suitable compress, easily made at home, would be a bag of frozen peas wrapped in a dish towel.*

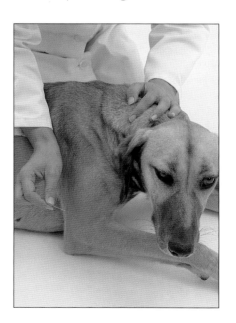

susceptible to this condition should always be x-rayed before breeding. Veterinarians will usually advise not to breed from dogs that show any signs of the disease.

CDRM

German Shepherd dogs are affected by a disease in which they develop a degeneration of the nerve bundles in the spinal cord (CDRM). The nerves that tell the dog where its feet are in space are affected first. This results in a painless paralysis of the hind legs and the dog sways as it walks; it can look similar to hip dysplasia. This is incurable, and progresses slowly to

stumbling on rough ground and dragging the top of the foot along the ground so that the nails are worn away. Healing massage therapies can help, while among the Bach Flowers *Crab Apple* helps if there are a lot of toxins in the dog's system, and *Oak* helps stoical dogs that try to ignore their problem. In homeopathy, *Conium maculatum* can delay progress but needs to be given in rising potencies as the case progresses, while *Plumbum*, for painless paralysis, is helpful if one side is more affected than the other. The tissue salt *Kali phos.* may be helpful to stimulate the nerves.

Neoplasia

The literal meaning of neoplasia is 'new growths'. The condition arises when cells in the body begin to multiply for no reason, causing tumours and cancers which may be either benign or malignant.

The term 'tumour' is generally reserved for the benign neoplasms, and cancer for the malignant ones. A benign tumour does not spread to other parts of the body and usually has a clearly defined edge, whereas a malignant growth sends tentacles of abnormal cells into the surrounding tissues so that it is impossible to tell what is healthy and what is abnormal tissue. The malignnant tumour also has a tendency to spread to other parts of the body by the blood or lymphatic system.

Tumours that are benign are generally not life-threatening, although a malignant but inactive growth can also be described as benign. On the other hand, a benign tumour, which has a defined shape and size and is not spreading to other parts of the body, may become life-threatening because of its size and/or because of the pressure it puts on a vital organ. This is what happens in the case of brain tumours, for example.

Neoplasm can include anything from harmless warts or papillomas at one end of the scale, to highly malignant cancers at the other that are capable of killing the patient in just a few weeks. Current medical science recognizes that neoplasms can develop after exposure to cancer-inducing agents (carcinogens), including some chemicals and tobacco, and to radiation from the sun and radioactive material. Neoplasms are also regarded as diseases in their own right.

▲ *Holistic treatment of neoplasms is more beneficial to the patient than conventional treatment alone.*

TREATMENT

Conventional veterinary treatment for malignant tumours focuses on fighting the cancer as vigorously as possible. Treatment is by sharp-knife surgery, laser surgery, chemotherapy and radiation therapy, or more likely than not, a combination of all of these.

From a holistic point of view, malignant neoplasms are viewed as an end-point of a disease process that may be of either long or short duration. The body is trying to store potentially toxic material that it cannot excrete by a normal route. These toxins are a result of the body's attempts to cope with the carcinogens. Its attempts may be adversely affected by stress factors, both physical and emotional. It is not known why the neoplasms develop in the first place – if it were purely a case of exposure to carcinogens, then everyone who smokes tobacco would

develop cancer. Neoplasms develop when the patient does not recognize the importance of apparently minor symptoms, when the patient's vitality is weak and it is unable to respond to therapy, or when the therapist fails to cure the early symptoms, allowing the neoplasm to manifest itself.

Good complementary therapy prevents many diseases from developing to the cancer stage. Some vets have reported a marked diminution in the number of cancer cases after introducing holistic methods. Good holistic treatment can also reverse the very early stages, or can induce long-lasting remissions in cases that would otherwise progress to death.

Deciding which therapies should be used is a personal choice. The subject should be discussed thoroughly with your vet and with a therapist chosen by you and your vet. Go through all the options together. The best approach is to use a mixture of complementary and conventional methods. If the dog is too weak to undergo conventional treatment, complementary support will be helpful. Surgery should always be supported by trauma remedies. Dogs undergoing chemotherapy or radiotherapy can be given treatment to help reduce the side effects, and all cases should be given treatment to deal with the underlying causes once the active treatment is over.

There has been plenty of discussion as to what type of result can be claimed to be successful in terms of holistic therapy. If the neoplasm disappears completely and does not return, that is a success, as is a case where the growth stops and does not reappear. For many people, if holistic treatment can lead to a calm, painless and natural death, rather than necessitating more suffering followed by euthanasia, then it too has been successful. For some, a treatment that leads to a longer but more painful life is not beneficial to the dog.

The Bach Flower remedies *Agrimony*, *Gentian*, *Gorse*, *Impatiens*, *Mustard*, *Oak* and *Olive* have all been found to help in cancer cases; the choice of remedy should depend on the dog's mental state at any particular stage of the disease.

Reiki, TTouch massage and acupuncture can be beneficial in helping to relieve pain and bring calmness and balance to the dog. In a condition as serious as cancer, consult a professional therapist for advice.

Homeopathy is helpful both in supporting conventional treatment and afterwards, when trying to treat the underlying cause of the illness. At the time of surgery, *Arnica*, *Hypericum* and *Calendula* will help to reduce bruising and pain, and will help the

broccoli

aloe vera

beetroot (beets)

carrots

garlic

royal jelly

▼ *If your unwell dog can bear to have its tummy touched, an aromatherapy massage can provide some much-needed comfort.*

skin to repair and heal. *Calc. phos.* and *Symphytum* can be given if bone surgery is needed. The side effects of chemotherapy can be alleviated by a skilled therapist, while *Uranium 30C* helps with radiation sickness and burns.

Viscum alb. will provide non-specific support. *Echinacea* will strengthen the immune system, and either *Hydrastis* or *Eupatorium Perfoliatum* will help to relieve pains. *Arsenicum alb.*, given in rising potencies, can remove the fear of dying from a terminally ill dog, and will allow an easy transition from life to death. If the dog's own constitutional remedy can be found, remarkable results are possible, but a consultation of up to an hour may be needed to find it.

Anthroposophical preparations of mistletoe (*Viscum abnova* and *Iscador*) are widely used for human cancers, and are now being requested for dogs by owners who have heard that humans respond well to it. The treatment is an injection given twice weekly, and only by the vet until the optimum dose is found. If you are

▲ *Diet is immensely important in the treatment of cancer. Providing your pet's body with the correct balance of energy and nutrition will give it the best chance possible to maintain its immune system and hold back the progression of the disease.*

interested in this treatment for your dog, discuss it with your vet. It will probably be a new approach for them and they may need to get more information before starting treatment.

Herbal infusions of *Red Clover*, a general anti-cancer agent, *Echinacea*, an immune system stimulant, and *Autumn Crocus*, for pain relief, are useful if given twice daily. Support from the tissue salt *Calc. phos.* to stimulate the body's metabolism may help. Nutrition is also vital. Broccoli, beetroot (beets) and carrots are traditional anti-cancer vegetables, and can be added to the puréed portion of the Billinghurst diet. Supplements of Vitamins A, B complex, C and E can slow the growth rate of tumours. Royal jelly, aloe vera and garlic are helpful in a non-specific way.

Massage

Massage is the oldest and simplest physical therapy. Giving your dog a massage will induce a feeling of well-being, and can help to establish a valuable non-verbal communication that conveys an attitude of loving care. This strengthens the bond between dog and owner, helping to heal not only the dog's physical body but its mind and spirit as well. The act of giving a massage is therapeutic for the owner too, and has been found to reduce people's stress levels.

Physically, massage improves the dog's circulation, relaxes the muscles and helps to balance muscle function and joint action, and can help to disperse scar tissue. It also helps the lymphatic system to speed up the rate at which it detoxifies the body. Massage may also increase the production of the body's natural pain killers (endorphins), which help to increase a feeling of well-being.

Massage can be used as an aid to keeping a healthy dog fit. It should not be used to treat sick animals unless they have first been checked by a vet. It should definitely not be used in cases where there is severe pain or the skin is damaged or infected, nor where there is muscle injury or where there are severe joint pains. Massage is also contra-indicated where the dog has recently had a high temperature (in the case of an acute infection, for example), and when the dog is known to have high blood pressure. The latter is difficult to recognize, as techniques for measuring the blood pressure of dogs are still being developed.

MASSAGE ROUTINE
A simple routine for an owner would be to begin with a few gentle strokes of even pressure along the body and limbs in the direction of the hair growth. These strokes should be slow and rhythmic, and will help to relax the dog. They also allow the owner to locate any tender spots. Lubricants are not normally required, but if they are, baby powder is preferred to the oils used on humans; these make the fingers slide too quickly over the skin for the massage to be effective, and they can get very messy.

Diagnostic massage points
This diagram shows the main pressure points in a dog. Note that too much pressure on these points can elicit a pain response.

a Ear
b Teeth and gums
c Throat and neck
d Back and spine
e Anal glands
f Hips
g Bladder
h Abdomen
i Lower abdomen and liver
j Ribs and lungs
k Ribs and lungs
l Elbow
m Shoulder
n Feet and toes
o Hoch (ankle)
p Stifle (knee)
q Kidney and ovary

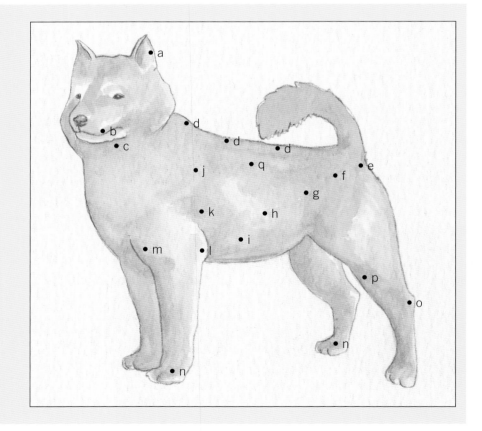

The pressure of the strokes should be gradually increased to a firmness that the dog will tolerate. Change the direction of the strokes to work towards the heart to stimulate venous and lymphatic drainage. Ideally, start at the feet and move upward and forward towards the head. If, however, the dog is foot-shy, start at the head and work back along the body.

The dog's feet should be massaged slowly and gently with the fingers, getting into the spaces between the toes. Massage the legs upward towards the body, starting just above the paw. Use your fingers for small dogs, and your palm for larger dogs.

To tackle the abdomen, either keep the dog standing or get it to roll over. Massage with circular movements, using either your palm or fingers depending on the size of the dog. The body and chest are best massaged first on one side and then the other. Start at the rear of the body and work towards the dog's head.

The spine should never be massaged. Instead, massage slightly to each side of the midline using the fingertips. It is here that you are most likely to find the tender trigger points. Do not massage these points vigorously, as this will cause the surrounding muscles to go into spasm. Light massage will help to reduce the reactivity of the point and to induce relaxation of the muscles. Finger pressure on a trigger point can deactivate it, while vigorous massage can increase the pain by stimulating further muscle contractions in an attempt to protect the damaged area.

Finally, move to the head and neck. This stage of the massage is a favourite with most dogs, and you may like to give a few minutes of extra attention here. Massage the head area gently, including around the eyes, nose, mouth and ears, rremembering to stroke and not to poke. The neck should be treated as an elongation of the back, and massage applied to the side, not the middle. End the session with a few light strokes along the body, from head to tail.

HOW TO MASSAGE

1 Place your hands on your dog's head and start with slow strokes, moving down over the ears. Repeat until you feel your dog relax. Extend the strokes over its head and around its eyes, nose, mouth and ears.

2 Move slowly down your dog's neck to the back area. Keep your hands on either side of the spine (never massage directly on the spine) and make long rhythmic stokes in the direction of the heart.

3 Slide your hands around the dog's sides to its abdomen and make circular movements over the belly and groin area, using either your fingers or the palms of your hands, depending on the size of the dog.

4 Massage your dog's shoulder and chest, then move down each leg towards the foot. The feet should be massaged very slowly and gently – try to rub between the toes if your dog will let you.

Physiotherapy

This therapy supplements the medical and surgical treatment of any condition that has a major impact on the musculoskeletal, or locomotor, system and the circulation. It includes everything from the simplest massage to the use of complex apparatus to stimulate muscle tissue. It is part of mainstream conventional medicine, yet also a vital component of holistic medicine. Good physiotherapy can help to control pain, speed up healing and preserve the function of injured tissue. It can be used alongside surgery, pharmaceutical medicines and all complementary therapies.

Training in animal physiotherapy usually begins with a course in human anatomy and physiology. Qualified physiotherapists are state-registered and are legally recognized. They are not allowed to diagnose the condition from which a patient is suffering (that is the province of the doctor), but once a medical diagnosis has been made, they are allowed to treat the patient under the doctor's supervision. In order to practise on animals, some physiotherapists undertake additional veterinary training. If you or your vet think that physiotherapy would help your dog, you are advised to enlist the help of a veterinary physiotherapist, if at all possible – not only will a qualified animal physiotherapist be

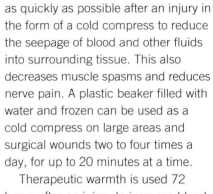

▲ *The H Wave machine passes warm currents of heat to the injured area to energize the tissue and encourage relaxtion. As the muscle tissue starts to relax, the tension is released.*

more familiar with the dog's anatomy, but they will also be better able to handle the animal.

Veterinary physiotherapy is commonly performed on professional sport animals such as racehorses and Greyhounds, and is becoming more widely used in general small animal veterinary practices. The objective of physiotherapy is to regain the strength and full range of movement, and this can be achieved either by manual manipulation or by a series of controlled exercises. The exercises are made more comfortable for the animal by the use of treatments such as cold and heat, electrical stimulation and laser therapy.

▼ *Laser equipment can be used to stimulate blood circulation in muscles. This soothes muscle tension and speeds up the healing process.*

Therapeutic use of cold is applied as quickly as possible after an injury in the form of a cold compress to reduce the seepage of blood and other fluids into surrounding tissue. This also decreases muscle spasms and reduces nerve pain. A plastic beaker filled with water and frozen can be used as a cold compress on large areas and surgical wounds two to four times a day, for up to 20 minutes at a time.

Therapeutic warmth is used 72 hours after an injury to increase blood circulation in the damaged tissue. This helps to remove waste products and increases nourishment of the area, speeding up healing, relieving tension and reducing pain.

Electrical stimulation has a variety of benefits. Special equipment can help with pain relief and stimulate muscle contractions. The latter can help to counteract muscle wastage, reduce spasm pains and increase

▼ *Palpation of the neck area. The therapist's hands feel the muscles for tightness, which indicates tension. The dog's response to the contact pressure may indicate painful areas.*

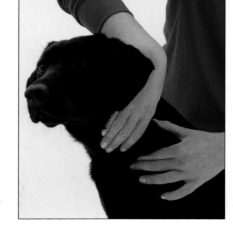

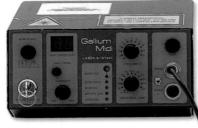

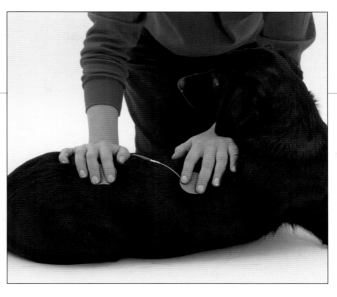

▲ *Palpation of the mid-spinal area. The physiotherapist's hands are placed at the sides of the spine to check for pain, muscle spasm, tension or heat swelling. The hand hold mobilizes the tight, painful soft tissues in order to release constriction and improve the circulation.*

▲ *Placing the pads of the H Wave machine over the dog's soft spinal tissue will stimulate the muscles in the same way as the hand hold. Heat from the machine will relax the muscle tissue, freeing the muscles from tension and reducing pain.*

muscle strength. It can also increase blood flow in damaged tissue and where there are certain forms of circulatory disease. This also aids healing.

Ultrasound is used to provide a form of heat therapy by using the energy of ultra-sonic vibrations to

▼ *Laser treatment uses light energy to stimulate the soft muscles in the lower back area. The laser increases the blood circulation to release tension in the damaged area.*

warm the tissues beneath the skin, which helps to increase the amount by which scar and other fibrous tissue can stretch. This allows the remodelling of scar tissue and helps to reduce the amount of scar tissue that does form. It can also help to deactivate painful muscular trigger points when properly used by trained operatives. Ultrasound treatment must never be used after exercise – it can have the opposite effect of increasing pain by overheating the tissue, causing further damage.

Exercise can be used in combination with physiotherapy to increase strength, endurance and flexibility. Dogs recuperating from injuries are often given stretching exercises, and these can be very useful; the physiotherapist will perform the manually assisted stretches after the dog has been warmed up by light exercise. Repeated gentle stretching will help to reduce muscle spasms and promote elongation of tissue, giving a greater range of movement.

Manual stretching must never overstretch the damaged tissues, or be done without the dog being warmed up first, or if there is an acute inflammation. If there is acute pain, ice packs should be applied. Hydrotherapy, or swimming in warm water, can help convalescing dogs to stretch their limbs safely without manual assistance. Exercise with weights and other equipment used in human physiotherapy is not easily adapted to canine therapy. However, under the right circumstances, malleable lead weights can be attached to the dog's limbs to give extra resistance to its movements.

Simple massage and the use of ice packs and gentle warmth may be tried by owners as self-help treatments at home. However, more specialist physiotherapy techniques can inflict further injury if misapplied, and these should only be used by a qualified physiotherapist; a physiotherapist without a veterinary qualification should always work under the guidance of a vet.

Osteopathy

This is a form of treatment based on the manipulation of the body's bony skeleton. Osteopathy is not a complete system of medicine. The basic premise is that disease results from the changes that occur in all parts of the body when one part of its structure is altered.

The American founder of osteopathy, Dr Andrew Taylor Still, saw the skeleton as having a dual purpose. The commonly recognized function was that it provided the physical framework for the body. By the action of the muscles that were attached to it, it allowed the mechanical movement of the body. Its other equally important function was to protect the vital organs of the body. Dr Still theorized that if the skeleton were out of alignment, the body it supported and protected would not be able to maintain a state of good health. The fundamental basis of all osteopathy is that structure governs function.

Osteopathy is recognized as a valid treatment that is complementary to and supportive of orthodox Western medicine. Osteopaths are trained to treat each patient as a complete structure, paying particular attention to the relationship between the musculoskeletal system and the function of the body. They are taught how to assess a patient's medical history, and how to examine the patient. From the patient's history, they will decide if osteopathy is a suitable treatment. A physical examination enables them to observe the ease and range of movement that the patient has in the limbs and spine. By carefully feeling the muscles and bones, the osteopath can locate painful areas and identify any

When to use osteopathy

In the absence of scientific research, it is difficult to evaluate the value of osteopathy on dogs. However, where vets have referred individual cases to human osteopaths, the results have been encouraging. Osteopathy appears particularly useful as a form of pain control for joint discomfort resulting from road traffic accidents, sports injuries and degenerative diseases.

If a dog refuses to cooperate once treatment begins, do not force it. You can either defer the session to a later date, or consider another therapy after discussing the options with your vet.

misalignments of the skeleton. The osteopath is then able to make a diagnosis of the problem and develop a treatment plan.

Osteopathic treatment for dogs uses soft-tissue massage techniques and joint manipulation to make adjustments to the damaged neuro-musculoskeletal structure. The techniques for dogs are similar to those used on humans. Manipulation techniques make corrections which repair the damage and allow healing to occur. Having given the first treatment, the osteopath will monitor improvements by sight and by feeling the changes that occur in the diseased area and in the dog's body in general.

The massage element of osteopathy is designed to increase blood flow and thereby increase the rate of elimination of toxic waste products that build up in damaged areas. It also

increases the oxygenation of the tissues, and this will help to relieve pain and stiffness.

The most common joint-manipulation technique used with osteopathy is the high-velocity thrust. Contrary to popular belief, although this causes popping or cracking noises, it does not realign bones and joints. It does, however, slightly separate the joint surfaces momentarily. This separation of the bone surfaces stretches the joint capsule and permits the joint to move more freely over a wider range of angles. At the time that the joint capsule is stretched, tiny bubbles of carbon dioxide come out of solution, and this is responsible for the audible popping sound.

The other techniques used in osteopathy are passive movement and articulation. Both of these techniques are designed to stretch the soft tissues gently and painlessly, to result in greater joint and limb mobility. Passive movement involves the osteopath gently moving the dog's limbs while the dog relaxes and makes no physical effort. Articulation takes this one stage further. It involves using the dog's limbs as levers by which to stretch the soft tissue. In all three techniques, the osteopath monitors the dog's response and makes adjustments to the treatment plan accordingly.

Osteopathy is officially recognized as a valid therapy for animals, although there are as yet no recognized schools of veterinary osteopathy. If you wish to have your dog treated osteopathically, it must have been examined initially by a vet. If the vet thinks the treatment would be beneficial, a qualified human osteopath will carry out treatment under the vet's direction. It is important that the vet and the osteopath cooperate with each other. The vet's notes, diagnosis and treatment schedule should be made available to the osteopath, and the osteopath should liaise about the proposed treatment, potential benefits and eventual outcome. Failure to liaise effectively can result in inappropriate treatment being given, and this may have an adverse effect on the dog.

Many osteopaths use other therapies in support of their treatment of human patients, such as aromatherapy essential oils. However, by law they are not allowed to use techniques other than osteopathy on dogs without the permission of the vet. It must be remembered that while the theory of osteopathy is valid for all species, its application in dogs is made more difficult because patient feedback is an impossibility and cooperation cannot be guaranteed from one session to the next. When the dog does cooperate, however, good results can be achieved.

GENERAL OSTEOPATHIC TREATMENT

1 Examination and articulation of the shoulder. The dog's front leg is extended by the ostepath in order to stretch the underlying muscles.

2 Examination and articulation of the hip, stifle and hoch. Each back leg is extended to stretch the muscles in the front of the thigh.

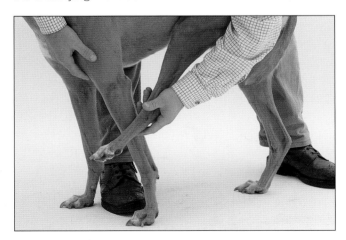

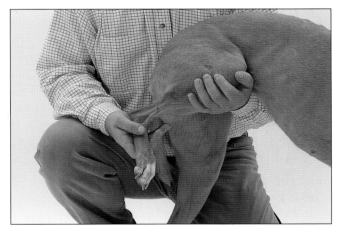

3 Examination and articulation of the hip in flexion. Each back leg is extended to stretch the hamstring muscles.

4 Examination and articulation of the hip in abduction, and of the pelvis and lumbar spine in rotation.

Chiropractic

Like osteopathy, chiropractic concentrates on the anatomy and physiology of the dog's musculoskeletal and nervous systems, and on the safe manipulation of the spine. The difference between the two therapies lies in their basic philosophy of disease. Chiropractic theory says that if vertebral segments of the spine are malaligned, there will be undue pressure on the spinal cord or spinal

When to use chiropractic

Chiropractic is not for home use. Because treatment involves manipulation of the spine, the consequences of misapplied techniques can be severe and could lead to the dog suffering paralysis. Even after observing the actions of a trained chiropractor during treatment sessions with your dog, never attempt to treat your dog yourself.

If you are having your dog treated, pay attention to its instinctive response to the practitioner. On subsequent visits to the clinic in particular, watch for signs of reluctance, the need to escape or defensive aggression. This may be your dog's way of telling you that it dislikes the treatment, and no matter how beneficial you and your vet and/or chiropractor have decided the treatment can be for your dog, if the animal does not feel comfortable with the treatment, you need to put an end to the sessions and reassess the alternatives. A resentful dog cannot be treated successfully.

nerves. This can cause interference with nerve transmissions, which may result in abnormal function and disease. If the malfunctioning vertebral segment can be repositioned by manipulation, the abnormal pressures on the spinal nerve roots are relieved and normal nerve function is restored to the affected area, including the tissues controlled by that segment.

The first stage of chiropractic treatment involves taking a detailed case history of the dog, and an examination of the nerves (nerologicial) and bones (orthopaedic). The neurological examination includes reflex and nerve stretch testing; the orthopaedic examination tests the range of movement of the various regions of the spine. At the same time, positions that cause pain are noted, as are any abnormal movement of the joints of the spine. Chiropractors are also trained to take x-rays. These are used to rule out the existence of any spinal disease that might cause a similar clinical condition, and to rule out the possibility of serious spinal damage, such as fractures.

The chiropractor is concerned with the physical effect created by any restriction of movement of the spine, however small and subtle this may appear. A change in alignment of the surfaces of the small vertebral joints, together with the associated nerve dysfunction, is known as a subluxation, a term used by vets to describe partial dislocations. Chiropractic diagnosis aims to recognize such restrictions and gives treatment to adjust them. The adjustment seldom results in total correction but initiates the body's natural healing processes, which slowly complete the realignment.

Chiropractic adjustment is carried out by carefully applying a high-velocity, short-amplitude thrust to the appropriate small facet joints of the vertebrae. Properly performed, an adjustment will correct the mechanical function of the joint and restore normal nerve function in the area.

As with osteopathy, this realignment of the joints is accomplished by a stretching of the joint capsule, and the same popping noise occurs due to the release of carbon dioxide within the joint. In severe or long-standing cases, treatment is often given in a series of adjustments designed to give a gradual return to normal function rather than in one or two more traumatic ones. Chiropractors are also taught deep-tissue massage techniques. These are used to support their manipulations, particularly in chronic cases. Drugs are never used in chiropractic treatment.

Few chiropractic colleges include veterinary training in the syllabus. The one veterinary chiropractic college in the UK is the McTimoney College of Chiropractic, while in the USA, the American Veterinary Chiropractic Association runs courses for vets and human chiropractors. As with osteopathy, the treatment of dogs (and other animals) by chiropractic is permitted by law, provided that treatment is given under the supervision of a vet.

Either a human chiropractor or an animal-trained one is allowed by law to treat a dog, but if you are given the choice, remember that the animal practitioner's training will have involved animal handling, and there is more chance that they will persuade the dog to cooperate.

If you are having your dog treated by a chiropractor, try to encourage a good level of communication between the practitioner and the vet. The vet may be required to take any x-rays needed by the chiropractor for the efficient treatment of the dog, but a full examination may not be possible because of the animal's dislike of it. Treatment can be difficult to give.

In spite of the difficulties involved, chiropractic does have a valuable place in modern holistic treatment of dogs who suffer the equivalent of back pain and spinal injuries. Because drugs are not involved, the treatment is entirely non-toxic. Adverse effects can sometimes occur after treatment, although these cases are rare. As with any therapy, however, it is worth discussing the possibility of things getting worse before they get better with both the vet and the chiropractor before starting treatment.

McTIMONEY CHIROPRACTIC

1 If a subluxation is located, the movements are adjusted accordingly. Both hands are placed behind the dog's neck as the practitioner first checks the Atlas at the base of the ears.

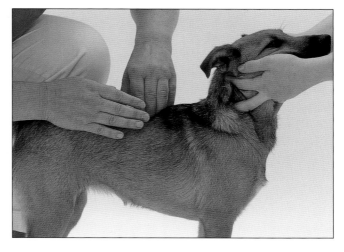

2 The next stage is to check the spine for subluxations. Here, the McTimoney chiropractic practitioner is making an adjustment of the thoracic spine.

3 The practitioner positions the dog's hind legs to check for subluxations in the pelvis area and the stifle (knee) joint.

4 The forelegs are then checked for signs of subluxations in the joints and elbow, which could be causing lameness.

Hydrotherapy

From the Greek word meaning 'water healing', hydrotherapy – whether by immersion in water or swimming – has been used for thousands of years as a method of healing and promoting fitness and a sense of well-being in humans. Since the 18th century, documentary evidence shows that walking in water was in common usage with lame horses. By the 19th century, Greyhounds were regularly exercised in water to improve their fitness levels. Modern research concludes that hydrotherapy is extremely beneficial in treating a variety of canine conditions. Unlike horses which are treated in cold water, dogs benefit from warm water.

Hydrotherapy is a form of low-impact physiotherapy which can be used for general fitness, after an injury or surgery, as an aid to treating medical conditions, and also to assist in weight loss. The use of water means that the

▼ *Before entering the water, dogs are fitted with a flotation jacket or harness.*

weight of the animal is supported, making it especially useful for animals that are lame or sore. Swimming or walking in water for 5 minutes is the equivalent to a dog going for an 8km (5-mile) run. If your dog has veterinary insurance, hydrotherapy costs are often covered within the policy.

This form of therapy is extremely beneficial for older dogs with arthritis or any form of degenerative joint disease. The warm water reduces the swelling in the joints, while the exercise helps to control any weight increase. Younger dogs with congenital conditions, such as hip or elbow dysplasia and slipping patella, also benefit, as the exercise helps to build muscle around the weakened joints. Increased muscle then provides support, acting as an internal bandage, helping joints to stay in place. In both cases, the water supports the weight of the dog, relieving pressure on the affected joints. Hydrotherapy is also useful in the rehabilitation of dogs with

▲ *If you are considering using hydrotherapy, check that the premises are clean and that staff are qualified before making a booking.*

neurological disorders, encouraging them to use their limbs without having to bear their weight.

Dogs are exercised either in a hydrotherapy pool or in a water treadmill. Hydrotherapy pools are normally smaller than a swimming pool and are heated to around 30°C (86°F). Non-slip steps or a ramp allow the dog to enter the pool, although there may be a manual or mechanical hoist to lower the dog into the water. Dogs enter the water wearing a flotation jacket and harness, and are accompanied by a trained therapist. The pool may have water jets, which increase the water resistance and also increase sensory awareness.

Water treadmills are small corridor-shaped raised pools with a moving treadmill floor and transparent walls. The speed of the treadmill and depth

◄ The therapist will assess the amount of time the dog needs in the pool.

of the water can be adjusted to suit each dog. The clear walls mean that the foot placement and gait of the dog can be seen. Again, the water is heated. In both the treadmill and the pool, the water is chlorinated or chemically treated.

Dogs are often referred by a veterinary surgeon for hydrotherapy, but in all cases they are required to have had a 'vet check' before they can attend. Some conditions, such as skin disorders, gastric upsets, open wounds and kennel cough, prohibit use of this therapy. Generally, bitches in season are also discouraged from attending. Dogs should not be fed for several hours before or at least an hour after their session. Ensure that your dog has had ample opportunity to relieve its self prior to each session. An 'accident' in the water will result in the pool being closed for use while it is emptied and cleaned, and this could result in an extra cost to the dog owner. Dogs should be brushed well before attending so that any loose coat is not shed in the water. Before entering the water, dogs are showered to remove any dust and debris from their coats. Most dogs love playing and chasing their toys while in the

pool, but those that are not so confident are gently encouraged by the therapist, who will be in the water with them. After each session, dogs are shampooed to remove any chemicals from their coats.

Free swimming in lakes, ponds or the sea does not have the same benefit as the use of a hydrotherapy pool. For dogs, immersion in warm water aids blood circulation, whereas cold water reduces circulation, increasing the chance of stiffness, leading to pain. There is also a risk

▲ The dog is under supervision at all times, even when leaving the pool.

of contracting a waterborne disease outdoors, such as eye, ear or gastric infections. Ultimately, there is also always the possibility of drowning, as the handler does not have the control of the dog afforded by swimming in a small pool wearing a flotation jacket.

▼ Dogs quickly get used to water treadmills, but the therapist will be close by in case of panic.

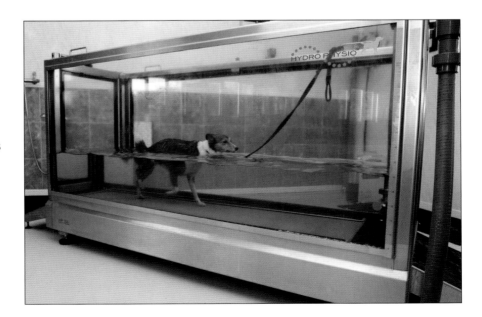

TTouch

This is a form of manipulation that differs from massage in that it affects the skin only and not the underlying tissues. Rhythmic, gentle finger touches are applied to the dog's body to calm and relax it and to improve its capacity for training. TTouch is particularly useful for frightened dogs.

The idea for the therapy was developed by Linda Tellington-Jones, a Canadian physiotherapist who worked with horses before extending the techniques to all other animals, including dogs. Tellington-Jones developed the therapy from the work of Dr Moshe Feldenkrais, an Israeli writer who was at the time teaching physical body awareness to humans.

The theory is that non-habitual movements combined with gentle manipulations can promote body awareness, and that this in turn can affect behaviour. The system behind the therapy is known as the Tellington-Jones Every Animal Method (TTeam), and the individual strokes are known as TTouch.

▼ *The Clouded Leopard is suitable for delicate areas such as the head. The secret here is for light pressure and a nimble hand movement.*

The basic principle behind the TTouch strokes is that the skin is moved in a circular motion through just over 360 degrees. If you imagine a clockface on the surface of the skin, the movement works clockwise from 6 o'clock, through 12 o'clock and continues to the 8 o'clock position.

Studies have shown that one effect of the technique is to change brain activity. Changes are seen in the *alpha*, *beta*, *delta* and *theta* waves of horses and the people who administer the therapy. It has the effect of stimulating the nervous system and benefiting both the mental and emotional spheres.

Skin manipulation is done with two or three fingers depending on the size of the dog; the thumb and heel of the hand rest on the body while the relaxed fingers move the skin. Only one circle is made in any one position; the hand is then slid to an adjacent area of skin and another circle made, with the sliding action connecting the circles. While one hand makes the circles, the other hand rests on the skin close to the working hand to complete the connection between owner and dog (it also helps the owner to balance as they perform the strokes).

There are 15 TTouch movements, each one using different parts of the fingers and hand, different pressures, and different speeds of movement. The techniques used include back

▲ *As its name suggests, the Tarantula Pulling the Plow manipulation involves moving the fingers in a spidery pathway across larger areas of the body, such as the neck and shoulders.*

and belly lifts, crossways movements across the belly, manipulation of the ears from base to tip (to stimulate the acupuncture points in the ear) and, if the dog will allow it, circles made in and around the mouth, lips and nose.

Dogs that resent being handled are often better if they are held on a halter rather than using a collar and lead, with the circles made with the end of a soft flexible wand or feather.

The main benefit of TTouch therapy is that it helps to increase the bond between dog and owner, and relaxes the animal when it is frightened and stressed. It can also be useful during recovery from accidents and surgery.

Several books and DVDs are available if you are interested in finding out more about it, and courses are also held which give a good introduction to the method.

TTouch hand movements

Clouded Leopard

Lying Leopard

Raccoon

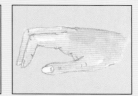
Snail's Pace

Bear

Feathering

Abalone

Lick of the Cow's Tongue

Tiger Touch

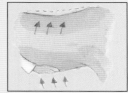
Noah's Ark

Python Lift

Butterfly

Tarantula Pulling the Plow

Belly Lifts

Back Lifts

Clouded Leopard So called because of the light and stealthy hand contact.

Lying Leopard Uses a firmer pressure and a flatter hand position to give a more defined contact.

Raccoon Use for smaller dogs for working around wounds, to speed healing, to increase circulation and activate neural impulses in the lower legs, and to reduce swelling.

Snail's Pace To relax back and neck muscles, to improve breathing and to reduce stress.

Bear For areas of heavy muscling, such as the shoulders, back and flank. The emphasis is on the fingernails making the contact, rather than the finger pads.

Feathering For dogs who are frightened of being touched. The movement should be light and fast.

Abalone This mimics the slow, circular motion of the sea abalone.

Lick of the Cow's Tongue A gentle, swiping movement upwards from the belly to the back to soothe and calm a nervous or anxious dog.

Tiger Touch A movement for heavily muscled dogs, and for itch relief. The fingernails are the point of contact, and because the fingers are raised and apart, the nails almost seem to make their own individual circles.

Noah's Ark Use these long, firm strokes to close a TTouch session. Using both hands, begin at the dog's head and make long, smooth strokes over the entire body.

Python Lift Use on the shoulders, legs, neck and chest areas to relieve muscular tension and spasms. Place both hands on either side of the dog's body or leg and slowly lift upwards for 1–2cm (½–1in). Hold for about 4 seconds, slowly come back down, then slowly release.

Butterfly Use this light movement alongside the Python Lift to increase circulation. The thumbs are pointed upwards with the fingers wrapped around the dog's leg. Lift the skin and muscle of the dog in the same way as for the Python Lift.

Tarantula Pulling the Plow Use light, nimble movements to gently roll the skin, working in a smooth pathway across the dog's shoulders, back and sides.

Belly Lifts Start behind the front legs and lift the dog's abdomen. Hold for 10–15 seconds, depending on the reaction. It is important that the pressure is released slowly and takes more time than the lift. Move gradually along the body towards the flank and repeat.

Back Lifts With fingers apart and curved upwards, start on the far side of the belly in the middle. In a raking motion, bring both hands across the belly and partway up the barrel of the body. Start gently and increase the pressure if the animal doesn't respond. You should be able to see the top of the back rise upwards.

Reiki

This is a hands-on therapy that bridges the gap between the physical therapies of massage and TTouch, and the pure energy therapies. It involves hand placements and movements that are designed more to direct the healing energies to strengthen the spirit or repair an injured area rather than to stimulate the skin and tissues themselves.

It is said that the healing energy of Reiki was first used in India by Buddha and later in the Middle East by Jesus. Its secrets were lost over the years, but were rediscovered in the late 19th century by a Japanese doctor, Dr Mikao Usui. It is said that when the doctor was close to death from cholera, he joined a Zen monastry and was taught the thoery of Reiki.

Practical knowledge of the application came to him in a vision, when he was shown symbols from the sutra and was taught how to use them. He was also given the ritual of attunement, which allows Reiki knowledge to pass from the initiated master to the uninitiated student. These rituals are still used in Reiki today.

The name Reiki is thought to originate from two Japanese symbols, 'Rei' meaning universal, and 'Ki' the non-physical life force. (Ki is similar to Q'i in acupuncture, the Vital Force of life.) The powerful healing energy Ki is freely available to those who are able to use it. Unfortunately, most of us are disconnected from it because of the stress and isolation of modern life. Reiki aims to reconnect people to life's energy force, thus enabling them to heal themselves, their family and friends, and their animals.

There are three degrees of Reiki. In the First Degree, the student is attuned to the life force and can begin to channel it where it is needed. The student is also taught the hand placements and movements that are

essential to direct the energy to the patient. In the Second Degree, the student is taught the symbols and mantras that allow the energy to be focused more strongly on the patient. It is also possible to use these for distant healing. The Third Degree, or Reiki Master level, is the teaching level. Knowledge of this degree is passed from master to student on a one-to-one level.

Because Reiki energy connects all life, it is universal and is used to heal

◄ If a dog's leg is broken, do not place your hands directly over the injury. Placing one hand on the dog near to the injury will help to take away the pain. The other hand should be held over the adrenals in order to energize the dog's response to stress. It is important to keep your palms parallel to the dog's body.

Some hand positions for treating dogs

Choose one of the following to give your dog the benefit of a Reiki experience at any time. If your dog is suffering physical or emotional distress, be sensitive to its response and stop treatment immediately if it appears to resent it. Do not place your hands directly on areas of acute inflammation, but hold them parallel to and just above the damaged area.

• Hold your hands either side of the ribcage, with the dog seated on your lap or in front of you on the floor. This will treat the whole body, and the Reiki will reach central parts immediately.

• Put one hand on the head of your dog as though you are going to stroke its ears, and one hand very lightly on the middle of the dog's back.

• Hold the dog between your hands, with one hand at the top of the spine and one by its tail at the base of the spine.

▲ Cupping your hands around the dog's ears will redirect the energy flow of the bud chakra at the base of the ears to benefit the dog.

▶ Giving the dog a whole body treatment will direct the flow of energy where it is most needed. Start at the top of the head with your hands over the bud chakra energy channel at the base of the dog's ears. Work from the head down the neck, back, abdomen and legs, and always end with the feet.

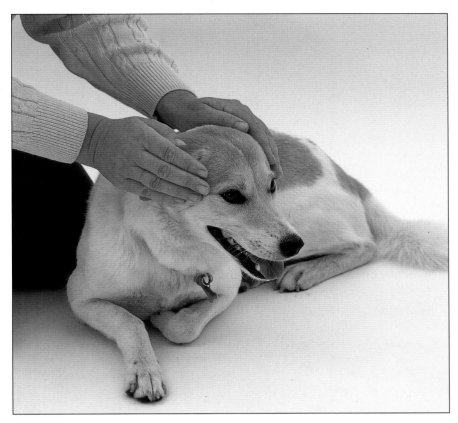

dogs in the same way as it is used on humans. Reiki can be used on dogs as an uplifting tonic or to ease actual suffering. Place your hands comfortably on the dog or over an injury or wound; the dog will move away or appear restless when it has had enough of the treatment. Reki can also be used to reassure dogs who are emotionally upset.

Reiki should not be used as the only means of treating a sick animal. If your dog appears ill, have it looked at by a vet and use Reiki to support the prescribed treatment, including surgery. The main use of Reiki should be to keep your dog in a state of optimum health and to prevent serious disease from becoming established.

◀ Reiki can be used on an unwell dog to support conventional treatment, and will help to reduce the stress of physical injuries, such as hip displasia. Where the dog is experiencing acute pain, move slowly and with relaxed movements – most dogs are frightened when in pain, and even a mild-mannered dog may become unpredictable.

Herbalism

This is probably the oldest form of healing still in use today. Herbal medicines are an essential part of the ancient medical systems of Traditional Chinese Medicine and the Indian Ayurvedic system. Western herbalism dates back to the ancient Greeks. It was the mainstay of English medicine until the 1930s and the introduction of the sulphonamides, a group of medicines that were the precursor of modern antibiotics.

Herbalism has made a resurgence, caused in part by the idea that the long-term effects of some modern drugs may not be totally beneficial to the patient. This has prompted a reappraisal of all medical therapies, and has encouraged an interest in holistic medicine and a desire for safe natural medicines that do not involve toxins or side effects – for both humans and animals. The fact that dogs and other animals are known to seek out and eat plants that are known to have medicinal properties supports the view that herbalism has an established place in orthodox veterinary medicine.

▼ *Herbal teas and decocotions can be stored for at least 2 days in a well-stoppered bottle.*

Condition	Herbal therapy
Cancer prevention	Lemon balm, mistletoe leaf, barberry bark, Roman chamomile flower, comfrey leaf, echinacea root, fenugreek seed
Itchy skin	German chamomile flower, burdock root, curled dock root, liquorice root, southernwood
Skin abrasions	Turmeric root, yarrow, peppermint, comfrey leaf
Colitis	Marsh mallow root, nutmeg seed, turmeric seed
Heart disease	Hawthorn, motherwort, dandelion leaf
Urinary tract disorders	Stone root, field horsetail, couch grass, bearberry leaf, juniper berry, marsh mallow root
Kidney impairment	Cinnamon bark, rehmannia root, comfrey leaf, celery seed

Many people take the view that since plants are natural, and natural products must be safer than manufactured ones, herbalism is therefore totally safe. This, however, is not the case. Some plants are poisonous in their natural form, and herbal medicines derived from an original plant source can be toxic if given in overdose. Always check the toxicity of your chosen plant.

▲ *Eucalyptus oil can be used in small quantities in cough mixtures.*

Some pharmacists object to the use of herbalism. This is because the chemical composition of individual plants of the same species varies according to the soil they are grown in and the season of the year in which they are harvested. This means that medicines derived from plants are by no means standardized. This is compounded according to which part of the plant is used and the method of extraction used on that plant material. Pharmacists would prefer to isolate the part of the plant that they consider to be the active ingredient, and use only that ingredient in a purified form. This is the only way to know exactly what action a single dose of medicine has on the body.

Unfortunately, few active agents have only one effect. They tend to have other unwanted actions or side effects. Herbalists believe that the active ingredients of herbal medicines work together to counteract harmful side effects. This allows a safe, effective dosage to be made.

Herbal medicines can be given in many forms. The traditional method is

poultices and compresses, however you should not use toxic herbs in this way, because a dog is likely to lick the dressing and it may poison itself.

There are very few practising veterinary herbalists, but some vets undertake courses in herbalism to combine this therapy with their veterinary knowledge. They can then carefully treat animals, monitoring their response to treatment before increasing the dose. With experience, their dosing regimes are becoming more accurate.

In cases of minor illness, you can treat your dog with herbs yourself. Keep up the treatment for one week before rejecting it as ineffective. In cases of chronic disease, it can take longer for improvement to be seen, although in these situations herbalism is best used to support conventional care. The health of your dog is paramount; if the dog's condition appears to deteriorate, stop the treatment and consult your vet.

▲ *Herbal teas are best given through the side of the dog's mouth, but not all animals appreciate them as much as this one does.*

in the form of herbal teas, which are made from bulk herbs that are available in loose form. Like all herbal preparations, bulk herbs should always be purchased from reputable companies. Herbal teas for dogs are made in the same way as they are for humans. The difference seems to be that dogs appear to need more in relation to their body weight than humans. A dose of 20ml (4 tsp) twice a day is generally accepted as suitable for a dog weighing about 50kg (20lb).

Good-tasting bulk herbs can be fed directly to the dog if mixed together with its usual food.

Commercial herbal extracts in the form of glycerine/water and alcohol/water tinctures are available from reputable suppliers, and can be given directly into the mouth of some dogs. Here, the dose rate is one drop per 13kg (5lb) of body weight. Herbal capsules and tablets are now being made for canine use, but some authorities believe that capsules of powdered herbs are not suitable for carnivorous animals. If using them, buy from a reputable company and follow the instructions carefully. Bulk herbs can also be used to make

▼ *Commercial extracts are standardized and will have a more constant effect than home-made teas. They can also be stored for longer periods.*

Aromatherapy

This is the use of volatile aromatic oils, which are derived from plant material, to cause physiological and psychological changes in the patient. The molecules of these essential oils are able to enter the body and the bloodstream by absorption through the lining of the nose and lungs or through the skin. This means that aromatherapy oils are as much medicinal substances as any conventional drug taken by mouth or given by injection.

Fragrant oils have been used medicinally in the Middle East for thousands of years. Their use is not taught in medical or veterinary schools at present, although some holistic veterinary clinics use aromatherapy, as do some human hospitals.

Several parts of the plant can be used as a source of the essential oil. The flowers, leaves, twigs, roots, seeds, bark and heartwood may be used according to the plant from which the oil is being extracted.

▶ *Essential oils should never be used undiluted on a dog's skin. Blend with a carrier oil before using oils for massage.*

There are several methods of extracting the oils, the commonest being steam distillation. This yields an oil and water mix that is cooled and separated into its two components. Pressing is used to squeeze the oil out of plants containing non-volatile oils. Carbon dioxide extraction is sometimes used, but is more expensive. Enfleurage is the traditional process of leaving petals on layers of fat for up to three weeks. During this time, the oils seep into the fat, from which they are separated by extraction with alcohol. This method is used for extracting delicate flower oils, such as rose and jasmine. It produces fine oils, but is very expensive. Solvent extraction produces oils known as absolutes, which may contain traces of the solvent. For this reason, they are disliked by some therapists. Synthetic oils are also produced. These are a much more standardized product,

▲ *Aromatic oils should be stored in well-stoppered bottles, away from the light and out of contact with homeopathic remedies or inquisitive children or pets.*

but are thought not to contain all the many components of the natural oil, which may reduce their therapeutic effect. They are believed by some therapists not to be as active as natural oils because they have a non-living chemical source which is devoid of the vitality of living materials.

There are hundreds of component oils in every extract. The final contents are governed by the geographical area and the soil in which the plant is grown, the climate, and the methods used in cultivation. Organically grown plants should be used to eliminate contamination with agrochemicals. Choose your supplier with care, and regard cheap oils with suspicion, although expense does not necessarily indicate good quality.

The dog has a highly developed sense of smell and can be expected to respond well to aromatherapy.

Condition	Essential oil
Lack of confidence, anxiety, panic	Ylang ylang, sandalwood
Loneliness, fear of being alone	Basil, bergamot or orange blossom
Restlessness, frustration	Chamomile
Liver problems	Rosemary
Kidney and bladder problems	Juniper
Skin allergies	Lavender, pine, terebinth
Respiratory problems	Cedarwood, eucalyptus, lemon, tea tree, lavender
Minor wounds, bites and stings	Lavender, tea tree
Toothache	Clove

▶ *Lavender oil is widely used for skin wounds and insect bites, but it should not be applied directly to areas of damaged skin.*

▶ *The relatively bare areas of the dog's belly, groin and armpit are the best sites for the application of essential oils by massage.*

Dogs instinctively use the secretions of their anal sacs and the glands of their feet, tails and cheeks, along with saliva, urine and faeces as a means of communication. This is to identify themselves, both for attracting mates and possibly deterring aggressors. It means that they are very suitable candidates for intranasal drug therapy.

Administration by massage is not really suitable for dogs except in the less hairy regions, such as the armpit and groin. Soaking the dog's body in a bath containing a few drops of oil is also unsuitable. It is difficult to get a dog to hold its head over an inhalation of oil in hot water. The best method is inhalation using a vaporizer. In this method, 5–10 drops of oil are floated on water that is being heated by a candle or night-light. The heating causes the oil/water mixture to evaporate, and the fragrant vapour fills the room, where it is inhaled by people and pets alike. This makes it suitable for the home treatment of sick dogs, especially those who resist oral medication. Inhalation is not suitable for treatment in a veterinary surgery

or hospital, however, because this would mean that other dogs would receive the same treatment, regardless of their symptoms.

Combinations of up to four oils can be used according to the symptoms. Such combinations should be freshly prepared by a professional aromatherapist. Aromatherapy can be used to support any mainstream or complementary therapy with the exception of homeopathy, because homeopathic remedies can be deactivated by aromatic substances.

It must be remembered that essential oils are concentrated chemicals and can be toxic in their neat form. They should never be used undiluted on the animal's skin. As well as absorbing the oil through the skin, the dog will also lick its fur and take in toxic doses through its mouth. Remember that a dog's nose is very sensitive. This may mean that what smells beautiful to a human nose may be unbearably strong for a dog, and may not have the desired therapeutic effect.

▶ *Vaporization is the easiest and gentlest method of using aromatherapy with dogs.*

Acupuncture

This is part of Traditional Chinese Medicine (TCM), which has been developed by the Chinese for over 3,000 years. It is based on the principle of the flow of energy, 'Q'i', (pronounced "chee") around the body through non-anatomical channels known as 'meridians'. If the flow of Q'i passing through any of these channels is disturbed, the health of the body is impaired, which leads to disease.

The body's energy flow increases and decreases in each meridian in a fixed cycle. These meridians also govern the function of an anatomical unit, although their function in TCM is different from Western medicine.

Conditions that respond best to acupuncture
• Musculoskeletal problems: arthritis, disc problems, hip displasia, spinal problems, lameness
• Chronic gastrointestinal diseases: chronic digestive disturbances such as chronic diarrhea or vomiting, distemper
• Neurological problems: nerve deafness, nerve injuries, epilepsy and some types of paralysis
• Skin diseases and allergic dermititis
• A variety of other problems, such as chronic pain syndrome, breeding problems, respiratory arrest and coma

Note: Acupuncture is not recommended for healing dogs with cancer, as it may unwittingly stimulate the disease.

Q'i has two opposite but complementary components: 'yin' and 'yang'. Everything in the universe contains yin and yang, but some things contain more yin than yang, and vice versa. The solid organs of the body – liver, spleen, kidney, heart, lungs and pericardium – are yin, while the hollow organs – stomach, small and large intestines, gall bladder and urinary bladder – are yang. One pair of meridians governs each organ, and there are two other non-paired meridians, the Governing Vessel and the Conception Vessel. These meridians run in pathways up the front and down the back of the body.

Acupuncture theory holds that everything in the universe is made from five basic philosophical elements: wood, fire, earth, metal and water. These elements relate in a positive or negative way to one another, so that wood produces fire, but restrains or destroys earth. Each element can change to the next in the course of a creative cycle.

Chinese acupuncture recognizes six environmental factors as the principal reasons for disease: wind, cold, summer heat, dampness, dryness and heat; each of these is associated with certain forms of disease. It also recognizes eight conditions composed of four pairs of opposites: yin and yang, internal and external, heat and cold, and excess and deficiency. The theory is that all disease is expressed by a combination of these eight conditions.

In acupuncture, no medicines are given, although Chinese herbs may be used in support of the treatment. Treatment itself is based on stimulating precise anatomical

▲ *In the West, acupuncture treatment begins with a thorough examination of the dog in order to make a correct diagnosis of the problem.*

positions along the meridians. These positions are based on the monitored results of stimulation over thousands of years. In the beginning, finger pressure was used, and later, thin slivers of bamboo or bone were inserted into underlying tissues. Today, fine surgical steel needles are used. The relationships between the five elements, the six environmental factors and the eight conditions of opposites indicate which points on which meridian should bring Q'i back into balance and allow the body's natural healing forces to complete the cure.

There is no structure or organ recognized by Western anatomists that could be responsible for the physical and physiological changes that result from acupuncture treatment. The effects of acupuncture cannot be explained in physical or biochemical terms, suggesting that they occur at a different level, somewhere in the invisible, energetic bodies that surround the physical level known to Western science. For many conventional Western-trained physicians, the philosophy of acupuncture and its approach to treatment is difficult to evaluate. A form of acupuncture has been developed in the West which uses fixed combinations of points for

▼ *The examination given to the dog may include x-rays and laboratory tests if the initial check-up does not identify the source of the problem.*

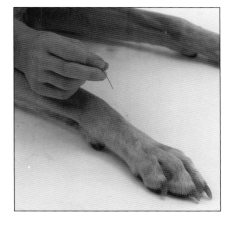

▲ *Needles are placed at various depths, depending on the size of the dog and the treatment being given.*

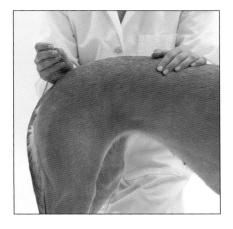

▲ *The points are chosen on the basis of an examination, the dog's history and the practitioner's experience.*

each diagnosis. This type of therapy is empirical, but cannot be used on as many conditions as traditional Chinese acupuncture.

Since Q'i, the philosophical elements, environmental factors and conditions of acupuncture are universal, its theory can be applied as easily to dogs as to humans. The positions of the meridian and acupuncture points varies from species to species, but the same positions can be used on dogs and humans alike.

Your dog is not likely to resist treatment. Most dogs find the therapy relaxing, and some have been known to fall asleep while the needles are in place. As a therapy, acupuncture is not as good as antibiotics at

dealing with acute infections, but it is very good with chronic diseases, including diseases of the immune system. Acupuncture is not for home use. Ask your vet to refer you to a qualified practitioner if you are interested in using it on your dog.

ACUPRESSURE

The use of needles is reserved by law to vets but, if you want to provide back-up care for your dog, simple training from a qualified practitioner will allow you to perform finger pressure, or 'acupressure', at home to support conventional treatment.

Like acupuncture, acupressure is based on the principle of Q'i, and is said to reduce pain by relaxing the muscles. It is applied with light fingertip or fingernail pressure on the acupuncture points; some styles of acupressure also involve rubbing, kneading and rolling. Note, however, that acupressure done incorrectly can actually increase pain. As with all therapies, do not proceed if your dog dislikes the treatment.

Homeopathy

The first holistic system of Western medicine to be developed, homeopathy can be very effective both on its own and in support of conventional medicine. Like acupuncture, it is at its best where conventional medicine is weakest.

The body has a natural healing force which is implemented in cases of illness or injury – small cuts and grazes heal on their own, and we soon get over minor coughs and colds. Scientists call this healing force 'homeostasis', and homeopaths believe that their medicine stimulates it. Samuel Hahnemann, an 18th-century German doctor and the originator of homeopathy, called the animal impulse for self-healing the 'Vital Force'. He saw this as an energetically active, living force that is essential to life. He took large doses

▼ *Homeopathic remedies come in the same form as more conventional medicines. To the casual observer, there is no difference in appearance between one homeopathic preparation and the next.*

When to use homeopathy
Remedies are available in different potencies, of which the most common are 6C and 30C. Use 6C potency for common or long-standing ailments, and 30C potency for emergencies and chronic symptoms.

Condition	Remedy
Panic attacks and emotional stress	Aconite
Prolonged grief	Ignatia
Flea bites and wasp stings	Apic
Bruises and swelling	Arnica
Flatulence and digestive disorders	Carbo Veg
Skin grazes and superficial wounds	Hypercium
Physical exhaustion	Arnica

of extract of *Chincona* bark (the tree from which quinine is extracted), and from his observations he deduced that a non-lethal quantity of a poison can stimulate healing of any disease for which the symptoms are similar to the effects of that poison.

The idea that 'like cures like' dates back to the ancient Greeks, but had never before been used as the basis for a medical therapy. Hahnemann tested substances on himself and his friends, and recorded the results in a volume he called the *Materia Medica*.

At first, Hahnemann used small, material doses, and found that some patients got worse before they got better, a phenomenon he called

'homeopathic aggravation'. To reduce the aggravations, he reduced the size of the dose, but although diluting reduced the aggravations, it also diminished the benefits. Next, liquid medicines were shaken after dilution in a method known as 'potentizing'. This reduced the aggravations while, at the same time, enhancing the healing property of the medicines or 'potencies'.

The potentizing process is unique to homeopathy. At each stage there are two procedures: the dilution in a fixed ratio of 1:9 or 1:99; and the succussion of the diluted solution by vigorous shaking. This is essential if the medical effects of the solution are to be enhanced or potentized as the concentration is reduced.

The starting point of a potency is the saturated solution of a soluble chemical, or the alcoholic extract of plant material known as the 'mother tincture'. Each succeeding potency is given a number for the quantity of dilutions made, and a letter for the Latin number of the degree of dilution, *X* or *D* standing for 10, *C* for 100, and *LM* for 50,000. For example, if you put

▼ *The gentle action of homeopathy remedies is always appreciated by the patient.*

one drop of the mother tincture of *Belladonna* with 99 drops of alcohol/water and shake it, you get a *1C* potency. One drop of the *1C* potency mixed with 99 drops of alcohol/water gives a *2C* potency, and one drop of a *2C* potency mixed with 99 drops of alcohol/water gives a *3C* potency, and so on. Potencies up to *30C* are still made by hand, and to these is added the suffix *H* for Hahnemann. Potencies from *30C* to *10M* are usually produced by mechanical methods.

The use of highly diluted medicines has led to two misconceptions: first, that the essence of homeopathy is the use of a very small dose rather than the use of a 'similar'; and second, that because there are no molecules left in potencies above *12X* or *6C*, the medicine could not possibly work. Observations over the last 200 years, however, have shown that these medicines do affect the living body. This phenomena is under scientific study, but the method by which homeopathy achieves its results will probably prove to be subatomic, at an energetic level. Like acupuncture, homeopathy is as applicable to sick dogs as to ailing humans.

A 'similar' is the medical agent with symptoms closely resembling those of the dog, and if the symptoms match completely, it is the 'similimum'. When a dog is treated, its physical, mental and emotional reactions to the world are used to identify the disease. The totality of the animal and its condition is treated, and the more you know about your dog in health, the more you can help. The smallest dose of the similimum that will stimulate the healing process is given. In acute cases, doses are repeated until benefits are seen. In chronic cases, each dose is left to have its full effect before it is repeated.

The second branch of homeopathic treatment is the removal of obstructions to a cure. This relates to the modern holistic idea that unless there is suitable nutrition, hygiene, living conditions and lifestyle, a complete and permanent cure is unlikely to result, no matter what the medicine. A good homeopath should enquire about these factors and give appropriate advice.

Tissue salts make up the third branch of homeopathy. In the 19th century, a German homeopathic doctor, Wilhelm Schüssler, identified 12 basic salts in the body and developed the idea that, if caught early and without complex symptoms, all disease could be treated with a combination of these salts. Biochemic tissue salts are often prescribed by homeopathic vets for use in low *6X* potencies to alleviate mild physical or emotional disease conditions, which may be caused by a mineral salt deficiency. Nutritional advice will also be given as part of the treatment.

▼ *Dogs will normally take powdered tablets without complaint. If your dog does object, however, the powder can be stirred into its drinking water.*

When to use tissue salts

Condition	Remedy
Emotional stress	Kali phos.
Allergies	Nat. sulph.
Neurological disorders	Silica
Dental problems	Calc. fluor.
Skin grazes and minor wounds	Hypercium 6C

Bach flowers

Plants and flowers play an essential part in many traditional healing systems. Flower essences, prepared from the stalks, petals and leaves of plants, can be used in response to canine emotional states.

The German homeopath Dr Samuel Hahnemann discovered a way of using the vibrational energy of plants to stimulate natural healing processes in his holistic system of homeopathy. A bacteriologist from Britain, Dr Edward Bach, took Hahnemann's ideas one stage further. His experience as a homeopathic doctor convinced him that physical disease was the result of the body's reaction to a non-material cause. Changes in the body's fundamental vibrational energy (what the acupuncturist calls 'Q'i' and the homeopath calls the 'Vital Force') resulted in a pathological change of mental state that could eventually lead to physical disease.

To Dr Bach, it appeared that mental attitude was more important in the choice of a medicine than physical symptoms. He believed that the mind showed the onset and cause of

▲ *Floating fresh flowers on 300ml (½ pint) of spring water in bright sunlight will yield 600ml (1 pint) of mother tincture when diluted with brandy. This is how Bach flower remedies are prepared.*

▲ *Only two drops of mother tincture are needed to produce 30ml (2 tbsp) of a stock solution that is further diluted before it is given to the patient.*

disease more definitely and sooner than the body. He closed his Harley Street practice in London in 1930, at the age of 43, to seek a means of healing that used non-toxic materials rather than potentized poisons.

Dr Bach was a sensitive, spiritual man who noted that his own moods could be influenced by the plants that he came into contact with. He started to look towards individual plants for his remedies, and his theory was that the natural vibrations of certain plants responded to the natural vibrations associated with certain mental states. Therefore, if the plants were appropriately prepared, they could correct distorted vibrations by the principle of resonance.

Initially, Bach used his intuition to discover 12 plants which affected pathological mental states. Later he increased the range to 37 plants, plus *Rock Water*, which is water from a natural spring (preferably a spring reputed to have healing properties). He also sanctioned the use of a

combination of five remedies in a preparation called *Rescue Remedy*. *Rescue Remedy* is the most popular essence for dogs, and is used in emergency situations for panic, shock and hysteria.

Bach chose two methods of preparation for his plants, based on the seasons. Flowers of plants which bloomed in the late spring and summer were picked at about 9.00am on sunny days. The flowers were floated on 300ml (½ pint) of spring water in a glass bowl and left in sunlight. If the sun clouded over, the batch was discarded. The flowers were removed using stems or branches of the same flower so that the energized water was not contaminated by human touch.

This energized water was used to fill bottles half-full of brandy. This was the mother tincture. Two drops of this added to 30ml (2 tbsp) of brandy gave what Bach called the 'stock solution'.

Plants that bloomed in the late winter and spring were processed by the boiling method. The flowers and stems were again picked on a bright, sunny morning before 9.00am. They were collected in a pan, and when the pan was three-quarters full, the lid was fitted and the material was taken home. The flowers and stems were covered with about 1.2 litres (2 pints) of spring water and simmered for 30 minutes, uncovered. The lid was then replaced and the covered pot put outside to cool. When cool, the stems were removed using twigs of the same plant, and the liquid filtered and used to make the mother tincture, as before.

The plants used for the remedies are ideally wild ones growing in unpolluted areas. If cultivated plants have to be used, they should be organically grown to avoid contamination with toxic chemicals. *Rock Water* (or 'holy' spring water) should be free from agrochemicals. Flowers from several plants should be

▲ *Flowers must be picked in bright, early morning sunshine if the mother tincture is to work. Wild flowers are preferred, and all flowers should be free of pollutants. Human contact with the plants should be minimal.*

used, rather than the flowers of one plant alone. Flower medicines can be prepared for the patient, although single remedies are now available in health-food stores and some chemists for use at home. Up to five remedies can be combined, depending on the patient's needs, using two drops of each essence in 30ml (2 tbsp) of spring water.

Bach Flowers are particularly valuable for behavioural problems, and while clinical tests have proved inconclusive in explaining how and why they work, positive results have been seen in both humans and dogs. The medicines are chosen according to the dog's mental state, using

▲ *Winter and early summer twigs, leaves and flowers are processed by the boiling method, and need to be simmered gently for at least 30 minutes to produce an effective mother tincture.*

human emotions as a guide. The owner talks in detail to the therapist about the dog's usual temperament. Treatment is based on the pathological mental state of the dog rather than the nature of its inappropriate behaviour. Dr Bach believed that his remedies covered all known emotional states.

▼ *Dogs with behavioural or emotional problems can respond better to Bach flowers than to pharmaceutical drugs.*

State of mind	Flower remedy
Shyness	Mimulus
Apathy	Wild Rose
Fear on behalf of the family	Red Chestnut
Lack of self-confidence	Larch
Lack of concentration	Clematis
Melancholy	Mustard
Aloofness	Water Violet
Excessive desire for companionship	Heather
Over-protectiveness	Chicory
Dominance	Vine

Crystal therapies

Crystals have been used for healing purposes for thousands of years. They have a regular, fixed, atomic structure as opposed to the chaotic arrangement of atoms in non-crystalline material. The natural energy of the atoms is harmonized by this structure, and every crystal has a natural frequency of vibration. This regularity is so stable that it is used to control electric clocks and the frequencies of radio receivers and transmitters. The vibration frequency of crystals is also a source of electrical energy, as demonstrated by the crystal radio sets of the 1930s.

Empirical studies indicate that through harmonic resonance the vibrational energy of a crystal can affect the basic energetic vibration of both people and animals. The energy of the crystal is believed to enter the body through the 'chakras', or energy-centres of the body, of Ayurvedic medicine. Each chakra is related to a hormone-producing gland of the body, and each has its own harmonic colour vibration. In turn, these correspond to seven layers or energy bands in the 'aura' – the invisible energy field that surrounds the physical body – which have been studied and identified over thousands of years. Because of the universality of life-energy, these factors are as valid for animals as they are for humans. The only difference is the location of the chakras within the body. They have been accurately mapped in humans, but the correspondences are not exactly the same for animals. There is some controversy over the location of the 'minor' and 'bud' chakras in dogs, although there is general agreement about the 'major' chakras.

▲ *Placing your hand over the major chakra at the crown of the dog's head will help to redirect the energy flow back into the body to restore a sense of equilibrium in the animal.*

As with the Bach Flowers, the mental state of the patient is the major factor in choosing which crystals should be used. Some crystals seem to have an affinity for certain body systems or symptoms. The factors quoted for crystal selection for humans can be applied to dogs.

Once the appropriate crystals have been selected, they are placed on the patient's resting body in set patterns. For a dog, the crystals can be taped to its collar or harness; special harnesses are available with pockets to hold crystals over the appropriate chakra for optimum healing. It is also possible to use liquefied crystal essences, which are produced in a similar way to the flower essences, and can be successfully used for mental and emotional problems.

Crystals can also be used in light therapy. Light is shone through coloured crystal filters in a darkened room on to the dog's body; the light

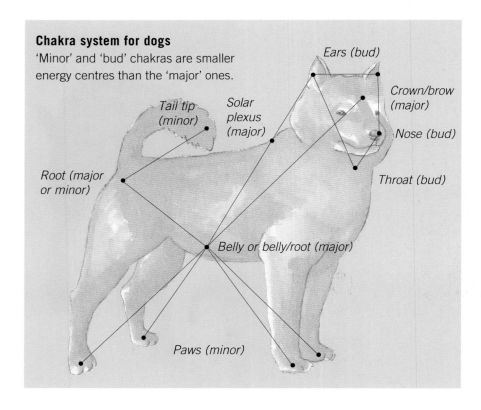

Chakra system for dogs
'Minor' and 'bud' chakras are smaller energy centres than the 'major' ones.

Ears (bud)
Crown/brow (major)
Tail tip (minor)
Solar plexus (major)
Nose (bud)
Throat (bud)
Root (major or minor)
Belly or belly/root (major)
Paws (minor)

Citrine quartz

Amythyst

Rose quartz

Choosing crystals

- Amethyst – a healing stone to calm the mind
- Bloodstone – to heal and energize the physical body
- Citrine quartz – an energizing stone, both physically and mentally
- Clear quartz – for general well-being
- Lapis lazuli – releases stress to focus and calm

- Moonstone – clears tension from the emotions and abdomen
- Rose quartz – to balance the emotions
- Rutilated quartz – to aid the healing of torn or broken tissue
- Smoky quartz – a grounding stone and a deep cleanser
- Tiger's eye – a practical, stable and stimulating energy

is directed on to a chakra, an acupuncture point, or the region of the affected organ. Colours have long been known to affect the mind and, increasingly, this phenomena is used when choosing colour schemes for high-stress areas, such as medical centres, hospitals and police cells.

Crystals contain metallic ions which can benefit the body's metabolic system. These are slowly absorbed by the body through the skin, if the crystal is in contact with it, in a similar way to the essential oils used in aromatherapy. It has been demonstrated that if a human holds a crystal in their hand for more than 30 minutes, their brain waves change from the alert *beta* waves to the more relaxed *alpha* waves. The deep relaxation pattern associated with *theta* and *delta* waves will increase if the crystals are held for periods of more than half an hour.

While crystals emanate healing vibrations, they also absorb negative and pain vibrations from the patient, and to maintain the healing potential

of crystals it is necessary to cleanse them regularly. They can be left outside for a 24-hour period when the moon is above the horizon; the dual action of sunlight and moonlight over this period is said to cleanse the crystal. Alternatively, the crystal can be put into salt water for 24 hours and

left with its point facing downwards for 8 hours to dry. Iron-containing crystals can be cleansed using spring water in the same way. Porous crystals, such as lapis lazuli and moonstone, should not be washed. They can be buried for 24 hours and then wiped clean using spring water, if necessary.

Crystal healing is very helpful for dogs whose illness is due to mental and emotional problems, and it can be used to complement all physical medical therapies. However, it is not advised to use crystal therapy on unset broken bones, or before surgery of any kind, because it can interfere with the anaesthetic. Crystal therapists should always discuss the case with the vet before treatment is started, and only proceed with the vet's approval.

▼ *To treat your dog with crystals, ask the animal to lie down, then scatter the crystals on the floor around it. Attach the crystals to the dog's collar if the dog becomes restless.*

Living with the veteran dog

When a dog reaches middle age (about 7), physical changes start to occur. Early symptoms will be detected by your vet during routine examinations, and prescribed drugs are available to combat some of the problems associated with aging. Simple changes in lifestyle and routine can do much to ensure that the older dog continues to lead an enjoyable and fulfilling life.

As the body slows down, less energy is used, and this can lead to obesity. Weighing your dog regularly, combined with careful control of diet and moving to a low-calorie food, will ensure this doesn't become a problem.

Joints start to deteriorate and the dog may become stiff or even lame after strenuous activity. Regular exercise is important, but should be done little and often. Arthritis is common and if suspected your vet will be able to prescribe drugs to reduce inflammation and pain. A memory-foam or orthopaedic bed will reduce pressure on painful joints and ensure the dog is comfortable when resting.

▲ *A correctly fitted coat will help to keep the older dog warm and dry on cold, damp days.*

Purpose-built ramps are available for dogs that are no longer able to jump into the car or manage garden steps.

The older dog may experience reduced sight or even go blind. There are many reasons for this, but age-related cataracts are common. Your vet will make a diagnoses and be able to assess just how much your dog can see. Most dogs adjust quickly to sight loss, but simple steps such as not moving the furniture or leaving things lying around can make this transition

▲ *Purpose-built ramps are available to buy if your veteran dog can no longer jump into back of the car.*

easier. Deafness can also be dangerous as the dog can't hear when it is called, nor can it hear danger such as traffic. In this case, unless in a safe enclosed area, walks should be on a lead or flexi-lead. Attaching a bell to your dog's collar will let you know where it is even if it is unable to hear you.

Weight loss, a cough, fits, incontinence or discharges are all indicators that you should consult your vet, as they may be a precursor to an organ failure.

◄ *Daily exercise is still important for older dogs, even if the pace is slower and the distance shorter.*

▼ *A raised bowl is of great benefit for dogs that have spinal discomfort and those that are not stable on their legs.*

The death of your dog

No living being, human or animal, is immortal. The cycle of birth, life and death is natural and unbreakable. Many people who are interested in complementary health take the view that the essential spirit of the organism continues to exist after the death of the physical body, perhaps rejoining with an invisible source from which all life manifests. Whatever the case, in due course it will be your responsibility to ensure that the transition from life to death is as easy and pain-free as possible for your dog.

Most owners hope that when the time comes for their dog to die, it will do so peacefully in its sleep, or they will be there to comfort it. Often dying is protracted, however. It is then the owner's task to decide if and when to euthanase their pet in order to relieve it from suffering.

Many owners find this an extremely difficult decision, and will ask their vet for advice. Any owner faced with this situation should consider their relationship with their dog as a two-way contract. They have undertaken to give their dog a good life, to care for it and to protect it. In return, the dog has

▶ *Remember the happy times that you spent together and all the things that you both enjoyed.*

rewarded them with the pleasure of its company. Vets are qualified to say when they think the suffering is too much for the dog to bear, but they cannot know how the owners are feeling or how family life is being affected. The owners must decide when to end the partnership, and usually they know when that time comes.

At this sensitive time, holistic care can help both dog and owners. The Bach Flower *Walnut* helps humans and animals cope with difficult changing circumstances and can help with the stress of dying. Homeopathic *Arsen. alb.* given in rising potencies helps to dispel the fear of dying that many feel towards the end of a long terminal illness. *Ignatia* is a good remedy for grief, and can be given to the dog's owners to help them adjust to and accept their loss. If your grief seems never-ending, *Natrum mur.* can help you finally come to terms with your loss.

DECISIONS AFTER DEATH

Whether we lose a dog after a tragic accident or to the gradual progression of old age, the moment of death always comes as a shock. This is made even worse by the fact that straight away we have to make decisions.

First, there is the decision of what to do with the remains of our much-loved companion. Your vet or a specialist company can make arrangements for cremation, either individual or communal, if this is what you wish. In individual cremation, the ashes are returned and can be kept or scattered in a place that your dog loved. Many owners prefer to bury their dog in the garden, but check

▲ *Choosing and growing a special plant in the garden in memory of your pet can involve the whole family.*

that this is not legally prohibited in your area. Pet cemeteries and are often the choice of people who worry about what might happen to a pet's grave if they have to move away.

Deciding when and what to tell children is always difficult. It is not a good idea to tell a child that a pet has gone to live in the country or similar. The child may feel betrayed by the dog's sudden desertion, or they may not understand why it hasn't come back home. Most children are more robust than we give them credit for, and can cope with death. Involving them in some way, for example getting them to choose a plant to put in the garden in memory of their canine friend, is helpful.

Coping with grief is difficult when all around life seems to continue as normal. Sadly, many people are dismissive of the pain caused by the loss of a pet. Free pet bereavement counselling is available from national animal charities, and it does help to talk to someone who understands how you feel.

After the death of a dog, you may feel you are not ready to go through the heartache again, or you may feel that you can't bear to be without a dog. Either way, this is your choice; don't let anyone push you into a decision that is not right for you.

Useful addresses

KENNEL CLUBS

UK
The Kennel Club (KC)
1–5 Clarges Street
Piccadilly, London W1J 8AB
www.thekennelclub.org.uk

USA
American Kennel Club (AKC)
260 Madison Avenue
New York, NY 10016
www.akc.org

United Kennel Club (UKC)
100 E Kilgore Road
Kalamazoo
MI 49002-5584
www.ukcdogs.com

Canada
Canadian Kennel Club (CKC)
200 Ronson Drive
Suite 400, Etobicoke, ON
M9W 5Z9
www.ckc.ca

Australia
Australian National Kennel
Council (ANKC)
ankc.org.au

South Africa
Kennel Union of Southern
Africa (KUSA)
PO Box 2659
Cape Town 8000
www.kusa.co.za

India
Kennel Club of India (KCI)
No.28/89 AA Block
First Street
Anna Nagar
Chennai 600 040
www.kennelclubofindia.org

Japan
Japan Kennel Club (JKC)
www.jkc.or.jp

Worldwide
Fédération Cynologique
Internationale (FCI)
Place Albert 1er, 13
B-6530 Thuin
Belgium
www.fci.be

CHARITABLE ORGANIZATIONS

UK
Blue Cross
Shilton Road, Burford
Oxon OX18 4PF
www.bluecross.org.uk

Dogs Trust
17 Wakley Street
London EC1V 7RQ
www.dogstrust.org.uk

RSPCA
Wilberforce Way
Southwater, Horsham
West Sussex RH13 9RS
www.rspca.org.uk

USA
ASPCA
424 E 92nd Street
New York
NY 10128-6804
www.aspca.org

Canada
Peoples Animal Welfare
Society (PAWS)
23000 Lawrence Avenue East
Box 73039
Toronto, ON
M1P 2R2
www.pawscanada.org

CANINE HEALTH

UK
British Veterinary
Association (BVA)
7 Mansfield Street
London W1G 9NQ
www.bva.co.uk

USA
Academy of Veterinary
Homeopathy (AVH)
PO Box 232282
Leucadia, CA 92023-2282
theavh.org

Canada
Canadian Veterinary Medical
Association (CVMA)
339 Booth Street
Ottawa, ON, K1R 7K1
www.canadianveterinarians.net

Worldwide
The World Small Animal
Veterinary Association
(WSAVA)
www.wsava.org

World Veterinary Association
(WVA)
Avenue de Tervueren 12
B-1040 Bruxelles, Belgium
www.worldvet.org

DOG TRAINING

UK
Association of Pet Dog
Trainers (APDT)
PO Box 17
Kempsford GL7 4WZ
www.apdt.co.uk

USA
Association of Professional
Dog Trainers (APDT)
2365 Harrodsburg Road A325
Lexington, KY 40504
apdt.com

Canada
Canadian Association of
Professional Pet Dog Trainers
(CAPPDT)
3226 Cambourne Crescent
Mississauga, ON
L5N 5G2
www.cappdt.ca

Australia
Australian Association of
Professional Dog Trainers
www.aapdt.org

National Dog Trainers
Federation
20 Havelock Road
Bayswater
VIC 3153
ndtf.net.au

Worldwide
COAPE Association of Applied
Pet Behaviourists & Trainers
www.capbt.org

NUTRITION

European College of
Veterinary and Comparative
Nutrition (ECVCN)
www.esvcn.com

FEDIAF
www.fediaf.org

American College of
Veterinary Nutrition
www.acvn.org

Index

Acknowledgements

This edition is published by Lorenz Books
an imprint of Anness Publishing Ltd.
info@anness.com
www.lorenzbooks.com
www.annesspublishing.com

If you like the images in this book and would
like to investigate using them for publishing,
promotions or advertising, please visit our website
www.practicalpictures.com for more information.

© Anness Publishing Ltd 2019

All rights reserved. No part of this publication may be
reproduced, stored in a retrieval system, or transmitted
in any way or by any means, electronic, mechanical,
photocopying, recording or otherwise, without the
prior written permission of the copyright holder.

A CIP catalogue record for this book
is available from the British Library.

Publisher: Joanna Lorenz
Senior Editor: Felicity Forster
Photography: Robert and Justine Pickett
Additional photography: Jane Burton and John Daniels
Additional text: Dr Peter Larkin and Mike Stockman
    (breeds), Patsy Parry (training) and John Hoare
    (holistic care)
Designer: Nigel Partridge
Production: Ben Worley

The publisher would like to thank the many dog owners
and breeders who provided animals for photography.

We would also like to thank the following for allowing their
photographs to be reproduced in this book (l=left, r=right,
t=top, m=middle, b=bottom). Alamy: 93t, 124m, 130br,
228m, 273br, 313tr. Animal Photography: 193t, 193b, 323t.
Ardea: 90m, 162, 166t, 166bl, 166br, 167br, 202t, 287b, 313tl,
313b, 324br. The Boykin Spaniel Club & Breeders Association
of America, Inc: 130t, 130bl. Corbis: 98t. DK Images: 85t,
85bl, 85br, 86t, 86bl, 86br, 90t, 90b, 96t, 96m, 96b, 114t,
114b, 117t, 117m, 117b, 119t, 119m, 119b, 124t, 124b,
129tl, 129tr, 129b, 142bl, 193m, 228t, 228b, 261b, 270t,
270bl, 273t, 273bl, 307tl, 317t, 317m, 317b, 325t, 325m.
Fotolia: 142br, 307tr. Hans Hilgenstock: 281b. iStock: 37b,
98bl, 231t, 231ml, 231mr, 231b, 265b, 307b, 324t, 404b,
414t, 414b, 424. Lucy Doncaster: 336tl, 350b, 384t. Rachel
Prince: 281t. SuperStock: 281m, 325b. Tracy Morgan Animal
Photography: 92t, 92m, 92b, 98br, 179br, 261tl, 261tr,
270br, 324bl.

PUBLISHER'S NOTE

Although the advice and information in this book are
believed to be accurate and true at the time of going to
press, neither the authors nor the publisher can accept
any legal responsibility or liability for any errors or omissions
that may have been made nor for any inaccuracies nor for
any loss, harm or injury that comes about from following
instructions or advice in this book.

The reader should not regard the recommendations,
ideas and techniques expressed and described in this
book as substitutes for the advice of a qualified vet
or dog training professional. Any use to which the
recommendations, ideas and techniques are put is
at the reader's sole discretion and risk.

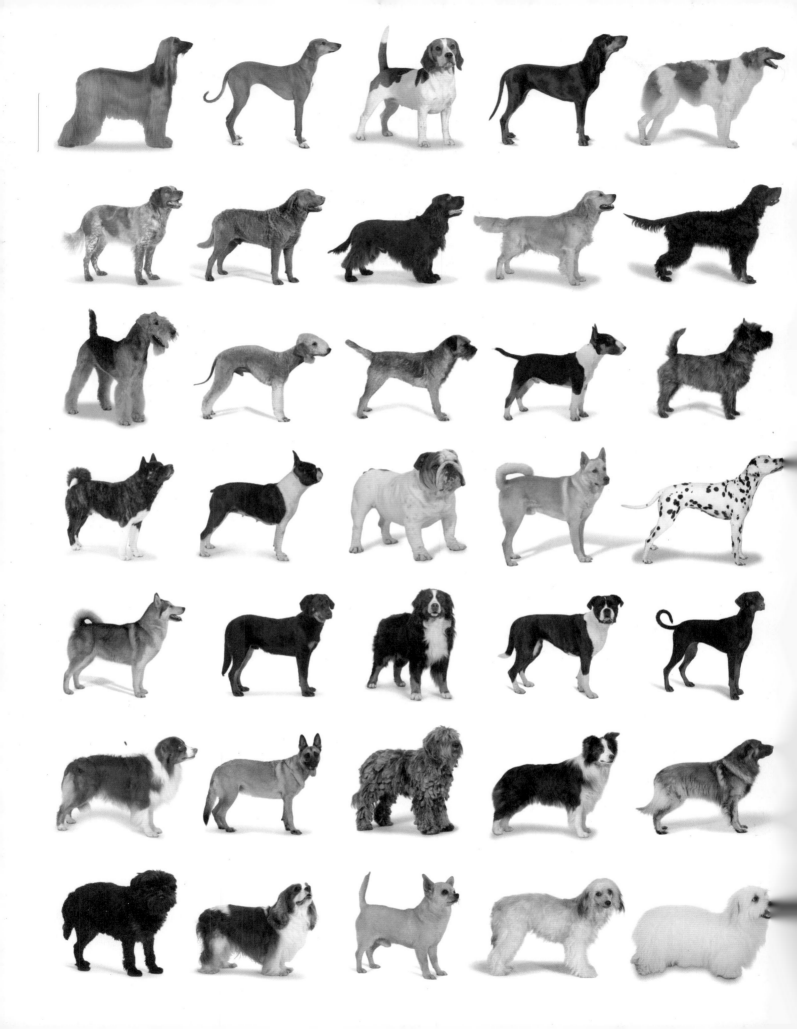